卷烟消费市场研究初探

杨 蕾 张 涛 陶 鹰 何雪峰 徐艳群 编著

JUANYAN XIAOFEI SHICHANG YANJIU CHUTAN

华中科技大学出版社
http://press.hust.edu.cn
中国·武汉

内 容 简 介

《卷烟消费市场研究初探》一书紧扣消费需求变化,在总结传统消费市场分析方法与应用现状的基础上,聚焦卷烟行业消费市场研究实践与方法,建立消费视角与卷烟研发视角的深度链接,旨在有效指导卷烟产品研发,满足消费市场需求。全书共五章,采用中英文对照模式撰写,从卷烟消费需求研究进展、消费需求分析、消费特征研究、需求转化机制及市场状态评估与预测等方面进行了全面系统的梳理。本书不仅提供了烟草行业领域消费市场研究丰富的系统性方法和分析技术,还提供了大量的消费市场研究指导产品研发的应用案例,具有行业聚焦、创新性强、实用性强、学术价值高等特点,可为卷烟企业产品策划、定向研发、市场策略制定、满足消费需求提供科学依据和实践指导。本书涵盖了经济学、市场营销学、心理学等领域,适合烟草行业从业者、市场营销与消费者行为研究人员等阅读。

图书在版编目(CIP)数据

卷烟消费市场研究初探 / 杨蕾等编著. -- 武汉:华中科技大学出版社,2024.12.
ISBN 978-7-5772-1409-2

Ⅰ. F426.89-53

中国国家版本馆 CIP 数据核字第 20242PU769 号

卷烟消费市场研究初探
Juanyan Xiaofei Shichang Yanjiu Chutan

杨蕾　张涛　陶鹰　何雪峰　徐艳群　编著

策划编辑:吴晨希	
责任编辑:陈　骏	
封面设计:原色设计	
责任校对:刘小雨	
责任监印:朱　玢	
出版发行:华中科技大学出版社(中国·武汉)	电话:(027)81321913
武汉市东湖新技术开发区华工科技园	邮编:430223
录　　排:华中科技大学惠友文印中心	
印　　刷:湖北新华印务有限公司	
开　　本:787mm×1092mm　1/16	
印　　张:22.75　插页:2	
字　　数:512 千字	
版　　次:2024 年 12 月第 1 版第 1 次印刷	
定　　价:209.00 元	

本书若有印装质量问题,请向出版社营销中心调换
全国免费服务热线:400-6679-118　竭诚为您服务
版权所有　侵权必究

编辑委员会

编委会主任	邓林昆				
编委会副主任	詹建波				
编　著	杨　蕾	张　涛	陶　鹰	何雪峰	徐艳群
副　主　编	冯洪涛	唐　军	张　伟	李　超	许春平
	夏建军	刘春波	何　俊	夏体渊	赵美威
	杨乾栩	张　玲	吴家灿	蒋梦菲	蔡　波
	周　博	杨建云	苏　杨	王文元	余　耀
	王　晋				
编　委	朱　明	胡　群	苗　崧	冷思漾	王希璇
	杨　玺	尹志豇	任宏光	郭丽娟	唐　丽
	邹　娟	郭　珺	刘　欣		

前言
PREFACE

在经济迅猛发展的浪潮中,消费者的卷烟消费习惯与需求正经历着深刻变革。理解并把握这些变化,对于烟草行业而言至关重要。随着烟草行业"136/345"发展目标的提出,国内中高端卷烟品牌迎来了新的发展机遇,整个行业的竞争力亦随之提升。为实现这一战略目标,在"稍紧平衡、总量控制"政策导向下,各大中烟企业纷纷将目光投向消费市场,致力于洞悉消费者需求,以期发掘潜在市场机遇,提高市场占有率和扩大品牌影响力,推动企业持续前行。

深入的市场研究是企业把握消费者喜好、需求及购买习惯的关键。它不仅能助力企业精准策划产品、推广市场,还能为制定科学合理的市场策略提供有力依据。同时,通过跟踪市场趋势和消费者需求的变化,企业能够迅速应对市场挑战,发掘新的增长点。结合政策环境分析,消费市场研究已成为企业实现可持续发展、提升市场竞争力的核心所在。

在此背景下,近年来学者们围绕消费者满意度、消费市场的构建等方面开展了广泛研究,旨在制定市场策略,提高消费购买率。然而消费购买决策影响因素较多,宏观层面,政策、社会环境、消费人群变化等决定了消费购买的外延;微观层面,消费者基本特征、需求偏好甚至心理及情感等都会直接影响其购买行为。

政策方面,受全球控烟趋势的影响,各国政府纷纷出台严格的烟草控制政策限制烟草广告、提高烟草税、加强烟草制品的质量监管等。中国亦调整了卷烟消费税率以控制吸烟率。与此同时,《"健康中国2030"规划纲要》提出了明确的控烟目标,到2030年,15岁以上人群吸烟率降低到20%;全面无烟法规保护的人口比例达到80%及以上。这些政策直接影响烟草制品的市场需求、价格和销售模式。

社会环境方面,消费者消费习惯改变、健康意识增强,消费者对烟草产品的健康属性要求越来越高,一定程度上推动了低焦油、低烟碱等新型卷烟产品的涌现。与此同时,电子烟等新型烟草制品也在不断发展,吸引着新一代消费者。

科技发展方面,工业4.0加快了数字化和智能化技术的发展,也在潜移默化地影响消费者的购物习惯和消费模式。产品品质不再是唯一评判标准,相反,诸如品牌、价格、包装设计、材质、促销、渠道等也在某一瞬间影响着他们的最终购买决定。

代际差异方面,随着国家生育政策逐步放开,主流消费群体正悄然发生变化。传统卷烟消费群体逐渐向中老年烟民转变,同时年轻消费者对新型烟草制品如电子烟等表现出浓厚的兴趣。受信息化、网络化、科技化影响,年轻一代自主意识更强,他们的一些消费理念也在影响着世人,成为不可忽视的力量。消费群体代际更替加快,使得消费需求代际差异越来越明显。这对企业如何平衡新老消费群体需求提出了挑战。

微观方面,消费市场研究涵盖多种细分维度,譬如:消费者基本特征研究,包括人口统计特征、生活方式、地理分布等,消费者基本特征一定程度反映了消费者的生活形态和消费习惯、购买力和购买偏好;消费者行为研究,包括购买行为、使用行为等,消费者行为研究可以帮助我们还原消费者的购买决策过程,分析消费者在产品使用过程中的行为,以评估产品的市场接受度和用户黏性,进而调整品牌策略;消费动机研究,分析消费者购买产品的动机,可以帮助我们制定针对性的营销策略;市场趋势及竞品研究,通过分析市场的整体趋势,分析竞争对手的产品、价格、渠道、促销等策略,有助于制定有效的竞争策略;此外,消费心理及情感研究也是研究的热点方向,了解消费者的深层次需求,研究消费者在购买过程中的心理变化,可以帮助我们制定更符合消费者心理需求的营销策略,与此同时,通过分析消费者与产品或品牌之间的情感联系,可以帮助建立强大的品牌情感连接。

综上所述,消费市场研究涵盖了宏观、微观多个视角、多个方面。这些研究旨在深入了解消费者的需求、偏好、购买行为以及市场趋势,为企业的产品策划、市场推广和营销策略制定提供科学依据。

本书在总结传统消费市场分析方法及应用现状基础上,聚焦于卷烟企业消费市场研究的实践与方法。与传统的洞察市场机会、调整市场策略不同,本书更侧重于从卷烟消费者视角指导产品研发,通过消费市场研究,挖掘消费需求,制定研发策略,进而满足市场需求。

本书共5章,采用中英文对照模式撰写,系统梳理了卷烟消费需求的研究进展、分析维度、消费特征、需求转化机制及市场状态评估与预测。第1章卷烟消费需求文献综述,总结国内外关于卷烟消费需求的研究进展,对目前卷烟消费需求主流研究方向、研究重点、研究方法进行总结;第2章卷烟消费需求分析,从消费者喜好的产品类型、消费者产品评价、消费者卷烟购买因素分析等不同维度进行阐述,给消费需求分析研究提供了方向及案例指导;第3章卷烟消费特征研究,契合研发需求,对消费指标与满意度、消费结构与行为、包装偏好与市场前景、风味偏好分析等分块进行了阐述分析,研究结论对于指导产品研发具有重要价值;第4章卷烟消费需求转化机制,对卷烟消费者评价与专家技术指标关联性、卷烟消费者内在质量需求转化路径进行了研究分析,对于建立消费需求向产品研发技术指标的转化链接模式及方法具有中烟参考价值;第5章卷烟市场状态评估与预测,介绍了移动平均方法、四象限法、时间序列等统计学方法在卷烟市场状态评估中的应用案例,实用性较强,可以帮助我们更深入地了解和把握卷烟市场状态趋势变化,为制定调整市场策略提供科学依据。

本书紧扣消费需求变化、市场研究方法、主流研究方向等,首次从卷烟研发视角出发,开展卷烟消费市场研究。本书立足"创新、实用、推广",总结多年研究经验及成果,具有以下特色。

1. 行业聚焦。目前国内关于"消费市场研究"方法的书籍较多,但针对卷烟消费需求指导产品研发的相关研究较少。本书首次从烟草行业视角系统性阐述卷烟消费需求调研的价值,特别是在产品研发、策略指导方面的意义。行业聚焦性、专业性较强。

2. 创新性强。本书在卷烟消费市场研究方面展现出突出的创新性。它首次从研发视角出发,将消费需求分析与产品研发紧密结合,为烟草行业提供了一种全新的研究思路和方法。

3. 实用性强。本书详细阐述了卷烟消费需求的各个方面,包括消费者喜好、产品评价、购买因素分析等,并提供了丰富的市场调研方法和分析技术,既可作为卷烟消费市场研究技术方法的参考用书,又可作为烟草行业市场调研的辅导材料。

4. 学术价值高。本书系统地总结了国内外卷烟消费市场研究的最新进展和主流研究方向,为读者提供了丰富的学术背景和理论支撑。书中不仅涵盖了国内外市场调研的前沿方法和分析技术,还通过大量的应用案例,展示了这些方法和技术在实际操作中的可行性和有效性,具有较高的学术价值。

本书由杨蕾、张涛、陶鹰、何雪峰、徐艳群编著而成,在编写过程中参考了大量的国内外相关领域的论文、专著、行业及非行业研究成果和案例,在此谨表谢意。

由于时间仓促,本书难免有不当之处,恳请读者给予批评指正。

编委会
2024 年 11 月

目录
CONTENTS

第 1 章 综述   1
卷烟消费需求的文献综述研究   1
A Literature Review on the Consumer Demand for Cigarettes   6

第 2 章 卷烟消费需求分析   13
消费者喜欢的卷烟产品类型研究   13
Research on the Types of Cigarette Products Preferred by Consumers   22
基于扎根理论的卷烟消费者产品评价和需求分析   32
Consumer Product Evaluation and Demand Analysis of Cigarettes based on Grounded Theory   43
基于自组织建模方法的卷烟购买因素分析   60
Cigarette Purchase Factors Analysis based on Self-Organizing Modeling   68

第 3 章 卷烟消费特征探究   79

消费指标与满意度   79
卷烟产品消费者满意度影响因素实证研究   79
An Empirical Study on the Influencing Factors of Cigarette Consumer Satisfaction   93
卷烟评价指标与消费者需求的关联度研究   114
Study on the Correlation between Cigarette Evaluation Indicators and Consumer Demand   123

消费结构与行为   135
卷烟消费者结构及其消费行为特征分析   135
Analysis of the Characteristics of the Cigarette Consumer Structure and Behavior   146

包装偏好与市场前景　　160

卷烟包装偏好的区域性及对象性差异分析　　160
Analysis of Regional and Object Differences in Cigarette Packaging Preferences　　167

卷烟包装特性与市场前景间的多序列相关分析　　177
Polyserial Correlation Analysis of Cigarette Packaging Characteristics and Market Prospects　　184

风味偏好分析　　193

基于 MFA 的消费者与专家卷烟抽吸感知及风味感知分析　　193
Analysis of Consumer and Expert Cigarette Smoking Perception and Flavor Perception based on MFA　　200

第 4 章　卷烟消费需求转化机制　　210

卷烟消费者评价与专家技术指标关联性研究　　210
Research on the Correlation between Cigarette Consumer Evaluation and Expert Technical Indicators　　226

基于层次分析法和 Shapley 值分解方法的卷烟消费者内在质量需求转化路径构建研究　　245
Research on the Transformation Path of Cigarette Consumers' Internal Quality Demand based on AHP and Shapley Value Decomposition　　262

第 5 章　卷烟市场状态评估与预测　　283

基于 R 语言编程的移动平均方法在卷烟产品销量状态分析中的应用　　283
Application of Moving Average Method based on R Programming in the Analysis of Cigarette Product Sales Status　　292

基于产品生命周期和四象限法的卷烟产品市场状态评价　　305
Evaluation of the Market Status of Cigarette Products based on the Product Life Cycle and the Four-Quadrant Method　　314

单规格卷烟月度销量的时间序列预测方法研究　　328
A Study on Time Series Forecasting Method for Monthly Sales of Cigarettes with Single Specification　　339

第 1 章

综述

卷烟消费需求的文献综述研究

摘要: 在经济发展和人民生活不断改善的背景下,人们的消费偏好发生了很大变化,卷烟消费者的卷烟消费习惯和需求也在不断变化。近几年,学者对卷烟消费需求的关注与探讨取得了丰富的研究成果。本文基于对相关文献的梳理,从卷烟消费需求影响因素、卷烟消费者行为、卷烟消费者满意度、卷烟消费市场的构建等方面分析了卷烟消费需求的研究进展。

关键词: 卷烟;消费需求;综述

在经济发展和人民生活不断改善的背景下,人们的消费偏好发生了很大变化,生活水平有了极大的提升,人们对卷烟的消费需求也快速增长。国家统计局官方网站记载,2000年到2019年,国内卷烟消费量从8161.6亿支增长到61983.7亿支,年均增长率达到了11.26%。随着烟草行业市场化机制的持续引入,传统的生产导向型营销观念已无法适应如今的营销环境,卷烟企业认识到基于消费者的价值诉求与消费需求开展生产和营销才是正确的经营之道。加强对卷烟消费需求的研究,对烟草商业企业高质量发展,提升卷烟消费者的品牌忠诚度具有重大意义[1],对于企业如何做好品牌培育,加强品牌与消费者之间的联系也具有重大意义[2]。近几年,学者对卷烟消费需求的关注与探讨取得了丰富的研究成果。本文基于对相关文献的梳理,探讨了卷烟消费需求的研究进展。

1 关于消费需求的研究

国内学者对消费需求的研究成果颇丰,主要从消费需求的影响因素、消费结构、心理因素对消费需求的影响等方面展开了研究。

在消费需求的影响因素方面,郑浩天、刘仙梅(2021)探讨了城乡收入差距对消费需求的动态影响[3];周国红、刘理豪、徐虹绯(2019)从品质消费视角探讨城市居民消费行为的影响因素,发现从众心理对品质消费购买意愿的影响最大[4];徐驰文(2021)在当前内循环背景下,对城乡消费者收入分配与消费需求的关系进行了实证分析,认为建立更加合理的分配制度,提高城乡消费者收入,是刺激消费需求的必要条件[5]。在消费结构的研究方面,周发明、杨婧(2010)分析发现我国城乡居民消费结构存在显著的差异[6];王少辉、李富有(2021)基于中国健康与养老追踪调查对城乡老年群体消费结构、需求特征及行为决策进行实证研究[7];师月荣(2021)在双循环新发展格局下探讨消费扩容提质,认为消费扩容提质要以满足人民需要为出发点[8]。在心理因素对消费需求的影响研究方面,李晨馨(2021)以母婴人群为切入点,通过构建心理因素作用于消费需求的影响机制,以基础模式和诱导模式的双重触发模式,解读心理因素对消费需求的具体作用[9];王建荣(2020)对C2C环境下服务承诺、消费者心理契约与消费意愿的互动关系进行了实证分析[10]。

2 关于卷烟消费需求的研究

2.1 国外关于卷烟消费需求的研究

Townsend J 等人(1994)对英国1972—1990年的吸烟数量和吸烟频率的变化情况进行研究,发现收入水平较低的人群对卷烟的价格变化更为敏感[11]。Chaloupka F J 等人(2012)对不同年龄段和不同收入人群对烟草的消费情况进行了实践调研,发现烟草消费税是减少烟草消费的有效工具[12]。

2.2 国内关于卷烟消费需求的研究

国内关于卷烟消费需求的研究主要从卷烟消费需求影响因素、卷烟消费者行为、卷烟消费者满意度、卷烟消费市场的构建等方面展开,取得了丰富的研究成果。

(1)关于卷烟消费需求影响因素的研究。周冀衡、张洲颖等(2008)通过定量分析发现卷烟价格在很大程度上会对卷烟消费需求产生影响[13]。张海峰、林细细、梁若冰(2021)提出,由于消费惯性的作用,同类商品不同价位间存在需求的"替代转移效应"[14]。

(2)关于卷烟消费者行为的研究。蒋海浪、范剑波(2019)通过分析决策树C4.5的算法,研究卷烟消费者的购买行为,利用问卷调查样本数据得出了卷烟消费者对卷烟的满意度[15]。郭立军、叶剑、闫东(2020)提出卷烟消费者档案库建立的基础在于构建长期性的数据采集形式[16]。陈浩、王诗航等(2019)研究了某卷烟企业消费者购买行为的区域聚集规律以及地点和时段偏好,为卷烟企业的产品投放和营销策略提供了参考[17]。李晓亮、闫晓雯、马晓敏等(2020)分析了卷烟目标消费者的特征及购买行为,提出基于目标消费者的卷烟品牌培育策略[18]。

(3)关于卷烟消费者满意度的研究。云南中烟工业有限责任公司科技项目组(2020)

分析发现,将PLS路径建模用于卷烟消费者满意度分析,能更准确地反映各指标间的直接及间接的影响关系[19]。杨蕾、杨乾栩、冯洪涛等(2019)研究发现,消费者最看重产品的内在属性,其他属性对消费者满意度的影响在不同区域会有所差别[20]。申言(2020)认为探索高端卷烟品牌培育模式,应坚持以消费者为中心,细分消费群体,把握消费诉求,有效适应、满足市场需求[21]。黎志红(2020)以贵州中烟"国酒香体验之旅"和四川中烟"万人进企业体验之旅"为例,提出开发并培育线上线下互动的消费者体验认知是企业推动品牌培育的有效路径[22]。

(4)关于卷烟消费市场的构建研究。严明、段淑娟(2020)提出,随着卷烟市场竞争的压力逐渐增大,烟草企业需要对消费者的需求、爱好以及影响其消费观的各种因素进行全面了解和分析,以制定更加科学有效的卷烟市场营销策略[23]。于梦吟、易瑜、蔡月香(2021)以三维三层卷烟为例,探讨了通过深入剖析卷烟市场逻辑和相关指标内涵,明确状态评价和策略评价相分离的思路,为实现卷烟市场状态"稍紧平衡"提供了决策参考[24]。邸辉(2020)认为,"邯烟新零消"终端服务平台的应用较好地解决了获取消费者真实数据的难题,将营销触角延展至消费者群体,实现了经营管理模式的转型升级[25]。颜凌(2020)基于经济新常态的背景,对我国烟草经济的卷烟品牌营销发展过程中出现问题进行了深入探讨与分析[26]。韦晶晶(2020)通过对体验式营销的理论研究,分析实施体验式营销的必要性和可行性,提出了卷烟品牌体验营销策略实施的保障措施[27]。

(5)关于卷烟消费税对消费需求的影响的研究。梁青山(2009)提出烟草价格和税收的提高可能带来加重吸烟者的经济负担、加大卷烟对部分吸烟者健康的危害、影响烟草经济和增加烟草走私行为等一系列不利的影响,因此认为提高烟草价格和税收的策略不宜在我国施行[28]。周冀衡、张洲颖和张一扬等人(2008)对我国2001年到2006年的烟草制品价格、税收以及烟草制品消费量进行了实证分析,发现烟草消费量并没有随着卷烟价格和税收的提高而降低[13]。郑榕、高松、胡德伟(2013)认为我国目前的卷烟价格和税负水平低于世界平均水平,中国的经济在不断发展,人均收入在增加,卷烟的价格却在下降,因此需要对烟草消费税进行大幅提高[29]。

3 研究评述与启示

通过对卷烟消费需求相关研究的梳理,发现相关研究主要有以下特点。

(1)研究视角:大部分学者都是基于消费者的地理分布、消费档次、消费心理、消费习惯和消费场所等视角来探讨卷烟消费需求的影响因素。

(2)研究内容:学者以满足卷烟消费者多重消费需求为关键点展开调查与探究,并基于卷烟消费者的诉求提出相应的对策。

(3)研究方法:以实证研究为主,大部分研究都是在完成市场调查和消费跟踪的基础上,获取大量的数据,从而深入分析消费群体、消费需求、消费行为和消费趋势。

综上可知,国外多数学者认为性别、年龄、社会地位等是影响卷烟消费需求的主要因素,并认为人们对卷烟的消费意愿主要受综合环境与个人条件的影响。国内学者研究视角较为广泛,不仅从卷烟消费者的消费心理、消费行为、消费习惯、消费需求等方面分析,而且从卷烟消费市场、卷烟消费税等视角探讨了卷烟消费需求对市场的影响。可见,对烟草工业企业来说,通过搭建平台等方式确保与卷烟消费者保持信息沟通顺畅,及时获取卷烟消费者的需求,并向广大消费者提供及时周到的服务,不仅能够显著提高消费者满意度,还能在发现和解决问题中提升企业竞争力。

参考文献

[1] 刘亚男.兰州市烟草公司兰州(桥)的消费者品牌忠诚提升策略研究[D].兰州:兰州大学,2021.

[2] 王静娟.烟酒消费税的消费效应研究[D].济南:山东财经大学,2021.

[3] 郑浩天,刘仙梅.城乡收入差距对居民基本消费需求的动态影响:基于ELES模型与VAR模型的实证分析[J].内蒙古财经大学学报,2021,19(5):82-88.

[4] 周国红,刘理豪,徐虹绯.城市居民品质消费行为的影响因素[J].城市问题,2019(10):98-103.

[5] 徐驰文.我国城乡消费者收入分配与消费需求的互动关系研究[J].商业经济研究,2021(20):50-53.

[6] 周发明,杨婧.基于ELES模型的中国城乡居民消费结构实证研究[J].江西农业大学学报(社会科学版),2010,9(3):84-89.

[7] 王少辉,李富有.中国老年群体消费结构、需求特征和行为决策[J].北京社会科学,2021(8):119-128.

[8] 师月荣.强化财政金融支持 助力内蒙古消费扩容提质[J].北方经济,2021(9):26-28.

[9] 李晨馨.心理因素对消费需求的影响分析:以新手爸妈群体为例[J].现代营销,2021(9):40-41.

[10] 王建荣.C2C环境下服务承诺、消费者心理契约与消费意愿分析[J].商业经济研究,2020(9):63-66.

[11] TOWNSEND J, RODERICK P, COOPER J. Cigarette Smoking by Socioeconomic Group, Sex, and Age: Effects of Price, Income, and Health Publicity[J]. Bmj, 1994, 309 (6959): 923-927.

[12] CHALOUPKA F J, YUREKLI A, FONG G T. Tobacco Taxes as a Tobacco Control Strategy[J]. Tobacco Control, 2012 (21): 172-180.

[13] 周冀衡,张洲颖,张一扬,等.2001—2006年中国卷烟价格与消费需求变化分析[J].湖南农业大学学报,2008(5):16-20.

[14] 张海峰,林细细,梁若冰.遵循普遍合意法则的有限理性消费行为选择:税负感知度与"替代转移效应"视角[J].管理世界,2021,37(2):51-65.

[15] 蒋海浪,范剑波.基于C4.5算法的卷烟消费者购买行为的研究与分析[J].宁波工程学院学报,2019,31(4):48-53.

[16] 郭立军,叶剑,闫东."互联网+卷烟营销"思维下的消费者档案库的建立[J].品牌研究,2020(1):29-30.

[17] 陈浩,王诗航,顾祖毅,等.基于POI数据的卷烟消费者行为研究[J].科技和产业,2019,19(1):76-80.

[18] 李晓亮,闫晓雯,马晓敏,等.基于目标消费者分析的卷烟品牌培育策略研究[J].中国管理信息化,2020,23(22):142-143.

[19] 云南中烟工业有限责任公司科技项目组.基于PLS路径建模的卷烟消费者满意度分析[J].中国市场,2020(25):127-131.

[20] 杨蕾,杨乾栩,冯洪涛,等.卷烟产品消费者满意度影响因素实证研究[J].云南农业大学学报(社会科学),2019,13(5):93-101.

[21] 申言.突出消费者导向 探索高端品牌培育模式[N].东方烟草报,2020-09-26(3).

[22] 黎志红.以体验认知为核心的卷烟品牌培育新策略[J].中国商论,2020(5):70-72.

[23] 严明,段淑娟.基于消费心理学的卷烟市场营销策略研究[J].商讯,2020(25):17.

[24] 于梦吟,易瑜,蔡月香.基于系统思维下的消费市场状态评价及调控体系初探[J].商展经济,2021(18):26-29.

[25] 邱辉.基于零消环节的消费数据获取研究[J].市场观察,2020(7):78.

[26] 颜凌.经济新常态下卷烟品牌营销策略分析[J].全国流通经济,2020(35):6-8.

[27] 韦晶晶.体验式营销在卷烟品牌培育应用的研究[C]//构建新体系 激发新活力:广西烟草学会2019年优秀论文集广西烟草学会专题资料汇编,2020:253-259.

[28] 梁青山.试论控烟策略:提高烟草价格和税收[J].职业与健康,2009,25(16):1767-1768.

[29] 郑榕,高松,胡德伟.烟草税与烟草控制:全球经验及在中国的应用[J].财贸经济,2013(3):44-54.

A Literature Review on the Consumer Demand for Cigarettes

Abstract: Significant changes in consumer preferences have occurred against continuous improvement in economic development and people's living standards. The smoking habits and demands of cigarette consumers are also constantly evolving. Scholars have made rich research achievements in studying cigarette consumption demand in recent years. Based on a review of relevant literature, this paper analyzes the research progress of cigarette consumption demand from the aspects of influencing factors, consumer behavior, consumer satisfaction, and market construction for cigarette consumption.

Keywords: Cigarettes; Consumer demand; Overview

Against the backdrop of continuous improvement in economic development and people's living standards, there has been a significant change in consumer preferences. With a substantial increase in the standard of living, there has been a rapid growth in the demand for cigarette consumption. According to the official website of the National Bureau of Statistics, from 2000 to 2019, domestic cigarette consumption increased from 816.16 billion sticks to 6198.37 billion sticks, with an average annual growth rate reaching 11.26%. With the continued introduction of market-oriented mechanisms in the tobacco industry, traditional production-oriented marketing concepts are no longer able to adapt to today's marketing environment. Cigarette companies have realized that conducting production and marketing based on consumer value demands and consumption needs is the correct way of operation. Strengthening research on cigarette consumption demand is significant for the high-quality development of tobacco commercial enterprises and enhancing brand loyalty among cigarette consumers[1]. It is also highly significant for enterprises to cultivate their brands effectively and strengthen connections between brands and consumers[2]. In recent years, scholars have achieved rich research results through their attention to and exploration of cigarette consumption demand. Based on a review of relevant literature, this article discusses the progress of research on cigarette consumption demand.

1　Research on Consumer Demand

Domestic scholars have made significant research achievements in consumer demand, focusing on factors influencing consumer demand, the structure of consumer and the impact of psychological factors on consumer demand. Regarding factors influencing consumer demand, Zheng Haotian and Liu Xianmei (2021) examined the dynamic impact of urban-rural income disparity on consumer demand[3]. Zhou Guohong, Liu Lihao, and Xu Hongfei (2019) explored the influencing factors of urban residents' consumption behavior from the perspective of quality consumption and found that conformity psychology significantly impacted purchase intention for quality consumption[4]. Xu Chiwen (2021) conducted an empirical analysis to study the relationship between income distribution and consumer demand among urban and rural consumers within the context of current internal circulation. It was concluded that establishing a more reasonable distribution system and increasing urban and rural consumers' incomes is essential for stimulating consumer demand[5]. Regarding consumption structure studies, Zhou Faming and Yang Jing (2010) analyzed significant differences in consumption structures between urban and rural residents in China[6]. Wang Shaohui and Li Fuyou (2021) conducted an empirical study on consumption structure, characteristics in demands, as well as behavioral decision-making among elderly groups in both urban and rural areas based on China's healthcare tracking survey[7]. Shi Yuerong (2021) discussed expanding consumption while improving quality under new dual-cycle development patterns. It was suggested that expansion should be based upon meeting people's needs[8]. Regarding studies into psychological factors impacting consumer demands, Li Chenxin (2021) starting with maternal-infant groups as a basis point, constructed an impact mechanism for psychological factors affecting customer demands. The specific effects were interpreted using a dual-trigger model consisting of basic models alongside induction models[9]. Wang Jianrong (2020) conducted an empirical analysis regarding interactions between service commitments, consumer psychological contracts, and intentions to consume in C2C environment[10].

2　Research on the Demand for Cigarette Consumption

2.1　Research on the demand for cigarette consumption abroad

Townsend J et al. (1994) studied the changes in smoking quantity and frequency in the UK from 1972 to 1990 and found that people with lower income levels are more sensitive to price changes of cigarettes[11]. Chaloupka F J et al. (2012) conducted practical research on tobacco consumption among different age groups and income groups. They found that tobacco consumption tax is an effective tool in reducing tobacco consumption[12].

2.2 Research on domestic cigarette consumption demand

Research on domestic cigarette consumption demand mainly focuses on factors influencing cigarette consumption demand, consumer behavior related to cigarettes, consumer satisfaction with cigarettes, as well as constructing a market for cigarette consumption. Rich research results have been achieved.

(1) Research on factors influencing cigarette consumption demand. Zhou Jiheng, Zhang Zhouying et al. (2008) found through quantitative analysis that cigarette prices significantly impact cigarette consumption demand[13]. Zhang Haifeng, Lin Xixi, Liang Ruobing (2021) proposed the "substitution transfer effect" of demand between different price ranges of similar products due to consumer inertia[14].

(2) Research on consumer behavior of cigarette consumption. Jiang Hailang and Fan Jianbo (2019) conducted a study on the purchasing behavior of cigarette consumers by analyzing the C4.5 decision tree algorithm. They utilized questionnaire survey sample data to determine the satisfaction of cigarette consumers towards their purchases[15]. Guo Lijun, Ye Jian, Yan Dong (2020) proposed that establishing a database for cigarette consumers is based on constructing long-term data collection forms[16]. Chen Hao, Wang Shihang et al. (2019) studied the regional clustering rules of consumer purchasing behavior of a cigarette company and their preferences for location and period, providing references for product placement and marketing strategies for cigarette companies[17]. Li Xiaoliang, Yan Xiaowen, Ma Xiaomin et al. (2020) analyzed the characteristics and purchasing behavior of target consumers of cigarettes, proposing brand cultivation strategies based on target consumers[18].

(3) Research on consumer satisfaction with cigarettes. The science and technology project team of China Tobacco Yunnan Industrial Co., Ltd. (2020) found that PLS path modeling used in analyzing consumer satisfaction with cigarettes can more accurately reflect the direct and indirect impact relationships between various indicators[19]. Yang Lei, Yang Qianxu, Feng Hongtao et al. (2019) found that consumers value the intrinsic attributes of products most, while other attributes may have different impacts on consumer satisfaction in different regions[20]. Shen Yan (2020) believes that exploring high-end cigarette brand cultivation models should adhere to a customer-centric approach by segmenting consumer groups and understanding their demands to adapt to and meet

market needs effectively[21]. Li Zhihong (2020), using examples such as "National Liquor Fragrance Experience Tour" by China Tobacco Guizhou Industrial Co., Ltd. and "Ten Thousand People Visiting Enterprise Experience Tour" by China Tobacco Sichuan Industrial Co., Ltd., proposed that developing interactive consumer experiences online and offline is an effective way for enterprises to promote brand cultivation[22].

(4) Research on the cigarette consumption market construction. Yan Ming and Duan Shujuan (2020) proposed that with the increasing pressure of competition in the cigarette market, tobacco companies need to comprehensively understand and analyze consumers' needs, preferences, and various factors influencing their consumption attitudes in order to develop more scientifically effective marketing strategies for the cigarette market[23]. Yu Mengyin, Yi Yu and Cai Yuexiang (2021) used three-dimensional three-layer cigarettes as an example to explore a clear approach to separating status evaluation from strategy evaluation by thoroughly analyzing the logic of the cigarette market and its related indicators, providing decision-making references for achieving a "slightly tight balance" in the cigarette market[24]. Di Hui (2020) believes that the application of the "Han Cigarette Retail Consumption" terminal service platform has effectively solved the problem of obtaining actual consumer data, extended marketing reach to consumer groups, and achieved transformational upgrading of business management models[25]. Yan Ling (2020) conducted an in-depth discussion and analysis of problems arising in the development process of cigarette brand marketing within China's tobacco economy against the background of new economic normalcy[26]. Wei Jingjing (2020) through theoretical research on experiential marketing, analyzed the necessity and feasibility of implementing experiential marketing and proposed safeguard measures for implementing cigarette brand experiential marketing strategies[27].

(5) Research on the impact of cigarette consumption tax on consumer demand. Liang Qingshan (2009) analyzed a series of adverse effects that may arise from raising tobacco prices and taxes, such as increased economic burden on smokers, more significant harm to some smokers' health from smoking cigarettes, impact on the tobacco economy, and increased tobacco smuggling activities. Therefore, it is believed that strategies to raise tobacco prices and taxes are not feasible in China[28]. Zhou Jiheng, Zhang Zhouying, Zhang Yiyang et al. (2008) conducted an empirical analysis of tobacco product prices, taxes, and consumption levels in China from 2001-2006. The research found that tobacco consumption did not decrease with higher cigarette prices or taxes[13]. Zheng Rong, Gao Song and Hu Dewei (2013) argued that China's current cigarette prices and taxes are still lower than the world average. China's economy is continuously developing, and per capita income is increasing, yet cigarettes have become cheaper. Therefore, it is necessary to

increase tobacco taxation significantly[29].

3 Research Review and Implications

Upon reviewing the relevant studies on cigarette consumption demand, it is found that the research has the following characteristics:

(1) Research perspective: Most scholars explore the influencing factors and for cigarette consumption demand from the perspectives of consumer geographic distribution, consumption levels, consumer psychology, consumption habits, and consumption locations.

(2) Research content: Scholars conduct investigations and explorations focusing on meeting the multiple consumption demands of cigarette consumers and propose corresponding strategies based on the appeals of cigarette consumption demand.

(3) Research method: Empirical research is predominant in terms of research methods, with most studies obtaining a large amount of data based on market surveys and consumer tracking to deeply analyze consumer groups, consumption demands, consumer behaviors, and consumption trends.

Most foreign scholars believe that gender, age, and social status influence cigarette consumption demand. They also believe that comprehensive environmental and personal conditions influence people's willingness to consume cigarettes. Domestic scholars have a broader research perspective. They analyze aspects such as consumer psychology, consumer behavior, consumption habits, and consumption demands and explore the impact of cigarette consumption demand on the market from perspectives such as cigarette consumer markets and cigarette consumer taxes. For tobacco industry enterprises, maintaining smooth communication with cigarette consumers through platform means, timely understanding of their needs, and providing timely and thoughtful services to consumers can improve customer satisfaction and enhance enterprise competitiveness by identifying and solving problems.

References

[1] LIU Y N. Research on the Promotion Strategy of Consumer Brand Loyalty in Lanzhou (Bridge) of Lanzhou Tobacco Company [D]. Lanzhou: Lanzhou University, 2021.

[2] WANG J J. Study on Consumption Effect of Alcohol and Tobacco Consumption Tax [D]. Jinan: Shandong University of Finance and Economics, 2021.

[3] ZHENG H T, LIU X M. Dynamic Impact of Urban-Rural Income Gap on

Residents' Basic Consumption Demand: An Empirical Analysis based on ELES and VAR Model [J]. Journal of Inner Mongolia University of Finance and Economics, 2021, 19 (5): 82-88.

[4] ZHOU G H, LIU L H, XU H F. The Influencing Factors of Urban Residents' Quality Consumption Behavior [J]. Urban Problems, 2019 (10): 98-103.

[5] XU C W. Study on the Interactive Relationship between Income Distribution and Consumption Demand of Urban and Rural Consumers in China [J]. Business Economics Research, 2021 (20): 50-53.

[6] ZHOU F M, YANG J. Empirical Study on Consumption Structure of Urban and Rural Residents in China based on ELES Model [J]. Journal of Jiangxi Agricultural University (Social Sciences Edition), 2010, 9 (3): 84-89.

[7] WANG S H, LI F Y. Consumption Structure, Demand Characteristics and Behavioral Decision of Chinese Elderly Groups [J]. Social Sciences in Beijing, 2021 (8): 119-128.

[8] SHI Y R. Strengthening Fiscal and Financial Support to Help Inner Mongolia's Consumption Expand and Improve Quality [J]. Northern Economy, 2021 (9): 26-28.

[9] LI C X. Analysis on the Influence of Psychological Factors on Consumer Demand: A Case Study of Novice Parents [J]. Modern Marketing, 2021 (9): 40-41.

[10] WANG J R. Analysis of Service Commitment, Consumer Psychological Contract and Consumption Intention under C2C Environment [J]. Business Economics Research, 2020 (9): 63-66.

[11] TOWNSEND J, RODERICK P, COOPER J. Cigarette Smoking by Socioeconomic Group, Sex, and Age: Effects of Price, Income, and Health Publicity [J]. Bmj, 1994, 309 (6959): 923-927.

[12] CHALOUPKA F J, YUREKLI A, FONG G T. Tobacco Taxes as a Tobacco Control Strategy[J]. Tobacco Control, 2012 (21): 172-180.

[13] ZHOU J H, ZHANG Z Y, ZHANG Y Y, et al. Analysis of Changes in Cigarette Price and Consumption Demand in China from 2001 to 2006[J]. Journal of Hunan Agricultural University, 2008 (5): 16-20.

[14] ZHANG H F, LIN X X, LIANG R B. Limited Rational Consumption Behavior Choice Following the Law of General Consent: the Perception of Tax Burden and the Perspective of "Substitution and Transfer Effect" [J]. Management World, 2021, 37 (2): 51-65.

[15] JIANG H L, FAN J B. Research and Analysis of Cigarette Consumers' Purchasing Behavior based on C4.5 Algorithms[J]. Journal of Ningbo Institute of Technology,

[16] GUO L J, YE J, YAN D. Establishment of Consumer Archive under "Internet＋Cigarette Marketing"[J]. Brand Research, 2020(1)：29-30.

[17] CHEN H, WANG S H, GU Z Y, et al. Research on Cigarette Consumer Behavior based on POI data[J]. Science and Technology Industry, 2019, 19(1)：76-80.

[18] LI X L, YAN X W, MA X M, et al. Research on Cigarette Brand Cultivation Strategy based on Target Consumer Analysis[J]. China Management Information Technology, 2020, 23(22)：142-143.

[19] Science and Technology project team of China Tobacco Yunnan Industrial Co., Ltd. Analysis of Cigarette Consumer Satisfaction based on PLS Path Modeling [J]. China Market, 2020(25)：127-131.

[20] YANG L, YANG Q X, FENG H T, et al. Empirical Study on Influencing Factors of Cigarette Consumer Satisfaction[J]. Journal of Yunnan Agricultural University (Social Sciences), 2019, 13(5)：93-101.

[21] SHEN Y. Highlight Consumer Orientation and Explore High-End Brand Cultivation Model[N]. Eastern Tobacco News, 2020-09-26(3).

[22] LI Z H. A New Strategy for Cigarette Brand Cultivation is Based on Experience Cognition[J]. China Business Review, 2020(5)：70-72.

[23] YAN M, DUAN S J. Research on Cigarette Marketing Strategy based on Consumer Psychology[J]. Business News, 2020(25)：17.

[24] YU M Y, YI Y, CAI Y X. Consumer Market State Evaluation and Regulation System based on System Thinking[J]. Business Exhibition Economics, 2021(18)：26-29.

[25] DI H. Research on Consumption Data Acquisition based on Zero Consumption Link[J]. Market Watch, 2020(7)：78.

[26] YAN L. Analysis of Cigarette Brand Marketing Strategy under the New Normal of the Economy[J]. National Circulation Economy, 2020(35)：6-8.

[27] WEI J J. Research on the Application of Experiential Marketing in Cultivating Cigarette Brands[C]//. Building a New System to Stimulate New Vitality：The 2019 Excellent Proceedings of Guangxi Tobacco Society, The Collection of Special materials of Guangxi Tobacco Society, 2020：253-259.

[28] LIANG Q S. Discuss Tobacco Control Strategy：Raising Tobacco Price and Tax [J]. Occupational and Health, 2009, 25(16)：1767-1768.

[29] ZHENG R, GAO S, HU D W. Tobacco Tax and Tobacco Control：Global Experience and Application in China[J]. Finance and Trade Economics, 2013(3)：44-54.

第 2 章
卷烟消费需求分析

消费者喜欢的卷烟产品类型研究

摘要：针对消费者需求进行卷烟的设计与改良，是进行市场化经营的重要基础。本次调查中，研究消费者喜欢的卷烟产品类型、包装风格、包装颜色、包装材质等，摸清卷烟消费者的真实需求，为卷烟新产品的开发提供具体工作指引。

关键词：消费者；卷烟产品；产品类型；包装

烟草行业作为国民经济的重要组成部分，近年来，随着市场经济的发展，已形成以消费者需求为导向的市场化经营理念。在该经营模式下，了解消费者的需求，针对消费者需求进行卷烟的设计与改良，是进行市场化经营的重要基础[1,2]。

长期以来，消费者都有一套他们自己的评价卷烟优劣的标准，深入分析消费者喜好，了解消费者的需求与消费特点，是卷烟经营者决策的重要依据[3]。按照当前市场化经营的理念，卷烟产品的设计、生产与营销，应该以消费者的需求为导向，根据消费者的消费行为与特征、消费者对各类卷烟产品的评价情况和满意度制定从设计、生产到营销的策略[4,5]。对于卷烟而言，消费情况常常因顾客的年龄、职业、收入、地域、偏好、品牌忠诚度、政策作用而变化，只有有效把握顾客的消费特点，准确掌握消费需求，才能为市场营销策略提供行之有效的指导。

伴随着我国市场的深化改革和卷烟零售终端的健全完善，大型的卷烟生产企业对数据的依赖性增加，零售点需要利用大数据对客户进行了解，企业需要了解消费者的感受和市场的发展动态，因此需要加强对卷烟消费者数据的分析与应用，提高卷烟企业的动态监控能力。本次调查中，对卷烟消费需求进行收集，研究消费者喜欢的卷烟产品类型，摸清卷烟消费者的真实需求,为卷烟新产品的开发提供具体工作指引。

1 研究方法

1.1 调查时间

2021年12月1日—2022年1月30日。

1.2 调查对象

以昆明、杭州、广州、成都、兰州、武汉、大理、上海、深圳、重庆、柳州、大连12个城市为调研城市,对居住在调研城市的卷烟消费者开展问卷调查,其中,主要以18～55岁卷烟消费者人群为调研对象。

1.3 调研方法

采用扫码自填的方法收集调查问卷。本次调查共收集到问卷8707份,其中有效问卷8077份,各城市有效样本量情况如表1所示。

表1 各城市有效样本量情况

城市	昆明	杭州	广州	成都	兰州	武汉	合计
有效样本量/份	810	812	801	810	801	424	4458
城市	大理	上海	深圳	重庆	柳州	大连	合计
有效样本量/份	401	806	805	802	405	400	3619

1.4 调查内容

消费群体基本特征涉及消费者居住城市、年龄、烟龄、性别、职业、文化程度、月均收入;消费者的消费喜好包括喜欢的卷烟类型、包装风格等。

本次调研中,满意度采用百分制计算,具体算法如下:

满意度=(选择"非常满意"的人数/总人数)×100+(选择"比较满意"的人数/总人数)×80+(选择"一般"的人数/总人数)×60+(选择"比较不满意"的人数/总人数)×40+(选择"非常不满意"的人数/总人数)×20

满意率=(选择"非常满意"的人数/总人数)+(选择"比较满意"的人数/总人数)

2 结果与分析

2.1 消费者基本信息描述

在受测样本中,卷烟消费者以男性居多,占总体的80.74%;年龄层方面,以18～55岁的卷烟消费者为主,其中26～45岁的消费者占63.80%;烟龄方面,烟龄普遍较长,平均烟龄为 10.62 年；职业方面，以"工人、普通人员、售货员、服务人员""企事业单位的一般职员"和"自由职业者"为主，共占 61.56%；受教育程度方面，除"硕士及以上"（占 3.24%）和"初中及以下"（占 9.36%）学历所占比重较小以外，其余学历层次的人数所占比重相当；收入水平方面，5000～7999 元居多，占 37.18%，2000～4999 元占 29.85%，累计达到 67.03%。

2.2 消费者喜欢的卷烟类型及原因

目前常规烟的消费群体仍然很庞大，但随着社会的发展，理性消费和注重健康成了卷烟消费的发展方向，细支烟、雪茄烟、中支烟、爆珠烟、电子烟将迎来更好的发展前景。如图 1 所示，本次调查中，虽然超过一半的消费者喜欢的卷烟类型为常规烟，但常规烟主要受中老年消费者喜爱，18～25 岁的青年消费者中仅有 37.18% 的消费者喜爱常规烟，由此推测，随着时代的发展，喜欢常规烟的消费者有逐渐减少的趋势。调查结果显示，常规烟更受 66 岁以上的消费者喜欢，而细支烟更受 18～25 岁的消费者喜欢。

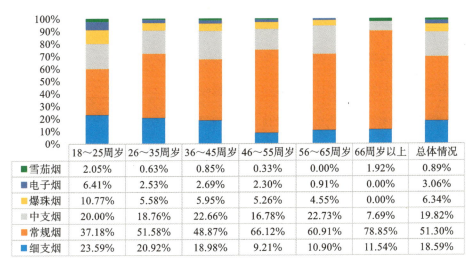

图 1 消费者喜欢的卷烟类型

从不同城市来看，各城市的多数消费者仍喜欢常规烟（见表 2）。

表 2 各城市消费者喜欢的卷烟类型

城市	昆明	杭州	广州	成都	兰州	武汉	大理	上海	深圳	重庆	大连	柳州
细支烟	20.10%	10.60%	32.20%	11.90%	9.50%	6.20%	16.50%	7.50%	17.90%	25.50%	27.80%	29.80%
常规烟	44.00%	78.80%	37.10%	33.90%	68.90%	56.70%	45.70%	65.10%	52.10%	58.30%	44.80%	43.90%
中支烟	22.20%	10.60%	26.20%	15.50%	14.20%	22.80%	17.30%	14.20%	25.90%	14.00%	22.00%	19.30%

续表

城市	昆明	杭州	广州	成都	兰州	武汉	大理	上海	深圳	重庆	大连	柳州
爆珠烟	8.90%	0.00%	1.10%	22.60%	7.40%	11.80%	9.40%	4.70%	2.70%	1.40%	4.00%	0.00%
电子烟	3.40%	0.00%	1.50%	13.70%	0.00%	2.40%	7.10%	8.50%	0.80%	0.70%	0.90%	7.00%
雪茄烟	1.40%	0.00%	1.90%	2.40%	0.00%	0.01%	3.91%	0.00%	0.78%	0.01%	0.41%	0.00%

2.2.1　消费者喜欢细支烟的原因

消费者喜欢细支烟的原因主要是认为"细支烟更健康""细支烟包装时尚、精美"。如图2所示，调查数据显示，选择"细支烟更健康"的消费者占33.87%。

图2　消费者喜欢细支烟的原因

2.2.2　消费者喜欢常规烟的原因

消费者对常规烟的偏好主要形成于消费者长期以来的习惯。如图3所示，调查数据显示，认为"习惯形成，一直以来都是"的消费者占51.08%。

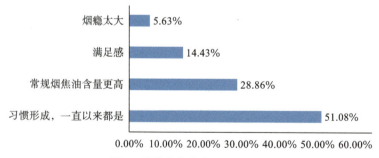

图3　消费者喜欢常规烟的原因

2.2.3 消费者喜欢中支烟的原因

消费者喜欢中支烟的原因主要是认为中支烟"浓度刚好,能够满足吸食需求"。如图4所示,调查数据显示,选择"浓度刚好,能够满足吸食需求"的消费者占37.77%。

图 4　消费者喜欢中支烟的原因

2.2.4 消费者喜欢爆珠烟的原因

消费者喜欢爆珠烟的原因主要是认为爆珠烟"味道清新,焦油含量低""口感醇厚,提神醒脑"。如图5所示,调查数据显示,选择"口感醇厚,提神醒脑"的消费者占26.17%。

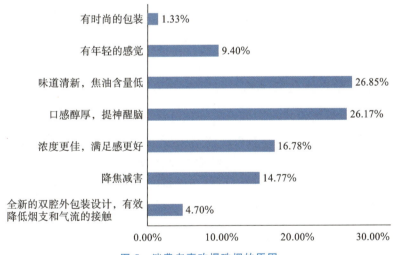

图 5　消费者喜欢爆珠烟的原因

2.2.5 消费者喜欢电子烟的原因

消费者喜欢电子烟的原因主要是"觉得有趣、时尚""想抽烟时应急备用""抽烟方便"。如图6所示,调查数据显示,选择以上三种原因的消费者人数占比均超过20%。

2.2.6 消费者喜欢雪茄烟的原因

消费者喜欢雪茄烟的原因主要是认为"雪茄烟口味独特"。如图7所示,调查数据显示,选择"雪茄烟口味独特"的消费者占47.62%。

图 6　消费者喜欢电子烟的原因

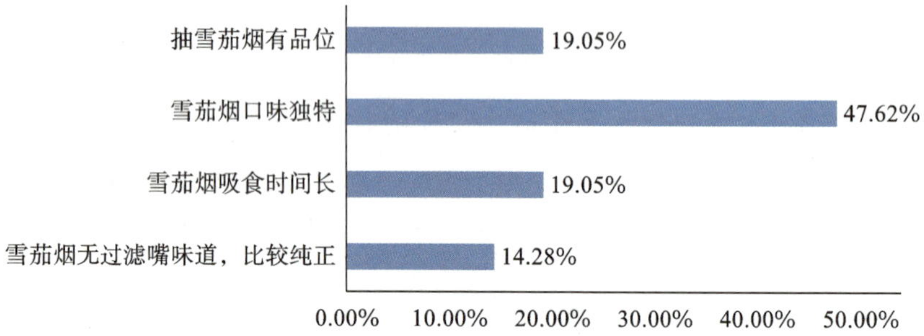

图 7　消费者喜欢雪茄烟的原因

2.3　消费者喜欢的包装风格

消费者喜欢的包装风格主要是"包装有文化内涵"（占 29.21％），"包装高档、时尚"（占 24.80％），"包装简约大方"（占 20.24％）。如图 8 所示，调查数据显示，18～25 岁的消费者主要喜欢"包装高档、时尚"的风格，26～45 岁的消费者主要喜欢"包装有文化内涵"的风格，66 岁以上的消费者主要喜欢"包装简约大方"的风格。针对这一调查结果以及青年消费者的消费特征，建议重点培育一种或几种危害性较低、彰显年轻个性等特点的中高档卷烟品牌，既满足了年轻人的需要，又提升了卷烟品牌结构。

2.4　消费者喜欢的包装颜色

消费者喜欢的包装颜色主要是"颜色素雅"（占 28.26％），"颜色高贵（比如以黑、金、红这三种颜色为主）"（占 26.42％）。如图 9 所示，调查数据显示，25 岁以下和 46 岁以上的消费者主要喜欢"颜色素雅"的包装颜色，26～45 岁的消费者主要喜欢"颜色高贵（比如以黑、金、红这三种颜色为主）"的包装颜色。

2.5　消费者喜欢的包装材质

消费者喜欢的包装材质主要是"材质为硬盒"（占 28.11％），"纹路有凹凸感"（占

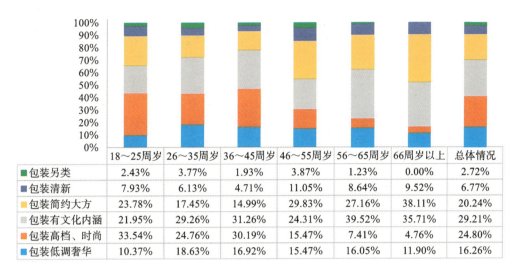

图 8　消费者喜欢的包装风格

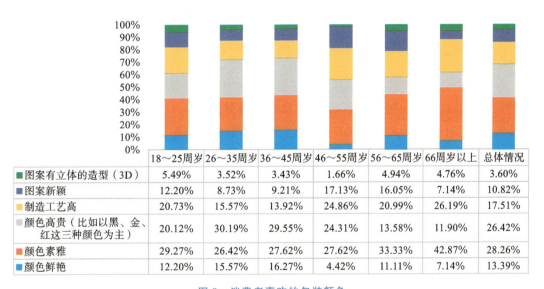

图 9　消费者喜欢的包装颜色

23.40%)。如图 10 所示,调查数据显示,总体而言,消费者均更喜欢材质为硬盒、开盒方式为翻盖的卷烟。

2.6　消费者喜欢的其他包装类型

包装风格方面:有创意、个性鲜明;内敛优雅;平淡素雅,简约大方;金碧辉煌,富贵豪气;大气尊贵,热情豪放,有富贵气息;国风,或者有地方特色;低调奢华,激情豪放等。

包装颜色方面:颜色深沉、颜色鲜艳、色彩多样化等。

包装材质方面:包装硬、不易压坏且打开方便;包装简便且严实;盒子薄,拿取方便;盒子为铁盒、铝盒;包装有质感等。

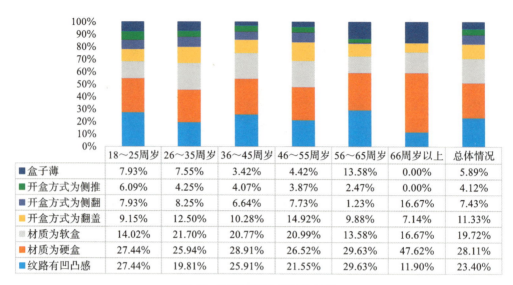

图 10 消费者喜欢的包装材质

3 结论与建议

卷烟产品的市场需求与卷烟品牌的信誉度成正比,当卷烟品牌信誉度提高时,消费者对卷烟产品的接受度也随之提高,卷烟产品会在消费者心中占据一定的位置,品牌信誉度较低的产品则不在考虑之列。此外,品牌信誉度提高后,情感系数也将增长,消费者对卷烟产品的需求就会继续增加。卷烟的价格弹性小,消费者对价格变动不敏感,这有助于提高企业的整体收益,因此品牌培育工作是企业的重点。品牌定位是品牌培育的前提,一个品牌定位的准确性决定了这个品牌是否能培育成功。品牌定位是品牌培育的方向标,它将直接引导品牌培育指向目标市场。任何一个卷烟品牌都不可能适合所有消费者,也不可能满足每位消费者的需求,这就要求烟草商业公司通过充分的市场调研,根据消费者对卷烟的不同需求、不同的购买行为和购买习惯,把整体市场划分为若干个具有类似属性的消费者群体组成的子市场,并从中确定目标市场,针对不同的目标市场进行卷烟品牌组合以适应消费者的需求。卷烟商业公司只有在综合考虑地理因素、人口因素、心理因素、行为因素后,有的放矢地锁定目标消费群体,品牌培育才能迈向成功。

参考文献

[1] 叶奕.面向零售商的烟草货源投放模式研究[D].杭州:浙江工业大学,2012.

[2] 段文婷.经济社会发展对卷烟消费需求的影响[C]//中国烟草学会2016年度优秀论文汇编——卷烟流通主题.山西省长治市平顺县烟草专卖局(营销部),2016:10.

[3] 王昊.卷烟企业顾客满意度指数模型设计及应用[C]//中国烟草学会.中国烟草学会2014年学术年会入选论文摘要汇编.江苏中烟工业有限责任公司企业管理部,2014:1.

[4] 杨蕾,杨乾栩,冯洪涛,等.卷烟产品消费者满意度影响因素实证研究[J].云南农业大学学报(社会科学),2019,13(05):93-101.

[5] 李豪.浅谈区域市场的卷烟消费者研究工作[C]//中国烟草学会.中国烟草学会2014年学术年会入选论文摘要汇编.上海烟草集团静安烟草糖酒有限公司,2014:1.

Research on the Types of Cigarette Products Preferred by Consumers

Abstract: Cigarette design and improvement according to consumer needs is an important basis for market-oriented management. The preferences of cigarette consumption such as cigarette product types, packaging styles, packaging colors and packaging materials were investigated and the real needs of cigarette consumers were figured out, in order to provide specific work guidance for the development of new cigarette products.

Keywords: Consumer; Cigarette products; Product type; Packaging

Tobacco industry is an important part of national economy. In recent years, a market-oriented management concept oriented by consumer needs has been formed, with the development of market economy. In this management mode, understanding consumers' needs and designing and improving cigarettes for consumers is an important basis for market-oriented management[1,2].

For a long time, consumers have their own standard to evaluate whether cigarettes are good or bad. In-depth analysis of consumer preferences and understanding of consumer needs and consumption characteristics are important basis for cigarette operators to make decisions[3]. According to the current concept of market-oriented management, the design, production and marketing of cigarette products should be oriented by consumer needs, and strategies from design, production to marketing should be carried out according to consumers, consumption behaviors and characteristics, as well as their evaluation and satisfaction of various cigarette products[4,5]. For cigarettes, consumption often changes due to the customers' age, occupation, income, region, cigarette preference, brand loyalty degree, and policy effect. Only by grasping the characteristics of customers' consumption effectively and mastering the consumption demand accurately can we provide effective guidance for marketing strategy.

With the deepening reform of Chinese market and the improvement of cigarette retail terminals, large cigarette production enterprises have become more dependent on data. Retail outlets need big data to understand customers, and enterprises need to understand consumers' feelings and the dynamics of the market. Therefore, it is necessary to strengthen the analysis and application of cigarette consumer data and to improve the dynamic monitoring ability of cigarette enterprises. In this survey, the consumption demand of cigarettes was collected to understand the types of cigarette products that consumers preferred, and the real demand of cigarette consumers was figured out, in order to provide specific work guidance for the development of new cigarette products.

1　Research Methods

1.1　Survey Time

The survey was conducted from December 1, 2021 to January 30, 2022.

1.2　Respondents

Taking Kunming, Hangzhou, Guangzhou, Chengdu, Lanzhou, Wuhan, Dali, Shanghai, Shenzhen, Chongqing, Liuzhou and Dalian as the research cities, a questionnaire was distributed to cigarette consumers living in the research cities, and the cigarette consumers aged 18-55 years were the main respondents.

1.3　Survey Methods

The questionnaire was collected by scanning code and self-filling method. A total of 8707 questionnaires were collected in this survey, 8077 of which were valid. The effective sample volume of each city is shown in Table 1.

Table 1　Effective Sample Volume of Each City

City	Effective sample volume	City	Effective sample volume
Kunming	810	Dali	401
Hangzhou	812	Shanghai	806
Guangzhou	801	Shenzhen	805
Chengdu	810	Chongqing	802
Lanzhou	801	Liuzhou	405
Wuhan	424	Dalian	400

1.4　Survey Content

The basic characteristics of consumer groups included the city where consumers live, age, length of smoking, gender, occupation, educational level and average monthly income. Consumer preferences included favorite cigarette types, packaging styles, etc.

In this survey, the degree of satisfaction was calculated by hundred-mark system.

The specific algorithm is as follows:

Degree of satisfaction=(number of people who choose "very satisfied"/total number of respondents)×100+(number of people who choose "relatively satisfied"/total number of respondents)×80+(number of people who choose "general"/total number of respondents)×60+(number of people who choose "relatively dissatisfied"/total number of respondents)×40+(number of people who choose "very dissatisfied"/total number of respondents)×20;

Satisfaction rate= (number of people who choose "very satisfied"/total number of respondents) + (number of people who choose "relatively satisfied"/total number of respondents).

2　Results and Analysis

2.1　Description of Basic Consumer Information

In the tested samples, cigarette consumers were mostly male, accounting for 80.74% of the total. In terms of age group, cigarette consumers mainly aged 18-55 years, 63.80% of them aged 26-45 years. In terms of length of smoking, the average length was 10.62 years. In terms of occupation, "workers, ordinary staff, salespeople, service personnel", "ordinary staff of enterprises and institutions" and "freelancers" accounted for 61.56%. In terms of educational level, except for master's degree or above (3.24%) and junior high school education or below (9.36%), the proportion of people at other different educational levels was equal. In terms of income level, people with an income of 5000-7999 yuan accounted for 37.18%, and those with an income of 2000-4999 yuan accounted for 29.85%, with an accumulative total of 67.03%.

2.2　Types of Cigarettes Consumers Prefer and the Reasons

At present, there is still very large consumer group of regular cigarettes, but with the development of society, rational consumption and health-conscious awareness has become the development direction of cigarette consumption, and slim cigarettes, cigars, medium cigarettes, cigarettes with capsule and electronic cigarettes will usher in a better prospect of development. In this survey, although more than half of consumers preferred regular cigarettes, regular cigarettes were mainly favored by middle-aged and elderly consumers, and only 37.18% of young consumers aged 18-25 years preferred regular cigarettes. Therefore, it is speculated that with the development of the times, the consumers who prefer regular cigarettes are gradually declining. The survey results showed that regular cigarettes were preferred by consumers over 66 years old, while slim cigarettes were preferred by consumers between 18 and 25 years old (Table 2).

Table 2 Types of Cigarette Preferred by Consumers   (Unit: %)

Type of cigarettes	Consumer age/(years old)					Overall situation
	18-25	26-35	36-45	46-55	56-65	Over 66	
Cigar	2.05	0.63	0.85	0.33	0.00	1.92	0.89
Electronic cigarette	6.41	2.53	2.69	2.30	0.91	0.00	3.06
Cigarette with capsule	10.77	5.58	5.95	5.26	4.55	0.00	6.34
Medium cigarette	20.00	18.76	22.66	16.78	22.73	7.69	19.82
Regular cigarette	37.18	51.58	48.87	66.12	60.91	78.85	51.30
Slim cigarette	23.59	20.92	18.98	9.21	10.90	11.54	18.59

In the perspective of different cities, the majority of consumers in each city still preferred regular cigarettes (Table 3).

Table 3 Types of Cigarettes Preferred by Consumers in Different Cities   (Unit: %)

Type of cigarettes	Kunming	Hangzhou	Guangzhou	Chengdu	Lanzhou	Wuhan	Dali	Shanghai	Shenzhen	Chongqing	Dalian	Liuzhou
Slim cigarette	20.10	10.60	32.20	11.90	9.50	6.20	16.50	7.50	17.90	25.50	27.80	29.80
Regular cigarette	44.00	78.80	37.10	33.90	68.90	56.70	45.70	65.10	52.10	58.30	44.80	43.90
Medium cigarette	22.20	10.60	26.20	15.50	14.20	22.80	17.30	14.20	25.90	14.00	22.00	19.30
Cigarette with capsule	8.90	0.00	1.10	22.60	7.40	11.80	9.40	4.70	2.70	1.40	4.00	0.00
Electronic cigarette	3.40	0.00	1.50	13.70	0.00	2.40	7.10	8.50	0.80	0.70	0.90	7.00
Cigar	1.40	0.00	1.90	2.40	0.00	0.01	3.91	0.00	0.78	0.01	0.41	0.00

2.2.1 Reasons Why Consumers Prefer Slim Cigarettes

The main reason why consumers preferred slim cigarettes was "slim cigarettes are healthier", "slim cigarettes are fashionable and exquisite pack". Survey data showed that there were 33.87% of consumers who believed "slim cigarettes are healthier" (Figure 1).

2.2.2 Reasons Why Consumers Prefer Regular Cigarettes

The main reason why consumers preferred regular cigarettes was the formation of consumers' habits all the time. According to the survey data, there were 51.08% of consumers who chose "habit formation, all through the way" (Figure 2).

2.2.3 Reasons Why Consumers Prefer Medium Cigarettes

The main reason why consumers preferred medium cigarettes was the concentration of medium cigarettes is "concentration is just enough to meet the demand for smoking".

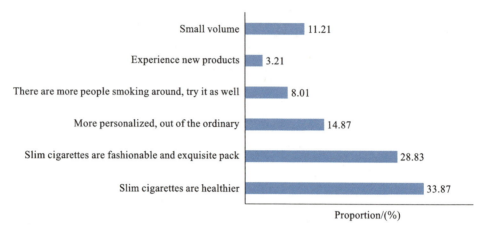

Figure 1　Reasons Why Consumers Prefer Slim Cigarettes

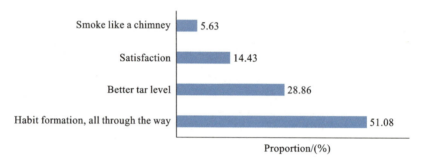

Figure 2　Reasons Why Consumers Prefer Regular Cigarettes

According to the survey data, there were 37.77% of consumers who believed "concentration is just enough to meet the demand for smoking" (Figure 3).

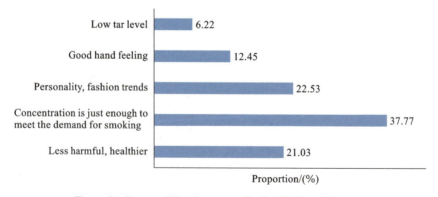

Figure 3　Reasons Why Consumers Prefer Medium Cigarettes

2.2.4　Reasons Why Consumers Prefer Cigarettes with Capsule

The main reasons why consumers preferred cigarettes with capsule were "fresh taste, low tar level", "mellow taste, refreshing". The survey data showed that there were

26.17% of consumers who felt "mellow taste, refreshing" (Figure 4).

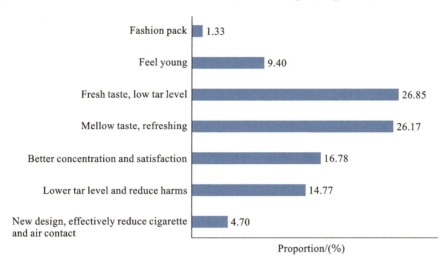

Figure 4   Reasons Why Consumers Prefer Cigarettes with Capsules

2.2.5   Reasons Why Consumers Prefer Electronic Cigarettes

The main reasons why consumers preferred electronic cigarettes were "find interesting, fashionable", "stand by when want to smoke", "convenient for smoking". Survey data showed that there were more than 20% of consumers who chose the three reasons above (Figure 5).

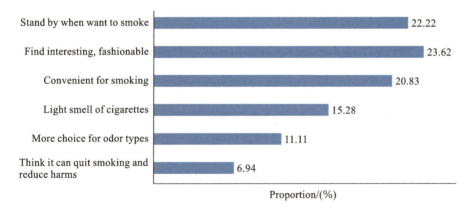

Figure 5   Reasons Why Consumers Prefer Electronic Cigarettes

2.2.6   Reasons Why Consumers Prefer Cigars

The main reason why consumers preferred cigars was cigar has a unique taste. According to the survey data, there were 47.62% of consumers who chose "unique taste" (Figure 6).

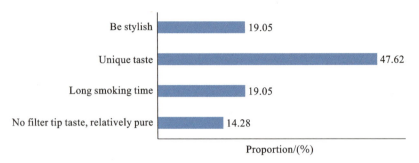

Figure 6　Reasons Why Consumers Prefer Cigars

2.3　The Packaging Styles Favored by Consumers

Consumers' favorite packaging styles were mainly "with cultural connotations" (29.21%), "high-end and fashionable pack" (24.80%), "simple and elegant pack" (20.24%). The survey data showed that consumers under 25 years old mainly preferred the style of "high-end and fashionable pack"; consumers aged 26-45 years mainly preferred the style of "pack with cultural connotations"; and consumers over 66 years old mainly preferred the style of "simple and elegant pack" (Table 4). In view of this result and the consumption characteristics of young consumers, it is suggested to focus on cultivating one or several medium and high-end cigarette brands with low harm and young personality. It not only meets the needs of young people, but also enhances the brand structure of cigarette.

Table 4　Packaging Styles Favored by Consumers　　　　　　　　　　(Unit:%)

Packaging style	Consumer age						Overall situation
	18-25	26-35	36-45	46-55	56-65	Over 66	
Weird	2.43	3.77	1.93	3.87	1.23	0.00	2.72
Fresh	7.93	6.13	4.71	11.05	8.64	9.52	6.77
Simple and elegant	23.78	17.45	14.99	29.83	27.16	38.11	20.24
With cultural connotations	21.95	29.26	31.26	24.31	39.52	35.71	29.21
High-end, fashion	33.54	24.76	30.19	15.47	7.41	4.76	24.80
Modest luxury	10.37	18.63	16.92	15.47	16.05	11.90	16.26

2.4　The Packaging Colors Favored by Consumers

The packaging colors favored by consumers were mainly "simple but elegant color" (28.26%) and "noble color (such as black, gold and red)" (26.42%). According to the survey data, consumers under 25 years old and above 46 years old mainly preferred the pack with "simple but elegant color", while consumers between 26 and 45 years old mainly preferred the pack with "noble color" (Table 5).

Table 5 Packaging Colors Favored by Consumers (Unit:%)

Packaging color	Consumer age						Overall situation
	18-25	26-35	36-45	46-55	56-65	Over 66	
Three-dimensional modeling of patterns	5.49	3.52	3.43	1.66	4.94	4.76	3.60
Novel patterns	12.20	8.73	9.21	17.13	16.05	7.14	10.82
High manufacturing technology	20.73	15.57	13.92	24.86	20.99	26.19	17.51
Noble color (such as black, gold and red)	20.12	30.19	29.55	24.31	13.58	11.90	26.42
Simple but elegant color	29.27	26.42	27.62	27.62	33.33	42.87	28.26
Bright color	12.20	15.57	16.27	4.42	11.11	7.14	13.39

2.5 The Packaging Materials Favored by Consumers

The packaging materials favored by consumers were mainly "hard pack" (28.11%) and "concave and convex pattern" (23.40%). Survey data showed that consumers preferred cigarettes with flip-top hard pack (Table 6).

Table 6 Packaging Materials Favored by Consumers (Unit:%)

Packaging material	Consumer age						Overall situation
	18-25	26-35	36-45	46-55	56-65	Over 66	
Thin pack	7.93	7.55	3.42	4.42	13.58	0.00	5.89
Side push	6.09	4.25	4.07	3.87	2.47	0.00	4.12
Side flip	7.93	8.25	6.64	7.73	1.23	16.67	7.43
Flip top	9.15	12.50	10.28	14.92	9.88	7.14	11.33
Soft pack	14.02	21.70	20.77	20.99	13.58	16.67	19.72
Hard pack	27.44	25.94	28.91	26.52	29.63	47.62	28.11
Concave and convex pattern	27.44	19.81	25.91	21.55	29.63	11.90	23.40

2.6 Other Pack Types Favored by Consumers

Pack style: creative, distinctive personality; introverted and elegant; plain and simple but elegant, simple and elegant; resplendent, rich and noble; noble and generous, warm and unrestrained, rich and noble flavor; national style, or with local characteristics; modest luxury; passionate and unrestrained, etc.

Pack color: deep color; bright color; diverse colors, etc.

Pack material: hard pack is not easy to crush and is easy to open; pack is simple and tight; pack is thin and easy to take; pack is iron box, or aluminum box; pack is of textural quality, etc.

3 Conclusions and Suggestions

The market demand for cigarette products is directly proportional to the reputation of cigarette brands. When the brand reputation increases, consumers also increase acceptance of cigarette products which will have a certain place in the psyche, those with low brand reputation will not be considered.

When the brand reputation is improved, the emotional coefficient will also increase upward, and the demand for cigarette products will keep increasing. Consumers have little price elasticity of products and are insensitive to price changes, which can improve the overall earnings of enterprises. Therefore, brand cultivation is the focus of enterprises. Brand positioning is the premise of brand cultivation.

The accuracy of a brand positioning determines whether the brand can be successfully cultivated. Brand positioning is the direction of brand cultivation, and it will directly guide brand cultivation to target market. No cigarette brand can be suitable for all consumers, nor can it meet the needs of every consumer. It requires tobacco commercial companies to divide the overall market into several different consumer groups with similar attributes according to different desires and demands, purchasing behaviors and habits of consumers in the target market through sufficient market research, and to determine the target market. Cigarette brands are combined according to different target markets, so as to meet the needs of consumers. Only after comprehensive consideration of geographical, demographic, psychological and behavioral factors can cigarette commercial companies lock the target consumer groups, so as to achieve success in brand cultivation.

References

[1] YE Y. The Research of Tobacco Retailer's Supply Mode[D]. Hanzhou: Zhejiang University of Technology, 2012.

[2] DUAN W T. Influence of Economic and Social Development on Cigarette Consumption Demand[C]//Proceedings of 2016 Annual Conference of China Tobacco Society, 2016:10.

[3] WANG H. Design and Application of Customer Satisfaction Index Model for Cigarette Enterprises[C]//Proceedings of 2014 Annual Conference of China Tobacco Society,2014:1.

[4] YANG L,YANG Q X,FENG H T,et al. Empirical Study on the Factors Affecting Consumer Satisfaction of Cigarette Products[J]. Journal of Yunnan Agricultural University(Social Sciences),2019(5):93-101.

[5] LI H. On the Research of Cigarette Consumers in Regional Market[C]//Proceedings of 2014 Annual Conference of China Tobacco Society,2014:1.

基于扎根理论的卷烟消费者产品评价和需求分析

摘要：为了从消费者和零售客户的角度真实客观地了解卷烟产品的市场现状、消费习惯差异、品牌销售趋势等信息,本文运用深度访谈法,在全国4个城市开展消费者需求信息收集和调研服务,记录并整理了32位受访者的访谈资料,引入扎根理论分析方法,借助NVivo 11.0软件,完成扎根理论三级编码,得到了涵盖个人情感、融入圈子、突出个性、娱乐、交际、工作、包装、品牌、口味、价格、卷烟类型、购买渠道等12个主范畴层次分析结果,并提炼为一个核心类属,即购买习惯,并围绕该核心类属进行详细分析。研究结果表明:消费者倾向于从习惯性光顾的店面购得卷烟产品,且更倾向于购买本地烟,还偏好大品牌如"云烟""玉溪"等,在外观上偏向于能反映当地文化、颜色鲜明、易开启、有高档感的包装;其次,不同地区消费结构存在差异,主要表现在各地区烟文化和主抽品牌不同,在产品吸味偏好上也存在较大差异。结论:烟草行业应完善品牌培育配套机制,从口味和包装上做相应的创新迭代,满足日益变化的消费需求,从而实现可持续发展。

关键词：消费者；扎根理论；卷烟；评价；需求分析

1 引言

作为国民经济的重要支柱产业,烟草行业的发展对国民经济的发展具有巨大的推动作用,也是实现我国烟草行业稳占国内市场,积极向外扩张,打造强势民族烟草业的关键所在[1]。因此,烟草经济应当尽快实现可持续发展的宏伟目标。目前,中国烟草行业的发展策略主要侧重于:一是确定明确的发展方向;二是强化体制创新和机制创新,在整个烟草行业完善现代企业管理制度和经营管理手段;三是重视科技创新,加大科研投入,充分发挥科技作为第一生产力的巨大作用[2,3]。

NVivo 11.0是一款计算机辅助质性数据分析软件,由澳大利亚QSR公司设计研发,是当前国际质性分析软件中的主要产品[4]。它构建了基于扎根理论的操作方法框架,即对现有数据进行提炼和深入分析,以发现核心要素,并探寻要素之间的关系,然后建立相关假设[5]。它具有强大的编码功能,可以概括许多文献和数据资料中与某个研究课题相关的信息,帮助研究人员快速捕捉文献中的信息点[6]。通过使用这款能够处理大量原始数据的软件进行定性研究,研究人员可以从海量的数据和文本信息中快速筛选出需要的信息,从而显著缩短研究周期,提高研究效果。根据Fassinger的研究,理论上样本量越大,饱和度越高,但实际工作中,为避免数据处理过于烦琐,最好的样本量在20~35之间[7]。因此,本文借助 NVivo 11.0,对昆明、广州、成都、杭州 4 个城市的 32 位卷烟消费者进行深度访谈,采用深度访谈和扎根理论分析相结合的方法,旨在了解消费者对产品口味、包装、价格、概念、产品满意度等卷烟指标的评价,并据此总结出消费者对产品外观、产品口味、产品价位等方面的需求信息。

2 材料与方法

2.1 数据来源

本文数据来源于 2021 年 10 月市场调研。调研过程中对昆明、成都、广州、杭州 4 个城市的 32 位受访者进行访谈,被访对象包括主抽云产卷烟的消费者、同价位竞品卷烟的消费者、女性消费者、零售商、35 岁以下的年轻烟民、35~55 岁资深烟民 6 个类别,每个城市每个类别 1 人。遵循"动态抽样"和"信息饱和"的原则[8],进行抽样及焦点访谈,其中男性 24 人,女性 8 人,年龄从 22~53 岁均匀分布。访谈时间为 105 分钟,使用开放式问题展开,提纲见表 1。

表 1　消费者消费动机及需求访谈提纲

序号	内容简介	时间/分钟	目的
1	自我介绍	5	相互认识,说明目的,活跃气氛
2	烟民烟史介绍	15	通过烟民的抽烟史了解烟民抽烟的动机与场合
3	品牌认知	15	了解烟民对卷烟品牌的认知程度
4	烟民消费习惯和态度	20	了解烟民的吸食习惯
5	卷烟产品评价	20	详细了解烟民对卷烟产品各方面的偏好
6	购买态度和习惯	20	了解烟民的购买习惯及购买决策过程
7	广告及促销	10	了解烟民对卷烟广告的认知度和记忆度,把握烟民的媒体接触习惯

2.2 数据处理

本研究采用 NVivo 11.0 版本,使用编码和层次分析功能,采用扎根理论,将重要节点进行编码汇总及深度的定性分析[9,10];构建了基于研究内容的理论框架,确定开放式编码、轴心式编码和核心编码[11],示意图详见图 1。

对编码进行饱和度与效度检验。按照理论饱和度原则,随机抽取 1/3 的样本资料作为理论饱和度的验证[12,13]。检验结果显示,各概念和范畴已相对完善,没有产生新的概念和范畴。数据编码方面,32 位受访者原始资料的概念提取参考依据强、内部效度高,符合研究要求。

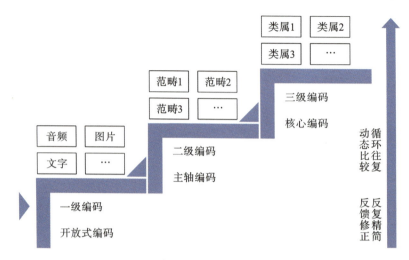

图 1　扎根理论三级编码示意图

3　结果与分析

3.1　编码结果

3.1.1　开放式编码

在反复研读访谈资料的基础上,对原始数据进行逐字逐句编码,贴标签,重新赋予概念并形成概括性更强的新范畴,本研究初步得到290个概念,由于存在重复与同义的标签,经比较、合并和遴选后,最终得到105个概念(表2)。

3.1.2　主轴编码

主轴编码是在开放式编码的基础上,通过比较不同概念之间的异同、厘清其相互关系,提炼归纳了12个更高层次的范畴和维度,它们分别是个人情感、融入圈子、突出个性、娱乐、交际、工作、包装、品牌、口味、价格、卷烟类型、购买渠道(表2)。

表 2　三级编码

开放编码	主轴编码	核心编码
释放压力、思绪混乱、闲暇无聊、对卷烟好奇、烦恼、心情低落、暴躁、萎靡不振	个人情感	接触卷烟的原因
周围流行、合群、朋友抽烟、家人抽烟	融入圈子	
认为抽烟可以突出个性、感觉抽烟好玩	突出个性	
唱歌、打麻将、打游戏、打牌、喝酒	娱乐	抽烟场合
聚会、庆祝活动、社交活动、聊天	交际	
加班、应酬	工作	

续表

开放编码	主轴编码	核心编码
吸引眼球、彰显个性、有内涵和档次、反映地域文化、颜色鲜明、国潮设计、另类图案、浮雕、烫金、凹凸纹路、立体、皮纹设计、激光图案设计、有质感、环保、素雅、低调、高档时尚、简约大方	包装	购买习惯
紫云、红河、金沙江、软珍、云烟、玉溪、悦刻、柚子、娇子、中华、双喜、黄鹤楼、红塔山、利群、和谐、苏烟、芙蓉王	品牌	
淡雅、浓烈、柔和、口味纯正、口感醇香、顺畅通透、饱满、烟草本香、清爽、中性、回甘、口不会干	口味	
奢侈品卷烟、高档、中档、低档、玉溪价位大众、云烟性价比高、娇子价位在可接受范围内、利群价格合适	价格	
粗支烟、中支烟、常规烟、细支烟、薄荷、果香、陈皮爆珠、陈皮、冬虫夏草、枇杷、蓝莓、甜香、茉莉绿茶、低焦油量、中焦油量、高焦油量、电子烟	卷烟类型	
超市、便利店、烟酒店、专卖店、同事、朋友、老板	购买渠道	

3.1.3 核心编码

在得到12个范畴的基础上,形成了接触卷烟的原因、抽烟场合、购买习惯三大核心编码(表2)。同时,层次分析结果显示(图2),在所有一级节点中,购买习惯占比最大,约四分之三;抽烟场合和接触卷烟的原因分别处于第二、第三位,两者差距较小。购买习惯所有二级节点中,口味占比最大,品牌和包装次之,且差距较小;购买渠道、价格和卷烟类型的占比较小。由此可知,在影响消费者购买卷烟的诸因素中,"购买习惯"分量最重,是核心编码,其重要性超过其他因素。

3.2 结果分析

3.2.1 口味的评价

不同地区消费者评价卷烟质量的标准基本一致,但仍有所差异。

杭州:抽吸顺畅,没有颗粒感,口感好,燃烧状态,烟灰不发黑。

广州:入口的最初口感,口腔无辣感,烟草味浓,吸进去顺畅,回味好,残留的烟味浓度,燃烧的程度,烟灰的颜色。

昆明:开包香味,烟丝不碎,颜色金黄,吸的时候不呛,燃烧速度。

成都:首先是烟丝味道,再看吸食的口感、香气、烟灰是否容易掉等。

可以看出,抽吸顺畅、口感、燃烧速度、烟灰颜色等是消费者关注的共性指标。

在对云产卷烟(又称云烟)口味评价方面,消费者认为云烟品牌不呛喉,烟草味纯正,口不干,档次高,品质好,系列多;认为玉溪品牌品质、口碑、影响力都非常高,抽吸起来不辛辣,顺畅,不刺激喉咙(表3)。

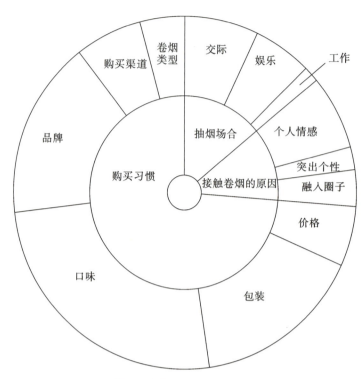

图 2 节点编码层次统计图

表 3 主要云产卷烟品牌评价

品牌	系列	选择原因	抽吸过程质量评价
云烟	云烟（细支珍品）	价格合适，历史悠久，旗下品牌比较多	劲头比较小，没有粗支烟的刺激性大，烟味比较香醇
	云烟（七彩印象）	细支烟比较有个性，很少人抽	口感是比较纯正的烟草味，没有添加太多香精，抽烟时吸力小，抽起来喉咙有回甘，喉咙比较舒服
	云烟（黑金刚印象）	知名度高，引人注目，包装设计好看，颜色独特（黑色的包装盒，字是金色，很炫酷，饱满度也很高）	烟的味道比较醇厚，只有烟草味，没有香精味
	云烟（云龙）	包装大气，档次高，价格适中，口味合适；本香味比较淡雅，烟气入口比较顺滑，抽多了也不容易上头，有云烟品牌特色；身边的朋友、同事都在抽这个烟	烟燃烧得比较慢，口感比较柔和，焦油含量稍微有点低，烟味清淡
	云烟（紫）	晚上工作的时候特别容易犯困，抽浓一点的烟可以提神；价格实惠，假货少，口味好	烟味比较重、比较浓

续表

品牌	系列	选择原因	抽吸过程质量评价
云烟	云烟（软珍品）	包装好看，牌子历史比较悠久，假烟很少，口味合适	抽吸顺畅，无杂质和异味
玉溪	玉溪（软）	软包装，口感不辛辣	口味较纯正，烟味适中，烟丝压得紧，抽起来阻力较小，比较顺畅，不凶不呛
	玉溪（硬）	价格合理，历史悠久，品牌规格齐全	口感不辣，不会口干

3.2.2 品牌形象感知

不同地区消费者对云产卷烟品牌形象的感知有所不同（表4）。总体上看，"历史悠久""老品牌""质量稳定""创新力强"为消费者对云烟品牌形象的感知；而"全国性""亲民""品质始终如一""潮流前卫"为消费者对玉溪品牌形象的感知。不同之处在于消费者认为云烟品牌知名度更广一些。同时，部分消费者认为玉溪品牌显"成熟稳重"，云烟品牌则更显"阅历丰富"。

表4 各地消费者对云产卷烟品牌形象的感知

品牌	项目	昆明	成都	广州	杭州
云烟	联想到的词语	代表云南；历史悠久；容易买到；口感不变；价格能接受	老品牌；历史悠久，有吸引力，全国各地均有销售；质量稳定，口感好	老品牌；保守；有民族特色；优雅；创新力强	历史悠久；代表云南；更适合年轻人（口感没有那么重）
	拟人化品牌形象	一位30～35岁的集领导能力、品位、爱好广泛于一身的全能型精英	一位50岁左右阅历丰富、性格豪爽、雷厉风行的中年人	一位40岁左右在旅游业行事稳重、生活安定、热情好客的企业家	一位刚刚踏入社会不久，对职业还处于探索阶段的年轻人
	品牌形象来源	与玉溪相比，低调而不失锋芒的包装	特定历史时刻时的必需品，被广泛用于重要场合	品牌的悠久历史和所使用材料的优良品质	品牌给消费者比较新潮的感觉

续表

品牌	项目	昆明	成都	广州	杭州
玉溪	联想到的词语	品质始终如一；历史悠久	相对云烟价格更为亲民；覆盖率高，全国各地都容易买到；劲头大；口碑不错，亲和力强	名气略逊于云烟，能联想到云南；包装好看	假货少；好抽；购买方便；销量不错
	拟人化品牌形象	一位穿着潮流、前卫的年轻普通职员	一位成熟稳重、亲和力强、气质适度得体的中年人	一位40岁左右思想相对传统保守的中年人	一位30岁左右有自己想法的创业者
	品牌形象来源	更加面向大众的市场价位；更加年轻化、迎合年轻人的心态的包装设计理念	品牌的悠久历史	旗下卷烟品种较少；包装较为普通	端庄秀丽的品牌名字；品牌的悠久历史

3.2.3 消费者对卷烟包装的喜好

包装在消费者购买卷烟时起到非常大的作用，因为它意味着内涵和档次。消费者喜欢的包装是能反映当地地域文化，而且颜色鲜明，容易在货架上找到，偏向国潮设计或者另类的图案。消费者认为包装的高档感应该从工艺上体现，比如浮雕、烫金、有凹凸感的纹路、立体效果、皮纹设计、激光图案设计等；包装盒子要硬且薄，手感好，可以采用环保材料；整体要偏向素雅，有文化底蕴，体现国潮风格。消费者不喜欢颜色花哨、印刷模糊、毫无特点的包装。详见表5。

表5 各地消费者对卷烟包装的喜好

项目	昆明	成都	广州	杭州
喜欢的包装	外包装为上翻盖或侧翻盖	高档时尚（从外观、颜色、纹路、装饰的图文体现），有文化内涵，有质感，有立体的造型，有凹凸感	颜色鲜艳，图案新颖，有水墨画和国潮风的感觉，能体现地方特色，盒子比较薄，表面有凹凸不平的纹理，吸引眼球（越高档的卷烟越能体现民族风格，越素雅）	包装简约大方，手感好，外观精美，有档次感；颜色基本上是黑、金、红这三种主打色，给人比较高贵的感觉

续表

项目	昆明	成都	广州	杭州
不喜欢的包装	包装摸起来比较软,手感不好,配色不协调	包装花里胡哨;包装普通,没有新意,没有特点	包装工艺比较粗糙,不精致	包装平淡无奇,颜色较素

3.2.4 购买渠道

各城市消费者主要通过超市、便利店、烟酒店、专卖店来购买卷烟,且以熟悉的、居住地附近的店为首选。购买价格较高的卷烟则倾向去大一点的超市。消费者对品牌的主要认知途径为:购买时烟店货架展示,朋友介绍,烟店或者网络推荐。购买优惠一般较少,消费者表示整条购买相对便宜,部分地区会送打火机。详见表6。

表6 各地区消费者购买卷烟渠道分析

项目	昆明	成都	广州	杭州
购买渠道	超市、便利店、烟酒店、商店、托朋友	超市、烟酒店、专卖店	便利店、超市、烟酒店、卷烟专卖店、商店	烟酒店、专卖店、超市、零售店
购买过程中与商家互动情况	过去整条购买折扣力度较大,但现在没有优惠了	整条购买折扣力度较大	整条购买有优惠,或者送打火机	价格是固定的,不会打折,偶尔整条购买的价格会便宜一点,但一般情况下不会有优惠
如何了解到新品牌的卷烟	烟店、超市买烟时看见或老板推介;朋友聚会时	从身边朋友了解;烟酒店、超市	从身边朋友了解;烟店货架展示	朋友聚会时;烟酒店老板推介

3.2.5 卷烟类型和价格

按口感分类:有比较辣的和比较呛的烟,比如云烟(紫)、红河和金沙江;也有相对比较温和的烟,比如云烟(软珍品)和女士烟。

按规格分类:粗支烟、中支烟或常规烟适合平常抽及作为婚宴用烟。细支烟主要是在娱乐的时候抽,或适合烟瘾不大的人抽。目前很多男性消费者出于健康考虑,也开始通过抽细支烟来减少吸烟量。

按香型分类:女性消费者比较愿意接受薄荷、果香等香型。男性消费者则比较愿意接受陈皮爆珠香型,尤其广州的消费者,他们认为陈皮、冬虫夏草等香型更为养生,对身体有益。成都消费者不太接受外加香型,成都女性消费者比较喜欢果香,比如枇杷、蓝莓、甜香、茉莉、绿茶等,并且表示抽起来舒服,不刺激喉咙,也没有烟草味,心理上可以获得满足感。

按焦油含量分类:8毫克以下是低焦油量,8~10毫克的焦油量比较适中,超过12毫克就是高焦油量。

按价格分类:广州、昆明和成都的消费者都认为50元以上的卷烟为高档卷烟,杭州的消费者认为80元以上的卷烟为高档卷烟。杭州和昆明的消费者认为30元以下的卷烟为低档卷烟,成都和广州的消费者认为20元以下的卷烟为低档卷烟。高档品牌主要用于商务应酬和送礼,比如中华、大重九。抽烟的档次和自身经济收入有关;注重健康、经济自由的人会选择高档卷烟,比如印象、软中华、苏烟。一般人群选择中档卷烟,比如软珍、和谐。大众消费的卷烟一般是低档卷烟,比如紫云、红塔山、软珍、利群、红河等。详见表7。

表7 各地区卷烟品牌价格分类　　　　　　　　　　　　　　　　（单位:元）

价格分类	昆明	成都	广州	杭州
奢侈品	>100	—	—	—
高档	50~60	50~80	>50	80~100
中档	30~49	30~49	20~50	30~79
低档	<30	<20	<20	<30

各城市卷烟消费者的第一选择一般会偏向本地烟,第二选择、第三选择会偏向于云烟、玉溪、中华、黄鹤楼等大品牌卷烟,详见表8。在本次调查中,消费者购买最多的品牌从高到低依次是中华、云烟、玉溪、黄鹤楼、双喜、南京、利群、芙蓉王、宽窄、大重九(说明:宽窄、大重九为副品牌名,其中宽窄主品牌为娇子,大重九主品牌为云烟),详见图3。

表8 各地区品牌选择意向表

地区	第一选择	第二选择	第三选择
成都	娇子	云烟	中华
广州	双喜、云烟	玉溪	黄鹤楼
昆明	云烟	玉溪	红塔山
杭州	利群	云烟	玉溪

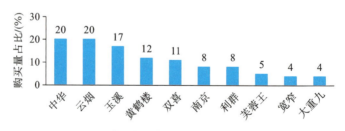

图3　购买量排名前十的品牌(可多选)

4 讨论

第一,从产品口味来看,由于各地区烟文化和主抽品牌的不同,各城市消费者喜欢的口味也不同。昆明消费者喜欢的卷烟口味:口味纯正、口感醇香、温和,烟味较重,不辣嗓子。成都消费者喜欢的卷烟口味:烟劲不大,口感偏柔和,抽起来顺畅通透、饱满,不刺激喉咙,烟草本味。广州消费者喜欢的卷烟口味:口感适中、淡雅,抽起来顺畅、顺滑,烟草味纯正,回甘好。杭州消费者喜欢的卷烟口味:口感厚一点和浓一点,抽起来有劲、不呛,抽吸清爽。

第二,从产品外观来看,各城市消费者喜欢的包装风格不同。昆明消费者喜欢低调奢华的包装,成都消费者喜欢高档、时尚、有质感的包装,广州消费者喜欢颜色鲜艳、有地方特色的包装,杭州消费者喜欢简约低调的包装。但在不喜欢的包装方面不同城市消费者意见较为统一,包括图案花哨、颜色平淡无奇、印刷模糊、缺乏质感。总体来看,消费者喜欢的包装是能反映当地地域文化,而且颜色鲜明,在货架上容易找到,能体现中华文化的国风设计。消费者认为包装的高档感应该从工艺上体现,比如浮雕、烫金、有凹凸感的纹路、立体效果、皮纹设计、激光图案设计等。在材质方面,包装盒要硬且薄,有手感。

第三,从品牌选择来看,卷烟消费者的第一选择会偏向本地烟,第二选择、第三选择一般偏向云烟、玉溪、中华、黄鹤楼等大品牌。品牌影响力是影响消费者购买的重要因素,石凤学等对我国16个城市3个价位档次4个卷烟规格的购买因素分析结果显示,品牌形象是第二影响因素,如"本地知名度高""老品牌,历史悠久""经典品牌"等[14]。烟草行业应该努力提升市场竞争能力,注重重点品牌的研发,规避强势品牌产品线老化和重点品牌大而不强的现象,可从完善工商协同营销机制、消费者品牌协同以及批零协同等方面入手,建立"消费者、零售商、工商企业"三位一体的品牌培育机制,提高卷烟企业对卷烟品牌的培育能力[15]。

第四,从购买渠道来看,各城市消费者购买渠道集中在超市、便利店、烟酒店、专卖店,且一般会选择比较熟悉的店或附近的店。选择这些渠道的原因是出于习惯及购买便利,且不容易买到假烟。而价格高一点的烟在品牌超市才能买到。

第五,从产品价位来看,大部分消费者普遍认为50~100元是高档卷烟,10~30元的卷烟为低档卷烟。20~30元的卷烟价格属于可接受范围。

参考文献

[1] 孙升.浅谈品牌效应的烟草经济发展分析[J].中国经贸,2021(20):149.

[2] 靳晓理.浅析中国烟草行业未来发展方向[J].中国市场,2013(29):82-83.

[3] 李媛.中国烟草产业发展现状及其改革方向探索[J].中国城市经济,2012(2):61-63.

[4] 姜勇,潘正旺.基于质性分析的体育学科核心素养培养影响因素研究[J].辽宁师范大学学报(自然科学版),2020,43(1):11.

[5] 杨锐,王光明.影响学生综合实践活动课程高效学习的因素探究——基于NVivo 11

的质性分析[J].教育导刊,2016(5):49-53.

[6] 王光明,佘文娟,宋金锦.基于NVivo 10质性分析的高效数学学习心理结构模型[J].心理与行为研究,2014,12(1):74-79.

[7] 常亮.消费者参与共享经济的行为归因和干预路径——基于扎根理论的分析框架[J].贵州社会科学,2017(8):89-95.

[8] 李建桥.重庆市某库区县留守中学生亚健康状态及其危险行为同伴教育干预效果评价[D].重庆:重庆医科大学,2014.

[9] 董津津,陈关聚.科技型企业创新行为决策动因与机理——基于扎根理论的溯源与模糊集定性比较分析的验证[J].中国科技论坛,2020(7):111-119.

[10] 段斌斌,许晓东,陈敏.我国高校科技人才培育制度的特征、问题与改进——基于36位科技人才访谈的分析[J].高校教育管理,2021,15(4):101-114.

[11] 王碧梅.科学学科核心素养结构及指标体系建构——基于15个国家课程标准和38位教师深度访谈内容的编码分析[J].外国教育研究,2021,48(9):43-56.

[12] FASSINGER R E. Paradigms, Praxis, Problems and Promise: Grounded Theory in Counseling Psychology Research[J]. Journal of Counseling Psychology, 2005, 52(2):156-166.

[13] 吕宁,韩霄,赵亚茹.旅游中小企业经营者创新行为的影响机制——基于计划行为理论的扎根研究[J].旅游学刊,2021(3):13.

[14] 石凤学,张涛,邹娟,等.基于自组织建模方法的卷烟购买因素分析[J].中国烟草学报,2017,23(3):124-132.

[15] 滕洁.新常态下卷烟品牌培育策略研究[J].现代商贸工业,2021,42(1):65-67.

Consumer Product Evaluation and Demand Analysis of Cigarettes based on Grounded Theory

Abstract: To objectively understand the market status, consumption habits differences, brand sales trends, and other information about cigarette products from the perspectives of consumers and retail customers, this study employed an in-depth interview method to conduct consumer demand information collection and research services in four cities nationwide. The interview data of 32 respondents were recorded and organized, and the grounded theory analysis method was introduced. With the assistance of NVivo 11.0 software, the grounded theory three-level coding was completed, resulting in the analysis of 12 main categories covering individual emotions, social integration, personality highlights, entertainment, socialization, work, packaging, brand, taste, price, cigarette type, and purchase channels. These results were refined into a core category, namely purchasing habits, around which detailed analysis was conducted. The research results indicate that consumers tend to purchase cigarette products from stores they habitually visit, and they are more inclined to purchase local cigarettes, with the second preference being major brands such as "Yunyan" and "Yuxi". Consumers also prefer packaging that reflects local culture, has vibrant colors, is readily available, and exudes luxury. Furthermore, there are regional differences in consumption structures, mainly manifested in different regional smoking cultures and preferred brands. Conclusion: The tobacco industry should improve brand cultivation supporting mechanisms, innovate and iterate on taste and packaging to meet the increasingly changing consumer demands, and thus achieve sustainable development.

Keywords: Consumers; Grounded theory; Cigarettes; Evaluation; Demand analysis

1 Introduction

As a vital pillar industry of the national economy, the development of the tobacco industry plays a significant role in promoting overall economic growth. It is crucial for ensuring the stable dominance of the domestic market by the tobacco industry in China, actively expanding overseas, and building a robust national tobacco industry[1]. Therefore, the development of the tobacco economy should strive to achieve grand sustainability goals as soon as possible. Currently, the development strategy of the Chinese tobacco industry mainly focuses on: first, determining clear development directions; second, strengthening institutional innovation and mechanism innovation to optimize the modern enterprise management system and operational management methods across the entire tobacco industry; third, emphasizing technological innovation, increasing research and development investment, and truly harnessing the enormous role of technology as the primary productivity[2, 3].

NVivo 11.0 is a computer-aided qualitative data analysis software developed by the Australian QSR company, which is a leading product among international qualitative analysis software[4]. It constructs an operational method framework based on grounded theory, refining and deeply analyzing existing data to discover core elements, explore relationships between elements, and then establish relevant hypotheses[5]. It has powerful "coding" functionality, enabling researchers to summarize information relevant to a research topic from many literature and data sources, helping researchers quickly capture information points in the literature[6]. By using this software, which requires processing large amounts of raw data for qualitative research, researchers can quickly sift through the massive data and textual information to extract the needed information, significantly shortening the research cycle and improving research effectiveness. According to Fassinger's study, theoretically, the larger the sample size, the higher the saturation, but in practical work, to avoid overly cumbersome data processing, the optimal sample size is between 20-35[7]. Therefore, this paper utilizes NVivo 11.0 to conduct in-depth interviews with 32 cigarette consumers in four cities: Kunming, Guangzhou, Chengdu, and Hangzhou. Based on the combination of in-depth interviews and grounded theory analysis, the aim is to understand consumers' evaluations of cigarette indicators such as taste, packaging, price, concept, and product satisfaction and to summarize consumers' demand information regarding product appearance, taste, and price.

2 Materials and Methods

2.1 Data Source

The data for this study were obtained from market research conducted in October 2021. Thirty-two respondents from four cities—Kunming, Chengdu, Guangzhou, and Hangzhou—were interviewed. The interviewees included followed item.

(1) Primary consumers of Yunnan-produced cigarettes.

(2) Competitive brand cigarettes of the same price range.

(3) Female consumers.

(4) Retailers.

(5) Young smokers under 35 years old.

(6) Senior smokers aged between 35 to 55 years old comprised eight categories, with one person per category per city.

Following the principles of "dynamic sampling" and "information saturation"[8], sampling and focus interviews were conducted, including 24 males and 8 females, with ages ranging from 22 to 53 years old. The interviews lasted for 105 minutes and were conducted using open-ended questions. The interview outline is provided in Table 1.

Table 1　Interview Outline for Consumer Motives and Demands

Serial No.	Brief introduction	Time (minutes)	Purpose
1	Self-Introduction	5	Get acquainted, state the purpose, and create an active atmosphere
2	Introduction of Smoking History	15	Understand the smoking history of smokers to comprehend their motivations and occasions for smoking
3	Awareness of Brand	15	Assess the level of awareness regarding cigarette brands among smokers
4	Smoking Consumers' Consumption Habits and Attitudes	20	Investigate smoking habits among smokers in detail
5	Evaluation of Cigarette Products	20	Gain insight into smokers' preferences for various aspects of cigarette products
6	Purchase Attitudes and Habits	20	Explore smokers' purchasing habits and decision-making processes
7	Advertising and Promotion	10	Examine the awareness and recall of cigarette advertisements and understand smokers' media consumption habits

2.2　Data Processing

This study utilized NVivo 11.0 software, employing coding and hierarchical analysis functions based on grounded theory to summarize important nodes and conduct in-depth qualitative analysis[9, 10]. A theoretical framework based on the research content was constructed, identifying open, axial, and core coding[11]. The schematic diagram is illustrated in Figure 1.

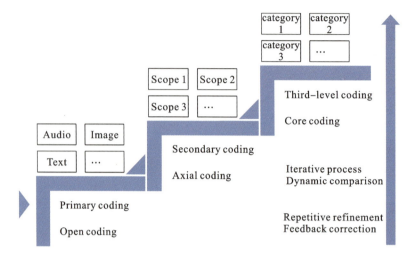

Figure 1　Schematic Diagram of Three-Level Coding based on Grounded Theory

The saturation and validity of the coding were examined. Following the principle of theoretical saturation, one-third of the sample data were randomly selected for validation of theoretical saturation[12, 13]. The examination results indicated that various concepts and categories were relatively complete, with no new concepts or categories emerging. Regarding data coding, the concept extraction from the original data of 32 participants was robust, had high internal validity, and met the requirements of the study.

3　Results and Analysis

3.1　Coding Results

3.1.1　Open Coding

Based on repeated reading of interview materials, the original data were coded verbatim, labeled, conceptualized, and formed into more generalized new categories. This study initially obtained 290 concepts, and after comparison, consolidation, and selection due to duplicate and synonymous labels, a final set of 105 concepts was obtained (Table 2).

3.1.2　Axial Coding

Building upon open coding, Axial coding involved comparing the differences and similarities between different concepts, clarifying their interrelationships, and refining and summarizing 12 higher-level categories and dimensions. These include personal emotions, social integration, individuality, entertainment, socialization, work, packaging, brand, taste, price, cigarette type, and purchase channels (Table 2).

Table 2 Third-Level Coding

Open Coding	Axial Coding	Core Coding
Stress relief, confused thoughts, boredom, curiosity about cigarettes, annoyance, low mood, irritability, and listlessness	Individual emotions	Reasons for contact with cigarettes
Popularity among peers, desire for social conformity, friends smoking, family members smoking	Social integration	
Perceiving smoking as a means to express individuality and finding it enjoyable	Emphasis on personality	
Engaging, mahjong, gaming, card playing, and drinking	Entertainment	Smoking occasions
Participating in gatherings, celebrations, social interactions, and chatting	Socialization	
Working overtime and attending social events	Work	
Attractiveness, showcasing personality, connotation and sophistication, reflecting regional culture, vivid colors, national trend design, alternative patterns, embossing, hot stamping, relief patterns, three-dimensional, leather texture design, laser design, textured, environmentally friendly, elegant, understated, high-end fashion, simple and generous	Packaging	Purchasing habits
Brands including Purple Cloud, Red River, Jinsha River, Ruanzhen, Yunyan, Yuxi, Yueke, Pomelo, Jiaozi, Zhonghua, Double Happiness, Huanghelou, Hongtashan, Liqun, Harmony, Suyan, Furongwang	Branding	
Subtle, strong, mild, pure flavor, rich and aromatic taste, smooth and clear, full-bodied, tobacco aroma, refreshing, neutral, lingering aftertaste, non-drying mouthfeel	Taste	
Luxury cigarettes, high-range, mid-range, low-range, Yuxi for mass consumption, Yunyan with high cost-effectiveness, Jiaozi with price ranges within acceptable limits, Liqun with suitable prices	Pricing	
Regular, medium, slim, menthol, fruity, tangerine burst bead, tangerine, caterpillar fungus, pipa, blueberry, sweet fragrance, jasmine green tea, low tar content, medium tar content, high tar content, electronic cigarettes	Types of cigarettes	
Supermarkets, convenience stores, tobacco shops, specialty stores, colleagues, friends, shop's owners	Purchasing channels	

3.1.3 Core Encoding

Building upon the 12 categories identified, three major categories emerged: reasons for cigarette initiation, smoking occasions, and purchasing habits (Table 2). Simultaneously, the hierarchical analysis results (Figure 2) indicate that among all primary nodes, purchasing habits constitute the largest proportion, approximately three-quarters; smoking occasions and reasons for cigarette initiation follow closely behind, with a relatively smaller gap between them. Within the hierarchy of purchasing habits, taste holds the largest proportion, followed by brand and packaging, with a minimal difference between them; purchasing channels, pricing, and cigarette types account for smaller proportions. Hence, it is evident that among the various factors influencing consumer cigarette purchases, "purchasing habits" carry the greatest weight, serving as the core encoding, surpassing the importance of other factors.

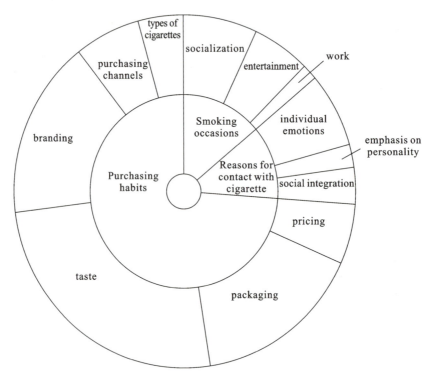

Figure 2　Node Encoding Hierarchy Statistics

3.2　Results Analysis

3.2.1　Evaluation of Taste

Consumers from different regions generally agree on the criteria for assessing the quality of cigarettes, yet variations still exist. In Hangzhou, smooth inhalation without any particle sensation, good taste, burning state, and absence of blackened cigarette ash are regarded as indicators of good quality. In Guangzhou, emphasis is placed on the initial taste upon inhalation, absence of spiciness in the mouth, strong tobacco flavor, smooth inhalation, good aftertaste, concentration of residual smoke odor, degree of combustion, and color of cigarette ash. In Kunming, characteristics such as a pleasant aroma upon opening the package, intact tobacco leaves, golden color, no irritation during inhalation, and burning speed are valued. Similarly, in Chengdu, the taste of tobacco leaves and the sensation during inhalation, aroma, and ease of cigarette ash detachment are considered. It can be observed that smooth inhalation, taste, burning speed, and color of cigarette ash are common indicators of consumer attention. Regarding the evaluation of Yunnan-produced cigarettes taste, consumers perceive Yunyan brand as non-irritating to the throat, with a pure tobacco flavor, non-drying, high-class, good quality, and diverse product series. The Yuxi brand is considered to have high quality, reputation, and influence, providing a non-pungent, smooth, and non-irritating throat sensation during inhalation (Table 3).

Table 3   Major Evaluations of Leading Yunnan-Produced Products

Brands	Series	Reason for selection	Quality evaluation of smoking process
Yunyan	Yunyan (Treasure-Slim)	Reasonable price, long history, wide range of subsidiary brands	The strength of the cigarette is relatively mild, lacking the strong stimulation of thick cigarettes, with a more aroma taste
	Yunyan (Colorful Impressions)	Thin cigarettes have unique personalities and are rarely smoked by people	The taste is characterized by a pure tobacco aroma, with minimal addition of flavorings, providing a gentle suction force during smoking, leaving a pleasant sensation in the throat
	Yunyan (Black Diamond Impressions)	High visibility, eye-catching, attractive packaging design with unique colors (black packaging with golden letters, visually striking, and high saturation)	The flavor of the cigarette is rich and full-bodied, solely tobacco-flavored without any artificial flavorings

continue

Brands	Series	Reason for selection	Quality evaluation of smoking process
Yunyan	Yunyan (Yunlong)	Grand packaging, high class, suitable price, appropriate taste. The aroma is relatively elegant, smoking is smooth in the mouth, and it doesn't get you high easily, even when smoked in large quantities, giving a Yunyan brand experience. Friends and colleagues around are smoking this brand	The cigarette burns slowly, offering a mild and smooth smoking experience with a slightly lower tar content and a light taste
	Yunyan (Purple)	It's easy to feel drowsy when working at night, so smoking a stronger cigarette helps stay alert. Affordable price, few counterfeit products, and good taste	The cigarette is slightly heavier and denser
	Yunyan (Treasure-Soft)	Attractive packaging with a long brand history; few fake products; suitable taste	It smokes smoothly without impurities or strange odors
Yuxi	Yuxi (Soft)	Soft packaging and a non-spicy taste	The taste is pure, with a moderate tobacco aroma, and tightly packed tobacco leaves provide minimal resistance when smoked, ensuring a smooth and comfortable experience without harshness or irritation
	Yuxi (Hard)	Reasonable price, long history, wide range of subsidiary brands	The taste is not spicy, preventing dryness of the mouth

3.2.2 Perception of Brand Image

Consumers in different regions have varying perceptions of Yunyan and Yuxi's brand image (see Table 4). Overall, consumers perceive Yunyan as having a "long history", being an "established brand", having "stable quality", and being "innovative". In contrast, Yuxi is perceived as a "national brand", "affordable", "consistent quality", and "trendy and avant-garde". The difference lies in the broader recognition of the Yunyan brand by consumers. Additionally, some consumers perceive the Yuxi brand as more "mature and stable", while the Yunyan brand is seen as more "experienced and worldly".

Table 4　Perception of the Yunyan Brand by Consumers in Various Regions

Brand	Project	Kunming	Chengdu	Guangzhou	Hangzhou
Yunyan	Associated words	Representative of Yunnan; with a long history; widespread availability; consistent taste; affordable pricing; moderate positioning	An old brand; with a long history; intellectual appeal; nationwide presence; stable quality; good taste	An old brand; conservative; with ethnic characteristics; elegance; and strong innovation	With a long history; representative of Yunnan, it is more suitable for young people (with a lighter taste)
	Anthropomorphic brand image	A person around 30-35 years old, embodying leadership, good taste, and with a wide range of hobbies	A middle-aged person around 50 years old, with a straightforward and decisive personality	An entrepreneur in his 40s engaged in the tourism industry, leading a stable life, exhibiting steadiness in actions, and being hospitable and enthusiastic	Young people in their early twenties, are still in the exploratory stage of their careers
	Source of brand image	Compared to Yuxi, the packaging is low-key yet sharp and distinctive	A necessity of specific historical moments, widely used for important occasions	Confidence stems from the brand's long history and use of pure and high-quality materials	The brand gives consumers a relatively trendy feeling

continue

Brand	Project	Kunming	Chengdu	Guangzhou	Hangzhou
Yuxi	Associated words	Consistent quality; with a long history	Yunyan's counterpart is affordable; widely available nationwide, with strong strength, good reputation, and strong affinity	Slightly less renowned than Yunyan, associated with Yunnan, with attractive packaging	Few counterfeit products; easy to smoke; convenient to purchase; and have good sales
	Anthropomorphic brand image	Slightly stable and young ordinary employees dress in trendy and avant-garde styles	A middle-aged person aged between 40 and 50, comparatively mature and stable	A middle-aged person aged around 40, with a relatively traditional and conservative mindset	An entrepreneur around 30 years old, with his ideas and thoughts
	Source of brand image	As consumers of mass-market cigarettes, they experience no pressure; the packaging design concept is more youthful and appealing to the mindset of young people	A brand with a long history	It has a relatively small variety of cigarette brands and relatively plain packaging	The name gives a feeling of homeliness and purity; this brand has a long history

3.2.3 Consumer Preferences for Cigarette Packaging

Packaging plays a significant role in consumers' cigarette purchasing decisions as it signifies the essence and class of the product. Consumers prefer packaging that reflects local cultural elements, with bright colors that make it easy to spot on shelves, leaning towards national-style designs or alternative patterns. Consumers believe that the high-end feel of packaging should be reflected in its craftsmanship, such as embossing, gold stamping, textured patterns, three-dimensional effects, leather patterns, and laser designs; packaging boxes should be firm yet thin, providing a pleasant tactile experience and utilizing eco-friendly materials. Packaging should lean towards a simple, elegant, culturally rich, and national-style aesthetic. Consumers dislike packaging with flashy colors, blurry printing, and lack of distinctive features. Refer to Table 5 for details.

Table 5 Consumer Preferences for Cigarette Packaging in Various Regions

Project	Kunming	Chengdu	Guangzhou	Hangzhou
Preferred Packaging	Subtle features flip and side flip outer packaging materials	High-end fashion (evident from appearance, color, patterns, and decorative graphics), with cultural connotations in craftsmanship, possessing texture, three-dimensional shapes, and concave-convex effects	Bright colors and innovative patterns are imbued with traditional Chinese painting and national style, representing local characteristics. The manufacturing process leaves uneven textures, with relatively thin boxes, attracting attention (The higher the grade of cigarettes, the closer they align with national characteristics, exuding elegance and simplicity)	The minimalist and elegant packaging offers a pleasing hand feel, exquisite appearance, and a sense of sophistication; colors predominantly include black, gold, and red, imparting a sense of nobility

continue

Project	Kunming	Chengdu	Guangzhou	Hangzhou
Non-preferred Packaging	The packaging feels soft, lacks tactile sensation, and has poor color coordination	Flamboyant; packaging is ordinary, lacking novelty and distinctive features	Craftsmanship appears blurry and rough, lacking refinement	Ordinary and plain, with relatively subdued colors

3.2.4 Purchasing Channels

Consumers in various cities primarily purchase cigarettes from supermarkets, convenience stores, tobacco and liquor shops, and specialty stores, with familiarity and proximity to their residential areas being the preferred choice. For higher-priced cigarettes, consumers tend to visit larger supermarkets. The main avenues of brand awareness for consumers include shelf displays in tobacco shops at the time of purchase and recommendations from friends, tobacco shops, or online sources. Regarding purchasing incentives, they are generally limited, with consumers indicating that purchasing entire packs is relatively cheaper, and in some regions, complimentary lighters are provided. Refer to Table 6.

Table 6 Analysis of Cigarette Purchasing Channels by Region

Project	Kunming	Chengdou	Guangzhou	Hangzhou
Purchasing Channels	Supermarkets, convenience stores, tobacco and liquor shops, general stores, through friends	Supermarkets, tobacco and liquor shops, specialty stores	Convenience stores, supermarkets, tobacco and liquor shops, cigarette specialty stores, and general stores	Tobacco and liquor shops, specialty stores, supermarkets, retail stores
Interaction with merchants during the purchase	Previously, buying a pack was cheaper, but now it is not	Significant discounts for purchasing entire packs make the price cheaper	Discounts are available for purchasing entire packs, or receiving a complimentary lighter	Prices are fixed and not subject to discounts; purchasing entire packs may be slightly cheaper, but discounts are generally not offered

continue

Project	Kunming	Chengdou	Guangzhou	Hangzhou
How to discover new cigarette brands	At tobacco shops or supermarkets, upon seeing or being recommended by the owner; During gatherings with friends	Learning from friends in one's social circle; Tobacco and liquor shops, supermarkets	Learning from friends in one's social circle; Display in tobacco shops	Discovering during gatherings with friends; Recommendations from tobacco and liquor shop owners

3.2.5 Cigarette Types and Prices

Classified by flavor. There are relatively spicy and pungent flavors, such as Yunyan (Purple), Red River, and Jinsha River, as well as relatively mild cigarettes, such as Yunyan (Treasures-Soft), and cigarettes targeted at women.

Classified by specification. Thick, medium, or regular cigarettes are suitable for regular smoking, banquets, and wedding gifts. Slim cigarettes are mainly smoked during leisure time or are suitable for individuals with low smoking habits. Currently, many male consumers, considering their health, also opt for slim cigarettes to reduce smoking quantity.

Classified by aroma type. Female consumers tend to accept mint, fruity, and other flavors. Male consumers are more receptive to citrus burst beads, especially in Guangzhou, where they believe flavors like citrus peel and Cordyceps are more beneficial to health. Consumers in Chengdu are less accepting of added flavors; Chengdu's female consumers prefer fruity flavors such as pipa, blueberry, sweet fragrance, jasmine, and green tea, which they find comfortable to smoke, non-irritating to the throat, without tobacco smell, and satisfying psychologically.

Classified by tar content. Below 8 milligrams is considered low tar, 8 to 10 milligrams is moderately tarred, and exceeding 12 milligrams is high tar.

Classified by price. Consumers in Guangzhou, Kunming, and Chengdu consider cigarettes priced above 50 yuan high-grade, while consumers in Hangzhou consider cigarettes priced above 80 yuan high-grade. Consumers in Hangzhou and Kunming consider cigarettes priced below 30 yuan low-grade, while consumers in Chengdu and Guangzhou consider cigarettes priced below 20 yuan low-grade. High-grade brands like Zhonghua and Dachongjiu are mainly used for business, social occasions, and gifting. The choice of cigarette grade is related to personal income; individuals prioritizing health and financial freedom may choose high-grade cigarettes such as Impression, Zhonghua-Soft, and Su Yan. The general populace opts for Medium-grade cigarettes like Treasures-Soft and Harmony. Mass consumption generally involves low-grade cigarettes, such as Ziyun, Hongtashan, Treasures-Soft, Liqun, Red River, etc. Refer to Table 7.

Table 7　Cigarette Brand Price Classification by Region　　　(Unit: Yuan)

Price Classification	Kunming	Chengdu	Guangzhou	Hangzhou
Luxury Goods	>100	—	—	—
High-grade	50-60	50-80	>50	80-100
Medium-grade	30-49	30-49	20-50	30-79
Low-grade	<30	<20	<20	<30

The first choice for cigarette consumers in each city tends to be local brands, while the second and third choices lean towards major brands such as Yunyan, Yuxi, Zhonghua, and Huanghelou. See Table 8 for details. In this survey, the most purchased brands by consumers, from highest to lowest, are Zhonghua, Yunyan, Yuxi, Huanghelou, Double Happiness, Nanjing, Liqun, Furongwang, Kuan Zhai, and Dachongjiu. (Note: "Kuan Zhai, Dachongjiu" are sub-brand names, with Kuan Zhai's main brand being "Jiaozi" and Dachongjiu's main brand being "Yunyan"). Refer to Figure 3.

Table 8　Intention of Brand Selection in Various Regions

Regions	First choice	Second choice	Third choice
Chengdu	Jiaozi	Yunyan	Zhonghua
Guangzhou	Double Happiness, Yunyan	Yuxi	Huanghelou
Kunming	Yunyan	Yuxi	Hongtashan
Hangzhou	Liqun	Yunyan	Yuxi

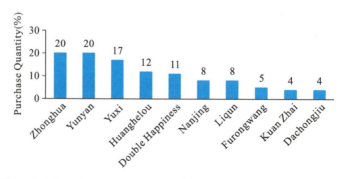

Figure 3　Top 10 Brands in Purchase Quantity Ranking (Multipe choice)

4　Discussion

Firstly, in terms of flavor preference, consumers in different cities have varying tastes due to the differences in tobacco culture and preferred brands among various regions. Consumers in Kunming prefer cigarettes with a pure flavor, smooth and mild taste, and strong tobacco flavor without irritation to the throat. Consumers in Chengdu prefer cigarettes with moderate strength, soft and smooth taste, smooth and full-bodied smoking experience without throat irritation, and authentic tobacco flavor. Consumers in Guangzhou prefer cigarettes with moderate and elegant taste, smooth and mellow smoking experience, authentic tobacco flavor, and good aftertaste, and dislike excessive addition of artificial flavors or other additives. Consumers in Hangzhou prefer cigarettes with a slightly thicker and stronger taste, powerful smoking sensation, no irritation, and a refreshing smoking experience.

Secondly, consumers in different cities favor different packaging styles regarding product appearance. Consumers in Kunming prefer low-key luxurious packaging, consumers in Chengdu prefer high-end fashion with texture, consumers in Guangzhou prefer bright-colored packaging with local characteristics, and consumers in Hangzhou prefer simple and low-key packaging. However, there is a consensus on disliked packaging, including flashy patterns, dull colors, blurry printing, and packaging lacking texture. Consumers prefer packaging that reflects local culture, has bright colors, is easy to find on shelves, and embodies Chinese cultural elements. Consumers believe that the luxury of packaging should be reflected in craftsmanship, such as embossing, gold stamping, textured patterns, three-dimensional designs, leather patterns, laser designs, etc. Regarding materials, packaging boxes should be hard and thin, with a tactile feel.

Thirdly, regarding brand selection, cigarette consumers prefer local brands as their first choice, with the second and third choices generally leaning towards major brands such as Yunyan, Yuxi, Zhonghua, and Huanghelou. Brand influence is a significant factor affecting consumer purchases. For instance, the analysis results of purchasing factors in 16 cities, three price ranges, and four cigarette specifications by Shi Fengxue et al. show that brand image is the second most influential factor, such as "high local visibility", "old brand, long history", "classic brand", etc.[14] The tobacco industry should strive to enhance market competitiveness, focus on the research and development of critical brands, and avoid aging product lines and the phenomenon of large but weak vital brands. This can be achieved by improving the mechanism of coordinated marketing between industry and commerce, consumer-brand coordination, and wholesale-retail coordination, establishing a three-in-one brand cultivation mechanism of "consumers, retailers, industrial and commercial enterprises", and improving the brand cultivation capability of cigarette companies.[15]

Fourthly, regarding purchasing channels, consumers in various cities primarily purchase cigarettes from supermarkets, convenience stores, tobacco and liquor shops, and specialty stores, usually choosing familiar or nearby ones. The reasons for choosing these channels are purchasing habits, convenience, and the difficulty of buying counterfeit cigarettes. Cigarettes with slightly higher prices are usually available only in larger supermarkets and convenience stores.

Lastly, in terms of product price, consumers in various cities generally consider cigarettes priced between 50-100 yuan high-grade and those priced between 10-30 yuan low-grade cigarettes. Cigarettes priced between 20 and 30 yuan are considered within an acceptable range.

References

[1] SUN S. Analysis of the Tobacco Economic Development based on Brand Effect[J]. China Economic Trade, 2021(20): 149.

[2] JIN X L. Analysis of the Future Development Direction of China's Tobacco Industry[J]. China Market, 2013(29): 82-83.

[3] LI Y. Exploration of the Current Situation and Reform Direction of China's Tobacco Industry[J]. China Urban Economy, 2012(2): 61-63.

[4] JIANG Y, PAN Z W. Research on Influencing Factors of Core Literacy Training in Sports Disciplines based on Qualitative Analysis[J]. Journal of Liaoning Normal University (Natural Science Edition), 2020, 43 (1): 11.

[5] YANG R, WANG G M. Investigation of Factors Affecting Students' Efficient Learning in Comprehensive Practice Courses—Qualitative Analysis based on NVivo 11[J]. Education Guide, 2016(5): 49-53.

[6] WANG G M, SHE W J, SONG J J. Psychological Structure Model of Efficient Mathematics Learning based on NVivo 10 Qualitative Analysis[J]. Psychological and Behavioral Research, 2014, 12 (1):74-79.

[7] CHANG L. Attribution and Intervention Paths of Consumer Participation in Sharing Economy Behavior—Analysis Framework based on Grounded Theory[J]. Guizhou Social Sciences, 2017(8):89-95.

[8] LI J Q. Evaluation of Sub-Healthy Status and Intervention Effect of Companion Education on Left-Behind Middle School Students in a Reservoir County in Chongqing[D]. Chongqing: Chongqing Medical University, 2014.

[9] DONG J J, CHEN G J. Research on Influencing Factors and Mechanism of

Innovation Behavior of Technology-Based Enterprises—Verification based on Root Theory and Fuzzy Set Qualitative Comparison Analysis[J]. China Science and Technology Forum,2020(7):111-119.

[10] DUAN B B, XU X D, CHEN M. Characteristics, Problems, and Improvement of Talent Cultivation System in Science and Technology Universities in China—Analysis based on Interviews with 36 Talents[J]. Higher Education Management, 2021, 15 (4):101-114.

[11] WANG B M. Construction of the Core Literacy Structure and Index System of Scientific Subjects—Based on Coding Analysis of 15 National Curriculum Standards and In-Depth Interviews with 38 Teachers[J]. Foreign Education Research,2021,48 (9):43-56.

[12] FASSINGER R E. Paradigms, Praxis, Problems and Promise: Grounded Theory in Counseling Psychology Research[J]. Journal of Counseling Psychology, 2005, 52 (2): 156-166.

[13] LV N, HAN X, ZHAO Y R. Influence Mechanism of Innovation Behavior of Entrepreneurs in Small and Medium-Sized Sports Enterprises—Root Research based on Planned Behavior Theory[J]. Journal of Tourism Studies, 2021(3):13.

[14] SHI F X, ZHANG T, ZOU J, et al. Analysis of Factors Influencing Cigarette Purchase based on Self-Organized Modeling Method[J]. Chinese Tobacco Science, 2017, 23 (3): 124-132.

[15] TENG J. Research on Brand Cultivation Strategy of Cigarette Brands under the New Normal[J]. Modern Commerce and Industry, 2021, 42 (1): 65-67.

基于自组织建模方法的卷烟购买因素分析

摘要：为了进一步了解不同卷烟规格消费人群的购买动机，本研究针对2015年4种卷烟规格，分品牌形象、价值（价格）、社交应酬、健康、新品、产品和渠道/宣传促销七个大类进行调研，并采用自组织GMDH分析进行购买因素分析。结果表明：不同卷烟规格最重要的购买因素主要分布在品牌形象和价值（价格）两个大类中，而4种产品的购买因素侧重点分别体现在产品价值、品牌历史形象、社交应酬优势和产品性价比上。该结果可为工业企业在老产品提质维护方面提供参考价值。

关键词：购买动机；自组织建模；GMDH；卷烟

基于自组织控制论提出的成组数据处理的神经网络算法——GMDH分析，主要通过寻找最优复杂度实现变量的自动筛选，并得到明确的模型结构，该算法具有以下特点：①能得到用函数解析式表示的清晰的模型结果；②建模过程实现自组织控制，不需任何初始假设；③具有最优复杂度及高精度预测能力[1]。目前自组织GMDH分析在复杂经济系统的模拟、预测、模式识别、样本聚类等诸多方面成为辅助人们进行经济系统分析和决策的一项强有力的工具，在国民经济GDP研究中已得到了一定程度的应用[2-4]。随着烟草行业区域市场壁垒被不断打破，烟草品牌在下游市场的竞争日趋激烈。因此，对于市场现有卷烟规格而言，亟须做好消费者购买动机分析以迎合消费者的购买心理，从而增强品牌的核心竞争力，稳定产品市场份额。利用自组织GMDH分析可以有效剖析消费者购买动机，但是该方法在卷烟市场调研中应用较少，仅有汪晨雪在分析南昌市场消费者选购"金圣"和"芙蓉王"卷烟的动机因素时进行了应用[5]。因此，本研究更为系统地对2015年4种卷烟规格的购买因素（梳理出七大类指标，总计34个选项）进行调研，采用自组织GMDH分析，获得4种卷烟规格消费群体的关键购买因素，以期为行业在老产品提质维护方面提供参考价值。

1　材料与方法

1.1　材料

本研究主要针对2015年的A、B、C、D四种产品的购买因素开展调研，其中A产品收集有效样本103条，B产品收集有效样本84条，C产品收集有效样本194条，D产品收集有效样本188条。选取了七大类指标作为问卷选项，包括品牌形象、价值（价格）、社交应酬、健康、新品、产品和渠道/宣传促销。

品牌形象大类包括以下8个选项。X_1：本地知名度高；X_2：全国知名度高；X_3：老品牌,历史悠久;X_4:品牌有文化内涵;X_5:品牌形象鲜明/有个性;X_6:经典品牌;X_7:与这个品牌有感情、有渊源;X_8:品牌名称好。

价值(价格)大类包括以下 3 个选项。X_9:性价比高,是我可以负担得起的;X_{10}:价格高、有档次;X_{11}:公认价值。

社交应酬大类包括以下 4 个选项。X_{12}:符合我的身份地位;X_{13}:在朋友/同事/他人中的口碑好;X_{14}:社会流行度高,抽的人很多;X_{15}:工作环境或社交场合认可这个产品。

健康大类包括以下 1 个选项。X_{16}:低焦、低危害,相对比较健康。

新品大类包括以下 1 个选项。X_{17}:是新出的产品,有吸引力。

产品大类包括以下 13 个选项。X_{18}:产品质量稳定;X_{19}:烟丝质量好;X_{20}:劲头大、过瘾;X_{21}:劲头适中;X_{22}:香气浓郁;X_{23}:香气清淡;X_{24}:入喉顺畅;X_{25}:吸后口腔无异味;X_{26}:包装经典;X_{27}:包装时尚、新颖;X_{28}:包装有档次;X_{29}:过滤嘴设计好;X_{30}:新品多。

渠道/宣传促销大类包括以下 4 个选项。X_{31}:购买方便;X_{32}:广告宣传力度大;X_{33}:有优惠或促销;X_{34}:假烟少。

1.2 统计方法

1.2.1 自组织数据挖掘

为了准确分析卷烟市场消费者选择购买 4 种卷烟产品时的动机,本研究对访谈问卷中所取得的数据通过自组织数据挖掘方法进行了细化分析。

自组织数据挖掘思想首先由乌克兰控制论学家 A. G. Ivachenko 在 1967 年提出,后来在 Adolf Müller、Frank Lemke 等科学家的努力下,自组织数据挖掘方法得到了较快的发展。而计算机技术日新月异的发展又使多变量复杂系统的自组织建模成为可能[6]。

1.2.2 自组织数据挖掘的工作原理

自组织数据挖掘的技术核心是 GMDH(group method of data handling),即成组数据处理法。它从参考函数构成的初始模型(函数)集合出发,按一定的法则产生新的中间候选模型(遗传、变异),再经过筛选(选择),重复这样一个遗传、变异、选择和进化的过程,使中间候选模型的复杂度不断增加,直至得到最优复杂度模型[7]。

自组织数据挖掘方法的特点是数据分组和贯穿于整个建模过程中的内、外准则运用。它将观测样本数据分为训练集(training set)和测试集(testing set):在训练集上利用内准则建立中间待选模型;在测试集上利用外准则进行中间候选模型的选择。在外准则达到最小时,相应的模型即为最优复杂度模型。这个模型表达了输入输出变量之间的关系。自组织算法的基本步骤见参考文献[6]。

本研究采用自组织数据挖掘软件(KnowledgeMiner 5.0)实现。

2 结果与分析

2.1 A 产品自组织建模的购买因素分析

以消费者购买 A 产品的影响因素作为输入变量 X,以经常购买 A 产品的消费者数量

作为输出变量 Y。算法类型为最小偏差准则。应用自组织数据挖掘软件（KnowledgeMiner 5.0），计算筛选出最优复杂度模型：

$$Y = 10.313939 + 4.686060X_{12} + 5.562724X_{19} + 5.415582X_{23} - 5.972193X_{25} + 7.455838X_{14} + 8.302585X_{28} - 9.474248X_{29} + 8.319394X_{5} + 10.198918X_{17} + 14.176303X_{3} + 15.010733X_{6} + 21.233309X_{1} + 37.411064X_{11}$$

$R^2 = 0.9189$；预测误差：0.0829；平均绝对百分比误差：13.90%；近似误差：0.0811。

从上述模型和图 1 可以看出，当消费者经常购买 A 产品时，影响其购买决策的主要因素有十一个，主要分布在五个大类里面，其中品牌形象大类主要为"本地知名度高""老品牌，历史悠久""品牌形象鲜明/有个性""经典品牌"；价值（价格）大类主要为"价值得到公认"；社交应酬大类主要为"符合我的身份地位""社会流行度高，抽的人很多"；新品大类主要为"是新出的产品，有吸引力"；产品大类主要为"烟丝质量好""香气清淡""包装有档次"。变量前面的系数越大，说明该因素对卷烟消费者数量的影响越大，或者说消费者在购买自己抽的卷烟时越看重该因素。很明显，"公认价值"是消费者购买该品牌卷烟时最看重的因素。模型中的常数项说明消费者在做购买决策时，除了主要受到模型中的几个因素的影响外，还受到很多其他因素的影响。常数越小，说明其他因素的影响越小。另外，影响因素的系数为负说明该因素对购买动机影响不大，主要体现在产品大类中的"吸后口腔无异味""过滤嘴设计好"上。

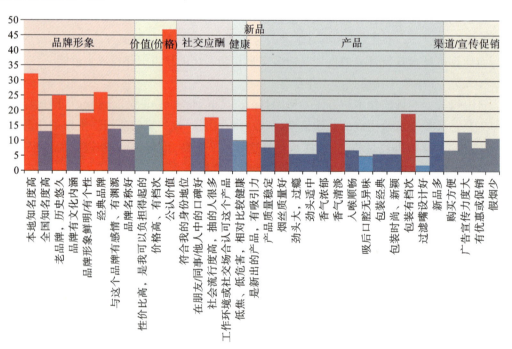

图 1　A 产品购买因素关注人数分布情况

2.2 B产品自组织建模的购买因素分析

以消费者购买B产品的影响因素作为输入变量X,以经常购买B产品的消费者数量作为输出变量Y。算法类型为最小偏差准则。应用自组织数据挖掘软件(KnowledgeMiner 5.0),计算筛选出最优复杂度模型。

$Y = 7.813154 + 4.186844X_2 + 5.080919X_{16} + 4.951341X_{10} - 5.403012X_8 - 6.189723X_{26} - 5.909407X_{27} + 6.249407X_{13} + 9.114269X_{17} + 7.934567X_{28} + 12.937182X_1 + 13.821937X_6 + 26.506128X_3 + 20.072275X_{11}$

$R^2 = 0.9149$;预测误差:0.0862;平均绝对百分比误差:14.56%;近似误差:0.0851。

从上述模型和图2可以看出,当消费者经常购买B产品时,影响其购买决策的主要因素有十个,主要分布在六个大类里面,其中品牌形象大类主要为"本地知名度高""全国知名度高""老品牌,历史悠久""经典品牌";价值(价格)大类主要为"价格高、有档次""公认价值";社交应酬大类主要为"在朋友/同事/他人中的口碑好";健康大类主要为"低焦、低危害,相对比较健康";新品大类主要为"是新出的产品,有吸引力";产品大类主要为"包装有档次"。变量前面的系数越大,说明该因素对卷烟消费者数量的影响越大,或者说消费者在购买自己抽的卷烟时越看重该因素。很明显,"老品牌,历史悠久"是消费者购买该品牌卷烟时最看重的因素。模型中的常数项说明消费者在做购买决策时,除了主要受到模型中的几个因素的影响外,还受到很多其他因素的影响。常数越小,说明其他因素的影响越小。另外,影响因素的系数为负说明该因素对购买动机影响不大,主要体现在品牌形象大类中的"品牌名称好"以及产品大类中的"包装经典""包装时尚、新颖"上。

2.3 C产品自组织建模的购买因素分析

以消费者购买C产品的影响因素作为输入变量X,以经常购买C产品的消费者数量作为输出变量Y。算法类型为最小偏差准则。应用自组织数据挖掘软件(KnowledgeMiner 5.0),计算筛选出最优复杂度模型。

$Y = 17.082209 + 7.917794X_2 + 8.713123X_{12} + 9.504688X_{13} + 10.293512X_{17} + 11.080136X_{23} - 12.233792X_{29} - 12.710546X_{21} + 12.400946X_{14} + 14.202927X_6 + 16.018333X_{30} + 33.780907X_1 + 34.906937X_3 + 45.933899X_{11} + 14.396142X_{15}$

$R^2 = 0.9398$;预测误差:0.0616;平均绝对百分比误差:10.04%;近似误差:0.0602。

从上述模型和图3可以看出,当消费者经常购买C产品时,影响其购买决策的主要因素有十二个,主要分布在五个大类里面,其中品牌形象大类主要为"本地知名度高""全国知名度高""老品牌,历史悠久""经典品牌";价值(价格)大类主要为"公认价值";社交应酬大类主要为"符合我的身份地位""在朋友/同事/他人中的口碑好""社会流行度高,抽的人很多""工作环境或社交场合认可这个产品";健康大类主要为"低焦、低危害,相对比较健康";新品大类主要为"是新出的产品,有吸引力";产品大类主要为"香气清淡""新品多"。变量前面的系数越大,说明该因素对卷烟消费者数量的影响越大,或者说消费者在购买自己抽

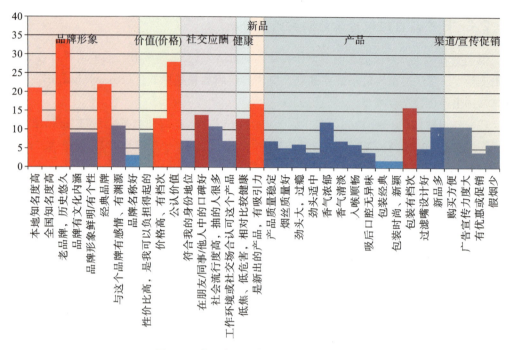

图 2　B 产品购买因素关注人数分布情况

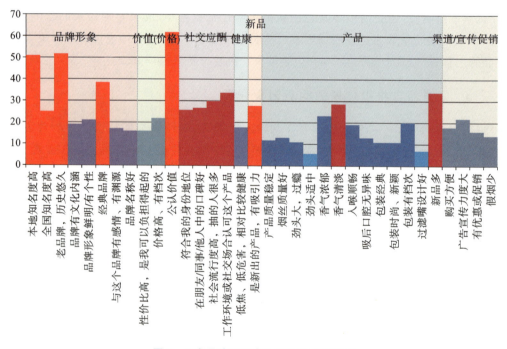

图 3　C 产品购买因素关注人数分布情况

的卷烟时越看重该因素。很明显,"公认价值"是消费者购买该品牌卷烟时最看重的因素。模型中的常数项说明消费者在做购买决策时,除了主要受到模型中的几个因素的影响外,还受到很多其他因素的影响。常数越小,说明其他因素的影响越小。另外,影响因素的系数为负说明该因素对购买动机影响不大,主要体现在产品大类中的"劲头适中""过滤嘴设计好"上。

2.4 D产品自组织建模的购买因素分析

以消费者购买D产品的影响因素作为输入变量X,以经常购买D产品的消费者数量作为输出变量Y。算法类型为最小偏差准则。应用自组织数据挖掘软件(KnowledgeMiner 5.0),计算筛选出最优复杂度模型。

$Y = 19.858166 - 10.858164X_7 - 11.380106X_{21} - 11.842220X_{27} - 11.271664X_{19} - 11.662505X_{34} + 15.257550X_9 + 15.938383X_8 + 20.541288X_2 + 19.285566X_{12} + 16.967615X_{30} + 40.735580X_1 + 30.868595X_6 + 25.461088X_3 + 38.781330X_{11}$

$R^2 = 0.9257$;预测误差:0.0754;平均绝对百分比误差:11.09%;近似误差:0.0743。

从上述模型和图4可以看出,当消费者经常购买D产品时,影响其购买决策的主要因素有九个,主要分布在四个大类里面,其中品牌形象大类主要为"本地知名度高""全国知名度高""老品牌,历史悠久""经典品牌""品牌名称好";价值(价格)大类主要为"性价比高,是我可以负担得起的""公认价值";社交应酬大类主要为"符合我的身份地位";产品大类主要为"新品多"。变量前面的系数越大,说明该因素对卷烟消费者数量的影响越大,或者说消费者在购买自己抽的卷烟时越看重该因素。很明显,"本地知名度高"是消费者购买该品牌卷烟时最看重的因素。模型中的常数项说明消费者在做购买决策时,除了主要受到模型中

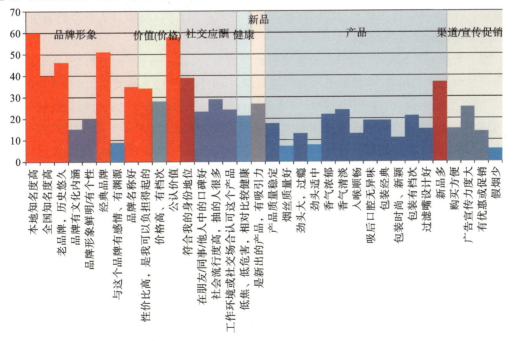

图4　D产品购买因素关注人数分布情况

的几个因素的影响外,还受到很多其他因素的影响。常数越小,说明其他因素的影响越小。另外,影响因素的系数为负说明该因素对购买动机影响不大,主要体现在品牌形象大类中的"与这个品牌有感情、有渊源"以及产品大类中的"烟丝质量好""劲头适中""包装时尚、新颖"和渠道/宣传促销大类中的"假烟少"上。

3 结论

当消费者经常购买 A 产品时,最重要的购买因素为价值(价格)大类中的"公认价值",其次为品牌形象大类中的"本地知名度高""老品牌,历史悠久""品牌形象鲜明/有个性""经典品牌",而社交应酬、新品以及产品大类中的"符合我的身份地位""社会流行度高,抽的人很多""是新出的产品,有吸引力""烟丝质量好""香气清淡""包装有档次"则位列其后,相对不重要的因素为产品大类中的"吸后口腔无异味""过滤嘴设计好"。因此,在进行该产品的提质维护时,主要考虑在保持较好的烟丝质量的同时突出体现产品价值,另外,在更新产品包装时,应在保持原有风格不变的同时提高档次感和新颖性,以增加对消费者的吸引力,而不必过多考虑过滤嘴的更新设计和口味改善等问题。

当消费者经常购买 B 产品时,最重要的购买因素为品牌形象大类中的"老品牌,历史悠久",其次为价值(价格)大类中的"价格高、有档次""公认价值",特别在健康大类中提出了"低焦、低危害,相对比较健康"的特殊关键因素,相对不重要的因素为品牌形象大类中的"品牌名称好"以及产品大类中的"包装经典""包装时尚、新颖"。因此,在进行该产品的提质维护时主要考虑该产品品牌形象的传承,可尝试进行低焦产品的改进,另外,在更新产品包装时,应在保持原有风格不变的同时提高档次感和新颖性,以增加对消费者的吸引力,而不必过多考虑时尚性等问题。

当消费者经常购买 C 产品时,最重要的购买因素为价值(价格)大类的"公认价值",其次为品牌形象大类中的"本地知名度高""老品牌,历史悠久""经典品牌",而"符合我的身份地位""在朋友/同事/他人中的口碑好""社会流行度高,抽的人很多""工作环境或社交场合认可这个产品"这四个因素在社交应酬大类中体现更为明显,相对不重要的因素为产品大类中的"劲头适中""过滤嘴设计好"。因此,在进行该产品的提质维护时,主要考虑在保持该产品在社交应酬环境中的优势的同时,突出体现产品价值,另外,在更新产品包装时,应在保持原有风格不变的同时提高新颖性,以增加对消费者的吸引力,而不必过多考虑过滤嘴的更新设计和劲头改善等问题。

当消费者经常购买 D 产品时,最重要的购买因素为品牌形象大类中的"本地知名度高",其次为价值(价格)大类中的"公认价值""性价比高,是我可以负担得起的",相对不重要的因素为产品大类中的"烟丝质量好""劲头适中""包装时尚、新颖"和渠道/宣传促销大类中的"假烟少"。因此,在进行该产品的提质维护时主要考虑突出体现产品价值,突出产品性价比高的特点,另外,在更新产品包装时不必过多考虑时尚性、新颖性等问题。

参考文献

[1] 刘光中,颜科琦,康银劳.基于自组织理论的 GMDH 神经网络算法及应用[J].数学的实践与认识,2001,31(4):464-469.

[2] 何跃,鲍爱根,贺昌政.自组织建模方法和 GDP 增长模型研究[J].中国管理科学,2004,12(2):139-143.

[3] 韩玉东,陈建中.自组织建模方法和贵州 GDP 增长影响因素模型研究[J].机械与电子,2006,8(1):255-258.

[4] 康银劳,颜科琦.自组织建模方法及西部 GDP 增长模型研究[J].西南交通大学学报,2001,36(2):206-211.

[5] 汪晨雪.消费者卷烟品牌选购动机因素研究——以南昌市场消费者选购"金圣"和"芙蓉王"卷烟为例[D].南昌:江西师范大学,2013.

[6] LEMKE F,MÜLLER J A. Self-Organizing Data Mining—An Intelligent Approach to Extract Knowledge from Data[M]. Berlin:Dresden, 1999.

[7] IVACHENKO A G,KOZUBOVSKI S F,Yu V K. Objective System Analysis of Macroeconomic Systems[J]. Systems Analysis Modelling Simulation,1990,7(3):201-206.

Cigarette Purchase Factors Analysis based on Self-Organizing Modeling

Abstract: In order to further understand the buying motivation of consumers with different cigarette specifications, this study surveyed four cigarette specifications in 2015 in seven categories: brand image, value (price), social entertainment, health, new products, products, and channels/promotion, and used the self-organizing GMDH analysis to analyze the buying factors. The results show that the most important buying factors of different cigarette specifications are mainly distributed in two categories: brand image and value (price). Among them, the emphasis on the buying factors of four products is reflected in product value, brand history image, social entertainment advantages, and product cost performance. The results can provide a reference value for the industry to improve the quality and maintenance of old products.

Keywords: Buying motivation; Self-organizing modeling; GMDH; Cigarette

The GMDH analysis, a neural network algorithm for group data processing proposed based on self-organizing cybernetics, mainly realizes automatic screening of variables and obtains a clear model structure by seeking optimal complexity. It has the following characteristics: ① obtaining a clear model result expressed analytically by functions; ② self-organizing control in the modeling process without any initial assumptions; ③ optimal complexity and high-precision prediction[1]. The self-organizing GMDH analysis has become a powerful tool to assist people in economic system analysis and decision-making in the simulation, prediction, pattern recognition, sample clustering, and many other aspects of complex economic systems. It has been applied to a certain extent in studying national economy GDP[2-4]. With the continuous breakdown of regional market barriers in the tobacco industry, fierce competition among tobacco brands in the downstream market has been created. Therefore, for the existing market cigarette specifications, it is urgent to do an excellent job in consumer purchase motivation analysis to cater to consumers' purchase psychology, enhance the core competitiveness of the brand, and stabilize the market share of the product. Self-organized GMDH analysis can effectively analyze consumers' purchasing motivation, but this method is rarely studied in cigarette market research; only Wang Chenxue applied it in the analysis of purchasing motive of consumers in the Nanchang market when choosing "Jinsheng" and "Furongwang" cigarettes[5]. Therefore, this study more systematically considers the purchasing factors of four cigarette specifications in 2015 (sorting out seven categories of questionnaires with a total of 34 options) and adopts self-organized GMDH analysis to obtain the critical purchasing factors of consumer groups of four cigarette specifications, in order to provide reference value for the industry in improving the quality and maintenance of old products.

1 Materials and Methods

1.1 Materials

This study focuses on the research situation of purchasing factors of four products A, B, C, and D in 2015, among which 103 effective samples were collected for product A, 84 effective samples were collected for product B, 194 effective samples were collected for product C, and 188 effective samples were collected for product D. Seven categories of indicators were selected as questionnaires, including brand image, value (price), social entertainment, health, new products, products and channels/promotion.

The brand phenomenon category includes the following 8 options. X_1: High local popularity; X_2: High national popularity; X_3: Old brand, long history; X_4: Brand has cultural connotation; X_5: Brand image is distinctive/individuality; X_6: Classic brand; X_7: Have feelings and connections with this brand; X_8: Good brand name.

The value (price) category includes the following 3 options. X_9: Good cost performance, I can afford it; X_{10}: High price, high grade; and X_{11}: Recognized value.

The social entertainment category includes the following 4 options. X_{12}: In line with my identity and status; X_{13}: Good reputation among friends/colleagues/others; X_{14}: High social popularity, many people smoke; X_{15}: The product is recognized in the work environment or social occasions.

The health category includes the following 1 option. X_{16}: Low tar, low harm, relatively healthy.

The new product category includes the following 1 option. X_{17}: It is an attractive new product.

The product category includes the following 13 options. X_{18}: Stable product quality; X_{19}: Good tobacco quality; X_{20}: Great strength; X_{21}: Moderate strength; X_{22}: Rich aroma; X_{23}: Light aroma; X_{24}: Smooth throat; X_{25}: No odor in the mouth after smoking; X_{26}: Classic packaging; X_{27}: Fashionable and novel packaging; X_{28}: High grade packaging; X_{29}: Good filter design; X_{30}: Many new products.

The channel/promotion category includes the following 4 options. X_{31}: Convenient to purchase; X_{32}: Strong advertising; X_{33}: Offers or promotions; X_{34}: Fewer fake cigarettes.

1.2 Statistical Methods

1.2.1 Self-Organizing Data Mining

In order to accurately analyze the motivation of cigarette market consumers in purchasing four cigarette products, this study further analyzed the data obtained from the interview questionnaire through the self-organizing data mining method.

The idea of self-organizing data mining was first proposed by the Ukrainian cybernetician A. G. Ivachenko in 1967. Later, with the efforts of scientists such as Adolf Müller and Frank Lemke, the self-organizing data mining method was rapidly developed. The rapid development of computer technology has made the self-organizing modeling of multivariate complex systems possible[6].

1.2.2 Working Principle of the Self-Organizing Data Mining Method

The technical core of self-organizing data mining is GMDH (group method of data handling), a group data processing method. It starts from the initial model (function) set composed of reference functions and generates new intermediate candidate models (genetic, mutation) according to certain rules. After screening (selection), the process of genetics, mutation, selection, and evolution is repeated so that the complexity of the intermediate candidate model constantly increases until the most complex model is obtained[7].

The characteristics of a self-organizing data mining algorithm are data grouping and the application of internal and external criteria throughout the modeling process. It divides the observed sample data into training and testing sets: the internal criteria are used to establish the intermediate candidate model on the training set, and the external criteria are used to select the intermediate candidate model on the testing set. When the external criteria reach the minimum, the corresponding model is the optimal complexity model. This model expresses the mutual relationship between input and output variables. The basic steps of a self-organizing data mining algorithm are referred to in reference[6].

This study adopts self-organizing data mining software (KnowledgeMiner 5.0) to achieve this.

2 Results and Analysis

2.1 Analysis of Purchase Factors for Product A based on Self-Organization Modeling

The influencing factors of consumers' purchase of Product A are input variable X, and the number of consumers who often purchase Product A is output variable Y. Algorithm type: Minimum Deviation Criterion. The optimal complexity model is screened by computer using self-organizing data mining software (KnowledgeMiner 5.0):

$Y = 10.313939 + 4.686060X_{12} + 5.562724X_{19} + 5.415582X_{23} - 5.972193X_{25} + 7.455838X_{14} + 8.302585X_{28} - 9.474248X_{29} + 8.319394X_5 + 10.198918X_{17} + 14.176303X_3 + 15.010733X_6 + 21.233309X_1 + 37.411064X_{11}$

$R^2 = 0.9189$; prediction error: 0.0829; mean absolute percentage error: 13.90%; approximation error: 0.0811.

As can be seen from the above model and Figure 1, when consumers often purchase product A, there are 11 main factors for their purchase decisions, mainly distributed in five categories, among which brand image category is mainly "High national popularity", "Old brand, long history", "Brand image/character", "Classic brand"; value (price) category is mainly "Recognized value"; social entertainment category is mainly "In line with my identity and status", "high social popularity, many people smoke"; new product category is mainly "It is a new product, attractive"; the main product categories are "Good tobacco quality", "Light aroma", and "Classic packaging". The larger the coefficient in front of the variable, the greater the factor's influence on the number of cigarette consumers or the more critical it is to consumers when purchasing cigarettes for themselves. It is obvious that "Recognized value" is the most critical factor for consumers in purchasing this brand of cigarettes. The constant term in the model indicates that when consumers make purchasing decisions, in addition to being mainly affected by several factors in the model, they are also affected by many other factors. The smaller the constant, the smaller the influence of other factors is. In addition, the negative coefficient of the influencing factor indicates that the factor has little influence on the motivation to purchase the product, mainly reflected in the product category of "No odor in the mouth after smoking" and "Good filter design".

2.2 Analysis of Purchase Factors for Product B based on Self-Organization Modeling

The influencing factors of consumers purchasing Product B are taken as input variables X, and the number of consumers who often purchase Product B is used as output variable Y. Algorithm type: Minimum Deviation Criterion. By applying self-organization data mining software (KnowledgeMiner 5.0), the computer screens out the optimal complexity model:

$Y = 7.813154 + 4.186844X_2 + 5.080919X_{16} + 4.951341X_{10} - 5.403012X_8 - 6.189723X_{26} - 5.909407X_{27} + 6.249407X_{13} + 9.114269X_{17} + 7.934567X_{28} + 12.937182X_1$

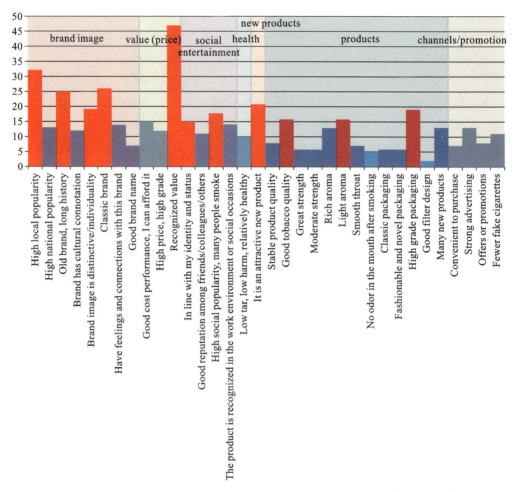

Figure 1　Distribution of the Number of People Concerned with Product A's Purchase Factors

$+ 13.821937 X_6 + 26.506128 X_3 + 20.072275 X_{11}$

$R^2 = 0.9149$; prediction error: 0.0862; mean absolute percentage error: 14.56%; approximation error: 0.0851.

As can be seen from the above model and Figure 2, when consumers often purchase Product B, there are ten main factors for their purchase decisions, mainly distributed in six categories, among which brand image category is mainly "High local popularity", "High national popularity", "Old brand, long history", "classic brand"; value (price) category is mainly "High price, high grade", "Recognized value"; social entertainment category is mainly "Good reputation of friends/colleagues/others"; health category is mainly "Low tar, low harm, relatively healthy"; new product category is mainly "It is a new product, attractive"; product category is mainly "High grade packaging". The larger the coefficient in front of the variable, the greater the factor's influence on the number of cigarette consumers or the more critical it is to consumers when they buy cigarettes. It is obvious that "Old brand, long history" is the most critical factor for consumers in buying this brand of cigarettes. The constant term in the model indicates that when consumers make purchase decisions, in addition to being mainly affected by several factors in the model, they are also affected by many other factors. The smaller the constant, the smaller the influence of other factors is. In addition, the negative coefficient of the influencing factor indicates that the factor has little influence on the purchase motivation of the product, mainly reflected in the "Good brand name" in the brand image category, and the "Classic packaging" and "fashionable and novel packaging" in the product category.

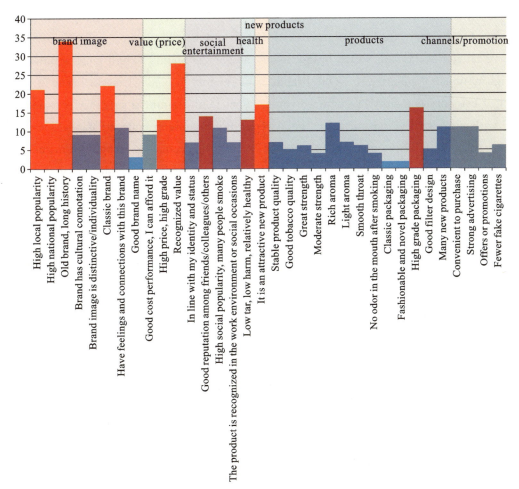

Figure 2　Distribution of the Number of People Concerned with Product B's Purchase Factors

2.3　Analysis of Purchase Factors for Product C based on Self-Organization Modeling

The influencing factors of consumers purchasing Product C are taken as input variables X, and the number of consumers who often purchase Product C is used as output variable Y. Algorithm type: Minimum Deviation Criterion. By applying self-organization data mining software (KnowledgeMiner 5.0), the computer screens out the optimal complexity model:

$$Y = 17.082209 + 7.917794X_2 + 8.713123X_{12} + 9.504688X_{13} + 10.293512X_{17} + 11.080136X_{23} - 12.233792X_{29} - 12.710546X_{21} + 12.400946X_{14} + 14.202927X_6 + 16.018333X_{30} + 33.780907X_1 + 34.906937X_3 + 45.933899X_{11} + 14.396142X_{15}$$

$R^2 = 0.9398$; prediction error: 0.0616; mean absolute percentage error: 10.04%; approximation error: 0.0602.

As can be seen from the above model and Figure 3, when consumers often purchase Product C, there are twelve main factors for their purchase decisions, mainly distributed in five categories, among which brand image category is mainly "High local popularity", "High national popularity", "Old brand, long history", and "Classic brand"; value (price) category is mainly "recognized value"; social entertainment category is mainly "in line with my identity and status", "good reputation among friends/colleagues/others", "High social popularity, many people smoke", and "the product is recognized in the work environment or social occasions"; The health category mainly includes "low tar, low harm, relatively healthy"; the new product category mainly includes "It is new products, attractive"; and the product category mainly includes "Light aroma" and "Many new products". The larger the coefficient in front of the variable, the greater the influence of the factor on the number of cigarette consumers, or the more consumers value the factor when purchasing their cigarettes. It is obvious that "recognized value" is the most critical factor for consumers when buying this brand of cigarettes. The constant term in the model indicates that when consumers make purchasing decisions, in addition to being mainly affected by several factors in the model, they are also affected by many other factors. The smaller the constant, the smaller the influence of other factors. In addition, the negative coefficient of the influencing factor indicates that the factor has little influence on the motivation to buy the product, mainly reflected in the product category of "Moderate strength" and "Good filter design".

2.4 Analysis of Purchase Factors for Product D based on Self-Organization Modeling

The influencing factors of consumers purchasing Product D are taken as input variables X, and the number of consumers who often purchase Product D is used as output variable Y. Algorithm type: Minimum Deviation Criterion. By applying self-organization data mining software (KnowledgeMiner 5.0), the computer screens out the

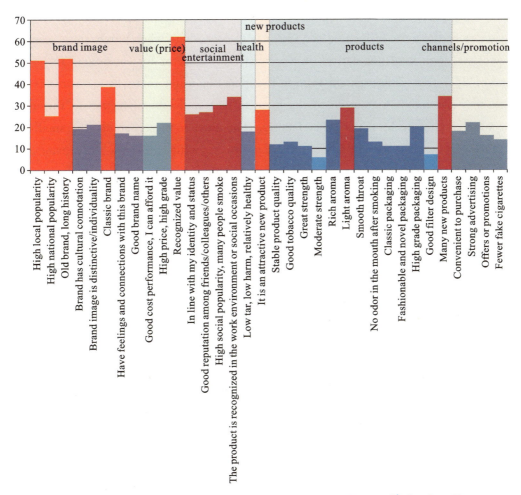

Figure 3　Distribution of the Number of People Concerned with Product C's Purchase Factors

optimal complexity model:

$Y = 19.858166 - 10.858164X_7 - 11.380106X_{21} - 11.842220X_{27} - 11.271664X_{19} - 11.662505X_{34} + 15.257550X_9 + 15.938383X_8 + 20.541288X_2 + 19.285566X_{12} + 16.967615X_{30} + 40.735580X_1 + 30.868595X_6 + 25.461088X_3 + 38.781330X_{11}$

$R^2 = 0.9257$; prediction error: 0.0754; mean absolute percentage error: 11.09%; approximation error: 0.0743.

As can be seen from the above model and Figure 4, when consumers often purchase Product D, there are nine main factors for their purchase decisions, mainly distributed in four categories, among which brand image category is mainly "high local popularity", "high national popularity", "old brand, long history", "classic brand", "good brand name"; value (price) category is mainly "good cost performance, I can afford it", "recognized value"; social entertainment category is mainly "in line with my identity and status"; product category is mainly "many new products". The larger the coefficient in front of the variable, the greater the factor's influence on the number of cigarette consumers or the more influential the factor is to consumers when purchasing cigarettes. Obviously, "high local popularity" is the most critical factor for consumers to buy this brand of cigarettes. The constant term in the model indicates that when consumers make purchasing decisions, in addition to the main influence of several factors in the model, they are also affected by many other factors. The smaller the constant, the smaller the influence of other factors. In addition, the negative coefficient of the influencing factor indicates that the factor has little influence on the motivation to buy the product, mainly reflected in the brand image category of "having feelings and connections with the brand", the product category of "good quality of tobacco", "moderate strength", "fashionable and novel packaging", and the channel/promotion category of "fewer fake cigarettes".

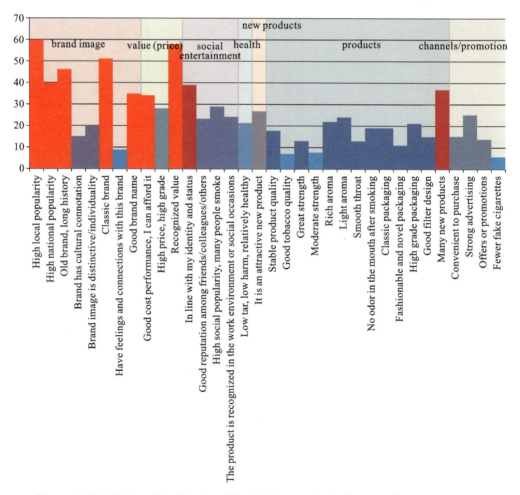

Figure 4　Distribution of the Number of People Concerned with Product D's Purchase Factors

3 Conclusion

When consumers often buy cigarettes of product A, the most critical purchasing factors are mainly "recognized value" in the value (price) category, followed by "high local popularity", "old brand, long history", "brand image is distinctive/individuality", "classic brand" in the brand image category. While "In line with my identity and status", "high social popularity, many people smoke", "It is an attractive new product", "good tobacco quality", "light aroma", and "classic packaging" are the third. The relatively unimportant factors are "no odor in the mouth after smoking" and "good filter design" in the product category. Therefore, when improving the quality and maintenance of the product, the main consideration is the prominent embodiment of the product value while maintaining good tobacco quality. In addition, when updating the product packaging, the original style should be maintained while improving the sense of class and novelty to increase the attraction to consumers, without too much consideration of the updated filter design and the improvement of oral odor.

When consumers regularly purchase cigarettes of product B, the most critical purchasing factors are mainly "old brand, long history" in the category of brand image, followed by "high price, high grade" and "recognized value" in the category of value (price). In particular, the special key factors of "low tar, low harm, relatively healthy" are proposed in the health category. The relatively unimportant factors are "good brand name" in the category of brand image, and "classic packaging" and "fashionable and novel packaging" in the category of product. Therefore, when improving the quality and maintenance of the product, the inheritance of the historical image of the product should be mainly considered. Improvements can be made to low-tar products. In addition, when updating the product packaging, the original style should be maintained while improving the sense of grade and novelty to increase consumer attraction without too much consideration of decisive packaging fashion.

When consumers often buy product C, the most critical purchasing factors are mainly "recognized value" in the value (price) category, followed by "high local popularity", "old brand with a long history", and "classic brand" in the brand image category. The four characteristics in the social entertainment category are more pronounced, including "in line with my identity and status", "good reputation among friends/colleagues/others", "high social popularity, many people smoke", and "the product is recognized in the work environment or social occasions". The relatively unimportant factors are "Moderate strength" and "Good filter design" in the product category. Therefore, when improving the quality and maintenance of the product, the main consideration is the prominent embodiment of the product's value while maintaining its advantages in the social entertainment environment. In addition, when updating the product packaging, it is necessary to maintain the original style while improving the novelty to increase the attraction to consumers, without too much consideration of the updated design of the filter and the improvement of momentum.

When consumers regularly purchase product D, the most critical purchasing factors are mainly "High local popularity" in the brand image category, followed by "Recognized value" and "Good cost performance, I can afford" in the value (price) category. The relatively unimportant factors are "Good tobacco quality", "Moderate strength", "Fashionable and novel packaging" in the product category, and "Few fake cigarettes" in the channel/promotion category. Therefore, when improving the quality and maintenance of the product, the main consideration is the prominent embodiment of the product's value, highlighting the characteristics of high-cost performance. In addition, when updating the product packaging, there is no need to consider too much about fashionable and novel packaging.

References

[1] LIU G Z, YAN K Q, KANG Y L. GMDH Neural Network Algorithm based on Self-Organization Theory and Its Application[J]. Mathematics in Practice and Theory, 2001, 31 (4): 464-469.

[2] HE Y, BAO A G, HE C Z. Research on Self-Organization Modeling Method and GDP Growth Model[J]. Chinese Journal of Management Science, 2004, 12 (2): 139-143.

[3] HAN Y D, CHEN J Z. Research on Self-Organization Modeling Method and GDP Growth Influencing Factor Model in Guizhou Province[J]. Mechanical and Electronic Engineering, 2006, 8 (1): 255-258.

[4] KANG Y L, YAN K Q. Research on Self-Organization Modeling Method and Western GDP Growth Model[J]. Journal of Southwest Jiaotong University, 2001, 36 (2): 206-211.

[5] WANG C X. Research on the Motivation Factors of Consumers' Cigarette Brand Choice: A Case Study of "Jinsheng" and "Furongwang" Cigarettes in Nanchang Market[D]. Nanchang: Jiangxi Normal University, 2013.

[6] LEMKE F, MÜLLER J A. Self-Organizing Data Mining—An Intelligent Approach to Extract Knowledge from Data[M]. Berlin: Dresden,1999.

[7] IVACHENKO A G, KOZUBOVSKI S F, YU V K. Objective System Analysis of Macroeconomic Systems[J]. Systems Analysis Modelling Simulation, 1990, 7 (3): 201-206.

第 3 章

卷烟消费特征探究

消费指标与满意度

卷烟产品消费者满意度影响因素实证研究

摘要：消费者满意度是影响卷烟购买意愿的重要因素。为了找出影响消费者对卷烟满意度评价的属性指标，本文以描述消费者满意度的 76 个卷烟指标为基础，通过正交因子旋转及偏最小二乘法回归分析，筛出 52 个卷烟属性指标，按照卷烟归属特征不同，将其分为内在属性、外在属性、抽象属性、表现属性。结果表明：①所确定的 52 个卷烟属性指标均与消费者满意度呈正相关，且内在属性、外在属性、表现属性、抽象属性与消费者满意度间的相关系数分别为 0.55～0.65、0.45～0.55、0.4～0.45、0.3～0.4；②偏最小二乘法分析结果表明，内在属性是卷烟产品最重要的属性，对消费者满意度影响最大，其次是抽象属性、外在属性和表现属性，影响度分别为 39.52%、25.76%、21.86%、12.86%；③对不同区域卷烟产品消费者满意度进行评价，结果表明，消费者最看重产品的内在属性，其他属性对消费者的满意度影响因区域不同而有所差别。

关键词：消费者满意度；产品属性；影响因素；卷烟指标

早在20世纪60年代,美国就开始了消费者满意度的研究。在营销学领域,美国学者Richard(1965)最早提出了顾客满意(CS)的概念,他认为,顾客满意是衡量顾客对产品预期和支付成本之间差距大小的指标,顾客满意会提高继续购买或消费的可能性[1]。Howard和Sheth(1969)认为顾客满意是顾客对其实际付出的价值与获得的感知价值之间匹配度的评价[2]。随着对消费者满意度结构的深入探索和研究,人们开始从行为学角度来研究消费者满意度。Cronin和Taylor(1992)通过对银行、餐饮和其他服务类行业的研究,得出消费者满意度是影响消费者重购意向的重要变量之一[3]。

国内关于消费者满意度的研究起步较晚,主要以美国消费者满意度指数(ACSI)和中国消费者满意度指数(CCSI)为研究基础,针对不同行业进行消费者满意度研究。孙庆莉等(2008)以北京市新发地农产品批发市场的客户作为调查对象,构建了农产品批发市场客户满意度模型[4];李金晖(2009)以汽车业为研究对象,根据汽车消费行为和产品特点研究了消费者满意度影响因素[5];徐晓萌(2011)以顾客让渡价值为切入点,以笔记本电脑消费行为为研究对象,构建了消费者满意度的评价指标体系[6];文兰等(2014)以云南特色农产品小粒咖啡的网络营销为研究对象,在ACSI模型中加入"品牌形象"这一维度,构建了消费者满意度测评模型[7]。

在卷烟产品的消费者满意度研究方面,于明芳等(2001)建立了卷烟产品用户满意度指数模型并进行应用[8];范军等(2013)以汉川市市场为调查依据,运用熵值法,对卷烟零售客户的满意度进行了评价分析[9];祖强(2017)立足卷烟消费者购买需求的角度,以卡诺模型为基础,从消费者需求研究、需求项目分类、零售客户评价标准、实际运用和管理等方面探索构建面向消费者的零售客户分类评价体系[10]。

随着消费者行为研究的不断深入,产品属性的概念也逐渐被不同领域和行业所理解和重视。特里·A.布里顿、戴安娜·拉萨利(2003)认为与体验相关的产品属性包含四个方面:物理属性,即组成产品的各个部件的特性;流程属性,与物理属性相对应,适用于服务型产品;美学属性,即产品的外观是如何影响我们的感官的;关联属性,如品牌、支持、促销等[11]。内在属性是指产品的物理组成,包括原材料、制造和形态等方面的内容;外在属性是指不是产品的物理组成部分,且可以在不使用产品的情况下进行评估的属性,包括品牌、包装、服务和价格等内容;表现属性是指产品发挥作用的方式,只有通过使用才能进行评估的属性(如汽车的耗油量);抽象属性是指将多种属性包含的信息集合而成的一种综合属性,包括加权多种属性、用户意向属性和使用情境属性[12]。吴长亮(2011,郑州大学)将产品属性从消费者决策角度直接分为成本属性和收益属性两大类。收益属性中,首先是功能属性,即产品提供的功能在多大程度上能满足消费者的期望;其次是质量属性,即产品能否顺利贡献某种功能和保持这种功能的持久性;再次是情感属性,即使用某种产品有何心理收益。成本属性则包括以下四个方面,即价格成本、使用前成本、使用成本、处置成本[13]。

本文采用马克·佩里博士的产品属性分类方法,从可反映卷烟产品的指标出发,探索对消费者满意度有影响的卷烟指标,形成卷烟产品属性指标体系,并考察卷烟产品属性对消费者满意度的影响度,确定主要产品属性,对指导卷烟攻关方向、构建新的卷烟产品消费者满意度评价方法均起到了积极作用。

1 材料与方法

1.1 数据来源

本次消费者调研针对消费水平在 100~1000 元/条价位段,年龄在 20~50 岁的卷烟消费群体,调研覆盖全国七大区域,每个区域两个城市,共计 14 个城市,具体如表 1 所示;对表 2 中涉及的 76 个细分指标及总体满意度进行问卷调研,每个城市问卷 100 份,共计 1400 份,每个城市备份问卷 10 份,最终问卷数量 1540 份,实际有效问卷为 1442 份。在调研样品选择上,选择不同区域畅销烟及不同价位段全国销量排名靠前的云烟、中华、玉溪、芙蓉王、双喜、利群、黄金叶等品牌卷烟产品为评价样品。

表 1 样本分布情况表

区域	华东	华北	华南	西南	西北	东北	华中
城市	上海	北京	广州	成都	西安	沈阳	郑州
样本量	100	105	100	105	100	102	102
城市	宁波	保定	深圳	昆明	兰州	哈尔滨	武汉
样本量	105	105	103	105	101	103	106

1.2 分析方法

1.2.1 指标收集

通过消费者定性访谈,获得 76 个用于描述消费者满意度的卷烟指标,根据卷烟特征将其归为 9 类,见表 2。

表 2 卷烟指标确定

卷烟指标大类	卷烟指标细分
嗅香 4 个	嗅香浓淡程度、嗅香舒适度、烟草纯正程度、嗅香新颖独特程度
口腔 7 个	口腔舒适度、口腔干燥程度、烟气浓度、口腔残留烟草浓度、口腔劲头接受程度、烟气平稳程度、口腔饱满程度
鼻腔 7 个	鼻腔舒适度、烟气细腻柔和度、鼻腔顺畅度、鼻腔劲头接受程度、鼻腔烟气纯净程度、烟气丰富程度、香气浓度
喉部 5 个	烟气顺滑度、喉咙舒适度、喉咙干燥程度、喉咙细腻柔和程度、烟气充足度
余味 6 个	余味干净程度、抽后口腔干燥程度、余味纯正程度、余味镇静程度、余味舒适程度、余味生津感

续表

卷烟指标大类	卷烟指标细分
烟支外观10个	烟支粗细、烟支图案喜好程度、烟支长度、烟身硬度、滤嘴长度、滤嘴抽吸顺畅程度、特殊滤嘴喜好程度、卷烟纸颜色喜好程度、烟支整体搭配协调性、烟支喜好程度
烟支物理7个	烟梗数量、烟丝颜色喜好程度、烟灰颜色喜好程度、烟灰易断程度、烟支燃烧速度、焦油量、劲头
包装11个	包装高档程度、包装素雅程度、包装材质喜好程度、包装颜色喜好程度、包装防伪程度、包装新颖独特程度、包装字体喜好程度、产品概念新颖程度、包装图案喜好程度、有情感共鸣、开合方式喜好程度
其他19个	口碑、母品牌口碑、营销宣传、悠久历史、怀旧的、高端/有档次、适合社交/适合送礼、大众化的、知名度、小众的/另类的、价格适中的、价格高的、烟丝产地、生产厂商、购买容易程度、渠道可信度、时尚的、适合自吸、性价比

1.2.2 指标筛选和验证

采用等量最大法对表2中的76个卷烟指标进行正交旋转,解决变量间的多重共线性问题;再将旋转后的结果采用最小二乘法进行回归,舍去 P 值大于0.05的卷烟指标,并通过关联度分析研究筛选出的指标与满意度之间的相关性,以验证筛选指标的合理性,最终完成卷烟技术指标的筛选。指标筛选和验证使用的分析方法具体如下所示。

(1) 正交因子旋转+回归分析用于指标筛选。

先对模型中的自变量进行正交因子旋转,并提取一定的主因子;然后用因变量对所取的主因子进行回归;最后将因变量对所提取的主因子的回归方程转化为对原自变量的回归方程,然后选取 $P<0.05$ 的指标集。

(2) 关联度分析用于指标验证。

采用关联度分析探究卷烟指标与消费者满意度的相关性。Pearson 相关系数作为简单相关系数,是用来度量两个变量间的线性关系的,Pearson 相关系数越大,说明变量间的线性关系越强,其计算公式为:

$$r(X,Y) = \frac{\text{cov}(X,Y)}{\sqrt{\text{var}(X)\text{var}(Y)}}$$

1.2.3 筛选指标在满意度分析上的应用

以卷烟产品属性为指标,对不同区域卷烟消费者满意度进行分析,确定不同区域消费者对卷烟产品需求指标的关注方向。本文采用偏最小二乘法对满意度进行分析。

在多元回归里, $y = \beta_0 + \beta_1 x_1 + \beta_2 x_2 + \cdots + \beta_p x_p + \varepsilon$,系数 β 代表各个自变量对因变量的影响程度,系数越大,因变量受这个自变量影响越明显。对卷烟指标和消费者满意度做偏最小二乘分析,通过变量系数,确定其对考察因素的影响度。

2 结果与分析

2.1 卷烟属性指标筛选

将消费者所能感知的 76 个卷烟指标作为描述消费者满意度的卷烟指标，采用等量最大法对所有自变量进行正交旋转，解决变量间的多重共线性问题，旋转成分载荷值见表 3。从表 3 中可以看出，所有的旋转成分载荷都在 0.7 以上，对原始变量的信息提取率很高，效果很好。其中购买容易程度的载荷达到了 0.877，值是最大的。载荷大于 0.8 的变量有 10 个，其余都在 0.7~0.8 区间内。

表 3 76 个卷烟指标旋转成分矩阵结果

指标	旋转成分矩阵	指标	旋转成分矩阵	指标	旋转成分矩阵
购买容易程度	0.877	鼻腔舒适度	0.747	嗅香舒适度	0.740
小众的/另类的	0.874	烟丝颜色喜好程度	0.760	烟梗数量	0.718
价格高的	0.836	烟灰颜色喜好程度	0.759	烟支燃烧速度	0.782
大众化的	0.835	烟气平稳程度	0.747	焦油量	0.702
价格适中的	0.830	喉咙舒适度	0.738	包装字体喜好程度	0.703
烟草纯正程度	0.813	包装图案喜好程度	0.751	烟身硬度	0.741
开合方式喜好程度	0.814	烟支图案喜好程度	0.754	滤嘴抽吸顺畅程度	0.781
滤嘴长度	0.808	口腔饱满程度	0.748	特殊滤嘴喜好程度	0.721
适合自吸	0.813	包装新颖独特程度	0.749	卷烟纸颜色喜好程度	0.733
悠久历史	0.807	包装材质喜好程度	0.751	烟支整体搭配协调性	0.762
嗅香浓淡程度	0.794	适合社交/适合送礼	0.745	烟支喜好程度	0.716
嗅香新颖独特程度	0.795	包装素雅程度	0.747	烟气浓度	0.775
烟灰易断程度	0.794	烟气丰富程度	0.741	口腔残留烟草浓度	0.726
性价比	0.798	烟丝产地	0.754	口腔劲头接受程度	0.701
知名度	0.790	口腔舒适度	0.729	鼻腔顺畅度	0.755
营销宣传	0.790	口腔干燥程度	0.728	鼻腔劲头接受程度	0.783
烟支粗细	0.784	产品概念新颖程度	0.744	鼻腔烟气纯净程度	0.762
渠道可信度	0.789	烟气细腻柔和度	0.723	香气浓度	0.754
劲头	0.771	烟气顺滑度	0.724	喉咙干燥程度	0.787
母品牌口碑	0.786	时尚的	0.736	喉咙细腻柔和程度	0.762
烟支长度	0.781	抽后口腔干燥程度	0.714	烟气充足度	0.765
生产厂商	0.783	口碑	0.732	余味纯正程度	0.768

续表

指标	旋转成分矩阵	指标	旋转成分矩阵	指标	旋转成分矩阵
怀旧的	0.781	余味舒适程度	0.710	余味镇静程度	0.755
包装颜色喜好程度	0.759	高端/有档次	0.720	余味生津感	0.789
有情感共鸣	0.772	余味干净程度	0.705		
包装防伪程度	0.765	包装高档程度	0.711		

将旋转后的自变量与因变量采用偏最小二乘法进行回归,将统计学检验 P 值大于 0.05 的卷烟指标舍去,同时结合专家建议、消费者需求,整理文献资料、对类似指标进行归类并对不重要的指标进行删除,共计获得 52 个卷烟指标,52 个指标对应的模型拟合结果见表 4。

从表 4 可以看出,模型回归系数为 0.803,拟合效果理想,R^2 为 0.645,也就是说,自变量能解释因变量 64.5% 的信息,作为一个自变量众多的模型,这个结果较为可观,调整后的 R^2 也达到了 0.641,模型拟合效果良好。

表 4 回归方程拟合优度

R	R^2	调整后的 R^2	标准估计的误差
0.803	0.645	0.641	0.693

2.2 卷烟属性指标的确定

通过 52 个卷烟指标与消费者满意度之间的关联度分析,得到表 5,从中可以看出,所有的卷烟指标与消费者满意度之间都是正相关,其中余味舒适程度与消费者满意度的相关性最强,达到了 0.643,这为当前卷烟感官质量提升指明了方向。按 52 个卷烟指标的不同属性,对卷烟指标进行归类,划分为内在属性、外在属性、表现属性和抽象属性(见表 5)。

表 5 Person 相关系数结果

内在属性 16 个	相关系数	Sig.	外在属性 15 个	相关系数	Sig.	抽象属性 14 个	相关系数	Sig.	表现属性 7 个	相关系数	Sig.
余味舒适程度	0.643	0.000	包装图案喜好程度	0.533	0.000	高端/有档次	0.301	0.000	性价比	0.438	0.000
喉咙舒适度	0.614	0.000	包装新颖独特程度	0.537	0.000	适合自吸	0.321	0.000	价格高的	0.415	0.000
口腔舒适度	0.618	0.000	包装颜色喜好程度	0.52	0.000	产品概念新颖程度	0.376	0.000	渠道可信度	0.432	0.000
抽后口腔干燥程度	0.634	0.000	包装高档程度	0.553	0.000	口碑	0.37	0.000	价格适中的	0.457	0.000

续表

内在属性 16个	相关系数	Sig.	外在属性 15个	相关系数	Sig.	抽象属性 14个	相关系数	Sig.	表现属性 7个	相关系数	Sig.
烟气细腻柔和度	0.621	0.000	包装材质喜好程度	0.529	0.000	适合社交/适合送礼	0.368	0.000	烟丝产地	0.435	0.000
劲头	0.598	0.000	包装素雅程度	0.543	0.000	有情感共鸣	0.346	0.000	生产厂商	0.401	0.000
口腔干燥程度	0.619	0.000	烟丝颜色喜好程度	0.537	0.000	时尚的	0.372	0.000	购买容易程度	0.407	0.000
口腔饱满程度	0.609	0.000	烟支图案喜好程度	0.532	0.000	母品牌口碑	0.319	0.000			
烟气平稳程度	0.608	0.000	烟灰颜色喜好程度	0.537	0.000	营销宣传	0.316	0.000			
烟气丰富程度	0.615	0.000	包装防伪程度	0.525	0.000	知名度	0.396	0.000			
余味干净程度	0.631	0.000	滤嘴长度	0.469	0.000	大众化的	0.322	0.000			
嗅香浓淡程度	0.555	0.000	烟灰易断程度	0.502	0.000	怀旧的	0.315	0.000			
烟气顺滑度	0.614	0.000	烟支长度	0.475	0.000	悠久历史	0.382	0.000			
鼻腔舒适度	0.596	0.000	烟支粗细	0.473	0.000	小众的/另类的	0.309	0.000			
烟草纯正程度	0.531	0.000	开合方式喜好程度	0.455	0.000						
嗅香新颖独特程度	0.536	0.000									

可以看出,产品内在属性与产品内在品质相关,如产品口味、产品质量、烟气指标、安全性指标、物理化学指标等;产品外在属性与产品外观相关,如烟支设计搭配、烟包、烟盒设计搭配、包装材质等;产品表现属性与产品的市场表现相关,如产品价格、市场接受度、认可度、时尚度、购买意愿等;产品抽象属性主要偏向于消费者对卷烟产品的认知度,如品牌认知度、产品设计创意、产品品名、健康关注度等。

图 1 为卷烟属性与消费者满意度相关系数盒状图,从图中可以看出内在属性、外在属性、表现属性、抽象属性与消费者满意度之间的相关性分别为 0.55~0.65、0.45~0.55、

0.4~0.45、0.3~0.4,相关系数逐渐降低。

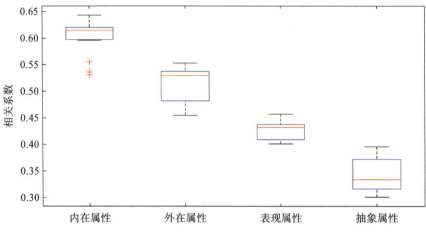

图 1　卷烟属性与消费者满意度相关系数盒状图

2.3　卷烟属性指标应用结果分析

2.3.1　基于卷烟属性的消费者满意度分析

对 52 个卷烟指标进行偏最小二乘分析,并提取其标准化相关系数,再将每个属性的标准化系数相加,获得卷烟属性对消费者满意度的影响度,结果见表 6。

表 6　卷烟属性对消费者满意度影响度

内在属性 16 个	标准化系数 ∑2.209	外在属性 15 个	标准化系数 ∑1.222	抽象属性 14 个	标准化系数 ∑1.439	表现属性 7 个	标准化系数 ∑0.719
余味舒适程度	0.161	包装图案喜好程度	0.101	高端/有档次	0.151	性价比	0.155
喉咙舒适度	0.152	包装新颖独特程度	0.098	适合自吸	0.142	价格高的	0.113
口腔舒适度	0.150	包装颜色喜好程度	0.097	产品概念新颖程度	0.120	渠道可信度	0.111
抽后口腔干燥程度	0.147	包装高档程度	0.093	口碑	0.110	价格适中的	0.106
烟气细腻柔和度	0.145	包装材质喜好程度	0.092	适合社交/适合送礼	0.110	烟丝产地	0.082
劲头	0.144	包装素雅程度	0.091	有情感共鸣	0.109	生产厂商	0.079
口腔干燥程度	0.142	烟丝颜色喜好程度	0.085	时尚	0.105	购买容易程度	0.073

续表

内在属性 16 个	标准化系数 ∑2.209	外在属性 15 个	标准化系数 ∑1.222	抽象属性 14 个	标准化系数 ∑1.439	表现属性 7 个	标准化系数 ∑0.719
口腔饱满程度	0.137	烟支图案喜好程度	0.084	母品牌口碑	0.104		
烟气平稳程度	0.137	烟灰颜色喜好程度	0.084	营销宣传	0.099		
烟气丰富程度	0.135	包装防伪程度	0.078	知名度	0.093		
余味干净程度	0.135	滤嘴长度	0.077	大众化的	0.083		
嗅香浓淡程度	0.131	烟灰易断程度	0.065	怀旧的	0.082		
烟气顺滑度	0.130	烟支长度	0.065	悠久历史	0.078		
鼻腔舒适度	0.130	烟支粗细	0.061	小众的/另类的	0.053		
烟草纯正程度	0.124	开合方式喜好程度	0.051				
嗅香新颖独特程度	0.109						

从表 6 中可以看出,内在属性的 16 个变量对满意度的总体影响值为 2.209,影响度达 39.52%,是最高的,内在属性平均每提升 1 个单位,满意度就会提升 2.209 个单位,说明在消费者评价里,产品的内在属性尤为重要;外在属性的 15 个变量对满意度的总体影响值为 1.222,影响度达 21.86%,低于抽象属性 14 个变量的影响值总和 1.439(影响度 25.76%),表现出消费者对产品的抽象属性的感知程度强于对外在属性的感知程度;而表现属性 7 个变量的影响值是 0.719,影响度为 12.86%,从总量上看最低,但是每个变量的平均影响力在 0.1 以上,特别是性价比变量,其系数高达 0.155。

2.3.2 卷烟属性指标重要程度的区域性差异

基于不同区域卷烟的 4 个属性指标,拟合 R^2,从表 7 可以看出,各地区的拟合优度基本在 0.6 以上,拟合优度较好,只有华北地区的拟合优度相比其他地区略低,但也在可接受的范围内。

表 7 不同卷烟属性重要程度的区域性差异

模型	标准化回归系数				拟合优度 R^2
	内在属性	外在属性	抽象属性	表现属性	
华东	2.088	1.049	1.702	0.737	0.693
华北	2.312	1.460	1.160	0.772	0.596
华南	2.551	1.208	1.534	0.697	0.672

续表

模型	标准化回归系数				拟合优度 R^2
	内在属性	外在属性	抽象属性	表现属性	
西南	2.365	1.152	1.300	0.732	0.708
西北	2.271	1.254	1.554	0.611	0.651
东北	2.138	1.116	1.167	0.768	0.646
华中	1.824	1.506	1.648	0.652	0.629
全国	2.691	1.222	1.439	0.719	0.645

表7还反映了不同地区卷烟指标四个属性的标准化回归系数,从中可以看到,四个属性中,每个地区内在属性的标准化回归系数都是最大的,因此可以认为每个地区的消费者在进行消费时都最看重卷烟产品带来的体验,因此各卷烟企业在生产时应该着重关注产品本身的质量。从表7中还可以看出,在七个区域中,华南地区内在属性的标准化回归系数值达到了2.551,在所有地区中最大,表明华南地区是所有区域中最看重内在属性的,之后依次为西南地区、华北地区、西北地区、东北地区和华东地区,华中地区内在属性的标准化回归系数最低。从外在属性来看,各个地区之间的差别不明显,其中华中地区和华北地区的标准化回归系数值较大。从抽象属性来看,华东地区和华中地区的标准化回归系数值最大,说明这两个地区相比其他地区而言比较注重抽象属性。表现属性方面,各个地区之间几乎没有差异。

表8是不同区域52个指标数据回归结果,可以从各个具体指标来分析消费者需求评价指标重要性的区域性差异。

表8 不同区域卷烟指标对消费者满意度影响

指标	华东	华北	华南	西南	西北	东北	华中
高端/有档次	0.182	0.132	0.207	0.139	0.151	0.085	0.173
嗅香浓淡程度	0.177	0.121	0.15	0.124	0.129	0.099	0.08
烟气平稳程度	0.165	0.129	0.177	0.12	0.108	0.156	0.107
生产厂商	0.163	0.045	0.114	0.1	0.043	0.072	0.079
产品概念新颖程度	0.163	0.063	0.125	0.114	0.128	0.14	0.125
劲头	0.154	0.158	0.138	0.162	0.143	0.15	0.12
余味舒适程度	0.15	0.197	0.18	0.2	0.123	0.123	0.162
母品牌口碑	0.145	0.083	0.14	0.051	0.082	0.06	0.152
口碑	0.144	0.106	0.058	0.097	0.14	0.078	0.175
喉咙舒适度	0.143	0.138	0.166	0.152	0.146	0.194	0.094
渠道可信度	0.141	0.099	0.125	0.155	0.078	0.034	0.092
烟支长度	0.14	0.077	0.124	0.025	0.04	0.026	0.062

续表

指标	华东	华北	华南	西南	西北	东北	华中
大众化	0.139	0.04	0.041	0.083	0.055	0.089	0.077
口腔干燥程度	0.136	0.141	0.18	0.149	0.161	0.155	0.084
抽后口腔干燥程度	0.136	0.196	0.163	0.159	0.147	0.099	0.107
适合社交/适合送礼	0.135	0.059	0.151	0.098	0.152	0.094	0.118
价格高	0.135	0.141	0.112	0.063	0.093	0.139	0.093
鼻腔舒适度	0.13	0.095	0.117	0.154	0.134	0.168	0.133
烟草纯正程度	0.128	0.082	0.168	0.127	0.157	0.07	0.15
口腔舒适度	0.125	0.144	0.194	0.169	0.159	0.148	0.107
烟灰易断程度	0.124	0.063	0.057	0.048	0.075	0.052	0.05
小众的/另类的	0.122	0.039	0.1	0.021	0.042	−0.016	0.098
烟气丰富程度	0.118	0.116	0.15	0.164	0.179	0.118	0.103
烟丝产地	0.117	0.084	0.083	0.11	0.059	0.095	0.084
烟气细腻柔和度	0.116	0.152	0.178	0.169	0.163	0.121	0.106
口腔饱满程度	0.115	0.181	0.142	0.136	0.177	0.123	0.127
怀旧的	0.114	0.042	0.073	0.082	0.073	0.072	0.062
知名度	0.113	0.095	0.031	0.082	0.082	0.12	0.144
时尚的	0.111	0.091	0.143	0.102	0.089	0.049	0.116
烟气顺滑度	0.109	0.188	0.158	0.174	0.073	0.127	0.117
包装素雅程度	0.107	0.068	0.098	0.075	0.079	0.107	0.117
包装防伪程度	0.107	0.056	0.062	0.07	0.115	0.081	0.073
余味干净程度	0.106	0.128	0.171	0.101	0.194	0.159	0.118
适合自吸	0.099	0.167	0.089	0.152	0.165	0.158	0.116
烟灰颜色喜好程度	0.089	0.155	0.061	0.076	0.117	0.022	0.058
有情感共鸣	0.086	0.076	0.132	0.065	0.19	0.122	0.139
包装高档程度	0.083	0.089	0.119	0.093	0.086	0.077	0.14
嗅香新颖独特程度	0.082	0.147	0.12	0.105	0.079	0.129	0.108
悠久历史	0.079	0.063	0.146	0.077	0.095	0.062	0.029
价格适中	0.077	0.18	0.048	0.091	0.093	0.089	0.09
滤嘴长度	0.072	0.106	0.083	0.091	0.08	0.059	0.077
包装新颖独特程度	0.071	0.136	0.084	0.077	0.101	0.104	0.075
营销宣传	0.069	0.104	0.1	0.138	0.109	0.038	0.124
包装材质喜好程度	0.068	0.089	0.078	0.107	0.113	0.065	0.172
烟丝颜色喜好程度	0.053	0.113	0.097	0.046	0.096	0.095	0.135

续表

指标	华东	华北	华南	西南	西北	东北	华中
烟支图案喜好程度	0.048	0.123	0.072	0.113	0.068	0.051	0.145
开合方式喜好程度	0.035	0.082	0.102	0.082	0.013	0.045	0.032
烟支粗细	0.03	0.067	0.07	0.058	0.023	0.061	0.102
包装图案喜好程度	0.022	0.103	0.071	0.103	0.152	0.132	0.116
包装颜色喜好程度	0	0.132	0.028	0.088	0.097	0.138	0.153
购买容易程度	−0.007	0.08	0.087	0.073	0.09	0.116	0.073
性价比	0.110	0.143	0.127	0.139	0.154	0.239	0.141

从表 8 可以得出，不同区域消费者评价卷烟时注重的评价指标有所差异，具体表现如下。

（1）华东地区的消费者评价卷烟时排名前五的评价指标分别为"高端/有档次""嗅香浓淡程度""烟气平稳程度""生产厂商""产品概念新颖程度"。总体上，华东地区消费者表现出更注重卷烟的抽象属性，更重视卷烟中包含的身份认同的价值和整体的知名度，同时也对母品牌和厂商有一定的归属感。在口味上，嗅香浓淡程度是华东地区消费者最注重的内在属性。

（2）华北地区的消费者评价卷烟的五个最重要的指标分别为"余味舒适程度""抽后口腔干燥程度""烟气顺滑度""口腔饱满程度""价格适中"。整体上，华北地区的消费者更注重卷烟的内在属性，强调口味和品质感。同时，在价格上，华北地区的消费者也更重视与品质相适应的价格，卷烟本身定位是否高端对他们的整体评价影响不大。与全国总体结果一样，余味是影响口味评价最主要的指标。

（3）华南地区的消费者最注重的五个指标分别为"高端/有档次""口腔舒适度""余味舒适程度""口腔干燥程度""烟气细腻柔和度"。他们对卷烟的内在品质和身份体现的特质同时表现出关注，也对卷烟的社交功能提出要求。

（4）西南地区的消费者注重"余味舒适程度""烟气顺滑度""烟气细腻柔和度""口腔舒适度""烟气丰富程度"。与华北地区消费者类似，西南地区的消费者更注重卷烟的内在品质。在抽象属性方面，西南地区的消费者同时在意营销宣传以及高端品质。

（5）西北地区的消费者看重的五个指标分别为"余味干净程度""有情感共鸣""烟气丰富程度""口腔饱满程度""适合自吸"。西北地区消费者在对卷烟的口感表现出关注的同时，也十分看重卷烟品牌是否能给他们带来情感共鸣。

（6）东北地区的消费者在评价卷烟时重视"喉咙舒适度""鼻腔舒适度""余味干净程度""适合自吸""烟气平稳程度"几个方面。这几个方面都属于内在属性指标，说明东北地区的消费者更看重卷烟产品的口感，同时性价比在该地区消费者的心目中占有很高的比重。

（7）华中地区的消费者评价卷烟时更注重"口碑""高端/有档次""包装材质喜好程度"

"余味舒适程度""包装颜色喜好程度"。华中地区的消费者对卷烟的知名度、高档程度提出了更高的要求,同时包装设计和烟支设计也在该地区的消费者心目中占有很高的分量。

总体而言,华北、西南、西北、东北的消费者对卷烟的内在品质有更高的要求,华东和华南的消费者更注重卷烟的社交属性和身份体现,而华中的消费者则十分注重卷烟的外观属性。华东的消费者较为注重品牌和厂商的归属感,而西北地区消费者更看重卷烟品牌带来的情感共鸣。

3 结论

消费者满意度是消费意愿的重要影响因素,而消费者满意度的评价又涉及产品的众多因素。本文采用数理统计方法对卷烟主要评价指标进行分析、归类,确定了对卷烟产品消费者满意度影响较大的4个产品属性及涵盖的52个评价指标。

(1) 通过52个卷烟指标与全国消费者满意度之间的相关系数分析可以看出,所有的卷烟指标与消费者满意度之间都是正相关,且余味舒适程度与消费者满意度的相关性最强,为当前卷烟感官质量提升指明了方向。

(2) 从四大属性指标与全国卷烟消费者满意度的偏最小二乘法分析结果可以看出,内在属性是卷烟产品最重要的属性,对消费者满意度影响最大,达到39.52%,属于消费者最为关注的重点。其次是抽象属性、外在属性和表现属性,影响度分别为25.76%、21.86%、12.86%。

(3) 将卷烟产品属性用于不同区域消费者卷烟满意度分析,结果表明不同区域消费者最看重内在属性,而对其他属性的关注度略有差异。其中,华北、西南、西北、东北的消费者对卷烟的内在品质有更高的要求,华东和华南的消费者更注重卷烟的社交属性和身份体现,而华中的消费者则十分注重卷烟的外观属性;此外,华东的消费者还较为注重品牌和厂商的归属感,而西北地区消费者更看重卷烟品牌带来的情感共鸣。

(4) 本文所开发的卷烟产品属性消费者满意度评价方法,精炼地反映了消费者对卷烟产品的满意度评价,更有利于对卷烟开发的整体把控,对于指导区域性产品开发具有实际意义。

参考文献

[1] RICHARD A C. An Expermental Study of Consumer Effort, Expectation and Satisfaction[J]. Journal of Marketing Research, 1965 (8): 19.

[2] HOWARD J A, SHETH J N. The Theory of Buyer Behaviour[M]. New York: John Wily & Sons, 1969: 218.

[3] CRONIN J J, TAYLOR S A. Measuring Service Quality: A Reexamination and Extension[J]. Journal of Marketing, 1992 (56): 55.

[4] 孙庆莉, 安玉发. 农产品批发市场客户满意度研究[J]. 商业研究, 2008(7): 181.

［5］ 李金晖.汽车消费行为与消费者满意度研究[J].市场研究,2009(1):26.

［6］ 徐晓萌.基于顾客让渡价值的笔记本电脑满意度研究[D].北京:北京化工大学,2011.

［7］ 文兰,赵璟.云南特色农产品小粒咖啡网络营销顾客满意度模型构建与分析[J].现代农业科技,2014(8):273.

［8］ 于明芳,雷樟泉.卷烟产品用户满意度指数的构建与应用[J].烟草科技,2001(3):24.

［9］ 范军,杨其刚.基于熵值的卷烟零售客户满意度评价[J].当代经济,2013(14):112.

［10］ 祖强.基于卡诺模型面向消费者的客户分类评价体系建设研究[J].中国烟草学报,2017,23(1):122.

［11］ 特里·A.布里顿,戴安娜·拉萨利.从平凡到卓越的产品策略[M].北京:中信出版社,2003:1.

［12］ 赵丽影.产品开发中顾客需求转化为产品属性的路径研究——基于QFD改进的思考[D].长春:东北师范大学,2005.

［13］ 吴长亮.消费者决策角度下的产品属性分类体系研究[J].商业时代,2011(19):24.

An Empirical Study on the Influencing Factors of Cigarette Consumer Satisfaction

Abstract: Consumer satisfaction is an essential factor affecting the purchase intention of cigarette consumption. In order to find out the attribute indicators that affect consumers' evaluation of cigarette satisfaction, this paper screens out 52 cigarette attribute indicators based on 76 cigarette indicators describing consumer satisfaction through orthogonal factor rotation and partial least squares regression analysis. According to the different characteristics of cigarette attribution, they are divided into internal attributes, external attributes, abstract attributes, and performance attributes. The results show that: ① The 52 cigarette attribute indicators determined are positively correlated with consumer satisfaction, and the correlation coefficients between internal attributes, external attributes, performance attributes, abstract attributes, and consumer satisfaction are 0.55-0.65, 0.45-0.55, 0.4-0.45, and 0.3-0.4 respectively; ② The results of partial least squares analysis show that internal attributes are the most critical attributes of cigarette products, and have the most significant impact on consumer satisfaction, followed by abstract attributes, external attributes, and performance attributes, with impact degrees of 39.52%, 25.76%, 21.86%, and 12.86% respectively; ③ Evaluation of consumer satisfaction of cigarette products in different regions shows that consumers value the internal attributes of products most, and the impact of other attributes on consumer satisfaction varies in different regions.

Keywords: Consumer satisfaction; Product attributes; Influencing factors; Cigarette indicators

As early as the 1960s, the United States began to study consumer satisfaction. In marketing, American scholar Richard (1965) first proposed the concept of customer satisfaction (CS). He believed that customer satisfaction was an indicator to measure the gap between customers' expectations of a product and the cost they paid and that customer satisfaction would increase the likelihood of continued purchase or consumption[1]. Howard & Sheth (1969) believed that customer satisfaction was the evaluation of the matching degree between the value customers paid and the perceived value they received[2]. With the in-depth exploration and research on the structure of consumer satisfaction, people began to study consumer satisfaction from the perspective of behavior. Through the study of banking, catering, and other service industries, Cronin and Taylor (1992) concluded that consumer satisfaction is one of the critical variables affecting repurchase intentions[3].

Domestic research on consumer satisfaction started late, mainly based on the American Customer Satisfaction Index (ACSI) and the Chinese Customer Satisfaction Index (CCSI), and conducted consumer satisfaction research for different industries. Sun Qingli et al. (2008) took the customers in Beijing Xinfadi agricultural products wholesale market as the research object and established a customer satisfaction model for agricultural products wholesale market[4]; Li Jinhui (2009) took the automobile industry as the research object and studied the influencing factors of consumer satisfaction according to the consumption tendency and product characteristics of automobiles[5]; Xu Xiaomeng (2011) took the customer transfer value as the breakthrough point and took the laptop consumption behavior as the research object to build an evaluation index system for customer satisfaction[6]; Wen Lan et al. (2014) took the online marketing of Yunnan featured agricultural products such as small grain coffee as the research object, added the dimension of "brand image" to the ACSI model and established a customer satisfaction evaluation model[7].

In terms of the research on consumer satisfaction with cigarette products, Yu Mingfang et al. (2001) established and applied the cigarette product user satisfaction index model[8]; Fan Jun et al. (2013) took the Hanchuan market as the research basis and evaluated and analyzed the satisfaction of cigarette retail customers by using the entropy method[9]; Zu Qiang (2017) explored the construction of a consumer-oriented retail customer classification and evaluation system from the perspective of cigarette consumers' purchasing needs and based on the Carnot model theory, from the perspectives of consumer demand research, demand item classification, retail customer evaluation standards, practical application and management[10].

With the deepening of consumer research behavior, different fields and industries have gradually understood and valued product attributes. Terry A. Britton and Diana LaSalle (2003) included four aspects of product attributes related to experience: physical attributes, namely the characteristics of the components that make up the product; process attributes, corresponding to physical attributes, which are suitable for service products; aesthetic attributes, namely how the appearance of the product affects our senses; association attributes, such as brand, support, promotion, etc.[11] Internal attributes refer to the physical composition of the product, including raw materials, manufacturing, and form; external attributes refer to attributes that are not physical components of the product and can be evaluated without using them, including brand, packaging, service, and price; performance attributes refer to the way the product functions, and can only be evaluated through using (such as the fuel consumption of a car); abstract attributes refer to a comprehensive attribute that is a collection of information contained in multiple attributes, including weighted multiple attributes, user intention attributes, and using context attributes[12]. Wu Changliang (2011, Zhengzhou University) directly divided product attributes into cost attributes and benefit attributes from the perspective of consumer decision-making. Among the benefit attributes, the first is functional attributes, that is, to what extent the function provided by the product can meet consumers' expectations; the second is quality attributes, that is, whether the product can successfully contribute a certain function and maintain the durability of this function; the third is emotional attributes, that is, what psychological benefits are there from using a certain product. The cost attributes include price cost, pre-use cost, use cost, disposal cost[13].

This paper adopts the classification method of Mark E. Paryr's commodity attributes, starts from the indicators that can reflect cigarette products, explores the cigarette indicators that have an impact on consumer satisfaction, forms the cigarette product attribute index system, and investigates the impact of cigarette product attributes on consumer satisfaction, determines the main product attributes, which plays a positive role in guiding the direction of cigarette public relations and building new cigarette product consumer satisfaction evaluation methods.

1 Materials and Methods

1.1 Data Sources

This consumer survey is aimed at the cigarette consumer group with a price range of 100 to 1000 yuan/piece, aged 20 to 50 years old, and covers seven regions and two cities in each region, a total of 14 cities, see Table 1. The questionnaire survey is conducted on the 76 sub-indicators and overall satisfaction in Table 2, with 100 questionnaires in each city, 1400 copies, and 10 backup questionnaires in each city. The final number of questionnaires is 1540, and the number of effective questionnaires is 1442. In terms of the selection of research samples, the best-selling cigarettes in different regions and the top-selling cigarette brands in different price ranges in China, such as Yunyan, Zhonghua, Yuxi, Furongwang, Double Happiness, Liqun, and Huangjinye, were selected as evaluation samples.

Table 1 Distribution of Samples

Region	East China	North China	South China	Southwest China	Northwest China	Northeast China	Central China
City	Shanghai	Beijing	Guangzhou	Chengdu	Xi'an	Shenyang	Zhengzhou
Sample size	100	105	100	105	100	102	102
City	Ningbo	Baoding	Shenzhen	Kunming	Lanzhou	Harbin	Wuhan
Sample size	105	105	103	105	101	103	106

1.2 Analytical Method

1.2.1 Indicators Collection

Through qualitative interviews with consumers, 76 cigarette indicators were obtained to describe consumer satisfaction, and they were classified into 9 categories according to the characteristics of cigarette attribution, as shown in Table 2.

Table 2 Determination of Cigarette Indicators

The categories of cigarette indicators	The characteristics of cigarette indicators
Olfactory 4	Intensity of olfactory, olfactory comfort, purity of tobacco, novelty and uniqueness of olfactory
Oral 7	Oral comfort, oral dryness, smoke concentration, oral residual tobacco concentration, oral strength acceptance, smoothness, oral fullness
Nasal 7	Nasal comfort, delicateness and softness of smoke, nasal smoothness, nasal strength acceptance, nasal smoke purity, smoke richness, aroma concentration
Throat 5	Smoke smoothness, throat comfort, throat dryness, throat delicate softness, smoke adequacy
Aftertaste 6	Aftertaste cleanliness, oral dryness after smoking, aftertaste purity, aftertaste sedation, aftertaste comfort, aftertaste sensation
Cigarette appearance 10	Thickness of cigarette, cigarette pattern preference, length of cigarette, cigarette hardness, filter length, filter smoking smoothness, preference for special filter, preference for cigarette paper color, cigarette overall coordination, preference for cigarettes
Cigarette physics 7	Number of tobacco stem, cut tobacco color preference, ash color preference, ash breaking degree, cigarette burning speed, tar content, strength

continue

The categories of cigarette indicators	The characteristics of cigarette indicators
Packaging 11	Packaging upscale degree, packaging elegance degree, preference for packaging material, preference for packaging color, security of packaging, packaging novelty and uniqueness degree, preference for packaging font, product concept novelty degree, preference for packaging pattern, emotional resonance, preference for opening and closing
Other 19	Word-of-mouth, reputation of parent brand, marketing and advertising, long history, nostalgic, top grade/flossy, suitable for social/suitable for gift opening, popular, popularity, niche/alternative, moderate price, high price, cut tobacco origin, manufacturers, ease of purchased, channel credibility, fashionable, suitable for self-smoking, cost-effective

1.2.2 Indicators Screening and Validation

Orthogonal rotation is performed on 76 cigarette indicators in Table 2 using the maximum equivalent method to solve the multiple collinearity problem between variables; the rotation results are regressed using the least square method, and the cigarette indicators with P values greater than 0.05 are discarded. The correlation between the selected indicators and satisfaction is studied using the correlation degree analysis to validate the screening indicators' rationality and complete the screening of cigarette technical indicators. The analysis methods used for indicators screening and validation are as follows:

1) Orthogonal factor rotation + regression analysis is used for indicator screening

Orthogonal factor rotation analysis is first performed on the independent variables in the model to extract a specific principal factor; then, the principal factor is regressed by the dependent variable; finally, the regression equation of the dependent variable on the extracted principal factor is transformed into the regression equation of the original independent variable, and then the indicator set with P value<0.05 is selected.

2) Correlation degree analysis is used for indicator validation

Correlation analysis explores the correlation between cigarette indicators and consumer satisfaction. As a simple correlation coefficient, the Pearson correlation coefficient is used to measure the linear relationship between two variables. The larger the Pearson correlation coefficient is, the stronger the linear relationship between variables is. The calculation formula is:

$$r(X,Y) = \frac{\mathrm{cov}(X,Y)}{\sqrt{\mathrm{var}(X)\mathrm{var}(Y)}}$$

1.2.3 Application of Screening Indicators in Satisfaction Analysis

Taking cigarette product attributes as indicators, this paper analyzes the satisfaction of cigarette consumers in different regions. It determines consumers' focus in different regions on cigarette product demand indicators. This paper uses the partial least squares method to analyze satisfaction.

In multiple regression $y = \beta_0 + \beta_1 x_1 + \beta_2 x_2 + \cdots + \beta_p x_p + \varepsilon$, the coefficient β represents the degree of influence of each independent variable on the dependent variable. The larger the coefficient, the more obviously the independent variable affects the dependent variable. By using a partial least squares analysis of cigarette indicators and consumer satisfaction, the variable coefficient determines the influence of these indicators on the factors under consideration.

2　Results and Analysis

2.1　Screening of Cigarette Attributes

Using 76 cigarette indicators perceived by consumers as cigarette indicators to describe consumer satisfaction, the maximum equivalent method is adopted to perform orthogonal rotation on all independent variables to solve the multicollinearity between variables. The loading values of the rotating components are shown in Table 3. As can be seen from the attached table, all the loading values of the rotating components are above 0.7, indicating a high information extraction rate of the original variables and a good effect. The loading of the ease of purchase reaches 0.877, the largest value. There are 10 variables with a loading greater than 0.8, and the rest are in the range of 0.7-0.8.

Table 3　Results of the Rotation Composition Matrix of 76 Cigarette Indicators

Indicators	Rotation component matrix	Indicators	Rotation component matrix	Indicators	Rotation component matrix
Ease of Purchase	0.877	Nasal comfort	0.747	Olfactory comfort	0.740
Niche/Alternative	0.874	Cut tobacco color preference	0.760	Number of tobacco stem	0.718
High price	0.836	Ash color preference	0.759	Cigarette burning speed	0.782
Popular	0.835	Smoothness of smoke	0.747	Tar content	0.702
Moderate price	0.830	Throat comfort	0.738	Preference for packaging font	0.703

continue

Indicators	Rotation component matrix	Indicators	Rotation component matrix	Indicators	Rotation component matrix
Purity of tobacco	0.813	Packaging pattern preference	0.751	Cigarette hardness	0.741
Preference for opening and closing	0.814	Cigarette pattern preference	0.754	Filter smoking smoothness	0.781
Filter length	0.808	Oral fullness	0.748	Preference for special filters	0.721
Suitable for self-Smoking	0.813	Novelty and uniqueness of packaging	0.749	Preference for cigarette paper color	0.733
Long history	0.807	Preference for packaging material	0.751	Cigarette overall coordination	0.762
Intensity of olfactory	0.794	Suitable for social/ Suitable for gift	0.745	Preference for cigarettes	0.716
Novelty and uniqueness of olfactory	0.795	Packaging elegant degree	0.747	Smoke concentration	0.775
Ash breaking degree	0.794	Richness of smoke	0.741	Oral residual tobacco concentration	0.726
Cost-effectiveness	0.798	Cut tobacco origin	0.754	Oral strength acceptance	0.701
Popularity	0.790	Oral comfort	0.729	Nasal smoothness	0.755
Marketing and advertising	0.790	Oral dryness	0.728	Nasal strength acceptance	0.783
Thickness of cigarette	0.784	Novelty of product concept	0.744	Nasal smoke purity	0.762
Channel credibility	0.789	Delicateness and softness of smoke	0.723	Aroma concentration	0.754
Strength	0.771	Smoothness	0.724	Throat dryness	0.787
Reputation of parent brand	0.786	Fashionable	0.736	Throat delicate softness	0.762

continue

Indicators	Rotation component matrix	Indicators	Rotation component matrix	Indicators	Rotation component matrix
Length of cigarette	0.781	Oral dryness after smoking	0.714	Smoke adequacy	0.765
Manufacturer	0.783	Word-of-mouth	0.732	Aftertaste purity	0.768
Nostalgic	0.781	Aftertaste comfort	0.710	Aftertaste calmness	0.755
Preference for packaging color	0.759	Top grade/classy	0.720	Aftertaste sensation	0.789
Emotional resonance	0.772	Aftertaste cleanliness	0.705		
Security of packaging	0.765	Packaging upscale degree	0.711		

We used rotated independent and dependent variables to perform a partial least squares regression and discarded cigarette indicators with statistically significant P-values greater than 0.05. We also combined expert recommendations, consumer needs, literature reviews, classification of similar indicators, and deletion of unimportant indicators to obtain 52 cigarette indicators. The model fitting results for the 52 indicators, which correspond to the 52 indicators, are shown in Table 4. From Table 4, it can be seen that the model's regression coefficient is 0.803, the fitting effect is ideal, R-squared is 0.645, which means that the independent variable can explain 64.5% of the information in the dependent variable. As one of the many independent variables in the model, this result is quite promising, and the adjusted R-squared also reached 0.641, indicating an excellent model-fitting effect.

Table 4　The Goodness of Fit for the Regression Equation

R	R^2	Adjusted R^2	Standard error of estimation
0.803	0.645	0.641	0.693

2.2　Determination of Cigarette Attributes Indicators

Through the correlation analysis between 52 cigarette indicators and consumer satisfaction, as shown in Table 5, it can be seen that there is a positive correlation between all cigarette indicators and consumer satisfaction. Among them, the aftertaste comfort is closely related to consumer satisfaction, with a correlation coefficient of 0.643. This also indicates the direction of current cigarette sensory quality development.

Table 5 Results of Person Correlation Coefficients

16 intrinsic attributes	Correlation coefficient	Sig.	15 extrinsic attributes	Correlation coefficient	Sig.	14 Abstract attributes	Correlation coefficient	Sig.	7 Performance attributes	Correlation coefficient	Sig.
Aftertaste comfort	0.643	0.000	Preference for packaging pattern	0.533	0.000	Top grade/classy	0.301	0.000	Cost-effectiveness	0.438	0.000
Throat comfort	0.614	0.000	Novelty and uniqueness of packaging	0.537	0.000	Suitable for self-smoking	0.321	0.000	High price	0.415	0.000
Oral comfort	0.618	0.000	Preference for packaging color	0.52	0.000	Novelty of product concept	0.376	0.000	Channel credibility	0.432	0.000
Oral dryness after smoking	0.634	0.000	Packaging upscale degree	0.553	0.000	Word-of-mouth	0.37	0.000	Moderate price	0.457	0.000
Delicateness and softness of smoke	0.621	0.000	Preference for packaging material	0.529	0.000	Suitable for social/suitable for gift opening	0.368	0.000	Cut tobacco origin	0.435	0.000
Strength	0.598	0.000	Packaging elegant degree	0.543	0.000	Emotional resonance	0.346	0.000	Manufacturer	0.401	0.000

continue

16 intrinsic attributes	Correlation coefficient	Sig.	15 extrinsic attributes	Correlation coefficient	Sig.	14 Abstract attributes	Correlation coefficient	Sig.	7 Performance attributes	Correlation coefficient	Sig.
Oral dryness	0.619	0.000	Cut tobacco color preference	0.537	0.000	Fashionable	0.372	0.000	Ease of purchase	0.407	0.000
Oral fullness	0.609	0.000	Preference for cigarette pattern	0.532	0.000	Reputation of parent brand	0.319	0.000			
Smoothness	0.608	0.000	Ash color preference	0.537	0.000	Marketing and advertising	0.316	0.000			
Richness of smoke	0.615	0.000	Security of Packaging	0.525	0.000	Popularity	0.396	0.000			
Aftertaste cleanliness	0.631	0.000	Filters length	0.469	0.000	Popular	0.322	0.000			
Intensity of olfactory	0.555	0.000	Ash breaking degree	0.502	0.000	Nostalgic	0.315	0.000			
Smoothness of smoke	0.614	0.000	Length of cigarette	0.475	0.000	Long history	0.382	0.000			

continue

16 intrinsic attributes	Correlation coefficient	Sig.	15 extrinsic attributes	Correlation coefficient	Sig.	14 Abstract attributes	Correlation coefficient	Sig.	7 Performance attributes	Correlation coefficient	Sig.
Nasal comfort	0.596	0.000	Thickness of cigarette	0.473	0.000	Niche/Alternative	0.309	0.000			
Purity of tobacco	0.531	0.000	Preference for opening and closing	0.455	0.000						
Novelty and uniqueness of olfactory	0.536	0.000									

According to the different attributes of the 52 cigarette indicators, the cigarette indicators were classified into intrinsic attributes, extrinsic attributes, performance attributes, and abstract attributes, which are shown in Table 5. The intrinsic attribute indicators of the product are related to the internal quality of the product, such as product taste, product quality, smoke indicators, safety indicators, physical and chemical indicators, etc. Product extrinsic attributes related to product appearance, such as cigarette design and collocation, cigarette package, box design and collocation, packaging materials, etc. Product performance attributes related to product market performance, such as product price, market acceptance, recognition, fashion, purchase intention, etc. Product abstract attributes mainly focus on consumers' abstract awareness of cigarette products, such as brand awareness, product design creativity, product name, health attention, etc.

Figure 1 shows different boxplots. It can be seen from the figure that the correlations between intrinsic attributes, extrinsic attributes, performance attributes, abstract attributes, and consumer satisfaction are between 0.55-0.65, 0.45-0.55, 0.4-0.45, 0.3-0.4 respectively, and the correlation coefficients are gradually decreasing.

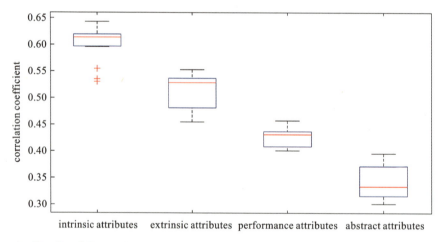

Figure 1 Boxplot of Correlation Coefficient Between Cigarette Attributes and Consumer Satisfaction

2.3 Analysis of Application Results of Cigarette Attribute Indicators

2.3.1 Analysis of Consumer Satisfaction Based on Cigarette Attributes

Partial least squares analysis was conducted on 52 indicators and their standardized correlation coefficients were extracted. The influence degree on consumer satisfaction was obtained by adding the standardized coefficients of each attribute. The results are shown in Table 6.

Table 6 Impact of Cigarette Attributes on Consumer Satisfaction

16 intrinsic attributes	Standardized coefficient ∑2.209	15 extrinsic attributes	Standardized coefficient ∑1.222	14 abstract attributes	Standardized coefficient ∑1.439	7 performance attributes	Standardized coefficient ∑0.719
Aftertaste comfort	0.161	Preference for Packaging pattern	0.101	Top grade/classy	0.151	Cost-effectiveness	0.155
Throat comfort	0.152	Novelty and uniqueness of packaging	0.098	Suitable for self-smoking	0.142	High price	0.113
Oral comfort	0.150	Preference for packaging color	0.097	Novelty of product concept	0.120	Channel credibility	0.111
Oral dryness after smoking	0.147	Top grade packaging	0.093	Word-of-mouth	0.110	Moderate price	0.106
Delicateness and softness of smoke	0.145	Preference for packaging material	0.092	Suitable for social/suitable for gift opening	0.110	Cut tobacco origin	0.082
Strength	0.144	Packaging elegant degree	0.091	Emotional resonance	0.109	Manufacturer	0.079
Oral dryness	0.142	Cut tobacco color preference	0.085	Fashionable	0.105	Ease of purchase	0.073
Oral fullness	0.137	Preference for cigarette pattern	0.084	Reputation of parent brand	0.104		

continue

16 intrinsic attributes	Standardized coefficient ∑2.209	15 extrinsic attributes	Standardized coefficient ∑1.222	14 abstract attributes	Standardized coefficient ∑1.439	7 performance attributes	Standardized coefficient ∑0.719
Smoothness	0.137	Ash color preference	0.084	Marketing and advertising	0.099		
Richness of smoke	0.135	Security of Packaging	0.078	Popularity	0.093		
Aftertaste cleanliness	0.135	Filters length	0.077	Popular	0.083		
Intensity of olfactory	0.131	Ash breaking degree	0.065	Nostalgic	0.082		
Smoothness of smoke	0.130	Length of cigarette	0.065	Long history	0.078		
Nasal comfort	0.130	Thickness of cigarette	0.061	Niche/Alternative	0.053		
Purity of tobacco	0.124	Preference for opening and closing	0.051				
Novelty and uniqueness of olfactory	0.109						

As shown in Table 6, the overall influence value of 16 variables of intrinsic attributes on satisfaction is 2.209, with an influence degree of 39.52%, which is the highest. For every unit increase of intrinsic attributes, satisfaction will increase by 2.209 units on average, indicating that intrinsic attributes of products are essential in consumer evaluation. The overall influence value of 15 variables of extrinsic attributes on satisfaction is 1.222, with an influence degree of 21.86%, which is lower than the sum of 14 variables of abstract attributes (1.439, with an influence degree of 25.76%), indicating that consumers' perception degree of abstract attributes is stronger than that of extrinsic attributes of products. The influence value of the 7 variables of performance attributes is 0.719, and the influence degree is 12.86%, which is the lowest in terms of total amount, but the average influence of each variable is above 0.1, especially the variable of cost performance, whose coefficient is as high as 0.155.

2.3.2 Regional Differences in the Importance of Cigarette Attributes

From Table 7, based on the fitting R^2 of the four attribute indicators of cigarette in different regions, it can be seen that the goodness of fit of almost all regions is above 0.6, which is relatively high and good. Only the goodness of fit of North China is slightly lower than that of other regions, but it is also within the acceptable range.

Table 7 Regional Differences in the Importance of Different Cigarette Attributes

Model	Standardized regression coefficients				Goodness of fit R^2
	Intrinsic properties	Extrinsic attributes	Abstract attributes	Performance attributes	
East China	2.088	1.049	1.702	0.737	0.693
North China	2.312	1.460	1.160	0.772	0.596
South China	2.551	1.208	1.534	0.697	0.672
Southwest China	2.365	1.152	1.300	0.732	0.708
Northwest China	2.271	1.254	1.554	0.611	0.651
Northeast China	2.138	1.116	1.167	0.768	0.646
Central China	1.824	1.506	1.648	0.652	0.629
Nationwide	2.691	1.222	1.439	0.719	0.645

Table 7 also reflects the summary of standardized regression coefficients of the four attributes of cigarette indicators in different regions. It can be seen that among the four attributes, the regression coefficients of intrinsic attributes in each region are the largest. Therefore, consumers in each region value the experience brought by cigarette products the most when they consume. Therefore, each cigarette enterprise should focus on the quality of the product itself when producing. It can also be seen from the table that among the seven regions, the standard value of the standardized regression coefficient of intrinsic attributes in South China reaches 2.551, which is the largest among all regions, indicating that South China values intrinsic attributes the most, followed by Southwest China, North China, Northwest China, Northeast China, and East China. The standardized regression coefficient of intrinsic attributes in Central China is the lowest. From the perspective of extrinsic attributes, there is no obvious difference among the regions, and the standardized regression coefficients of Central China and North China are relatively large. From the perspective of abstract attributes, the regression coefficients of East China and Central China are the largest, indicating that these two regions pay more attention to abstract attributes than other regions. In terms of performance attributes, there is almost no difference among regions.

Table 8 shows the regression results of 52 indicators in different regions, which can analyze the regional differences in the importance of consumer demand evaluation indicators from each indicator.

Table 8 Influence of Cigarette Indicators in Different Regions on Consumer Satisfaction

Indicators/Regions	East China	North China	South China	Southwest China	Northwest China	Northeast China	Central China
Top grade/classy	0.182	0.132	0.207	0.139	0.151	0.085	0.173
Intensity of olfactory	0.177	0.121	0.15	0.124	0.129	0.099	0.08
Smoothness	0.165	0.129	0.177	0.12	0.108	0.156	0.107
Manufacturer	0.163	0.045	0.114	0.1	0.043	0.072	0.079
Novelty of product concept	0.163	0.063	0.125	0.114	0.128	0.14	0.125
Strength	0.154	0.158	0.138	0.162	0.143	0.15	0.12
Aftertaste comfort	0.15	0.197	0.18	0.2	0.123	0.123	0.162
Reputation of parent brand	0.145	0.083	0.14	0.051	0.082	0.06	0.152
Word-of-mouth	0.144	0.106	0.058	0.097	0.14	0.078	0.175
Throat comfort	0.143	0.138	0.166	0.152	0.146	0.194	0.094
Channel credibility	0.141	0.099	0.125	0.155	0.078	0.034	0.092
Length of cigarette	0.14	0.077	0.124	0.025	0.04	0.026	0.062
Popular	0.139	0.04	0.041	0.083	0.055	0.089	0.077
Oral dryness	0.136	0.141	0.18	0.149	0.161	0.155	0.084
Oral dryness after smoking	0.136	0.196	0.163	0.159	0.147	0.099	0.107
Suitable for social/ suitable for gift opening	0.135	0.059	0.151	0.098	0.152	0.094	0.118
High price	0.135	0.141	0.112	0.063	0.093	0.139	0.093

continue

Indicators/Regions	East China	North China	South China	Southwest China	Northwest China	Northeast China	Central China
Nasal comfort	0.13	0.095	0.117	0.154	0.134	0.168	0.133
Purity of tobacco	0.128	0.082	0.168	0.127	0.157	0.07	0.15
Oral comfort	0.125	0.144	0.194	0.169	0.159	0.148	0.107
Ash breaking degree	0.124	0.063	0.057	0.048	0.075	0.052	0.05
Niche/Alternative	0.122	0.039	0.1	0.021	0.042	−0.016	0.098
Richness of smoke	0.118	0.116	0.15	0.164	0.179	0.118	0.103
Cut tobacco origin	0.117	0.084	0.083	0.11	0.059	0.095	0.084
Delicateness and softness of smoke	0.116	0.152	0.178	0.169	0.163	0.121	0.106
Oral fullness	0.115	0.181	0.142	0.136	0.177	0.123	0.127
Nostalgic	0.114	0.042	0.073	0.082	0.073	0.072	0.062
Popularity	0.113	0.095	0.031	0.082	0.082	0.12	0.144
Fashionable	0.111	0.091	0.143	0.102	0.089	0.049	0.116
Smoothness of smoke	0.109	0.188	0.158	0.174	0.073	0.127	0.117
Elegant packaging	0.107	0.068	0.098	0.075	0.079	0.107	0.117
Security of packaging	0.107	0.056	0.062	0.07	0.115	0.081	0.073
Aftertaste cleanliness	0.106	0.128	0.171	0.101	0.194	0.159	0.118
Suitable for self-smoking	0.099	0.167	0.089	0.152	0.165	0.158	0.116
Ash color preference	0.089	0.155	0.061	0.076	0.117	0.022	0.058
Emotional resonance	0.086	0.076	0.132	0.065	0.19	0.122	0.139
Top grade packaging	0.083	0.089	0.119	0.093	0.086	0.077	0.14
Novelty and uniqueness of olfactory	0.082	0.147	0.12	0.105	0.079	0.129	0.108
Long history	0.079	0.063	0.146	0.077	0.095	0.062	0.029
Moderate-priced	0.077	0.18	0.048	0.091	0.093	0.089	0.09
Filters length	0.072	0.106	0.083	0.091	0.08	0.059	0.077
Novelty and uniqueness of packaging	0.071	0.136	0.084	0.077	0.101	0.104	0.075
Marketing and advertising	0.069	0.104	0.1	0.138	0.109	0.038	0.124
Preference for packaging material	0.068	0.089	0.078	0.107	0.113	0.065	0.172
Cut tobacco color preference	0.053	0.113	0.097	0.046	0.096	0.095	0.135

continue

Indicators/Regions	East China	North China	South China	Southwest China	Northwest China	Northeast China	Central China
Preference for cigarette pattern	0.048	0.123	0.072	0.113	0.068	0.051	0.145
Preference for opening and closing	0.035	0.082	0.102	0.082	0.013	0.045	0.032
Thickness of cigarette	0.03	0.067	0.07	0.058	0.023	0.061	0.102
Packaging pattern preference	0.022	0.103	0.071	0.103	0.152	0.132	0.116
Preference for packaging color	0	0.132	0.028	0.088	0.097	0.138	0.153
Ease of purchase	−0.007	0.08	0.087	0.073	0.09	0.116	0.073
Cost-effectiveness	0.110	0.143	0.127	0.139	0.154	0.239	0.141

From Table 8, it can be concluded that the evaluation indicators which consumers pay attention to when evaluating cigarettes are different in different regions. The specific performance is as follows:

(1) For consumers in East China, the top five evaluation indexes are "top grade/classy", "intensity of olfactory", "smoothness", "manufacturer", and "novelty of product concept". Consumers in East China pay more attention to the abstract attributes of cigarettes, the value of identity contained in cigarettes, and the overall popularity of cigarettes, and they also have a certain sense of belonging to the parent brand and manufacturer. Regarding taste, the degree of aroma intensity is the most important intrinsic attribute for consumers in East China.

(2) The five most important indicators for consumers in North China to evaluate cigarettes are "aftertaste comfort", "oral dryness after smoking", "smoke smoothness", "oral fullness", and "moderate price". Overall, consumers in North China pay more attention to the internality of cigarettes and emphasize the sense of taste and quality. At the same time, in terms of price, consumers in North China also pay more attention to prices that are compatible with quality. Whether the positioning of the cigarette itself is high-end has little impact on their overall evaluation. As with the overall results in China, the aftertaste is the most important indicator that affects the taste evaluation.

(3) The five indicators that consumers in South China pay the most attention to are "top grade/classy", "oral comfort", "aftertaste comfort", "oral dryness", and "delicacy and softness of smoke". They also pay attention to the intrinsic quality of cigarettes and the characteristics of identity and put forward requirements for the social function of cigarettes.

(4) Consumers in Southwest China pay attention to "aftertaste comfort", "smoke

smoothness", "smoke delicacy and softness", "oral comfort", and "smoke richness". Similar to consumers in North China, consumers in Southwest China pay more attention to the intrinsic quality of cigarettes. Regarding abstract attributes, consumers in Southwest China also care about marketing publicity and high-end quality.

(5) The five indicators valued by consumers in Northwest China are "aftertaste cleanliness", "emotional resonance", "richness of smoke", "oral fullness", and "suitable for self-smoking". Consumers in Northwest China pay attention to the taste of cigarettes and attach great importance to whether the cigarette brand can bring them emotional resonance.

(6) When evaluating cigarettes, consumers in Northeast China attach importance to "throat comfort", "nasal comfort", "cleanliness of aftertaste", "suitable for self-smoking", and "smoothness". All these aspects belong to intrinsic attribute indicators, indicating that consumers in Northeast China pay more attention to the taste of cigarette products. At the same time, the cost-performance ratio occupies a high proportion in the minds of consumers in this region.

(7) Consumers in Central China pay more attention to "oral idiom", "top grade/classy", "perference for packaging material", "aftertaste comfort", and "perference for packaging color" when evaluating cigarettes. Consumers in Central China have put forward higher requirements for the popularity and high-grade level of cigarettes. Meanwhile, packaging design and cigarette design also occupy a high proportion of the minds of consumers in this region.

Consumers in North China, Southwest China, Northwest China, and Northeast China have a higher demand for the intrinsic quality of cigarettes. Consumers in East China and South China pay more attention to the social attributes and identity embodiment of cigarettes, while consumers in Central China pay more attention to the appearance attributes of cigarettes. Consumers in Eastern China pay more attention to the sense of belonging to brands and manufacturers, while consumers in Northwestern China pay more attention to the emotional resonance brought by cigarette brands.

3 Conclusion

Consumer satisfaction is an important factor affecting consumption intention, and the evaluation of consumer satisfaction involves many product factors. In this paper, the main evaluation indicators of cigarette products were analyzed and classified using the mathematical statistics method, and four product attributes and 52 evaluation indicators were identified that greatly impacted consumer satisfaction with cigarette products.

(1) By analyzing the correlation coefficients between the 52 cigarette indexes and the

national consumer satisfaction, it can be seen that all the cigarette indexes are positively correlated with consumer satisfaction, and the aftertaste comfort degree has the strongest correlation with consumer satisfaction, which indicates the direction that the current development of cigarette sensory quality is pursuing.

(2) The results of partial least square analysis of the four attribute indicators and national cigarette consumer satisfaction show that the intrinsic attribute is the most important attribute of cigarette products, which has the greatest impact on consumer satisfaction, reaching 39.52%, and is the focus of consumers' most attention. Abstract, extrinsic, and apparent attributes were the most important attributes, with influence degrees of 25.76%, 21.86%, and 12.86%, respectively.

(3) The cigarette product attributes were used to analyze the cigarette satisfaction of consumers in different regions. The results showed that consumers in different regions valued the intrinsic attributes most but paid slightly different attention to others. Consumers in North China, Southwest China, Northwest China, and Northeast China have a higher demand for intrinsic quality cigarettes. Consumers in East China and South China pay more attention to the social attributes and identity of cigarettes, while consumers in Central China pay more attention to the appearance attributes of cigarettes. In addition, consumers in East China also pay more attention to the sense of belonging of brands and manufacturers, while consumers in Northwest China pay more attention to the emotional resonance of cigarette brands.

(4) The evaluation method of consumer satisfaction with cigarette product attributes developed in this paper can simplify consumers' overall control of cigarette products, which is more conducive to the overall control of cigarette development and has practical significance for guiding regional product development.

References

[1] RICHARD A C. An Experimental Study of Consumer Effort, Expectation and Satisfaction[J]. Journal of Marketing Research, 1965(8): 19.

[2] HOWARD J A. SHETH J N. The Theory of Buyer Behaviour[M]. New York: John Wily & Sons, 1969: 218.

[3] CRONIN J J, TAYLOR S A. Measuring Service Quality: A Reexamination and Extension[J]. Journal of Marketing, 1992(56): 55.

[4] SUN Q L, AN Y F. Research on Customer Satisfaction in Agricultural Product Wholesale Markets[J]. Business Research, 2008(7): 181.

[5] LI J H. Research on Automobile Consumption Behavior and Consumer Satisfaction [J]. Market Research, 2009(1): 26.

[6] XU X M. Research on Laptop Satisfaction based on Customer Delivered Value[D]. Beijing: Beijing University of Chemical Technology, 2011.

[7] WEN L, ZHAO J. Construction and Analysis of Customer Satisfaction Model of Yunnan Special Agricultural Product Small Coffee Bean Network Marketing[J]. Modern Agricultural Science and Technology, 2014 (8): 273.

[8] YU M F, LEI Z Q. Construction and Application of Tobacco Product User Satisfaction Index[J]. Tobacco Science and Technology, 2001 (3): 24.

[9] FAN J, YANG Q G. Customer Satisfaction Evaluation based on Entropy Value in Tobacco Retail[J]. Contemporary Economy, 2013 (14): 112.

[10] ZU Q. Construction of Consumer-oriented Customer Classification and Evaluation System based on the Kano Model[J]. Chinese Journal of Tobacco Science. 2017, 23 (1): 122.

[11] BRITTON T A, LASALLE D. Product Strategy from Average to Greatness[M]. Beijing: CITIC Press, 2003: 1.

[12] ZHAO L Y. A study on the Path of Customer Needs Transforming into Product Attributes in Product Development-Reflections on the Improvement of QFD[D]. Changchun: Northeast Normal University, 2005.

[13] WU C L. Research on the Classification System of Product Attributes from the Perspective of Consumer Decision-Making[J]. Business Era, 2011 (19): 24.

卷烟评价指标与消费者需求的关联度研究

摘要: 本文基于对卷烟消费者需求的深度诊断,从不同品类、不同场景、不同用途对消费者需求进行标准化收集,采用相关系数和回归分析的方法遴选了13项卷烟评价指标,通过结构方程模型探究卷烟评价指标与消费者需求的关联度。研究发现:消费者主要关注的卷烟评价指标为品质、口感、吸味、价格、包装、第一印象、容易购买程度等。

关键词: 卷烟评价指标;消费者需求;关联度

前言

为了更好地了解卷烟消费需求,进一步了解卷烟消费者对卷烟产品的各类需求,本文对传统卷烟的口味、包装、价格、概念、产品满意度等内容进行收集分析。通过对卷烟消费者服务过程的深度诊断,从不同品类、不同场景、不同用途对消费者需求进行标准化收集,遴选了13项卷烟评价指标,并运用数学方法探索将卷烟消费者需求转化为产品研发的系统思路与方向。采用定量调查来解析影响卷烟消费者的关键指标,确定卷烟具有显著相关性的消费者需求指标的相对权重,论证消费者需求指标体系的合理性,为卷烟销售与产品研发提供依据。

1 数据来源及调查对象

本文涉及的信息数据包括社会经济数据、热点数据、受试省份卷烟销售数据,均采用间接调研法获得。社会经济数据主要从各省份统计局官网获取,热点数据通过互联网搜索获取。

定量调查主要在昆明、杭州等12个城市开展,调查对象主要为18~55岁的烟民人群,共需要收集8000份样本,各城市样本量详见表1。

表1 调查城市及取样数量

城市	昆明	杭州	广州	成都	兰州	武汉	大理	上海	深圳	重庆	柳州	大连
样本量	800	800	800	800	800	400	400	800	800	800	400	400
总计样本量	8000											

2 研究方法

2.1 产品属性指标与消费体验产品测试数据的关联度分析方法

探究卷烟评价指标与消费者需求的关联度,一般采用相关系数分析和回归分析的方法[1-6]。Pearson相关系数作为简单相关系数,是用来度量两个变量间的线性关系的,相关系数越大,说明变量间的线性关系越强。其计算公式为:

$$r(X,Y) = \frac{\text{cov}(X,Y)}{\sqrt{\text{var}(X)\text{var}(Y)}}$$

基于消费者需求的产品满意度测试指标调查结果,本研究运用数据挖掘方法,对产品属性指标与消费体验产品测试数据进行关联度分析。卷烟产品评价一般包括卷烟外在属性评价、卷烟产品口味评价。卷烟外在属性评价包括对烟盒形式、烟支长度、烟嘴长度、特殊卷烟、特殊烟嘴、烟丝等的评价;卷烟产品口味评价包括嗅香、口腔、鼻腔、喉咙、余味等方面,并对当前产品整体进行评价。

卷烟产品评价应详细了解烟民对卷烟产品各方面的偏好。首先询问消费者对卷烟产品的满意度评价,之后请消费者对主抽品牌进行口味评价,最后询问消费者对卷烟包装的偏好、价格的可接受度以及有关产品的概念认知和评价。

2.2 基于结构方程的卷烟消费者需求转化路径的管理要素分析方法

使用结构方程(SEM)来探索消费者需求(评价指标)间的结构关系和互相影响作用,构建简易转化路径模型,验证与确定消费者需求关注的信息,并建立消费者需求评价体系。

(1) 模型表达式。

结构方程包括测量模型和结构模型,一般结构方程可用3个基本方程表达。

测量模型:
$$X = \Lambda_x \xi + \delta \tag{1.1}$$

$$Y = \Lambda_y \eta + \varepsilon \tag{1.2}$$

结构模型:
$$\eta = B\eta + r\xi + \gamma \tag{1.3}$$

式(1.1)中的 $X=(x_1,\cdots,x_q)'$ 代表观测模型中的外生显变量,$\xi=(\xi_1,\cdots,\xi_n)'$ 代表外生潜变量,矩阵 $\Lambda_x(q\times n)$ 代表显变量 X 与潜变量 ξ 间的因子载荷,是一个 $q\times n$ 维的矩阵,$\delta=(\delta_1,\cdots,\delta_q)'$ 代表 X 的测量误差。式(1.2)中的 $Y=(y_1,\cdots,y_q)'$ 代表观测模型中的内生显变量,$\eta=(\eta_1,\cdots,\eta_q)'$ 代表内生潜变量,矩阵 $\Lambda_y(p\times m)$ 代表显变量 Y 与潜变量 η 间的因子载荷,是一个 $p\times m$ 维的矩阵,$\varepsilon=(\varepsilon_1,\cdots,\varepsilon_p)'$ 代表 Y 的测量误差。式(1.3)中的 $B\eta$ 代表内生潜变量间的结构系数矩阵,$r\xi$ 代表内生潜变量与外生潜变量的结构系数矩阵,γ 代表结构方程的干扰项。

η 和 ξ 均为潜变量,也被称作概念或因子,是由多个可以观测的显变量来测量的。内生潜变量与外生潜变量的关系由系数矩阵 B、r 以及误差项的线性关系来连接。

(2) 模型的基本假定。

在传统结构方程中,为简化模型推导,没有设定截距项,所以整个模型的表述和估计都不是在原始估测值上进行的,而是需要对数据进行中心化,即带入模型的数据都是估测值的均数离差。同时作为线性模型的估计,还要考虑线性方程的基本假设。基于这些条件,测量模型式(1.1)、式(1.2)须满足以下四条:

①$E(\boldsymbol{\eta})=0, E(\boldsymbol{\xi})=0, E(\boldsymbol{\delta})=0, E(\boldsymbol{\varepsilon})=0$;

②$\boldsymbol{\varepsilon}$ 与 $\boldsymbol{\eta}$、$\boldsymbol{\xi}$、$\boldsymbol{\delta}$ 不相关;

③$\boldsymbol{\delta}$ 与 $\boldsymbol{\eta}$、$\boldsymbol{\xi}$、$\boldsymbol{\varepsilon}$ 不相关;

④X、Y 服从多元正态分布。

在结构模型式(1.3)中,方程左右两边都出现了 $\boldsymbol{\eta}$,在对方程进行转换时,必定会出现 $(\boldsymbol{I}-\boldsymbol{B})^{-1}$,其中 $\boldsymbol{I}$ 为单位矩阵。只有在 $(\boldsymbol{I}-\boldsymbol{B})^{-1}$ 存在时,模型才能进行估计,因此,对结构模型来说,也要满足以下假设:

①$E(\boldsymbol{\eta})=0, E(\boldsymbol{\xi})=0, E(\boldsymbol{\gamma})=0$;

②$\boldsymbol{\xi}$ 与 $\boldsymbol{\gamma}$ 不相关;

③$(\boldsymbol{I}-\boldsymbol{B})$ 为非奇异矩阵。

(3) 模型估计。

与一般的多元回归模型不同,结构方程不是通过极小化均方误差 MSE(即拟合值与真实值偏差的平方和)来取得最优解,而是基于协方差来求解,即通过计算极小化样本协方差与模型估计协方差之间的差距来进行求解。用 $\sum$ 表示观测变量 Y 和 X 的总体协方差,这是一个真实值,即

$$\sum = E(YY')E(YX')$$

用 $\sum(\theta)$ 来表示其估计值,而这个估计值是自由参数的函数。那么,在 SEM 中,为使数据的拟合程度最大,就要找到最优的参数 θ,使得 $\sum - \sum(\theta)$ 的值最小。

事实上,$\sum$ 与 $\sum(\theta)$ 均为已知,可分别由样本来估计,常见的估计方法为最大似然估计。

SEM 的目标是求出使 F 最小的参数值 θ,其中 F 称作最小差异函数。

3 结果与分析

3.1 卷烟评价指标与消费者需求的关联度分析

经过变量筛选,挑选出 13 个卷烟评价指标,计算其与消费者满意度之间的相关系数,得到表 2。

表 2　卷烟评价指标与消费者满意度之间的 Pearson 相关系数结果

指标	Pearson 相关系数	指标	Pearson 相关系数	指标	Pearson 相关系数
杂气	0.271**	包装盒型	0.292**	香气	0.313**
余味	0.251**	包装体现的文化内涵	0.278**	价格	0.090**
谐调	0.258**	烟丝光泽	0.271**	容易买到	0.045**
包装材质	0.266**	刺激性	0.301**	第一印象	0.050**
包装美观程度	0.322**				

从表 2 可以看出，所有的卷烟评价指标与消费者满意度之间都呈显著正相关，相关系数在 0.045～0.322 之间，其中包装美观程度与消费者满意度的相关性最强，达到了 0.322，而容易买到与消费者满意度的相关性较弱，为 0.045。

按照相关系数大小分类，可以看出以下几点。

①相关系数在 0.3～0.4 的卷烟评价指标有包装美观程度、香气、刺激性。这些指标与消费者满意度呈现出较强的相关性，表明其与消费者需求联系紧密。

②相关系数在 0.2～0.3 的卷烟评价指标有杂气、谐调、烟丝光泽、包装体现的文化内涵、包装材质、包装盒型、余味。这些指标大部分都是卷烟品质相关，与消费者满意度呈现出略强的相关性，表明其与消费者需求联系较紧密。

③相关系数在 0.2 以下的卷烟评价指标有价格、容易买到、第一印象。这些指标与消费者满意度呈现出较低的相关性，表明其与消费者需求存在一定的联系。

在多元回归里，$y = \beta_0 + \beta_1 x_1 + \beta_2 x_2 + \cdots + \beta_p x_p + \varepsilon$，系数 β 代表各个自变量对因变量的影响程度，系数越大，因变量受这个自变量影响越明显。在多元线性模型里，x_1、x_2、$\cdots$、x_p 之间只有不相关时，即 $(X'X)^{-1}$ 存在时，其最小二乘估计（OLS）参数 β 才存在。当 x_1、x_2、$\cdots$、x_p 之间高度相关时，计算出的值会有很大的方差，估计值不稳健，这种现象称作多重共线性。

要检测多重共线性，可以计算各观测变量之间的 Pearson 相关系数。当 Pearson 相关系数值很大时，变量之间相关性特别强，若是把它们都作为自变量进行回归分析，多重共线性会干扰参数估计的准确性。所以，Pearson 相关系数可以作为一个检验指标。通过计算，得出以下 Pearson 相关系数表格，如表 3 所示。

表 3　卷烟评价指标间 Pearson 相关系数

指标	香气	烟丝光泽	刺激性	杂气	余味	谐调	包装材质	包装美观程度	包装盒型	包装体现的文化内涵
香气	1	0.605**	0.527**	0.427**	0.445**	0.423**	0.527**	0.509**	0.440**	0.496**

续表

指标	香气	烟丝光泽	刺激性	杂气	余味	谐调	包装材质	包装美观程度	包装盒型	包装体现的文化内涵
烟丝光泽	0.605**	1	0.542**	0.476**	0.485**	0.485**	0.504**	0.513**	0.464**	0.490**
刺激性	0.527**	0.542**	1	0.609**	0.545**	0.488**	0.466**	0.461**	0.422**	0.440**
杂气	0.427**	0.476**	0.609**	1	0.615**	0.528**	0.431**	0.409**	0.403**	0.381**
余味	0.445**	0.485**	0.545**	0.615**	1	0.638**	0.491**	0.465**	0.457**	0.427**
谐调	0.423**	0.485**	0.488**	0.528**	0.638**	1	0.523**	0.500**	0.490**	0.452**
包装材质	0.527**	0.504**	0.466**	0.431**	0.491**	0.523**	1	0.675**	0.572**	0.496**
包装美观程度	0.509**	0.513**	0.461**	0.409**	0.465**	0.500**	0.675**	1	0.621**	0.590**
包装盒型	0.440**	0.464**	0.422**	0.403**	0.457**	0.490**	0.572**	0.621**	1	0.552**
包装体现的文化内涵	0.496**	0.490**	0.440**	0.381**	0.427**	0.452**	0.496**	0.590**	0.552**	1

注:"**"表示在0.01级别(双尾)相关性显著。

从Pearson相关系数结果可看出,以上卷烟评价指标之间均存在显著正相关关系,表明各指标之间不存在多重共线性问题。从包装外观来看,包装材质与包装美观程度相关性最大,达到0.675,包装美观程度和包装盒型也有着很高的相关性。从卷烟品质来看,谐调和余味存在很高的相关性,达到0.638,余味和杂气相关性达到0.615。

在确定了无多重共线性问题后,对自变量和因变量进行回归,模型拟合优度和回归系数结果见表4、表5。

表4 模型拟合优度结果

模型	R	R^2	调整后 R^2	标准估算的错误
1	0.475	0.225	0.223	0.882

表5 回归系数结果(系数 a)

模型	标准化系数 Beta	t	显著性	模型	标准化系数 Beta	t	显著性
第一印象	0.051	3.491	0.000	包装盒型	0.057	3.029	0.002
容易买到	0.037	2.516	0.012	包装美观程度	0.119	6.524	0.000

续表

模型	标准化系数 Beta	t	显著性	模型	标准化系数 Beta	t	显著性
价格	0.071	4.835	0.000	包装材质	0.050	2.918	0.004
刺激性	0.083	4.695	0.000	谐调	0.066	3.664	0.000
烟丝光泽	0.059	3.523	0.000	余味	0.027	1.417	0.157
香气	0.161	9.885	0.000	杂气	0.052	2.855	0.004
包装体现的文化内涵	0.062	3.398	0.001	a 因变量:整体满意程度			

对卷烟评价指标进行分类,可以得到以下关系,如图 1 所示。

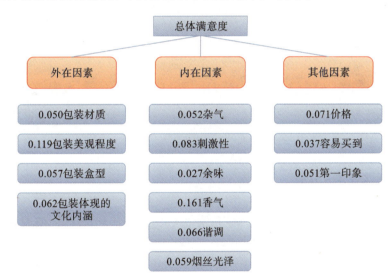

图 1　卷烟技术指标对总体满意度的影响程度图

从卷烟外在因素指标来看,"包装美观程度"对消费者的满意度打分影响程度最大,标准化系数达到了 0.119。结合消费者购买习惯分析,消费者在购买卷烟时往往是会在意卷烟包装的美观程度,因此"包装美观程度"对于消费者评价卷烟具有很大的影响。此外,"香气"是卷烟内在因素中最为重要的指标,标准化系数达到了 0.161。

3.2　消费者语言调研指标体系框架构建

3.2.1　模型初步设定

在确定观察变量与潜在变量之间的关系后,需要通过构建模型来研究各潜在变量之间的关系。将因子(CFA)模型用代表因果关系的箭头连接起来,就成了结构方程(SEM)。

值得注意的是,构建消费者评价指标体系的主要目的在于找到消费者对卷烟需求的具体结构和原因,因此一切指标都将围绕总体满意度来进行分析,以了解消费者是如何进行卷烟评价的。所以,构建出的模型必须结合实际业务运作情况,贴近真实消费者的思维模式。

潜变量之间的因果关系需以实际的具体指标之间的相关性为依托,同时进行大胆假设。初步构建的模型仅仅只是假设,可能存在错误和需要修改的地方,如果验证后的结果显示两个潜变量之间的关联性不成立,则需要对模型加以修改以符合验证结果。

用 Amos 软件构建出如下消费者评价模型(图 2)。

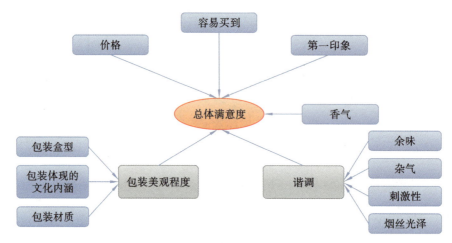

图 2　消费者评价建模

3.2.2　信度与效度分析

1) 问卷的信度分析

本研究中 13 个变量的 Cronbach's α 值为 0.752,表明问卷信度高,具有较强的稳定性及内部一致性。

2) 结构模型效度分析

(1) 内容效度。

本次调查问卷是在参考相关文献中量表的基础上设计而成的,因此具有相当的内容效度。

(2) 效标效度。

表 6 中的标准化路径系数全是显著的。从标准化路径系数可以看出,变量之间的标准化路径系数与之前的信度和效度分析关系很紧密,只要信度良好,效度可以接受,这里的标准化路径系数就是可靠的。

表 6 路径参数的计算结果

路径设置		标准化路径系数 P
包装美观程度	包装体现的文化内涵	0.1***
包装美观程度	包装盒型	0.299***
包装美观程度	包装材质	0.348***
谐调	余味	0.425***
谐调	杂气	0.118***
谐调	烟丝光泽	0.092***
谐调	刺激性	0.05***
总体满意度	容易买到	0.039**
总体满意度	第一印象	0.053***
总体满意度	价格	0.075***
总体满意度	谐调	0.151***
总体满意度	包装美观程度	0.212***
总体满意度	香气	0.234***

注："**"表示在 0.05 相关性显著。"***"表示在 0.01 相关性显著。

3) 模型的拟合效果评估

从表 7 中可以看出,均方根残差(RMR)为 0.195,拟合优度指数(GFI)为 0.707,调整的拟合优度指数(AGFI)为 0.614,节俭拟合优度指数(PGFI)为 0.536,卡方除以自由度为 78.176。RMR 越小越好,拟合较为合适;GFI、AGFI、PGFI 均越接近 1 越好,这里分别为 0.707、0.614 和 0.536,虽然没有达到 0.9 以上,但考虑样本量(8000),模型的拟合效果在可接受范围。

表 7 模型的拟合效果评估指数

模型	RMR	GFI	AGFI	PGFI	CMIN/DF
评估指数	0.195	0.707	0.614	0.536	78.176

对以上的模型结果进行梳理,把外生显变量的具体名字和标准化路径系数也添加在模型里。消费者调研指标体系结构方程的模型图如图 3 所示。

4 结论

(1) 能够直接影响到消费者对一款卷烟的总体满意度的因素包括包装美观程度、价格、容易买到、第一印象、谐调以及卷烟香气六个方面。在这六个方面中,卷烟香气对总体满意度的贡献最大,其次是包装美观程度。

(2) 与包装有关的因素中,包装材质影响程度最高,其次是包装盒型。

(3) 与卷烟口感有关的因素中,余味对卷烟口感的影响最大,其次是卷烟的杂气。

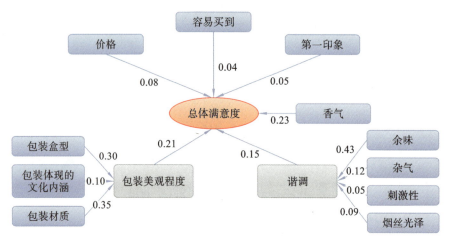

图 3　消费者调研指标体系结构方程模型图

综上,消费者主要关注的卷烟评价指标为品质/口感/吸味(余味、刺激性、杂气、香气、烟丝光泽、谐调)、价格、包装(包装材质、包装美观程度、包装盒型、包装体现的文化内涵)、第一印象、容易购买程度等。在消费者管理要素上,可以考虑卷烟的主要内在属性(香气、余味等口感/吸味指标)、外在属性(包装材质等指标)、表现属性(价格等指标)、抽象属性(第一印象等指标)。

参考文献

[1] 张素平.基于乘法模型的内蒙古乌兰察布市卷烟总销量预测研究[J].内蒙古科技与经济,2012(21):33-34+36.

[2] 赵旻,张丹枫,曾中良.基于组合模型的云南省卷烟需求预测与结果评价研究[J].中国烟草学报,2019,25(1):93-98.

[3] 王光明,佘文娟,宋金锦.基于NVivo 10质性分析的高效数学学习心理结构模型[J].心理与行为研究,2014,12(01):74-79.

[4] 王碧梅.科学学科核心素养结构及指标体系建构——基于15个国家课程标准和38位教师深度访谈内容的编码分析[J].外国教育研究,2021,48(09):43-56.

[5] 张静.数据挖掘聚类分析综述[J].价值工程,2014(15):226-227.

[6] 孔造杰,郝永敬.用权重概率综合系数法确定QFD中用户要求重要性[J].计算机制造系统,2001(2):65-67.

Study on the Correlation between Cigarette Evaluation Indicators and Consumer Demand

Abstract: In this paper, based on the depth diagnosis of the cigarette consumer demand, from different categories, different scenarios, and different purposes, this paper collected standardized way of consumer demand, the method of correlation coefficient and regression analysis to select the evaluation indicators, 13 cigarettes cigarette evaluation were selected through a structural equation model to explore the correlation of cigarette consumer demand and evaluation indicators. The study found that: consumers focus on cigarette evaluation indicators for quality, taste, flavor, price, packing, the first impression, ease of purchase, etc.

Keywords: Cigarette evaluation indicators; Consumer demand; Degree of relativity

Preface

In order to better understand the consumption demand for cigarettes and further understand the various demands of cigarette consumers for cigarette products, this paper collects and analyzes the contents of traditional cigarettes, including taste, packaging, price, concept, and product satisfaction. Through in-depth diagnosis of the consumption demand service process of cigarette consumers, by collecting standardized consumption demand methods from different categories, different scenarios, and different purposes, 13 evaluation indicators of cigarettes are selected, and mathematical methods are used to explore the systematic idea and direction of the transformation of cigarette consumer demand into product research and development. Quantitative research are used to analyze the critical indicators that affect cigarette consumers, determine the relative weight of consumer demand indicators with significant correlation for cigarettes, demonstrate the rationality of the consumer demand indicator system, and provide a basis for cigarette sales and product research and development.

1 Data Source and Survey Object

This paper involves the information data, including the social and economic data, the hot spot data, and a province's cigarette sales data, and adopts an indirect survey method. The social and economic statistics were mainly obtained from the official website of the provincial Bureau of Statistics, and the hot data were obtained through Internet searches.

Quantitative research was mainly conducted in 12 cities, including Kunming and Hangzhou, with respondents 18 to 55 years old smokers. The sample survey was conducted to collect 8000 samples from city to city, of the sample size, as shown in Table 1.

Table 1　The Sample Size of Each City

Cities	Kun ming	Hang zhou	Guang zhou	Cheng du	Lan zhou	Wu han	Da li	Shang hai	Shen zhen	Chong qing	Liu zhou	Da lian
Sample size	800	800	800	800	800	400	400	800	800	800	400	400
Total sample size	8000											

2　Research Methods

2.1　Correlation Analysis Method of Product Attribute Indicators and Consumer Experience Product Testing Data

Correlation coefficient analysis and regression analysis are generally used to explore the degree of relativity between cigarette evaluation indicators and consumer demand[1-6].

As a simple correlation coefficient, the Pearson correlation coefficient is used to measure the linear relationship between two variables. The larger the correlation coefficient is, the stronger the linear relationship between variables is. The calculation formula in this paper is as follows:

$$r(X,Y) = \frac{\text{cov}(X,Y)}{\sqrt{\text{var}(X)\text{var}(Y)}}$$

Based on the survey results of product satisfaction test indicators of consumer demand, this paper uses data mining to analyze the correlation between product attribute indicators and consumer experience product testing data. The evaluation of cigarette products generally includes the evaluation of cigarette appearance and external attributes and the evaluation of cigarette product taste. The requirements and evaluation of the external attributes of cigarettes include the form of cigarette packaging, cigarette length, filter rod length, unique cigarette, unique filter rod, and tobacco cut. The taste evaluation of cigarette products was carried out from several aspects: smell, oral cavity, nasal cavity, throat and aftertaste, and the overall evaluation of the current product.

Cigarette product evaluation should have a detailed understanding of smokers' preferences for all aspects of cigarette products. First, consumers were asked to evaluate their satisfaction with cigarette products; then, they were asked to evaluate the taste of their main smoking brands. Finally, consumers were asked to evaluate their preference for cigarette packaging, price acceptability, and product concept cognition and evaluation.

2.2 Management Factor Analysis Method of Cigarette Consumer Demand Transformation Path based on Structural Equation Model

Using structural equation modeling (SEM) to explore the structure of the relationship between consumer demand (evaluation) and interaction, to build a simple transformation path model, validate and determine consumer demand attention information, and establish the evaluation system of consumer demand.

(1) Model Expression.

Structural equation model including measurement model and structural model, the general structure equation can be used three basic equations.

Measurement model:
$$X = \Lambda_x \xi + \delta \tag{1.1}$$
$$Y = \Lambda_y \eta + \varepsilon \tag{1.2}$$

Structure model:
$$\eta = B\eta + r\xi + \gamma \tag{1.3}$$

Equation (1.1) of $X = (x_1, \cdots, x_q)'$ on behalf of the observation model of exogenous variables $\xi = (\xi_1, \cdots, \xi_n)'$. Represents the exogenous latent variable, the matrix $\Lambda_x(q \times n)$ represents the factor loading between the explicit variable X and the latent variable ξ, is a $q \times n$ dimensional matrix, and $\delta = (\delta_1, \cdots, \delta_q)'$ represents the measurement error of X. Equation (1.2) of $Y = (y_1, \cdots, y_q)'$ on behalf of the observation model of endogenous variables, $\eta = (\eta_1, \cdots, \eta_q)'$ represents endogenous latent variable, matrix $\Lambda_y(p \times m)$ on behalf of eta show variable Y and latent variables η between the factor loading, is a $p \times m$ dimensional matrix, $\varepsilon = (\varepsilon_1, \cdots, \varepsilon_q)'$ representative Y measurement error. In equation (1.3), $B\eta$ represents the matrix of structural coefficients between endogenous latent variables, $r\xi$ represents the matrix of structural coefficients between endogenous latent variables and exogenous latent variables, and γ represents the disturbance term of the structural equation.

Among them, the η and ξ are latent variables, also known as the concept or factor, composed of multiple variables to measure what can be observed. The coefficient matrix B, r, and the linear relationship, and the error term are connected the relationship between endogenous latent variables and exogenous latent variables.

(2) Basic Assumptions of the Model.

In the traditional structural equations, there is no predetermined intercept item to simplify the model deduction. Therefore, the entire model and estimation expression are not based on original estimates but require centralized data, i. e., data input into the model consists of estimated values of mean deviation. Additionally, when considering linear model estimation, it is important to take into account the basic assumptions of linear equations. Under these conditions, the observation model (1.1, 1.2) must satisfy the following four criteria:

① $E(\boldsymbol{\eta})=0, E(\boldsymbol{\xi})=0, E(\boldsymbol{\delta})=0, E(\boldsymbol{\varepsilon})=0$;

② the $\boldsymbol{\varepsilon}$ and $\boldsymbol{\eta}, \boldsymbol{\xi}, \boldsymbol{\delta}$ irrelevant;

③ the $\boldsymbol{\delta}$ and $\boldsymbol{\eta}, \boldsymbol{\xi}, \boldsymbol{\varepsilon}$ irrelevant;

④ the X, Y, obey the multivariate normal distribution.

In the structural model Equation (1.3), $\boldsymbol{\eta}$ appears on both the left and right sides of the equation, and $(\boldsymbol{I}-\boldsymbol{B})^{-1}$ must be included when transforming the equation, where $\boldsymbol{I}$ represents the identity matrix. It is essential for $(\boldsymbol{I}-\boldsymbol{B})^{-1}$ to be present in order to estimate the model accurately. Therefore, for a structural model, it is also necessary to satisfy the following assumptions:

①$E(\boldsymbol{\eta})=0, E(\boldsymbol{\xi})=0, E(\boldsymbol{\gamma})=0$;

②$\boldsymbol{\xi}$ is uncorrelated with $\boldsymbol{\gamma}$;

③$(\boldsymbol{I}-\boldsymbol{B})$ for nonsingular matrix.

(3) Model Estimation.

In contrast to the general multiple regression model, the structural equation is not solved by minimizing the mean square error (MSE), which involves minimizing the sum of the squares of deviations between the fitted value and true value. Instead, it is solved by minimizing covariance, specifically reducing the gap between sample covariance and model estimated covariance. Let $\sum$ represent the overall covariance of observed variables Y and X, which serves as a true value.

$$\sum = E(\boldsymbol{YY'})E(\boldsymbol{YX'})$$

Denote by $\sum(\theta)$ its estimate, which is a function of the free parameters. In structural equation modeling (SEM), the optimal parameters of θ need to be found in order to achieve the best data fitting, resulting in the minimum value of $\sum - \sum(\theta)$.

Both $\sum$ and $\sum(\theta)$ are known and can be estimated. The common estimation method used is maximum likelihood estimation.

The goal of SEM is to find the parameter values θ to minimize the minimum difference function F.

3 Results and Analysis

3.1 Correlation Analysis between Cigarette Evaluation Indicators and Consumer Demand

Following variable screening, the correlation between 13 cigarette evaluation indicators and consumer satisfaction was examined. The results are presented in Table 2.

Table 2 Pearson Correlation Coefficient Results between Cigarette Evaluation Indicators and Consumer Satisfaction

Indicators	Pearson correlation coefficient	Indicators	Pearson correlation coefficient	Indicators	Pearson correlation coefficient
Offensive odor	0.271**	Box type	0.292**	Aroma	0.313**
Aftertaste	0.251**	The cultural connotation of packaging	0.278**	The price	0.090**
Harmonic	0.258**	Cut tobacco gloss	0.271**	Ease of purchase	0.045**
Packing material	0.266**	Irritant	0.301**	First impression	0.050**
Aesthetics of packing	0.322**				

It is evident from the table that all the evaluation indicators of cigarettes are significantly and positively correlated with consumer satisfaction, with correlation coefficients ranging between 0.045 and 0.322. Among these, packaging aesthetics exhibits the strongest correlation with consumer satisfaction, at 0.322, while the correlation between ease of purchase and consumer satisfaction is weak, at 0.045.

According to the correlation coefficient of size classification, the following observations can be made.

(1) The correlation coefficient for cigarette evaluation indicators, packaging aesthetics, aroma, and irritant within the range of 0.3-0.4. These indicators exhibit a strong correlation with consumer satisfaction, indicating their close relationship with consumer demand.

(2) Cigarette evaluation indicators with a correlation coefficient between 0.2-0.3 include offensive odor, harmony, cut tobacco gloss, cultural connotation of packaging, packaging material, box type and aftertaste. These indicators are mostly related to cigarette quality and demonstrate a slightly stronger correlation with customer

satisfaction, suggesting their close connection to consumer demand.

(3) Cigarette quality evaluation indicators with a correlation coefficient below 0.2 encompass price, ease of purchase and first impression. There is a low correlation between these evaluation indices and consumer satisfaction, indicating a certain level of association between the evaluation indices and consumer demand.

In multiple regression, the equation $y = \beta_0 + \beta_1 x_1 + \beta_2 x_2 + \cdots + \beta_p x_p + \varepsilon$, β represents the extent of influence of each independent variable on the dependent variable. The greater the influence of the independent variable on the dependent variable, the more pronounced it is. In a multivariate linear model, if x_1, x_2... up to x_p are not related to each other (i.e., $(X'X)^{-1}$ exists), then there will be exist least squares estimation (OLS) parameter. However, when x_1, x_2... up to x_p are highly correlated with each other, the calculated value will have a large variance and the estimate will not be robust. This phenomenon is known as multicollinearity.

To detect multicollinearity, one can calculate the Pearson correlation coefficient between the observed variables. A large Pearson correlation value indicates a particularly strong relationship between variables. If all of these variables are used as independent variables in regression analysis, multicollinearity may disrupt the accuracy of parameter estimation. Therefore, the Pearson correlation coefficient can be utilized as a test index. Upon calculation, it is determined that the Pearson correlation coefficient takes the form Table 3.

Table 3 Pearson Correlation Coefficients between Cigarette Evaluation Indicators

Indicators	Aroma	Cut tobacco gloss	Irritant	Offensive odor	Aftertaste	Harmonic	Packing material	Aesthetics of packaging	Box type	The cultural connotation of packaging
Aroma	1	0.605**	0.527**	0.427**	0.445**	0.423**	0.527**	0.509**	0.440**	0.496**
Cut tobacco gloss	0.605**	1	0.542**	0.476**	0.485**	0.485**	0.504**	0.513**	0.464**	0.490**
Irritant	0.527**	0.542**	1	0.609**	0.545**	0.488**	0.466**	0.461**	0.422**	0.440**
Offensive odor	0.427**	0.476**	0.609**	1	0.615**	0.528**	0.431**	0.409**	0.403**	0.381**
Aftertaste	0.445**	0.485**	0.545**	0.615**	1	0.638**	0.491**	0.465**	0.457**	0.427**
Harmonic	0.423**	0.485**	0.488**	0.528**	0.638**	1	0.523**	0.500**	0.490**	0.452**

continue

Indicators	Aroma	Cut tobacco gloss	Irritant	Offensive odor	Aftertaste	Harmonic	Packing material	Aesthetics of packaging	Box type	The cultural connotation of packaging
Packing material	0.527**	0.504**	0.466**	0.431**	0.491**	0.523**	1	0.675**	0.572**	0.496**
Aesthetics of packaging	0.509**	0.513**	0.461**	0.409**	0.465**	0.500**	0.675**	1	0.621**	0.590**
Box type	0.440**	0.464**	0.422**	0.403**	0.457**	0.490**	0.572**	0.621**	1	0.552**
The cultural connotation of packaging	0.496**	0.490**	0.440**	0.381**	0.427**	0.452**	0.496**	0.590**	0.552**	1

** At the 0.01 level (two-tailed), the correlation is significant.

The results of the Pearson correlation coefficient indicate that there is a significant positive correlation among above cigarette evaluation indicators, suggesting the absence of multicollinearity issues. Specifically, there is a strong correlation (up to 0.675) between aesthetics of packaging, and packing material. Additionally, the aesthetics of packaging has a significant influence on the choice of box type. In terms of cigarette quality, high correlations are observed between harmonic and aftertaste (0.638), as well as aftertaste and offensive odor (0.615), while the remaining indicators have correlation coefficients below 0.6.

After confirming the absence of multicollinearity issues, regression analysis was conducted with independent and dependent variables. The regression equation results and model goodness-of-fit are presented in Tables 4 and 5 for reference.

Table 4 Goodness of Fit Model

Model	R	R^2	R^2 after adjustment	Error in standard estimates
1	0.475	0.225	0.223	0.882

Table 5　The Results of Regression Coefficient (Coefficient α)

Model	Standardized coefficients Beta	t	Sig.	Model	Standardized coefficients Beta	t	Sig.
First impression	0.051	3.491	0.000	Box type	0.057	3.029	0.002
Ease of purchase	0.037	2.516	0.012	Aesthetics of packaging	0.119	6.524	0.000
The price	0.071	4.835	0.000	Packing material	0.050	2.918	0.004
Irritant	0.083	4.695	0.000	Harmonic	0.066	3.664	0.000
Cut tobacco gloss	0.059	3.523	0.000	Aftertaste	0.027	1.417	0.157
Aroma	0.161	9.885	0.000	Offensive odor	0.052	2.855	0.004
The cultural connotation of packaging	0.062	3.398	0.001	α Dependent variable: overall satisfaction			

According to the classification of cigarette evaluation indicators, the following relationship can be obtained in Figure 1.

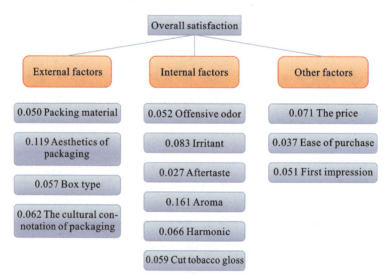

Figure 1　Influence Degree of Cigarette Technical Indicators on Overall Satisfaction

From an external perspective, the "aesthetic of packaging" has the greatest impact on consumer satisfaction scores for cigarettes, with a standard coefficient of 0.119. When analyzing consumers' purchasing habits, it is evident that they prioritize the aesthetic appeal of cigarette packaging when making their purchases. As a result, "aesthetic of packaging" significantly influences consumers' evaluation of cigarette indicators. Furthermore, among internal factors, "aroma" holds the most important indicator, with a standard coefficient of 0.161.

3.2 Development of a Framework for Consumer Language Survey Indicators System Construction

3.2.1 Preliminary Model Setting

Once the relationship between observed variables and latent variables has been determined, it is essential to examine the relationship between latent variables through model construction. The factor (CFA) model is connected by arrows representing causality, which then evolves into the structural equation model (SEM).

It is important to note that the primary objective of constructing the consumer evaluation indicators system is to understand the specific structure and reasons behind consumers' demand for cigarettes. Therefore, all indicators will revolve around overall satisfaction to comprehend how consumers evaluate cigarettes. As a result, the constructed model must align with actual business operations and reflect real consumer thought processes.

The causal relationship between latent variables should be established based on the correlation between specific indicators, and bold assumptions must be made. The initial model is a hypothesis, which may contain errors and require modification. If the verification results indicate that the relationship between the two latent variables is invalid, the model must be adjusted to align with the verification findings.

Amos software has been utilized to construct the consumer evaluation model depicted in Figure 2.

3.2.2 Analysis of Reliability and Validity

1) Questionnaire reliability analysis

The Cronbach's α value for the 13 variables in this study was 0.752, indicating high reliability, strong stability, and internal consistency of the questionnaire.

2) Structural model validity analysis

(1) Content validity.

The questionnaire design is primarily based on scale suggestions from relevant literature, ensuring a considerable degree of content validity.

(2) Criterion validity.

Figure 2　Consumer Evaluation Modeling

All standardized path coefficients in the Table 6 are significant, demonstrating close relationships between variables as indicated by previous reliability and validity analyses. With good reliability and acceptable validity, the path coefficients are also reliable.

Table 6　Path Parameters Calculation Results

Path settings		Standardized path coefficients P
Aesthetics of packaging	The cultural connotation of packaging	0.1***
Aesthetics of packaging	Box type	0.299***
Aesthetics of packaging	Packing material	0.348***
Harmonic	Aftertaste	0.425***
Harmonic	Offensive odor	0.118***
Harmonic	Cut tobacco gloss	0.092***
Harmonic	Irritating	0.05***
Overall satisfaction	Ease of purchase	0.039**
Overall satisfaction	First impression	0.053***
Overall satisfaction	The price	0.075***
Overall satisfaction	Harmonic	0.151***
Overall satisfaction	Aesthetics of packaging	0.212***
Overall satisfaction	Aroma	0.234***

Note: "**" indicates significant correlation at the 0.05 level. "***" indicates significance at the 0.01 level.

3) Evaluation of the model's fit effect

Table 7 presents the evaluation of the model's fitting effect. The root mean square residual (RMR) is 0.195, indicating a good fit. The goodness-of-fit index (GFI) is 0.707, the adjusted goodness-of-fit index (AGFI) is 0.614, and the parsimonious goodness-of-fit index (PGFI) is 0.536, all of which are close to 1 and within an acceptable range considering the sample size of 8,000. The chi-square divided by the degrees of freedom is also calculated as 78.176. While some indices may not exceed 0.9, given the large sample size, it can be concluded that the model fitting falls within an acceptable range for analysis purposes.

Table 7　Evaluation Index of the Model's Fitting Effect

Model	RMR	GFI	AGFI	PGFI	CMIN/DF
Default model	0.195	0.707	0.614	0.536	78.176

After organizing the results of the above model, the specific names and path coefficients of exogenous visible variables are incorporated into the model. Subsequently, the following structural equation model of the survey indicators system is constructed (see Figure 3).

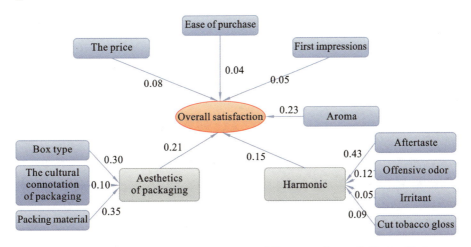

Figure 3　Structural Equation Model Diagram of Consumer Survey Indicators System

4　Conclusion

(1) Various factors directly impact overall satisfaction, including packaging, price, ease of purchase, first impression, harmonic, and aroma. Among these aspects, cigarette aroma has the greatest influence on overall satisfaction, followed by aesthetics of packaging.

(2) The influence of "packaging" factors can be seen in the packaging material with the highest impact, followed by the box type.

(3) When considering factors related to the "cigarette taste", it is evident that aftertaste has the most significant influence on cigarette taste, followed by cigarette offensive odor.

In summary, consumers pay attention to critical evaluation indicators such as quality/taste/flavor (including aftertaste, irritation, offensive odor, aroma, cut tobacco gloss, and harmony), price and packaging (including packing material, aesthetics of packaging, box type and cultural connotation of packaging), first impression and ease of purchase. In terms of consumer management factors internal attributes (such as aroma and aftertaste), external attributes (such as packaging materials), and performance attributes (such as price) should be considered when evaluating cigarettes. Abstract attributes like first impressions should also be taken into account.

References

[1] ZHANG S P. Prediction of Total Cigarette Sales in Ulanqab City of Inner Mongolia based on Multiplicative Model[J]. Inner Mongolia Science and Technology and Economy, 2012 (21): 33-34+36.

[2] ZHAO M, ZHANG D F, ZENG Z L. Model based on Combination of Cigarette Demand Forecast and Evaluation of the Results of Yunnan Province[J]. Journal of China tobacco, 2019, 25 (1): 93-98.

[3] WANG G M, SHE W J, SONG J J. A Psychological Structure Model for Efficient Mathematics Learning based on NVivo 10 Qualitative Analysis[J]. Psychological and Behavioral Research, 2014, 12 (01): 74-79.

[4] WANG B M. Construction of Core Literacy Structure and Index System of Science Subjects: Coding Analysis based on 15 National Curriculum Standards and In-Depth Interviews with 38 Teachers[J]. Foreign Education Research, 2021, 48 (09): 43-56.

[5] ZHANG J. Review of Data Mining Clustering Analysis[J]. Value Engineering, 2014 (15): 226-227.

[6] KONG Z J, HAO Y J. Determining the Importance of User Requirements in QFD Using Weighted Probability Comprehensive Coefficient Method[J]. Computer Manufacturing System, 2001(2): 65-67.

消费结构与行为

卷烟消费者结构及其消费行为特征分析

摘要: 在消费升级背景下,卷烟消费者的需求呈现多元化趋势,影响其购买卷烟的因素越来越多。基于此,结合卷烟消费市场的特殊性,对昆明等12个城市的卷烟消费者结构特征进行调研。结果显示,卷烟消费者的平均烟龄为10.62年,一般在17岁到34岁开始吸烟,月均购烟支出占平均月收入的7.45%。同时从消费动机、购买能力、消费习惯、购买数量等方面探讨了卷烟消费者消费行为特征。对卷烟消费者结构及其消费行为特征进行分析,有利于卷烟企业根据消费者的特征划分目标市场,提升市场占有率。

关键词: 卷烟;消费市场;消费者结构;消费行为

随着我国市场经济改革的不断深化、新型消费内涵的拓展以及消费主体需求的提升与变化,卷烟企业必须充分了解消费者的消费趋势与消费规律,不断提升产品的专业化和差异化水平,从而在消费升级的背景下迅速占有市场。传统卷烟不仅品牌繁多,档次、口味和价格也多种多样,此外,卷烟消费者的需求已逐步呈现多元化趋势,因此卷烟企业的市场营销不应再局限于单纯的产品推广,而应该利用大数据技术对消费者的消费行为进行分析,把握传统卷烟消费者的消费需求及动向,立足于现有的营销服务体系进行创新,并以此影响消费者行为。

近年来,学者们针对卷烟消费行为的研究成果颇丰,郭立军等[1]以消费者卷烟消费数据档案库为切入点,提出卷烟消费者档案库建立的基础在于构建长期性的数据采集形式;陈浩等[2]研究了某卷烟企业消费者消费行为的区域聚集规律以及地点和时段偏好,其研究结果可为卷烟企业的产品投放和营销策略提供参考;李晓亮等[3]分析了卷烟目标消费者的特征及消费行为,提出基于目标消费者的卷烟品牌培育策略。显然,卷烟消费者的消费行为会直接影响卷烟品牌的健康发展,因此,应通过零售行业的大数据对客户进行了解,掌握消费者的感受和市场发展动态,加强对卷烟消费者消费行为数据的分析与应用,提高卷烟企业对卷烟品牌的动态监控。

综上，在消费升级背景下，影响卷烟消费者消费行为的因素复杂多样，加之卷烟消费者的消费心理和消费动机具有随机性和多变性，从而使其消费行为复杂化。分析卷烟消费者的消费行为，挖掘消费者的潜在需求，是开展市场营销的基础。因此，本文结合卷烟消费市场的特殊性，以昆明等12个城市为调研城市，总结分析消费者消费行为的规律，探讨卷烟消费者结构及其消费行为特征，以期为卷烟企业根据消费者的特征划分目标市场、提升市场占有率提供参考。

1 材料与方法

1.1 调查范围及对象

传统卷烟消费者的人口结构可以在一定程度上反映传统卷烟消费者的市场结构，对其进行分析可以协助我们准确把握卷烟消费群体的基本特征。因此，本文以昆明、杭州、广州、成都、兰州、武汉、大理、上海、深圳、重庆、柳州、大连12个城市为调研城市，对居住在调研城市的18岁以上的卷烟消费者开展问卷调查。

1.2 调查方法

本文采用扫码自填的方法收集调查问卷。调查问卷主要包括两个部分，即消费者结构特征与消费者消费行为。其中，消费者结构特征涉及消费者居住城市、年龄、烟龄、性别、职业、文化程度、月均收入；消费者消费行为包括消费者购买决策、购买过程、购买能力以及购买活动，主要从购烟目的、卷烟信息获取渠道、购烟时的影响因素、购烟态度、卷烟满意度评价等进行分析。

本次调查共收回问卷8707份，其中有效问卷8088份，各城市有效样本量情况见表1。

表1 调研城市有效样本量基本情况

城市	昆明	杭州	广州	成都	兰州	武汉	大理	上海	深圳	重庆	柳州	大连	合计
样本量/份	810	812	801	810	801	424	412	806	805	802	405	400	8088

2 结果与分析

2.1 卷烟消费者结构特征

2.1.1 卷烟消费者年龄、性别、收入等结构特征

从表2可以看出，18～55岁的卷烟消费者占93.95%，其中26～45岁的卷烟消费者占63.80%，卷烟消费者的平均年龄为36.76岁。此外，昆明、大理的卷烟消费者中，年龄为18～25岁的卷烟消费者均超过35%，且大理18～25岁的卷烟消费者占48.6%。

表2　调研城市卷烟消费者年龄分布及占比　　　　　　　　　　　　　　　　单位：%

年龄	昆明	杭州	广州	成都	兰州	武汉	大理	上海	深圳	重庆	大连	柳州
18～25岁	36.3	8.1	13.8	15.3	5.6	13.2	48.6	13.9	10.7	13.7	11.3	12.3
26～35岁	38.5	22.9	38.8	38.5	32.5	33.3	19.0	47.1	39.6	29.7	33.3	35.8
36～45岁	16.2	28.3	37.0	29.8	34.2	28.8	18.0	30.8	37.6	24.9	28.8	26.4
46～55岁	6.7	30.5	7.1	13.5	20.8	14.9	9.7	6.1	7.5	20.4	19.8	14.1
56～65岁	2.0	6.9	2.2	2.8	5.9	7.3	4.0	1.7	3.4	7.6	5.2	8.9
>66岁	0.3	3.3	1.1	0.1	1.0	2.5	0.7	0.4	1.2	3.7	1.6	2.5

从性别来看(图1)，卷烟消费者以男性居多，占总数的80.74%；男女比例接近8∶2，而成都的男女比例接近7∶3，杭州和兰州的男女比例接近9∶1。

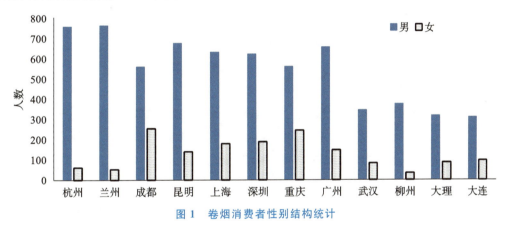

图1　卷烟消费者性别结构统计

从图2可以看出，受教育程度方面，除硕士及以上学历和初中及以下学历占比较小外，其他学历层次的卷烟消费者人数占比相当，且卷烟消费者的学历主要集中在高中/中专/技校、大专和本科学历层次，共占82.31%。

在职业方面，"工人、普通人员、售货员、服务人员"占比最高(24.78%)，离退休人员占比最低(3.33%)，各城市间无明显差异(图3)。

从图4可知，收入水平方面，卷烟消费者平均月收入为7096.87元。其中月收入为5000～7999元的居多，占37.18%，收入为2000～4999元的占29.85%，两者合计达到67.03%。从城市来看，上海市的卷烟消费者月均收入最高(9136.48元)，昆明市的卷烟消费者月均收入最低(5438.27元)。

2.1.2　卷烟消费者烟龄分布特征

由调查数据可知(表3和图5)，卷烟消费者的烟龄普遍较长，平均烟龄为10.62年。杭州的卷烟消费者的平均烟龄最长(13.35年)，昆明的最短(8.06年)。杭州、兰州和重庆的卷烟消费者中，烟龄为10年以上的超过50%；大理、广州和深圳的卷烟消费者中，烟龄在5

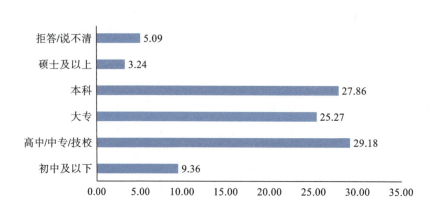

图 2　卷烟消费者受教育程度统计

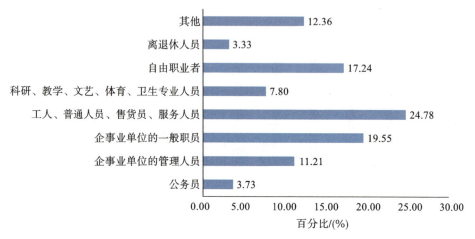

图 3　卷烟消费者职业情况统计

图 4　各城市卷烟消费者平均月收入统计

年内的超过 40%。从不同年龄卷烟消费者的平均烟龄可知，卷烟消费者一般在 17 岁到 34 岁之间开始吸烟。

表 3 各年龄段消费者的平均烟龄

年龄/岁	平均烟龄/年
18~25	3.96
26~35	7.91
36~45	11.60
46~55	17.20
56~65	22.39
>66	27.88
平均	10.62

图 5 各城市卷烟消费者的平均烟龄

2.2 卷烟消费者的消费动机

2.2.1 卷烟能够满足个人的生理和社交需求

由表 4 可以看出,消费者购买卷烟的原因主要是个人生理需求和社交需求。其中,工作需要占 19.44%,好奇占 12.80%,突出个性占 10.63%,社交需求占 13.23%。此外,通过调研了解到,深圳和广州的消费者购烟主要是用于个人消费;杭州有 0.76% 的消费者购烟是为了社交需求;柳州的消费者接触卷烟的原因主要是社交需求、好奇、缓解压力;上海的消费者接触卷烟的原因是受周围吸烟人的影响、借助卷烟突出个性。从职业来看,超过一半的离退休人员购烟是用于个人消费,公务员,企事业单位管理人员,科研、教学、文艺、体育和卫生专业人员中,超过一半的消费者购烟是用于个人消费和社交。可见,卷烟虽非公众必需品,但是从国内传统卷烟消费者的消费行为来看,吸烟能够满足个人的生理需求和社交需求。

表 4 消费者购买卷烟的主要原因

原因	人数	占比/(%)
好奇	301	12.80

续表

原因	人数	占比/(%)
突出个性	250	10.63
周围吸烟人的影响	730	31.05
工作需要	457	19.44
社交需求	311	13.23
缓解压力	150	6.38
记不清	152	6.47

2.2.2　卷烟消费者获取卷烟信息的渠道

从图6可知,有35.04%的消费者通过柜台陈列获取卷烟信息,29.19%的消费者通过朋友介绍获取卷烟信息。从城市来看,昆明、杭州、广州和兰州等城市的消费者主要是通过柜台陈列和朋友介绍获取卷烟信息,成都的消费者主要是通过朋友介绍和网络渠道(比如中国烟草网)获取香烟信息,深圳和柳州的消费者主要是通过柜台陈列和网络渠道获取卷烟信息。由此可知,消费者接触卷烟的原因主要是受周围环境的影响。

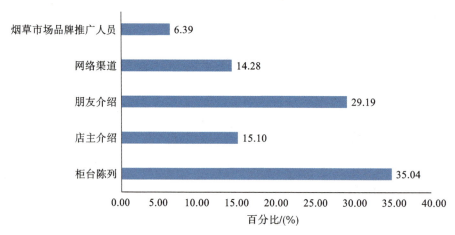

图6　获取卷烟信息的渠道

2.3　消费者的卷烟消费水平

2.3.1　卷烟消费者购烟价位分布

经济发展水平决定一个城市的消费特点,不同收入的消费者对卷烟的消费水平可能不同。本调查主要从常购卷烟价位和每月购烟支出来探讨消费者的卷烟消费水平。

调查数据显示,柳州、大理的消费者中,超过60%的消费者均购买20元/包以下的卷烟;杭州、广州和深圳的消费者中,超过65%的消费者购买20元/包以上的卷烟。同时发现,不论卷烟消费者出于何种目的购买卷烟,其选择的卷烟价位多在10～30元/包。可见,卷烟购买力在全国不同城市呈现出不同的数据,消费者购烟价位多集中在10～30元/包

(表 5)。而经济发展相对落后的城市,其卷烟消费水平相对较低。

表 5 消费者购烟价位分布

价格/(元/包)	人数	百分比/(%)
<10	757	9.36
10~20	3487	43.11
20~30	2291	28.33
30~40	723	8.94
40~60	487	6.02
60~80	222	2.74
>80	121	1.50

2.3.2 消费者的收入对卷烟消费的影响

从表6和表7可以看出,月收入在1999元以下的消费者,平均每月购烟支出为246.08元;月收入在20000元以上的消费者,平均每月购烟支出为856.40元。12个城市卷烟消费者平均每月购烟支出为529.02元,占平均每月收入的7.45%。

表 6 不同收入消费者购买卷烟的情况

项目	金额					
月收入/元	<1999	2000~4999	5000~7999	8000~11999	12000~19999	>20000
月购烟支出/元	246.08	410.31	511.82	662.54	849.81	856.40

表 7 各城市消费者平均每月购烟支出统计

城市	月收入/元	月购烟支出/元	占比/(%)
昆明	5438.27	465.86	8.57
杭州	8216.13	499.32	6.08
广州	6611.11	489.95	7.41
成都	7526.54	665.68	8.84
兰州	6326.35	526.17	8.32
武汉	6089.62	410.61	6.74
大理	5826.68	550.75	9.45
上海	9136.48	639.52	7.00
深圳	8486.96	595.47	7.02
重庆	6808.60	496.82	7.30
大连	5807.50	380.25	6.55
柳州	7150.62	485.68	6.79
平均	7096.87	529.02	7.45

综上,消费者的收入影响其卷烟消费水平。收入较高的消费者,可自由支配资金较为充足,会提高其卷烟消费水平;收入较低的消费者,能够自由支配的资金相对较少,限制了其卷烟消费水平。

2.4 卷烟消费者的消费习惯

2.4.1 消费者购烟以习惯型为主

消费者的卷烟消费行为主要表现为习惯型。调查数据显示,超过40%的消费者对某些卷烟有特殊感情,并长期购买;仅有不到4%的消费者购买卷烟时比较谨慎,选择困难。

由表8可知,杭州、武汉、大连和柳州有超过50%的消费者的购烟习惯为"对品牌有特殊感情,长期购买";昆明有近30%的消费者的购烟习惯为以"价格高低决定是否购买";杭州、上海和深圳有近30%的消费者的购烟习惯为"比较不同卷烟性价比后购买"。

表8　各城市消费者购烟习惯　　　　　　　　　　　　　　单位:%

购烟习惯	昆明	杭州	广州	成都	兰州	武汉	大理	上海	深圳	重庆	大连	柳州
对品牌有特殊感情,长期购买	32.1	57.1	40.7	43.6	39.8	54.6	38.9	38.7	37.0	48.3	52.5	51.4
比较不同卷烟性价比后购买	24.8	31.4	27.0	21.5	26.7	25.2	27.7	29.5	30.6	24.3	27.3	22.0
价格高低决定是否购买	30.0	6.7	23.1	13.7	24.9	13.4	15.7	11.8	18.8	11.0	11.8	14.3
根据柜台陈列情况购买	10.7	4.1	6.6	13.6	7.1	5.9	11.2	11.7	9.0	12.5	7.0	9.4
选择困难	2.4	0.7	2.6	7.6	1.6	0.9	6.5	8.3	4.6	3.9	1.4	2.9

2.4.2 口感是影响消费者购烟的主要因素

从图7可以看出,卷烟消费者购买卷烟时,口感无疑是影响其购烟的主要因素(占66.83%),其次为价格、品牌、包装、口碑等因素。通过调查了解到,有超过20%的消费者选择常吸品牌烟的主要原因是"品牌知名度高""喜欢品牌文化""历史悠久""品牌口碑好""烟香纯正""品牌档次高"。

2.5 消费者购买卷烟的数量

2.5.1 日吸烟量与购烟需求的影响

从区域来看,各城市的消费者每次购烟的数量略有差异。调查数据显示,上海有58.49%的消费者每次购烟量为1条;深圳有49.43%的消费者每次购烟量为1包。消费者每次的购烟数量主要与个人日吸烟量有关,日吸烟量越高的消费者,每次购烟的数量就越多。从表9可知,绝大多数消费者以每次1包或1条的方式购买卷烟,两者占比高达

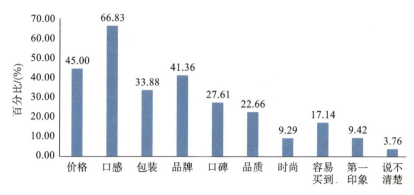

图 7 消费者购买卷烟的影响因素

58.70%。调查数据显示,日吸烟量在 5 支以下的,购烟数量为每次 1 包;日吸烟量在 2 包以上的,购烟数量为每次 4 条以上。

表 9 消费者每次购烟数量统计

数量	人数	占比/(%)
1 包	579	24.63
2～3 包	416	17.69
4～5 包	229	9.74
6～9 包	101	4.30
1 条	801	34.07
2～3 条	168	7.15
4 条以上	27	1.15
说记不清了	30	1.27

2.5.2 购烟地点影响购烟数量

消费者每次购烟的数量还与购烟地点有关,其在烟草专卖店购买的数量多为 1 条以上。调查数据显示,42.21%的消费者在烟草专卖店以 1 条的方式购买卷烟,31.36%的消费者在便利店以 1 包的方式购买卷烟。

从图 8 可以看出,有超过 23%的消费者通常在烟酒店和商场、超市购买卷烟,在小卖部购买卷烟的较少,仅占 10.51%。从城市来看,上海有超过一半的消费者经常在烟草专卖店购烟,柳州有 40%的消费者常常在便利店购烟,成都有 30%的消费者经常在小卖部购烟。

3 讨论与结论

目前,研究者[2,4-6]对卷烟消费者消费行为的研究,通常采用 POI 数据分析技术、决策树 C4.5 算法、对应分析方法、PSM 模型等方法进行实证分析,其研究结果显示,性别、年龄、社会地位等是影响卷烟消费者消费行为的主要因素,人们的卷烟消费行为主要受综合

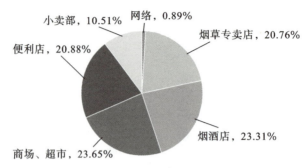

图 8　消费者购买卷烟的地点分布

环境与个人条件的影响。

本文在消费升级背景下,对卷烟消费者的结构特征及其消费行为进行调查与分析,结果如下所示。

(1) 卷烟消费者的结构特征为:卷烟消费者的年龄主要集中在 18～55 岁,以男性为主,男女比例接近 8∶2,平均烟龄为 10.62 年,一般在 17～34 岁开始吸烟;月均购烟支出占平均收入的 7.45%;学历主要集中在高中/中专/技校、大专、本科,占 82.31%。

(2) 影响卷烟消费者消费动机的因素主要有个人生理需求和社交需求。同时还应注意到,群体动力显著影响卷烟消费者的购买决策,有必要将群体动力作为影响卷烟消费行为的一个重要因素。

(3) 决定消费者购买能力的关键因素是月收入与可支配资金。卷烟定价对品牌的发展影响很大,合理制定卷烟价格可提升消费者的购买能力。但定价又是一个复杂的问题,除了考虑成本因素外,更要考虑价格是否能够被消费者所接受。在推出新品时,应先进行价格测试,把价格定在消费者普遍认同的价格之下,让消费者产生"物超所值"的感觉。

(4) 影响卷烟消费者消费行为的因素较多,如卷烟的口感、消费者的消费习惯、个人日吸食量以及购烟的地点等。因此,提升卷烟品牌的信誉度,培养消费者的认可度和消费习惯,可进一步提高产品的销量和市场稳定性。

综上所述,分析卷烟消费者结构及其消费行为特征,培育相应产品品牌,分类制定营销策略,打造卷烟品牌组合以适应传统卷烟消费者的消费需求,有利于卷烟企业根据消费者的特征划分目标市场,提升企业的市场占有率,实现企业健康可持续发展。

参考文献

[1] 郭立军,叶剑,闫东."互联网+卷烟营销"思维下的消费者档案库的建立[J].品牌研究,2020(1):29-30.

[2] 陈浩,王诗航,顾祖毅,等.基于 POI 数据的卷烟消费者行为研究[J].科技和产业,2019,19(1):76-80,85.

[3] 李晓亮,闫晓雯,马晓敏,等.基于目标消费者分析的卷烟品牌培育策略研究[J].中国管理信息化,2020,23(22):142-143.

[4] 蒋海浪,范剑波.基于C4.5算法的卷烟消费者购买行为的研究与分析[J].宁波工程学院学报,2019,31(4):48-53.

[5] 孙艳玲,张伟.消费者个体差异对卷烟消费动机、品牌偏好与购买行为的影响分析[J].特区经济,2016(5):144-146.

[6] 韩亚君,杨万青.湖南卷烟消费市场特征及发展方向:基于消费者行为角度分析[J].全国流通经济,2020(5):133-134.

Analysis of the Characteristics of the Cigarette Consumer Structure and Behavior

Abstract: Against consumer upgrading, there has been a noticeable trend towards diversification in cigarette consumer demand, with an increasing number of factors influencing their purchasing decisions. In light of this, and considering the unique characteristics of the cigarette consumption market, this paper surveys the structural features of cigarette consumers in 12 cities, including Kunming. The results indicate that the average duration of cigarette smoking among consumers is 10.62 years, with smoking usually starting between the ages of 17 and 34, and monthly cigarette expenditure accounting for 7.45% of the average monthly income. Additionally, this study delves into consumer behavior characteristics related to consumption motives, purchasing power, and habits to gain insights into quantity and expenditure patterns among cigarette consumers. By analyzing these consumers' structure and behavior traits, tobacco enterprises can effectively target specific market segments and increase their market share accordingly.

Keywords: Cigarette; The consumer market; Consumer structure; Consumer behavior

With the deepening of our country's market economy reform, the connotation of new consumption development, and changes in consumption patterns and demand improvement, it is imperative for cigarette enterprises to understand consumer trends and consumption patterns fully. They must continuously improve product specialization and differentiation in order to quickly capture the market amidst the backdrop of an upgraded consumption environment. Traditional cigarette brands not only vary in terms of variety, grade, taste, and price, but also face a gradually diversifying consumer demand. Therefore, tobacco enterprise marketing should no longer be limited to mere product promotion; instead, it should utilize big data technology to analyze consumer behavior and grasp traditional cigarette consumer demand trends. Innovation should be based on the existing production marketing service system to influence consumer behavior effectively.

In recent years, scholars have made significant research achievements in the study of cigarette consumption behavior. Guo Lijun et al.[1] proposed the establishment of a cigarette consumer data archive as a fundamental means for long-term data collection.

Chen Hao et al.[2] investigated the regional aggregation patterns, as well as the location and time preferences of consumer behavior within a cigarette enterprise. The findings from this research can offer valuable insights for informing product launches and marketing strategies within the cigarette industry. Li Xiao liang et al.[3] conducted an analysis on the characteristics of target consumers and their consumer behaviors, which informed strategies for cultivating cigarette brands based on these specific consumer segments. It is evident that consumer spending behaviors directly impact the sustainable development of cigarette brands. Therefore, it is essential to leverage big retail industry data to gain a deeper understanding of customers, grasp consumer sentiments, and monitor market developments effectively. Strengthening data analysis and application related to consumer spending behaviors will enable dynamic monitoring and facilitate growth within the cigarette brand enterprises.

In conclusion, against the backdrop of consumer upgrading, the intricate factors influencing cigarette consumer behavior, combined with the unpredictability of consumers' psychological and motivational drivers for cigarette consumption, contribute to the frequent and regular nature of their consumer behavior. Analyzing cigarette consumer behavior and identifying potential demand is fundamental to marketing development. Therefore, this article conducts research in 12 cities, including Kunming, to examine the patterns of consumer buying behavior and explore the structure and characteristics of consumer behavior within the cigarette consumption market. This will enable differentiation among cigarette enterprises based on consumer characteristics and target markets in order to increase market share.

1 Materials and Methods

1.1 Survey Scope and Object

Based on the demographic characteristics of traditional cigarette consumers, practical questionnaire analysis can reflect the market structure of traditional cigarette consumers and accurately capture the characteristics of the cigarette consumption group. Therefore, this study conducted a questionnaire survey on cigarette consumers over 18 years old living in Kunming, Hangzhou, Guangzhou, Chengdu, Lanzhou, Wuhan, Dali, Shanghai, Shenzhen, Chongqing, Liuzhou and Dalian.

1.2 Investigation Method

The questionnaire was collected using the code from the filling method. It mainly consists of two parts: consumer structural characteristics and consumer behavior. The structural characteristics include consumers' city of residence, age, smoking history, gender, occupation, educational level, and average monthly income. Consumer behavior includes the purchase decision-making process, buying power, and buying activities. It primarily analyzes purchase purpose, access to information about cigarettes, purchase factors influencing smoking habits, attitudes towards purchasing cigarettes, and satisfaction evaluation with cigarettes. A total of 8707 questionnaires were collected in this survey; 8088 were deemed valid. The effective sample size for each city is shown in Table 1.

Table 1 Basic Situation Investigation City Effective Sample Size

The City	Kunming	Hangzhou	Guangzhou	Chengdu	Lanzhou	Wuhan	Dali	Shanghai	Shenzhen	Chongqing	Liuzhou	Dalian	Total
Sample size	810	812	801	810	801	424	412	806	805	802	405	400	8088

2 Results and Analysis

2.1 Structural Characteristics of Cigarette Consumers

2.1.1 Age, Gender, and Income Distribution of Cigarette Consumers

Table 2 illustrates that the majority (93.95%) of cigarette consumers are between the ages of 18 to 55, with the highest percentage (63.80%) falling within the 26 to 45 age range of cigarette. The average age of cigarette consumers is 36.76. Furthermore, it is worth noting that over 35% of cigarette consumers in Kunming and Dali are aged between 18 to 25 years old, while in Dali specifically, this demographic accounts for approximately half (48.6%) of all cigarette consumers.

Table 2 Age Distribution of Cigarette Consumers

Age	Kunming	Hangzhou	Guangzhou	Chengdu	Lanzhou	Wuhan	Dali	Shanghai	Shenzhen	Chongqing	Dalian	Liuzhou
18-25	36.3	8.1	13.8	15.3	5.6	13.2	48.6	13.9	10.7	13.7	11.3	12.3
26-35	38.5	22.9	38.8	38.5	32.5	33.3	19.0	47.1	39.6	29.7	33.3	35.8
36-45	16.2	28.3	37.0	29.8	34.2	28.8	18.0	30.8	37.6	24.9	28.8	26.4
46-55	6.7	30.5	7.1	13.5	20.8	14.9	9.7	6.1	7.5	20.4	19.8	14.1
56-65	2.0	6.9	2.2	2.8	5.9	7.3	4.0	1.7	3.4	7.6	5.2	8.9

continue

Age	Kun ming	Hang zhou	Guang zhou	Cheng du	Lan zhou	Wu han	Da li	Shang hai	Shen zhen	Chong qing	Da lian	Liu zhou
>66	0.3	3.3	1.1	0.1	1.0	2.5	0.7	0.4	1.2	3.7	1.6	2.5

The table presents the age distribution and proportion of cigarette consumers in surveyed cities, represented as a percentage.

From a gender perspective (Figure 1), the majority of cigarette consumers are male, accounting for 80.74% of the total. The male-to-female ratio is close to 8∶2 overall, while in Chengdu, it is close to 7∶3, and in Hangzhou and Lanzhou, it is close to 9∶1.

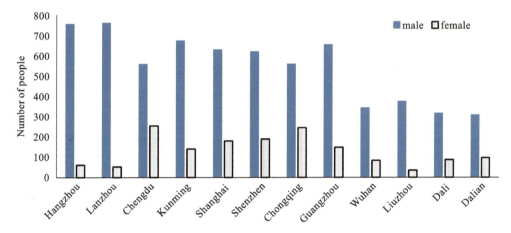

Figure 1　Gender Structure of Cigarette Consumers

As shown in Figure 2, the distribution of education levels among cigarette consumers is as follows: individuals with a master's degree or higher and individuals with junior high school education or lower account for 3.24% and 9.36%. The remaining percentage represents individuals with various levels of formal education, with the majority concentrated at the high school, technical secondary school, technical school, and college/university bachelor's degree level, totaling 82.31%.

Regarding career, priority is given that the highest proportion was represented by "workers, general staff, assistants and service personnel" at 24.78%, while retired personnel accounted for the lowest at 3.33%. No significant differences were observed between cities (Figure 3).

Figure 4 shows that the average monthly income of cigarette consumers is 7096.87 yuan, with 37.18% of consumers earning between 5000 to 7999 yuan per month. Additionally, 29.85% of consumers earn between 2000 to 4999 yuan monthly. Regarding specific cities, Shanghai has the highest average monthly income among cigarette

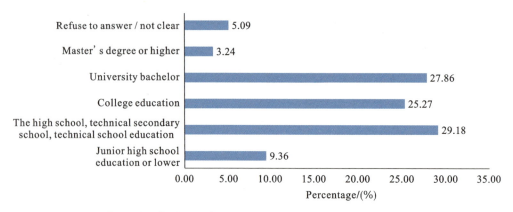

Figure 2　Statistics of Education Level of Cigarette Consumers

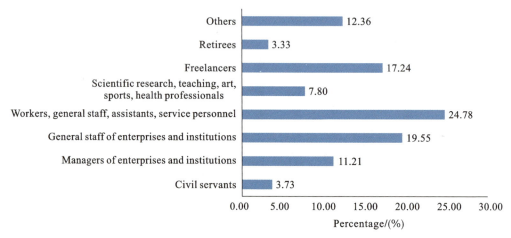

Figure 3　Cigarette Consumers' Professional Statistical Condition

consumers at 9136.48 yuan, while Kunming has the lowest at 5438.27 yuan.

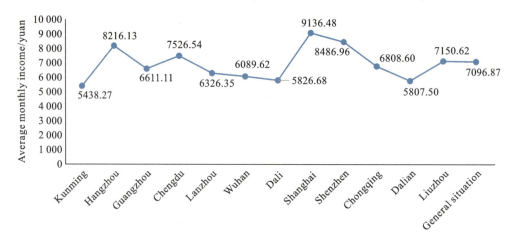

Figure 4　Statistics of Average Monthly Income of Cigarette Consumers in Each City

2.1.2 Distribution of Cigarette Consumers by Smoking History

The survey data (Table 3 and Figure 5) indicates that the average smoking history among cigarette consumers is relatively long, with an average of 10.62 years. The longest average smoking history was found in Hangzhou (13.35 years), while the shortest was in Kunming (8.06 years). In Hangzhou, Lanzhou, and Chongqing, over 50% of consumers have been smoking for more than 10 years; in Dali, Guangzhou, and Shenzhen, over 40% have been smoking for more than 5 years. On average, cigarette consumers tend to start smoking between the ages of 17 to 34.

Table 3 Average Years of Smoking History for Consumers of All Age Groups

Age	Average smoking history/years
18-25	3.96
26-35	7.91
36-45	11.60
46-55	17.20
56-65	22.39
>66	27.88
Average	10.62

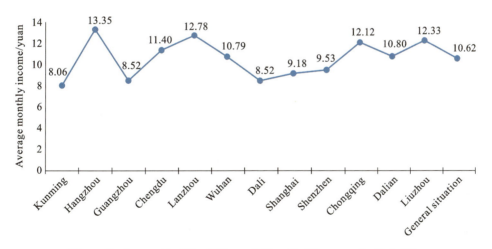

Figure 5 Average Smoking History of Cigarette Consumers in Each City

2.2 Consumption Motivation of Cigarette Consumers

2.2.1 Cigarettes Can Fulfill the Physical and Social Needs of Individuals

Table 4 illustrates that consumers purchase cigarettes primarily for physical needs and social needs. Specifically, work needs account for 19.44%, curiosity for 12.80%, outstanding personality for 10.63%, and social needs for 13.23%. Furthermore, the survey indicates that in Shenzhen and Guangzhou, the main reason for cigarette purchases is personal consumption; in Hangzhou, 0.76% of consumers buy cigarettes for social needs; in Liuzhou, consumers are driven by social communication needs, curiosity about cigarettes, and stress relief through smoking to purchase cigarettes; while in Shanghai, consumers are influenced by smokers around them and use cigarettes to showcase their personality. In terms of occupation, over half of retired individuals purchase cigarettes for personal consumption. In contrast, more than half of civil servants, enterprise managers, public institution managers, as well as professionals in scientific research, teaching, arts, sports, and health industries buy cigarettes both for personal use and social interaction purposes. It is evident that although optional to the general public's well-being or livelihoods, from a traditional perspective on cigarette consumer's consumption behavior in China, smoking can satisfy both the physiological and social requirements of individuals.

Table 4 Top Reasons Why Consumers Buy Cigarettes

Reasons	The number of people	Proportion/(%)
Curiosity	301	12.80
Outstanding personality	250	10.63
The effects of smoking people around you	730	31.05
Work needs	457	19.44
Social needs	311	13.23
To relieve stress	150	6.38
Can't remember	152	6.47

2.2.2 Cigarette Consumers Obtain Information through Various Channels

According to Figure 6, 35.04% of consumers acquire cigarette information from counter displays, while 29.19% rely on friends for introductions. In terms of specific cities, consumers in Kunming, Hangzhou, Guangzhou, and Lanzhou primarily receive cigarette information through counter displays and friends' recommendations. On the other hand, consumers in Chengdu mainly relies on friend introductions and online channels such as China Tobacco Net, while consumers in Shenzhen and Liuzhou predominantly use counter displays and online channels. Their surrounding environment largely influences consumers' exposure to cigarettes.

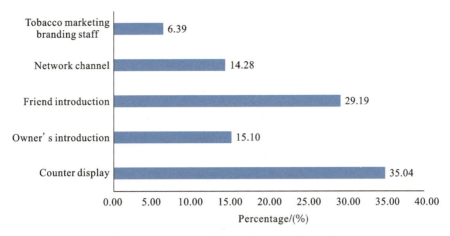

Figure 6 Access to Information about Cigarettes

2.3　The level of Cigarette Consumption by Consumers

2.3.1　Distribution of Purchase Prices for Cigarette Consumers

The level of economic development determines the consumption characteristics of a city, with different income consumers exhibiting varying levels of cigarette consumption. This investigation primarily focuses on the price of commonly purchased cigarettes and cigarette consumption patterns to explore the level of consumer consumption.

Survey data reveals that in cities such as Liuzhou and Dali, over 60% of consumers purchase cigarettes for under 20 yuan per package, while in Hangzhou, Guangzhou, and Shenzhen, more than 65% of consumers buy cigarettes priced at over 20 yuan per package. It was also observed that regardless of the purpose for which cigarette consumers make their purchases, their choice is largely influenced by price range (10-20 yuan per package followed by 20-30 yuan per package). The purchasing power for cigarettes varies across different cities nationwide; however, it is evident that consumer spending on purchasing and smoking cigarettes is concentrated within the price range of 10-30 yuan per package (see Table 5). In relatively economically underdeveloped cities, cigarette consumption levels tend to be lower.

2.3.2　The Influence of Income on Cigarette Consumption Among Consumers

As shown in Tables 6 and 7, consumers with a monthly income below CNY 1999 spend an average of CNY 246.08 on cigarettes each month. In contrast, those with a monthly income exceeding CNY 20000 have an average monthly expenditure of CNY 856.40 on cigarettes. Across twelve surveyed cities, cigarette-consuming individuals spend approximately CNY 529.02 monthly-accounting for about 7.45% of their average monthly income.

Table 5 Distribution of Purchase Prices for Cigarette Consumers

Price/(Yuan/package)	The number of people	Percentage/(%)
<10	757	9.36
10-20	3487	43.11
20-30	2291	28.33
30-40	723	8.94
40-60	487	6.02
60-80	222	2.74
>80	121	1.50

Table 6 The Purchasing Behavior of Cigarettes among Consumers with Varying Income Levels

Items	Amount					
Monthly income/yuan	<1999	2000-4999	5000-7999	8000-11999	12000-19999	>20000
Monthly expenditure on purchasing cigarettes/yuan	246.08	410.31	511.82	662.54	849.81	856.40

Table 7 Statistics on the Average Monthly Expenditure on Purchasing Cigarettes by Consumers in Each City

Cities	Monthly income/yuan	Monthly expenditure on purchasing cigarettes/yuan	Proportion/(%)
Kunming	5438.27	465.86	8.57
Hangzhou	8216.13	499.32	6.08
Guangzhou	6611.11	489.95	7.41
Chengdu	7526.54	665.68	8.84
Lanzhou	6326.35	526.17	8.32
Wuhan	6089.62	410.61	6.74
Dali	5826.68	550.75	9.45
Shanghai	9136.48	639.52	7.00
Shenzhen	8486.96	595.47	7.02
Chongqing	6808.60	496.82	7.30
Dalian	5807.50	380.25	6.55
Liuzhou	7150.62	485.68	6.79
Average	7096.87	529.02	7.45

In conclusion, the level of consumer cigarette consumption is influenced by their income. Higher-income consumers have more discretionary funds and tend to increase their cigarette consumption. On the other hand, lower-income consumers have limited disposable income, which restricts their cigarette consumption.

2.4 Cigarette Consumption Habits of Consumers

2.4.1 Consumers Primarily Purchase Cigarettes Out of Habit

The consumer behavior when it comes to cigarettes is primarily habitual. Survey data indicates that over 40% of consumers have a special affinity for certain brands and make long-term purchases. Less than 4% are more cautious in their buying habits and carefully consider their choices.

According to Table 8, in Hangzhou, Wuhan, Dalian, and Liuzhou, over 50% of consumers have a habit of purchasing and smoking a specific brand long-term; in Kunming, nearly 30% base their purchasing decisions on price; in Hangzhou, Shanghai, and Shenzhen, almost 30% compare different cigarette prices before making a purchase.

Table 8 Cigarette Purchasing Habits of Consumers in Different Cities (Unit: %)

Purchase and smoking habits	Kunming	Hangzhou	Guangzhou	Chengdu	Lanzhou	Wuhan	Dali	Shanghai	Shenzhen	Chongqing	Dalian	Liuzhou
Brands	32.1	57.1	40.7	43.6	39.8	54.6	38.9	38.7	37.0	48.3	52.5	51.4
Cost performance	24.8	31.4	27.0	21.5	26.7	25.2	27.7	29.5	30.6	24.3	27.3	22.0
Price level	30.0	6.7	23.1	13.7	24.9	13.4	15.7	11.8	18.8	11.0	11.8	14.3
The counter display	10.7	4.1	6.6	13.6	7.1	5.9	11.2	11.7	9.0	12.5	7.0	9.4
Selection difficulty	2.4	0.7	2.6	7.6	1.6	0.9	6.5	8.3	4.6	3.9	1.4	2.9

This study aims to examine the patterns of cigarette consumption habits across various urban areas.

2.4.2 Taste is the Primary Factor Influencing Consumer Purchasing Behavior of Cigarettes

As depicted in Figure 7, taste is the predominant factor influencing consumer cigarette purchases (66.83%), followed by price, brand, packaging, and public praise. The investigation revealed that over 20% of consumers frequently choose a particular brand due to high brand awareness, brand culture, classical appeal, long-standing history, good brand reputation, pure aroma smoke, and high-grade branding.

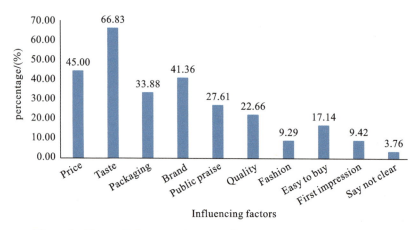

Figure 7　Factors Influencing Consumers' Decision to Purchase Cigarettes

2.5　The Number of Consumers Purchasing Cigarettes

2.5.1　Influenced by Daily Consumption and Consumer Demand

From a regional perspective, the purchasing behavior of consumers in each city varies slightly. According to survey data, 58.49% of consumers in Shanghai purchase by one piece, while 49.43% buy cigarettes by one pack in Shenzhen. The quantity of cigarettes purchased at one time is primarily associated with an individual's daily smoking habits; those who smoke more tend to purchase a larger quantity at once. As shown in Table 9, most consumers (58.70%) prefer to buy cigarettes in one pack or one piece. Survey data indicates that individuals who smoke less than five cigarettes per day typically purchase one pack at a time, while those who smoke over two packs per day tend to buy more than four pieces at once.

Table 9　Statistics on the Quantity of Cigarettes Purchased by Consumers Per Transaction

Quantity	The number of peoples	Proportion/(%)
1 package	579	24.63
2-3 packages	416	17.69
4-5 packages	229	9.74
6-9 packages	101	4.30
1 piece	801	34.07
2-3 pieces	168	7.15
more than 4 pieces	27	1.15
Say don't remember	30	1.27

2.5.2 The Location of Tobacco Purchase Influences the Quantity of Cigarettes Purchased

The quantity of cigarettes consumers purchase also correlates with the purchase location, the number bought at tobacco shops exceeds one piece. According to survey data, 42.21% of consumers bought cigarettes in 1 piece from tobacco shops, and 31.36% made their purchases 1 pack from convenience stores.

As depicted in Figure 8, over 23% of consumers typically purchase cigarettes at tobacco and liquor stores, and shopping malls, supermarkets, while a smaller percentage buy them at grocery stores, accounting for only 10.51%. In specific cities, more than half of consumers in Shanghai frequently buy cigarettes at tobacco shops, 40% in Liuzhou often make their purchases at convenience stores, and 30% in Chengdu usually buy cigarettes from grocery stores.

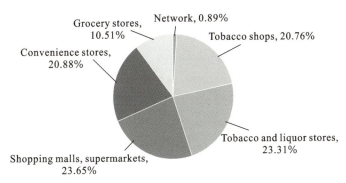

Figure 8 Distribution of Cigarette Purchasing by Consumers

3 Discussion and Conclusion

Currently, researchers[2, 4-6] commonly utilize POI data analysis technology, the decision tree C4.5 algorithm, the correspondence analysis method, the PSM model, and other methods to empirically analyze the consumption behavior of cigarette consumers. The research findings indicate that gender, age, social status, and other factors influence cigarette consumer behavior. Additionally, the integrated environment and individual conditions predominantly influence cigarette consumption behavior.

In this paper, against the backdrop of consumption upgrade, an investigation and analysis of the structural characteristics and consumer behavior of cigarette consumers was conducted. The results revealed the following:

(1) The structural characteristics of cigarette consumers are as follows: the age range of cigarette consumers is primarily 18-55 years old, with a predominantly male demographic (male to female ratio close to 8∶2). The average smoking history is 10.62

years, with the majority starting between the ages of 17-34. On average, monthly cigarette expenditure accounts for 7.45% of their income. Education levels are mainly concentrated in high school, technical secondary school, technical school, college, or university degree programs, accounting for approximately 82.31%.

(2) Major factors influencing consumer motivation for cigarette consumption include physiological needs and social needs. Additionally, it is essential to note that group dynamics significantly influence purchasing decisions among cigarette consumers, thus necessitating consideration as a critical factor affecting consumption behavior.

(3) Their income is critical in determining consumers' purchasing ability and disposable income. Cigarette prices significantly impact brand development, as reasonable pricing can enhance consumer purchasing power. However, pricing is a complex issue that requires consideration of not only cost factors but also whether it is acceptable to consumers. When launching new products, it is important to test the price and set it at a level generally recognized by consumers to create a sense of "material value" for them.

(4) There are various factors influencing consumer behavior towards cigarettes, including the taste of cigarettes, habits, personal daily consumption, and locations. Building credibility for cigarette brands can cultivate consumer recognition and consumption habits, ultimately improving product sales and market stability.

In conclusion, analyzing the structural characteristics and consumer behavior of cigarette consumers helps develop corresponding product brands and classifications while formulating marketing strategies. This enables cigarette brands to adapt to traditional consumer demands and allows tobacco enterprises to target specific markets based on consumer characteristics to improve market share and achieve sustainable development for the company.

References

[1] GUO L J, YE J, YAN D. "Internet + Cigarette Marketing" Thinking of the Consumer of the Archive Establishment[J]. Brand Research, 2020 (1): 29-30.

[2] CHEN H, WANG S H, GU Z Y, etc. Based on the POI Data of Cigarette Consumer Behavior Research[J]. Science and Technology and Industry, 2019, 12 (1): 76-80, 85.

[3] LI X L, YAN X W, MA X M, et al. Based on the Analysis of the Target Consumers Cigarette Brand Cultivation Strategy Research [J]. Management information in China, 2020, 23 (22): 142-143.

[4] JIANG H L, FAN J B. Algorithm based on C4.5 the Cigarette Consumer Buying Behavior Research and the Analysis[J]. Journal of Ningbo College of Engineering,

2019, 31 (4): 48-53.

[5] SUN Y L, ZHANG W. Influence of Individual Differences on Cigarette Consumption Motivation, Brand Preference and Purchase Behavior[J]. Special Zone Economy, 2016 (5): 144-146.

[6] HAN Y J, YANG W Q. Characteristics and Development Direction of Cigarette Consumption Market in Hunan Province: Based on the Perspective of Consumer Behavior[J]. The Circulation Economy, 2020 (5): 133-134.

包装偏好与市场前景

卷烟包装偏好的区域性及对象性差异分析

摘要：本研究以14种卷烟新品包装在昆明、南京等10个城市的市场调研数据为基础,分析了卷烟包装偏好的区域性差异和对象性差异。结果表明,卷烟包装偏好的区域性差异和对象性差异明显。不同城市在包装色彩、构图、总体印象和市场前景态度的评估上均存在明显差异,且西南地区和东部沿海地区差异明显;不同访问对象对包装色彩、构图、总体印象和市场前景态度的评估存在明显差异,零售户评价较高,商业公司从业人员评价适中,卷烟市场营销人员评价较低。

关键词:卷烟包装;偏好型;区域性差异;对象性差异

卷烟消费具有明显的区域性差异,不同类型消费者的卷烟消费倾向也有所不同,而卷烟包装形象和吸味是影响卷烟消费的两个重要因素,因此,对卷烟包装形象和吸味偏好进行区域性和对象性差异研究,对卷烟新产品的研发和销售有重要意义。

目前,国内关于卷烟吸味或烟叶品质差异性的研究较多[1-10],国内外很多研究及销售数据均表明卷烟消费倾向有明显的区域性差异,而对卷烟包装偏好的区域性和对象性差异研究却很少。为此,本研究从卷烟包装角度出发,对卷烟包装偏好的区域性和对象性差异进行研究,以期为卷烟新产品的研发和销售提供参考。

1 材料与方法

1.1 数据的采集及性状指标确定

在南京、杭州、昆明、广州、南宁、西安、成都、青岛、济南、石家庄10个城市对云南中烟14种卷烟新品的包装进行调研,调研对象为商业公司从业人员、卷烟市场营销人员和零售户。

性状指标包括定量指标和定性指标。定量指标为色彩(X_1)、构图(X_2)、总体印象

(X_3);定性指标为市场前景态度(X_4)。由于在问卷调查中定量部分和定性部分的某些样本存在信息缺失,为了保证信息得到最大限度的保留,分定量和定性两部分样本进行分析,其中定量分析有效样本数 3562 条,定性分析有效样本数 3362 条。详见表 1 和表 2。

表 1 云南中烟 14 种卷烟新品包装定量指标市场调查有效样本数 （单位:条）

调查城市	零售户	商业公司从业人员	市场营销人员	有效样本总数
成都	303	193	14	510
广州	84	112	70	266
杭州	112	210	238	560
济南	140	111	75	326
昆明	56	154	126	336
南京	97	186	97	380
南宁	112	112	84	308
青岛	140	56	14	210
石家庄	112	0	111	223
西安	136	233	74	443
合计	1292	1367	903	3562

表 2 云南中烟 14 种卷烟新品包装定性指标市场调查有效样本数 （单位:条）

调查城市	零售户	商业公司从业人员	市场营销人员	有效样本总数
成都	281	179	13	473
广州	78	104	65	247
杭州	104	195	221	520
济南	130	103	70	303
昆明	55	141	114	310
南京	90	197	102	389
南宁	104	104	78	286
青岛	130	52	13	195
石家庄	104	0	103	207
西安	115	242	75	432
合计	1191	1317	854	3362

1.2 分析方法

包装色彩、构图、总体印象 3 个定量指标均为百分制,分数越高代表受访者满意度越高;定性指标市场前景态度包括访问对象认为该产品市场前景良好、市场前景一般和市场前景不好这 3 个选项。针对定量指标,主要采用两因素方差分析结合多重比较方法对不同城市和不同访问对象的评分进行分析;针对定性指标,则采用列联表分析和卡方检验进行分析。

采用统计软件 R 和 Excel 进行数据分析。

2 结果与分析

2.1 不同城市之间卷烟包装色彩、构图和总体印象评价差异分析

从表3可以看出,不同城市之间卷烟包装色彩、构图和总体印象评价的差异均不能满足方差齐性要求($P<0.001$),说明在后续的多重比较分析中,需采用 Games-Howell 多重比较方法(不用假定方差齐性)进行差异分析。

表3 不同城市之间卷烟包装色彩、构图和总体印象评价的方差齐性分析结果

包装指标	Levene 统计量	自由度1	自由度2	P
色彩	11.305	28	3534	<0.001
构图	12.742	28	3534	<0.001
总体印象	12.939	28	3534	<0.001

从表4可以看出,不同城市之间卷烟包装色彩、构图和总体印象评价的方差分析均存在显著差异($P<0.001$),说明后续可采用 Games-Howell 多重比较方法进一步统计不同城市之间卷烟包装评价的具体差异。

表4 不同城市之间卷烟包装色彩、构图和总体印象评价的方差分析结果

包装指标	平方和	自由度	均方	F	P
色彩	16108.892	9	1789.877	22.361	<0.001
构图	17004.748	9	1889.416	23.309	<0.001
总体印象	16414.397	9	1823.822	22.968	<0.001

从图1可以看出,在色彩方面,昆明市的卷烟包装评分最高,并与其余城市之间差异显著($P<0.05$);杭州市和南京市的卷烟包装评分最低,并与其余城市之间差异显著($P<0.05$)。从图2可以看出,在构图方面,昆明市的卷烟包装评分最高,并与其余城市之间差异显著($P<0.05$);杭州市和南京市的卷烟包装评分最低,并与其余城市之间差异显著($P<0.05$)。从图3可以看出,在总体印象方面,昆明市的卷烟包装评分最高,并与其余城市之间差异显著($P<0.05$);石家庄市、杭州市和南京市的卷烟包装评分最低,并与其余城市之间差异显著($P<0.05$)。分析结果说明不同城市在卷烟包装色彩、构图和总体印象的评分上均存在差异,且3个指标差异情况趋势基本一致,大致表现为西南地区(如昆明、成都)评分较高,而东部沿海地区(如杭州、南京)评分较低。

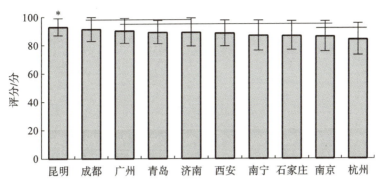

图 1　不同城市之间卷烟包装色彩均值-标准差 Games-Howell 多重比较

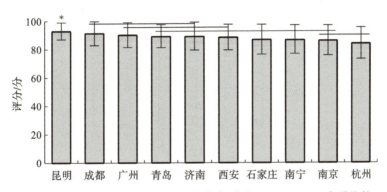

图 2　不同城市之间卷烟包装构图均值-标准差 Games-Howell 多重比较

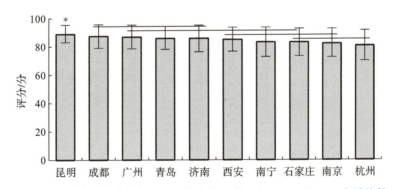

图 3　不同城市之间卷烟包装总体印象均值-标准差 Games-Howell 多重比较

2.2　不同访问对象对卷烟包装色彩、构图和总体印象评价的差异分析

从表 5 可以看出,不同访问对象对卷烟包装色彩、构图和总体印象评价的方差分析均存在显著差异($P<0.001$),说明后续可采用 Games-Howell 多重比较方法进一步统计不同访问对象之间的具体差异。

表 5　不同访问对象对卷烟包装色彩、构图和总体印象评价的方差分析结果

包装指标	平方和	自由度	均方	F	P
色彩	4591.384	2	2295.692	28.681	<0.001
构图	4796.234	2	2398.117	29.585	<0.001
总体印象	5454.623	2	2727.312	34.345	<0.001

从图 4 至图 6 可以看出,在卷烟包装色彩、构图、总体印象方面,均为零售户评分最高,商业公司从业人员评分适中,市场营销人员评分最低,且三者之间差异显著($P<0.05$)。分析结果说明不同访问对象对卷烟包装色彩、构图和总体印象评价均存在差异,且 3 个指标差异情况趋势完全一致。

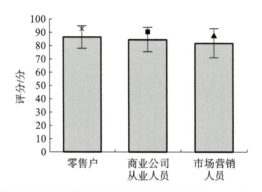

图 4　不同访问对象之间卷烟包装色彩均值-标准差 Games-Howell 多重比较

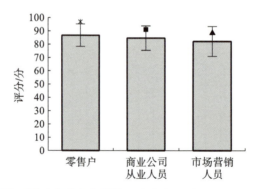

图 5　不同访问对象之间卷烟包装构图均值-标准差 Games-Howell 多重比较

2.3　不同城市对市场前景态度的列联表分析

对表 6 进行 χ^2 检验,结果显示 $P<0.05$,即不同城市对卷烟新品的市场前景看法不一致。成都和济南认为市场前景良好的占比较高,均超过 50%,而杭州认为市场前景良好的占比较低,仅 30.4%。认为市场前景良好的占比相对高的城市仅有 3 个,而认为市场前景一般的占比相对高的城市有 6 个,认为市场前景良好和市场前景一般的占比基本相同的城市为广州。

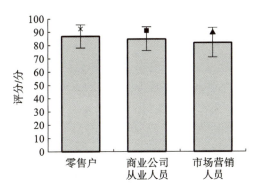

图 6 不同访问对象之间卷烟包装总体印象均值-标准差 Games-Howell 多重比较

表 6 不同城市对 14 种卷烟新品市场前景态度的调研结果　　　　　　　　　　　（单位：条）

调查城市	市场前景良好	市场前景一般	市场前景不好	合计	市场前景良好占比/(%)
南京	171	190	28	389	44.0
南宁	133	116	37	286	46.5
广州	113	110	24	247	45.7
成都	271	158	44	473	57.3
昆明	130	166	14	310	41.9
杭州	158	286	76	520	30.4
济南	154	127	22	303	50.8
石家庄	89	106	12	207	43.0
西安	172	233	27	432	39.8
青岛	83	105	7	195	42.6

2.4　不同访问对象对市场前景态度的列联表分析

对表 7 进行 χ^2 检验,结果显示 $P<0.05$,即不同访问对象对卷烟新品的市场前景看法不一致。零售户认为市场前景良好的占比超过 50%,而市场营销人员认为市场前景良好的占比较低,仅 34.7%。

表 7 不同访问对象对 14 种卷烟新品市场前景态度的调研结果　　　　　　　　　（单位：条）

访问对象	有效样本数				市场前景良好占比/(%)
	市场前景良好	市场前景一般	市场前景不好	合计	
商业公司从业人员	540	681	96	1317	41.0
市场营销人员	296	421	137	854	34.7
零售户	638	495	58	1191	53.6

3 小结

本次研究主要针对卷烟新品的包装色彩、构图和总体印象以及市场前景态度进行不同城市和不同访问对象间的差异分析和列联表分析。结果表明，不同城市在卷烟新品包装色彩、构图和总体印象的评分上均存在差异，且3个指标差异情况趋势基本一致，大致表现为西南地区（如昆明、成都）评分较高，而东部沿海地区（如杭州、南京）评分较低；在市场前景态度方面也存在同样的趋势，即成都认为市场前景良好的占比较高，杭州认为市场前景良好的占比较低，大部分城市认为市场前景一般。不同访问对象对卷烟新品包装色彩、构图和总体印象的评分也存在差异，且3个指标差异情况趋势一致，均表现为零售户评分较高，商业公司从业人员评分适中，市场营销人员评分较低；在市场前景态度方面也存在同样的趋势，即零售户认为市场前景良好的占比最高，商业公司从业人员认为市场前景良好的占比居中，市场营销人员认为市场前景良好的占比最低。

参考文献

[1] 宋旭艳,柯炜昌,张耀华,等.环境湿度对卷烟理化指标及感官质量的影响[J].烟草科技,2007(10):9-13.

[2] 林永明,杨国荣,缪明明,等.香烟评吸质量指标的地理区域差异分析[J].湖北农业科学,2009,48(12):3063-3067.

[3] 李向阳,邓云龙,邓建华,等.普洱市烤烟评吸质量特性及其区域差异研究[J].中国农学通报,2010,26(11):86-91.

[4] 高川川,赵瑞峰,刘珊,等.区域环境对卷烟主流烟气化学特性和感官质量的影响[J].烟草科技,2010(6):51-56.

[5] 杨君,邱杰,胡安福,等.吸烟人群饮食习惯引起的吸烟（烟气）偏好分析[J].科技通报,2014,30(9):42-46.

[6] 张斌.卷烟包装设计与卷烟营销的关系[J].湖南包装,2003(1):14-16.

[7] 白振松.浅述中式卷烟包装设计的发展方向[J].当代经济,2009(4):16-17.

[8] 冯和平.浅析卷烟包装的创意与文化品位[J].中国科技博览,2009(9):112.

[9] 杨君,胡安福,肖卫强,等.卷烟包装形象区域性差异分析[J].安徽农学通报,2011,17(21):137-138.

[10] 马永峰.浅析卷烟包装设计[J].发展,2012(6):119-120.

Analysis of Regional and Object Differences in Cigarette Packaging Preferences

Abstract: Based on market research data of 14 new cigarette packages in 10 cities, including Kunming and Nanjing, this paper analyzes the regional and object differences in cigarette packaging preferences. The results show that there are significant regional and object differences in cigarette packaging preferences; there are significant differences in the evaluation of color, composition, overall impression of packaging, and market prospects attitude in different cities, and there are significant differences between southwest and eastern coastal regions; there are significant differences in the evaluation of color, composition, overall impression of packaging, and market prospects attitudes among different interviewees, with retailers having a higher evaluation degree, commercial company employees having a moderate evaluation degree, and cigarette marketers having a lower evaluation degree.

Keywords: Cigarette packaging; Preference type; Regional differences; Object differences

Cigarette consumption has noticeable regional differences, and different types of consumers have different consumption tendencies. Cigarette packaging image and smoking preference are two critical factors affecting cigarette consumption. Therefore, the research on regional and object differences in cigarette packaging image and smoking preference is of great significance to develop and sell new cigarette products.

There are many domestic studies on cigarette smoking or tobacco leaf quality differences[1-10]. Many domestic and foreign studies and sales data show apparent regional differences in cigarette consumption tendencies, but few studies have examined regional and object differences in cigarette packaging. Therefore, this study studies the regional and object differences in cigarette packaging from the perspective of cigarette packaging to provide a reference for developing and selling new cigarette products.

1 Materials and Methods

1.1 Data Collection and Determination of Character Indicators

The packaging of 14 new cigarette products of China Tobacco of Yunnan Corporation was investigated in 10 cities, including Nanjing, Hangzhou, Kunming, Guangzhou, Nanning, Xi'an, Chengdu, Qingdao, Jinan, and Shijiazhuang. The respondents were employees of commercial companies, cigarette marketing personnel, and retail households.

The character indicators included quantitative indicators and qualitative indicators. The quantitative indicators are color (X_1), composition (X_2), and overall impression (X_3); the qualitative indicator is market prospects attitude (X_4). Because some samples in the quantitative part and the qualitative part of the questionnaire survey have information missing, in order to ensure the maximum retention of information, the quantitative and qualitative samples are analyzed, among which the quantitative analysis has 3562 effective samples, and the qualitative analysis has 3362 effective samples. See Table 1 and Table 2 for details.

Table 1 Quantitative Indicators of Package of 14 New Cigarette Products of China Tobacco of Yunnan Corporation Effective Sample Number of Market Survey   (Unit: pack)

Survey cities	Retail households	Employees of commercial companies	Cigarette marketing personnel	Total number of effective samples
Chengdu	303	193	14	510
Guangzhou	84	112	70	266
Hangzhou	112	210	238	560
Jinan	140	111	75	326
Kunming	56	154	126	336
Nanjing	97	186	97	380
Nanning	112	112	84	308
Qingdao	140	56	14	210
Shijiazhuang	112	0	111	223
Xi'an	136	233	74	443
Total	1292	1367	903	3562

Table 2 Qualitative Indicators of Package of 14 New Cigarette Products of China Tobacco of Yunnan Corporation Effective Sample Number of Market Survey   (Unit: pack)

Survey cities	Retail households	Employees of commercial companies	Cigarette marketing personnel	Total number of effcctive samples
Chengdu	281	179	13	473
Guangzhou	78	104	65	247

continue

Survey cities	Retail households	Employees of commercial companies	Cigarette marketing personnel	Total number of effective samples
Hangzhou	104	195	221	520
Jinan	130	103	70	303
Kunming	55	141	114	310
Nanjing	90	197	102	389
Nanning	104	104	78	286
Qingdao	130	52	13	195
Shijiazhuang	104	0	103	207
Xi'an	115	242	75	432
Total	1191	1317	854	3362

1.2 Analysis Method

Among the three quantitative indicators, color, composition, and overall impression of packaging are all based on a hundred-mark system, with the higher the score, the higher the respondent's satisfaction; market prospect attitude of the qualitative indicator, includes the three options of optimistic market prospect, general market prospect and poor market prospect of the product. For the quantitative indicators, two-factor variance analysis combined with multiple comparison methods are mainly used to analyze the scores of different cities and interviewees; for the qualitative indicators, contingency table analysis and chi-square test are used for statistical analysis.

Statistical software R and Excel are used for data analysis.

2 Results and Analysis

2.1 Analysis of Differences in Cigarette Packaging Color, Composition, and Overall Impression Evaluation among Different Cities

As can be seen from Table 3, the differences in cigarette packaging color, composition, and overall impression evaluation among different cities cannot meet the requirements of variance homogeneity ($P < 0.001$), indicating that in the subsequent multiple comparison analysis, the Games-Howell multiple comparison method (without assuming variance homogeneity) should be used for difference analysis.

Table 3　Variance Homogeneity Analysis Results of Cigarette Packaging Color, Composition, and Overall Impression Evaluation among Different Cities

Packaging indicators	Levene statistic	df_1	df_2	P
Color	11.305	28	3534	<0.001
Composition	12.742	28	3534	<0.001
Overall impression	12.939	28	3534	<0.001

As can be seen from Table 4, the variance analysis of cigarette packaging color, composition, and overall impression evaluation among different cities showed significant differences ($P<0.001$), indicating that the Games-Howell multiple comparison method can be used to further statistically analyze the specific differences in cigarette packaging evaluation among different cities.

Table 4　Variance Analysis Results of Cigarette Packaging Color, Composition, and Overall Impression Evaluation among Different Cities

Packaging indicators	SS	df	MS	F	P
Color	16108.892	9	1789.877	22.361	<0.001
Composition	17004.748	9	1889.416	23.309	<0.001
Overall impression	16414.397	9	1823.822	22.968	<0.001

As can be seen from Figure 1, in terms of color, the cigarette packaging score of Kunming is the highest and significantly different from that of other cities ($P<0.05$), while the scores of Hangzhou and Nanjing are the lowest and significantly different from those of other cities ($P<0.05$). As can be seen from Figure 2, in terms of composition, the cigarette packaging score of Kunming is the highest and significantly different from that of other cities ($P<0.05$), while the scores of Hangzhou and Nanjing are the lowest and significantly different from those of other cities ($P<0.05$). As can be seen from Figure 3, in terms of overall impression, the cigarette packaging score of Kunming is the highest and significantly different from that of other cities ($P<0.05$), while the scores of Shijiazhuang, Hangzhou, and Nanjing are the lowest and significantly different from those of other cities ($P<0.05$). This indicates differences in the cigarette packaging scores of color, composition, and overall impression in different cities. The differences in the three indicators are consistent, roughly showing that the scores of southwest region (such as Kunming and Chengdu) are higher. In comparison, the scores of eastern coastal region (such as Hangzhou and Nanjing) are lower.

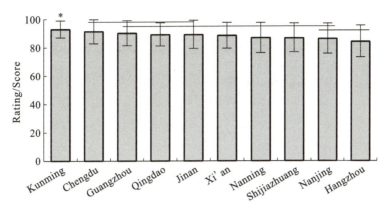

Figure 1　Mean-Standard Deviation Games-Howell Multiple Comparison of Cigarette Packaging Color among Different Cities

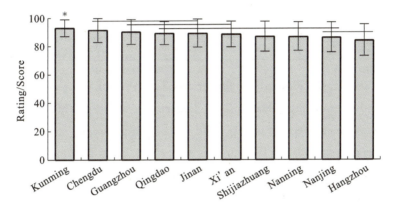

Figure 2　Mean-Standard Deviation Games-Howell Multiple Comparison of Cigarette Packaging Composition among Different Cities

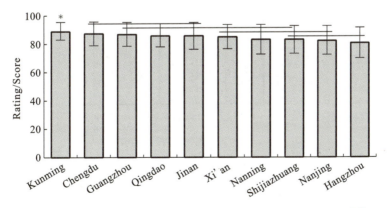

Figure 3　Mean-Standard Deviation Games-Howell Multiple Comparison of Cigarette Packaging Overall Impression among Different Cities

2.2 Difference Analysis of Different Interviewees' Impressions on Cigarette Packaging Color, Composition, and Overall Impression Evaluation

As can be seen from Table 5, the variance analysis of the differences in cigarette packaging color, composition, and overall impression among different interviewees has significant differences ($P < 0.001$), indicating that the Games-Howell multiple comparison method can be used to further calculate the specific differences among different interviewees.

Table 5 Variance Analysis Results of Different Interviewees' Impressions on Cigarette Packaging Color, Composition, and Overall Impression Evaluation

Packaging indicators	SS	df	MS	F	P
color	4591.384	2	2295.692	28.681	<0.001
composition	4796.234	2	2398.117	29.585	<0.001
overall impression	5454.623	2	2727.312	34.345	<0.001

As can be seen from Figure 4 to Figure 6, in terms of cigarette packaging color, composition, and overall impression, retail households score the highest, employees of commercial companies score moderately, and marketing personnel score the lowest, with significant differences among the three indicators ($P<0.05$). This indicates that different interviewees have different opinions on cigarette packaging color, composition, and overall impression, and the differences among the three indicators are entirely consistent.

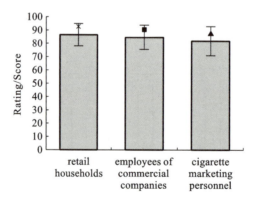

Figure 4 Mean-Standard Deviation Games-Howell Multiple Comparison of Cigarette Packaging Color among Different Interviewees

2.3 Analysis of the Market Prospects Attitude of Different Cities

The χ^2 test was performed in Table 6, and the result showed $P<0.05$, indicating that different cities had different views on the market prospects of new cigarette brands.

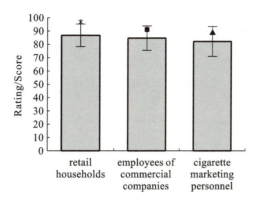

Figure 5 Mean-Standard Deviation Games-Howell Multiple Comparison of Cigarette Packaging Composition among Different Interviewees

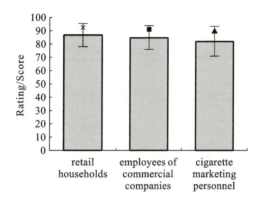

Figure 6 Mean-Standard Deviation Games-Howell Multiple Comparison of Cigarette Packaging Overall Impression among Different Interviewees

Chengdu and Jinan had a higher proportion of people who believed that the market prospects were promising, exceeding 50%. In comparison, Hangzhou had a lower proportion of people who believed that the market prospects were promising, only 30.4%. Only 3 cities had a relatively high proportion of people who believed the market prospects were promising. In comparison, 6 cities had a relatively high proportion of people who believed that the market prospects were general. The proportion of people who believed that the market prospects were promising and general was the same in Guangzhou.

Table 6 Survey Results of Different Cities' Attitudes toward the Market Prospects of 14 New Cigarette Brands (Unit: packs)

Survey city	Optimistic market prospect	General market prospect	Poor market prospect	Total	Market prospect is optimistic (accounting for %)
Nanjing	171	190	28	389	44.0

continue

Survey city	Optimistic market prospect	General market prospect	Poor market prospect	Total	Market prospect is optimistic (accounting for %)
Nanning	133	116	37	286	46.5
Guangzhou	113	110	24	247	45.7
Chengdu	271	158	44	473	57.3
Kunming	130	166	14	310	41.9
Hangzhou	158	286	76	520	30.4
Jinan	154	127	22	303	50.8
Shijiazhuang	89	106	12	207	43.0
Xi'an	172	233	27	432	39.8
Qingdao	83	105	7	195	42.6

2.4 Contingency Table Analysis of Market Prospects Attitude of Different Interviewees

The χ^2 test was performed in Table 7, and the result showed $P < 0.05$, indicating that different interviewees had different opinions on the market prospects of new cigarette brands. More than 50% of retailers believed that the market prospects were promising, while the proportion of marketers who believed that the market prospects were promising was relatively low, only 34.7%.

Table 7　Survey Results of Different Interviewees' Attitudes toward the Market Prospects of 14 New Cigarette Brands　　　　　　　　　　　(Unit: packs)

Interviewees	Number of Effective samples				Market prospect is optimistic (accounting for %)
	Optimistic market prospect	General market prospect	Poor market prospect	Total	
commercial company employees	540	681	96	1317	41.0
cigarette marketing personnel	296	421	137	854	34.7
retail households	638	495	58	1191	53.6

3　Summary

This study mainly conducted difference and contingency table analyses among cities and interviewed objects on the color, composition, overall impression, and market prospects attitude of new cigarette packaging. The results show that there are differences in the color, composition and overall impression of new cigarette packaging in different cities, and the trend of the three indicators is basically consistent, roughly showing that the southwest region (such as Kunming, Chengdu) has a higher score, while the eastern coastal region (such as Hangzhou, Nanjing) has a lower score; the same trend also exists in the market prospects attitude, namely, the proportion of optimistic market prospects in Chengdu is higher, the proportion of optimistic market prospects in Hangzhou is lower, and most cities think that the market prospects are general; different interview objects also have differences in the color, composition and overall impression of new cigarette packaging, and the trend of the three indicators is consistent, showing that retailers have a higher score, commercial company employees have a moderate score, and marketing personnel have a lower score; the same trend also exists in terms of market prospects, with retailers accounting for the highest proportion of optimistic market prospects, commercial company employees in the middle, and marketing personnel accounting for the lowest proportion of optimistic market prospects.

References

[1] SONG X Y, KE W C, ZHANG Y H, et al. Effects of Environmental Humidity on Physical and Chemical Indexes and Sensory Quality of Cigarettes[J]. Tobacco Science and Technology, 2007(10): 9-13.

[2] LIN Y M, YANG G R, MIAO M M, et al. Analysis of Geographic Regional Differences in Smoking Quality Indexes of Cigarettes[J]. Hubei Agricultural Sciences, 2009, 48(12): 3063-3067.

[3] LI X Y, DENG Y L, DENG J H, et al. Research on Pu'er Flue-Cured Tobacco's Smoking Quality Characteristics and Regional Differences[J]. Chinese Agricultural Science Bulletin, 2010, 26(11): 86-91.

[4] GAO C C, ZHAO R F, LIU S, et al. Effects of Regional Environment on Mainstream Cigarette Smoke Chemical Characteristics and Sensory Quality[J]. Tobacco Science and Technology, 2010(6): 51-56.

[5] YANG J, QIU J, HU A F, et al. Analysis of Smoking (Smoke) Preference Caused by the Smoking Population's Dietary Habits[J]. Science and Technology Bulletin, 2014(9): 42-46.

[6] ZHANG B. The Relationship between Cigarette Packaging Design and Cigarette Marketing[J]. Hunan Packaging, 2003(1): 14-16.

[7] BAI Z S. Brief Analysis of the Development Direction of Chinese Cigarette Packaging Design[J]. Contemporary Economy, 2009(4): 16-17.

[8] FENG H P. Brief Analysis of Cigarette Packaging Innovation and Cultural Taste [J]. China Science and Technology Expo, 2009 (9): 112.

[9] YANG J, HU A F, XIAO W Q, et al. Analysis of Regional Differences in Cigarette Packaging Image[J]. Anhui Agricultural Science Bulletin, 2011, 17 (21): 137-138.

[10] MA Y F. Brief Analysis of Cigarette Packaging Design[J]. Development, 2012 (6): 119-120.

卷烟包装特性与市场前景间的多序列相关分析

摘要：本文以云产卷烟 14 种新品在广州等 10 个城市的市场调研数据为基础，采用多序列相关分析方法分析了卷烟产品包装特性与市场前景的相关性，结果表明：①卷烟包装的总体印象评价得分基本由色彩得分和构图得分所决定，且色彩和构图得分对总体印象得分具有协同作用；②卷烟包装色彩、构图和总体印象评分越高，其市场前景越偏向于看好的趋势，而评分越低，其市场前景越偏向于不好的趋势。

关键词：包装特性；市场前景；多序列相关分析

卷烟包装是产品的一部分，是用来传递信息、出售卷烟、维护质量和品牌信誉的，同时，其与卷烟品牌一样，对消费者起到知觉线索的作用。我国人口众多，对卷烟的需求量也特别大，而我国的卷烟品牌也不少，那么如何提升一个卷烟品牌的销售量呢？除了卷烟的质量以外，价格和包装质量也是消费者购买卷烟的重要参考条件[1]。如果品牌的作用是使目标消费群体能够清晰记住品牌的特征和品牌的核心价值，那么包装设计就是实现这种功能的有效途径[2]。

色彩和构图在包装设计中占有特别重要的地位。不同的色彩能引起消费者不同的心理反应。因而，正确运用包装色彩的搭配方法，对保持卷烟产品的风格和对消费者心理的诱导起着良好的作用[3]。构图可以细致刻画和着力渲染产品的质感、形态和功能用途，将产品精美的质地引人入胜地呈现出来，给人以逼真的现实感，使消费者对所宣传的产品产生一种亲切感和信任感[3,4]。目前已有卷烟包装对于消费者群体的影响的相关研究报道，其中徐晓文[5]对昆明市场的研究调查显示，有超过半数的消费者注重香烟的包装；石凤学等人[6]研究发现，包装特性中色彩、构图、质感、铝箔纸和过滤嘴与吸味特性中香气、舒适度和口感存在极显著中度相关关系；另外，凤伟[7]研究发现，不同的人对包装设计中的色彩有着不同的心理感受，因此特定颜色的受众范围也不同；杨君等人[8]研究发现，不同地区的卷烟消费者对包装形象的偏好有着明显的差异，可以根据各地域卷烟消费者的颜色偏好，进行主配色调的设计，选取大多数目标消费群体青睐的风格；云南重点高端卷烟品牌消费调查研究[9]中发现，在广东省，包装为首选消费因素的比例是天津、重庆、辽宁、浙江等省市的 2 倍以上，重要性排位也比较靠前。

但是在卷烟新产品市场测试中，其包装设计上的色彩、构图与消费者对其总体印象和市场前景态度是否存在关联性，却没有进行相关研究。因此，本研究进一步分析卷烟包装设计上的色彩、构图与消费者对其总体印象和市场前景态度的关联性，从包装评价的角度为提高新产品的上市成功率提供理论参考。

1 材料与方法

1.1 数据的采集及性状指标确定

本文的研究数据来源于云产卷烟 14 种新品包装的市场调研(表 1),调研地点为南京、杭州、昆明、广州、南宁、西安、成都、青岛、济南、石家庄 10 个城市,调研对象为商业公司从业人员、卷烟市场营销人员和零售户。采集有效问卷 264 份,有效数据 3696 条。

性状指标包括定量指标和定性指标,定量指标为色彩 X_1、构图 X_2、总体印象 X_3,定性指标为市场前景态度 X_4。

表 1　云产卷烟 14 种新品包装市场调查概况　　　　　　（单位:份）

调查城市	商业公司从业人员	市场营销人员	零售户	有效问卷数
南京	16	7	8	31
杭州	15	18	8	41
昆明	11	9	4	24
广州	8	5	6	19
南宁	8	6	8	22
西安	20	6	10	36
成都	14	1	21	36
青岛	4	1	10	15
济南	8	5	10	23
石家庄	0	8	9	17
有效问卷数	104	66	94	264

1.2 分析方法

包装色彩、构图、总体印象三个定量指标(包装特性指标)均为百分制,分数越高代表受访者满意度越高;定性指标市场前景态度主要包括访问者认为该产品市场前景看好、市场前景一般和市场前景不好这三个选项。对包装特性指标内部的统计分析主要采用相关分析和逐步回归分析来进行;对于包装特性指标与市场前景态度(定性指标)之间的统计分析,由于市场前景态度特征变量属于分类变量类型,且包装特性指标数据属于连续变量类型,研究它们之间的关系应采用多序列相关分析[10]来找出包装特性指标中与市场前景态度具有相关性的指标。多序列相关分析是一种修正的 Pearson 相关分析,其计算公式如下:

$$\rho_s = \frac{\rho_p \sigma_y}{\sum_{j=1}^{r-1} \Phi(\tau_j)(y_{j+1} - y_j)}$$

式中,ρ_s 是 X(例如:色彩或者构图)和潜在变量 Y(市场前景态度)的多序列相关系数;ρ_p 是 X 和 Y 的 Pearson 相关系数;σ_y 是 Y 的标准差;$\Phi(\tau_j)$ 是第 j 类别的正态密度函数值的上限;y_{j+1} 和 y_j 是分类性状的值;r 是类别的数目。

本文采用的多序列相关分析利用 R 软件中的 polycor 程序包实现。

2 结果与分析

2.1 包装特性指标的相关分析和逐步回归分析

从表 2 可以看出,三个包装特性指标(色彩、构图和总体印象)之间均具有较高的正相关性且达到了 $P<0.01$ 的显著性水平,说明卷烟包装在色彩、构图和总体印象方面的关联程度较高。

表 2 包装特性指标之间的相关分析表

项目	色彩	构图	总体印象
色彩	1		
构图	0.910**	1	
总体印象	0.955**	0.958**	1

注:** 表示相关系数显著性水平达到 $P<0.01$。

对包装特性指标中的色彩、构图(自变量)与总体印象(因变量)进行逐步回归分析后建立了线性回归方程,发现方程达到 $P<0.01$ 的显著性水平,且 R^2 为 0.959,标准误为 1.947。从表 3 可知,两个包装特性指标(色彩、构图)回归系数均达到 $P<0.01$ 的显著性水平,说明卷烟包装的总体印象得分基本是由色彩得分和构图得分所决定的,知道了色彩得分和构图得分,可以通过回归方程预测出总体印象得分。

表 3 包装特性指标构图、色彩与总体印象的回归方程检验表

回归项	回归系数	标准误	通径系数	t	P
常数项	0.746	0.307	—	2.430	0.015
构图	0.510	0.008	0.517	60.375	<0.001
色彩	0.483	0.009	0.485	56.673	<0.001

从图 1 可以看出,增加色彩或构图的得分均可以提升总体印象得分,但是要达到总体印象得分的最大提升,需要同时增加色彩和构图的得分,两者具有协同作用。

图 2 表示所构建的回归方程的实测值和预测值离散程度,可以看出,两者基本位于对角线附近(点位于对角线上表示没有差异),差异较小。

2.2 包装特性指标与市场前景态度的多序列相关分析

对消费者对卷烟新品市场前景的态度(看好、一般、不看好)进行调查后,采用多序列相

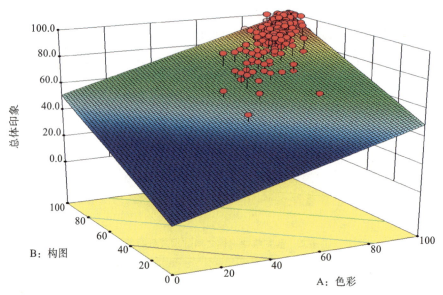

图 1 包装特性指标构图、色彩与总体印象的反应面图

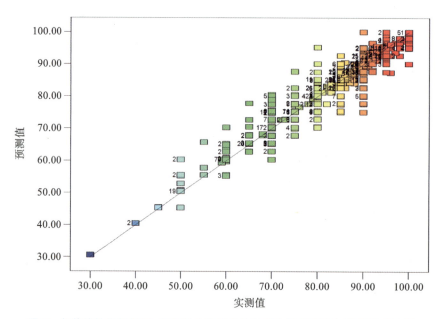

图 2 包装特性指标构图、色彩与总体印象的回归方程实测值与预测值对比图

关分析来评估三种态度与三个包装特性定量指标(色彩、构图和总体印象)之间的关系。从表 4 可知，三种市场前景态度与三个包装特性指标间的多序列相关系数均在 0.75 左右，且达到 $P<0.001$ 的显著性水平，说明色彩、构图和总体印象与三种市场前景态度具有较高的相关性，卷烟包装色彩、构图和总体印象评分越高，其市场前景越偏向于看好的趋势，而评分越低，其市场前景越偏向于不好的趋势。

表 4　包装特性指标与市场前景态度之间的多序列相关分析检验表

包装特性指标	与市场前景态度的多序列相关系数	标准误	卡方值	P 值
色彩	－0.738	0.009	821.1	<0.001
构图	－0.750	0.009	772.9	<0.001
总体印象	－0.769	0.008	833.4	<0.001

进一步通过箱线图(图 3~图 5)对三种市场前景态度与三个包装特性指标间的关系进行探索,箱体表示值在 95%的置信区间内,三角形表示均值,平行粗线表示中位数。从图上可知,色彩、构图和总体印象的均值水平由市场前景看好至市场前景不好有明显下降的趋势且分值下降较为明显(90→80→70)。认为市场前景看好的群体对色彩、构图和总体印象的评分均在 80~100 分范围内,其评分范围较窄;认为市场前景一般的群体对色彩和构图的评分均在 65~100 分范围内;而对总体印象的评分在 70~95 分范围内,其评分范围较为适中;而认为市场前景不好的群体对色彩、构图和总体印象的评分均在 40~95 分范围内,评分范围较宽。

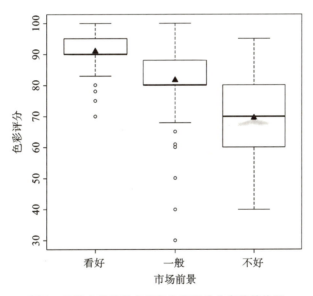

图 3　三种市场前景态度与色彩评分分布的箱线图

3　结论

首先,在三个包装特性指标(色彩、构图和总体印象)之间关系的研究中,发现三者评分的关联程度较高,卷烟包装的总体印象得分基本是由色彩得分和构图得分所决定的,知道了色彩得分和构图得分,可以通过建立的回归方程预测出总体印象得分,且色彩得分和构图得分对总体印象得分具有协同作用。其次,在对市场前景态度(看好、一般、不好)与包装特性指标(色彩、构图和总体印象)之间关系的研究中,发现卷烟包装色彩、构图和总体印象

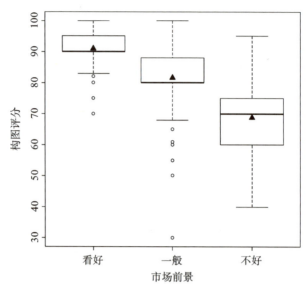

图 4　三种市场前景态度与构图评分分布的箱线图

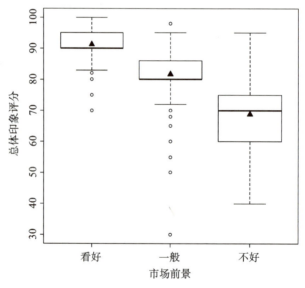

图 5　三种市场前景态度与总体印象评分分布的箱线图

评分越高,其市场前景越偏向于看好的趋势,而评分越低,其市场前景越偏向于不好的趋势。色彩、构图和总体印象的均值水平由市场前景看好至市场前景不好有明显下降的趋势且分值下降较为明显(90→80→70),认为市场前景看好的群体对色彩、构图和总体印象的评分范围相对较窄(80～100 分),而认为市场前景不好的群体对色彩、构图和总体印象的评分范围相对较宽(40～95 分)。

参考文献

[1] 张世博.影响卷烟包装质量的因素探析[J].商场现代化,2013(17):63.

[2] 魏星.香烟包装中的广告品牌塑造[J].包装工程,2012,33(20):129-132.

[3] 竹石.卷烟包装人性化的设计理念探讨[J].湖南包装,2009(1):23-25.

[4] 冯和平.浅析卷烟包装的创意与文化品位[J].中国科技博览,2009(9):112.

[5] 徐晓文.昆明香烟消费调查报告[J].企业与市场(月刊),2006(3):39-41.

[6] 石凤学,邹娟,陶鹰,等.卷烟包装特性与吸味特性间的相关性[J].食品工业,2015(6):263-265.

[7] 凤伟.卷烟包装颜色的探析[J].中国包装工业,2013(10):102.

[8] 杨君,胡安福,肖卫强,等.卷烟包装形象区域性差异分析[J].安徽农学通报,2011,17(21):137-138.

[9] "云南重点高端卷烟品牌消费调查研究"项目组.云南重点高端卷烟品牌消费调查研究[J].经济研究参考,2010(68):19-22.

[10] MATHUR P K,NAPEL J,BLOEMHOF S,et al. A Human Nose Scoring System for Boar Taint and Its Relationship with Androstenone and Skatole[J]. Meat Science,2012,91(4):414-422.

Polyserial Correlation Analysis of Cigarette Packaging Characteristics and Market Prospects

Abstract: Based on the market research data of 14 newly developed Yunnan cigarettes in 10 cities, such as Guangzhou, this paper uses polyserial correlation analysis to analyze the correlation between cigarette packaging characteristics and market prospects. The results show that: ① The overall impression evaluation score of cigarette packaging is determined by color score and composition score, and color and composition scores have synergistic effects on the overall impression; ② The higher the score of color, composition, and overall impression is, the more optimistic the market prospects attitude is, and the lower the score is, the more pessimistic the market prospects attitude is.

Keywords: Packaging characteristics; Market prospects; Polyserial correlation analysis

Cigarette packaging is a part of the cigarette product used to convey information, sell cigarettes, and maintain quality and brand reputation. At the same time, like cigarette brands, it has the role of perceptual clues for consumers. Due to the large population in China, there is a significant demand for cigarettes, and many cigarette brands exist in China. How to promote the sales of a cigarette brand? In addition to the quality of cigarettes, price and packaging quality are also necessary reference conditions for consumers to purchase goods[1]. If the role of the brand is to make the target consumer group clearly remember the characteristics and core values of the brand, then packaging design is just an effective way to achieve this function[2].

Color and composition play a critical role in packaging design. Different colors have different psychological reactions to consumers. Therefore, the correct use of packaging color collocation methods plays a good role in maintaining the style of cigarette products and inducing consumers' psychological awareness[3]. Composition can describe and focus on rendering the texture, shape, and functional use of the product in detail and present the exquisite texture of the product attractively. Give people a vivid sense of reality so that consumers have a sense of familiarity and trust in the advertised products[3, 4]. There are currently research reports on cigarette packaging for influence on consumer groups, among which Xu Xiaowen's[5] research on the Kunming market showed that more than half of the consumers pay attention to the packaging of cigarettes; Shi Fengxue et al.[6] found that there is a significant moderate canonical correlation between color, composition, texture, aluminum foil and filter in packaging characteristics and aroma, comfort and taste in smell characteristics; Feng Wei[7] also found that different people have different psychological feelings towards color in packaging design, so the audience range of a specific color is also different; Yang Jun et al.[8] found that cigarette consumers in different regions have significant differences in their preference for packaging image, and the main color design can be carried out according to the color preferences of cigarette consumers in various regions, and the style favored by most target consumer groups can be selected; a survey on the consumption of critical high-end cigarette brands in Yunnan[9] found that the proportion of packaging as the preferred consumption factor in Guangdong Province is more than twice that of Tianjin, Chongqing, Liaoning, Zhejiang and other provinces and cities, and the importance rank is also relatively high.

However, in the market test of new cigarette products, there is no research on whether the color and composition of packaging design are related to consumers' overall impression and attitude toward the market prospect. Therefore, this study further analyzes the correlation between the color and composition of packaging design and consumers' overall impression and attitude towards the market prospect and provides a theoretical reference for improving the success rate of new products from the perspective of packaging evaluation.

1 Materials and Methods

1.1 Data Collection and Determination of Properties

The research data of this paper comes from the market survey of 14 new packaging products developed by Yunnan Tobacco (Table 1). The survey sites are in 10 cities, including Nanjing, Hangzhou, Kunming, Guangzhou, Nanning, Xi'an, Chengdu, Qingdao, Jinan, and Shijiazhuang. The survey objects are employees of commercial companies, cigarette marketers, and retailers. 264 valid questionnaires and 3696 valid data were collected.

The properties include quantitative indicators and qualitative indicators, quantitative indicators such as color X_1, composition X_2, the overall impression of packaging X_3, and qualitative indicators such as market prospects attitude X_4.

Table 1 Survey Overview of 14 Cigarette Brands' Packaging Market (Unit: portion)

Survey city	Employees of commercial companies	Cigarette marketers	Retailers	Number of valid questionnaires
Nanjing	16	7	8	31
Hangzhou	15	18	8	41

continue

Survey city	Employees of commercial companies	Cigarette marketers	Retailers	Number of valid questionnaires
Kunming	11	9	4	24
Guangzhou	8	5	6	19
Nanning	8	6	8	22
Xi'an	20	6	10	36
Chengdu	14	1	21	36
Qingdao	4	1	10	15
Jinan	8	5	10	23
Shijiazhuang	0	8	9	17
Number of valid questionnaires	104	66	94	264

1.2 Analysis Method

The three quantitative indicators, color, composition, and overall impression of packaging, are all hundred-mark system, and the higher the score, the higher the respondents' satisfaction. The qualitative indicators of market prospects mainly reflect three options: optimistic, general, and poor. Statistical analysis within packaging traits is mainly conducted by correlation and stepwise regression analyses. For statistical analysis between packaging traits and market prospects attitude, since the variable of market prospects attitude characteristics belongs to the type of categorical variable and the data of packaging traits belong to the type of continuous variable, polyserial correlation analysis[10] is needed to study the relationship between them to find out the indicators that are correlated with market prospects attitude. Polyserial correlation analysis is a modified Pearson correlation analysis, and its calculation formula is as follows:

$$\rho_s = \frac{\rho_p \sigma_y}{\sum_{j=1}^{r-1} \Phi(\tau_j)(y_{j+1} - y_j)}$$

In formula, ρ_s is the polyserial correlation coefficient of X (e. g. color or composition) and the latent variable Y (market prospect attitude); ρ_p is the Pearson correlation coefficient of X and Y; σ_y is the standard deviation of Y; $\Phi(\tau_j)$ is the upper limit of the value of the normal density function of the jth category; y_{j+1} and y_j are the values of the categorical traits; r is the number of categories.

The polyserial correlation analysis used in this paper is implemented using the polycor package in R software.

2 Results and Analysis

2.1 Correlation Analysis and Stepwise Regression Analysis of Packaging Indicators

As can be seen from Table 2, the three packaging indicators (color, composition, and overall impression) have a high degree of positive correlation with each other, reaching the significant level of $P<0.01$. This indicates that the correlation degree of cigarette packaging in color, composition, and overall impression is high.

Table 2 Correlation Analysis Table of Packaging Indicators

terms	color	composition	overall impression
color	1		
composition	0.910**	1	
overall impression	0.955**	0.958**	1

"**" indicates significant correlation at the $P<0.01$ level

After stepwise regression analysis of color, composition (independent variable), and overall impression (dependent variable) in packaging indicators, a linear regression equation was established, and it was found that the equation reached the significant level of $P<0.01$, with R^2 being 0.959 and standard error being 1.947. As shown in Table 3, the regression coefficients of the two packaging indicators (color and composition) both reached the significant level of $P<0.01$. This indicates that the color score and composition score determine the overall impression evaluation score of cigarette packaging, and the overall impression score can be predicted by the regression equation based on the color score and composition score.

Table 3 Regression Equation Test Table of Packaging Traits Composition, Color and Overall Impression

Regression term	Coefficient	Standard error	Path coefficient	t-value	P-value
Constant term	0.746	0.307	—	2.430	0.015
Composition	0.510	0.008	0.517	60.375	<0.001
color	0.483	0.009	0.485	56.673	<0.001

As can be seen from Figure 1, increasing the scores of color and composition can both improve the overall impression evaluation score, but to achieve the maximum improvement of the overall impression score, the scores of color and composition need to be increased at the same time, and the two have a synergistic effect.

In addition, Figure 2 shows the dispersion degree of the measured values and predicted values of the regression equation constructed. It can be seen that the two are basically located near the diagonal (points on the diagonal represent no difference), with small differences.

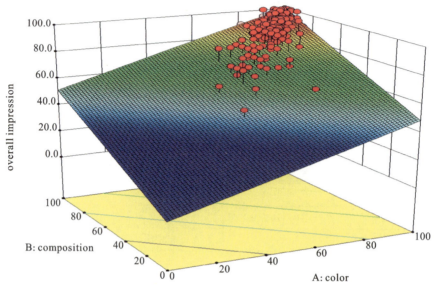

Figure 1 Response Surface Diagram of Packaging Indicators Composition, Color, and Overall Impression

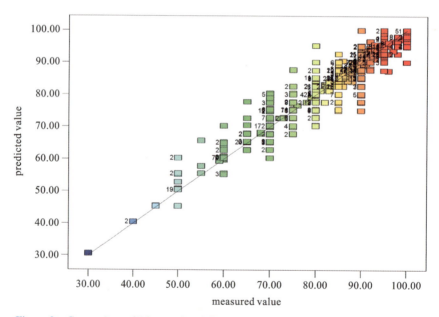

Figure 2 Comparison of Measured and Predicted Values of Regression Equations for Packaging Indicators Composition, Color, and Overall Impression

2.2 Polyserial Correlation Analysis of Packaging Indicators and Market Prospect Attitude

Polyserial correlation analysis was used to evaluate the relationship among three attitudes (optimistic, general, and poor) and three packaging indicators (color, composition, and overall impression) after a survey on cigarette market prospect attitudes of consumer (optimistic, general, and poor). Table 4 shows the polyserial correlation coefficients between the three market prospect attitudes and the three packaging indicators were around 0.75. They reached a significant level of $P<0.001$, indicating that color, composition, and overall impression had a high correlation with the three market prospect attitudes. The higher the score of cigarette packaging's color, composition, and overall impression, the more optimistic the market outlook attitude was, and the lower the score, the more pessimistic the market prospect attitude was.

Table 4   Polyserial Correlation Analysis Test Table between Packaging Indicators and Market Prospect Attitudes

Packaging indicators	Polyserial correlation coefficient with market	Standard error	Chi square value	P-value
color	−0.738	0.009	821.1	<0.001
composition	−0.750	0.009	772.9	<0.001
overall impression	−0.769	0.008	833.4	<0.001

Box plots will further explore the relationship between the three market prospect attitudes and the three packaging indicators (Figure 3 to Figure 5). Boxes represent 95% confidence interval values, triangles represent means, and parallel thick lines represent medians. As can be seen from the figure, the mean levels of color, composition, and overall impression have a significant descending trend from an optimistic market prospect to a poor market prospect, and the scores are relatively obvious (90→80→70). The group evaluating an optimistic market prospect scores about 80-100 in color, composition, and overall impression, which is a narrow range. The group evaluating a moderate market prospect scores about 65-100 in color and composition and about 70-95 in overall impression, which is a moderate range. The group evaluating a poor market prospect scores about 40-95 in color, composition, and overall impression, which is a wide range.

3   Conclusion

Firstly, in the study of the relationship among the three packaging indicators (color,

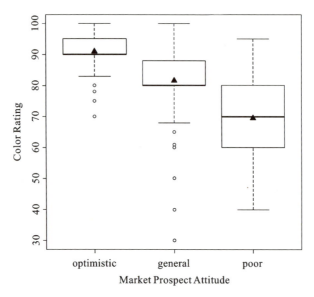

Figure 3　Box Plot of Three Market Prospect Attitudes and Color Rating Distributions

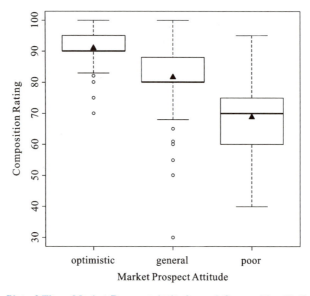

Figure 4　Box Plot of Three Market Prospect Attitudes and Composition Rating Distributions

composition, and overall impression), it is found that the correlation degree of the three indicators' scores is high. The color and composition scores determine the overall impression evaluation score of cigarette packaging. The overall impression score can be predicted by the established regression equation by knowing the color score and the composition score, and the color score and the composition score have a synergistic effect on the overall impression. Secondly, in the study of the relationship between the market prospect attitude (optimistic, general, poor) and the packaging indicators (color,

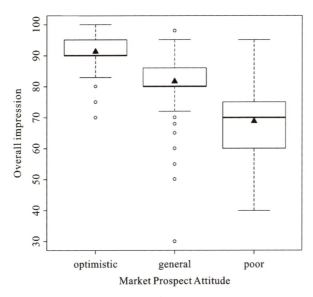

Figure 5　Box Plot of Three Market Prospect Attitudes and Overall impression Distributions

composition, and overall impression), it is found that the higher the cigarette packaging's color, composition, and overall impression score, the more optimistic the market prospect attitude is. The lower the score, the more negative the market prospect attitude is. The mean level of color, composition, and overall impression has a significant descending trend from the optimistic market prospect to the poor market prospect, and the score is relatively obvious (90→80→70). The group with an optimistic market prospect has a relatively narrow range of color, composition, and overall impression scores (80-100), while the group with a poor market prospect has a relatively wide range of color, composition, and overall impression scores (40-95).

References

[1] ZHANG S B. Analysis of Factors Affecting Cigarette Packaging Quality[J]. Market Modernization, 2013 (17): 63-63.

[2] WEI X. Advertising Brand Building in Cigarette Packaging [J]. Packaging Engineering, 2012,33 (20): 129-132.

[3] ZHU S. Discussion on the Design Concept of Humanized Cigarette Packaging[J]. Hunan Packaging, 2009 (1): 23-25.

[4] FENG H P. Brief Analysis of Creativity and Cultural Grade of Cigarette Packaging [J]. China Science and Technology Expo, 2009 (9): 112-112.

[5] XU X W. Kunming Cigarette Consumption Survey Report[J]. Enterprise and Market Monthly, 2006 (3): 39-41.

[6] SHI F X, ZOU J, TAO Y, et al. Correlation between Cigarette Packaging Characteristics and Cigarette Taste Characteristics[J]. Food Industry, 2015 (6): 263-265.

[7] FENG W. Analysis of Cigarette Packaging Color[J]. China Packaging Industry, 2013 (10): 102-102.

[8] YANG J, HU A F, XIAO W Q, et al. Analysis of Regional Differences in Cigarette Packaging Image[J]. Anhui Agricultural Science Bulletin, 2011, 17 (21): 137-138.

[9] Project Team of "Yunnan Key High-End Cigarette Brand Consumption Survey Research". Yunnan Key High-End Cigarette Brand Consumption Survey Research [J]. Economic Research Reference, 2010 (68): 19-22.

[10] MATHUR P K, NAPEL J, BLOEMHOF S, et al. A Human Nose Scoring System for Boar Taint and Its Relationship with Androstenone and Skatole[J]. Meat Science, 2012, 91(4): 414-422.

风味偏好分析

基于 MFA 的消费者与专家卷烟抽吸感知及风味感知分析

摘要： 多重因子分析（MFA）是一种能够用于描述和总结具有复杂结构和多方来源的多元数据的统计分析方法，其在食品和化妆品的感官分析以及消费者偏好调研中具有良好效用。本文运用 MFA 方法，针对消费者与专家卷烟抽吸感知及风味感知的调研数据，从强度和适宜度两个方面进行一致性分析和原因探析，结果发现：①消费者与专家在卷烟抽吸感知及风味感知方面均不具有一致性；②消费者专业知识的欠缺是造成不一致性的主要原因；③消费者对常吸烟在抽吸感知和风味感知评价上给予高度认可。鉴于上述结论，在风味偏好的调研中建议以实体物质辅助消费者准确把控卷烟风味偏好，在感知强度方面可借鉴常吸烟进行分析。

关键词： 卷烟抽吸感知；风味感知；多重因子分析；知识图谱

一直以来，卷烟消费者风味喜好度是行业亟待破解的难题，它不仅要求关注消费者感兴趣的"香气、吸味、刺激性、余味、舒适性、甜感、润感、余味、凉味"等抽吸感受与行业层面的"光泽、香气、谐调、杂气、刺激性、余味"等感官评价要求[1,2]，还需从卷烟风味方面入手，譬如卷烟香型、个性化嗅香、外加香、表香等特征来进行消费者偏好的收集[3-11]。更为关键的是，要确定消费者与专家在卷烟抽吸感知和风味感知方面是否具有一致性，以及弄清如何将消费者的抽吸感知和风味感知转化为专家感知并应用于产品定向研发，才能提高上市成功率。本文基于调研数据进行消费者与专家在卷烟抽吸感知及风味感知方面的一致性分析，剖析其影响因素，探寻解决思路。

1 数据采集与分析方法

1.1 数据采集

卷烟抽吸感知及风味感知初期调研以焦点小组座谈会的方式，分别针对消费者和业界专家进行，旨在了解有关消费者和专家在卷烟抽吸感知的强度和适宜度、风味感知的强度和适宜度方面的数据资料，分析消费者与专家在卷烟抽吸感知评价、风味感知评价方面的关联，寻找消费者与专家之间的桥梁，从而为后续依据消费者风味喜好进行产品研发打好基础。

1.1.1 调研的前期准备与要求

测试产品的选择原则：依据卷烟产品不同价格分类进行产品选取，覆盖高三类、二类、普一类、中一类、高一类及超一类，每一类选品 5 种，共计 30 种卷烟产品。要求所选产品覆盖不同品牌，在香型上有所差异，测试产品应有一定的全国市场渗透率，且品牌所在区域不能过于集中在某几个省份。首先，我们组织了 30 位评吸专家开展了 5 场评吸品鉴会，参考行业标准 YC/T 497—2014[2]，对上述 30 种产品进行评价。接着，在全国华东、华南、华中、西北、华北、东北、西南七大区域选取 10 个大中型城市，组织了 10 场座谈会，每场座谈会选取 6 名消费者，测试 6 个产品，对 30 种产品进行评价。

为了避免熟悉程度对测试结果的影响，每个城市测试的 6 个产品将剔除当地销量靠前的产品。为了减少测试产品顺序造成的影响，每个产品在不同组别的测试顺序不同，具体采用"平衡会场测试中呈现顺序和一阶延滞效应"[12]的实验设计。为了减少品牌、包装等因素对消费者抽吸感知评价和风味感知评价的影响，测试前对测试产品的 logo 进行遮挡。

1.1.2 调研内容

在卷烟抽吸感知调研中，分抽吸前、抽吸中和抽吸后三个阶段，从视觉感受、嗅觉感受、抽吸中感受和抽吸后感受几个方面对测试产品进行抽吸感知的强度和适宜度评价。在卷烟风味感知调研中，将针对 14 种香型风格，通过嗅香进行香型感知体验，利用抽吸进行香型感知强度、适宜度和诱人度评价。具体指标如表 1 所示。

表 1 消费者与专家卷烟抽吸感知和风味感知指标集

抽吸感知指标			风味感知指标		
油润	口部刺激性	劲头	烤烟烟香	木香	可可香
香气质	喉部刺激性	通透性	晾晒烟香	青滋香	奶香
香气量	鼻腔刺激性	细腻、柔和	清香	花香	膏香
丰富性	杂气	圆润、润度	果香	药草香	烘焙香
优雅度	甜度	成团、绵柔	辛香	豆香	
干净度	浓度				

注：抽吸感知指标从强度、适宜度两方面进行评价；风味感知指标从强度、适宜度和诱人度三方面进行评价。

1.2 分析方法

多重因子分析（multiple factor analysis，MFA）是一种能够运用于多组多维数据上的主成分分析方法，可用来探寻多组多维变量间的一致性问题，其在食品和化妆品的感官分析以及消费者偏好调研中具有良好效用[13,14]。在消费者与专家卷烟抽吸感知及风味感知分析中,我们以卷烟品类为样本,以消费者与专家的抽吸感知强度及适宜度,以及消费者与专家风味感知强度及适宜度为变量,运用多重因子分析(MFA)方法,分析消费者与专家在卷烟抽吸感知及风味感知的强度及适宜度评价中是否具有一致性。

2 消费者与专家抽吸感知与风味感知强度、适宜度的MFA分析及原因探析

2.1 基于MFA的消费者与专家抽吸感知强度及适宜度的一致性分析

为了分析消费者与专家的抽吸感知强度和适宜度评价的对应关系,我们依据测试产品对消费者和专家的评价数据分别进行了分类汇总,得出了消费者和专家对每一个测试产品在抽吸感知强度指标和适宜度指标方面的平均评价(均值),再运用MFA分析技术进行消费者与专家抽吸感知强度及适宜度的一致性分析,得出了消费者与专家抽吸感知强度及适宜度的MFA分析结果(图1)。

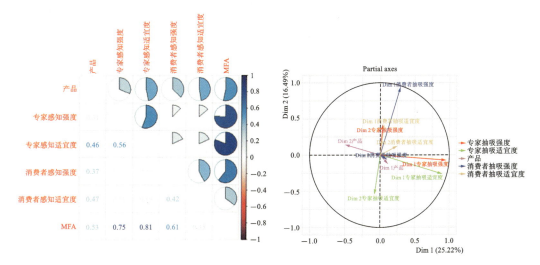

图1 基于MFA的消费者与专家抽吸感知强度及适宜度的分析结果

由图1可以看出,无论是在抽吸感知强度(适宜度)的指标体系层面,还是在抽吸感知强度(适宜度)的具体指标层面,消费者与专家的评价均没有表现出显著的线性相关关系,也就是说,消费者与专家在抽吸感知强度及适宜度方面均不具有一致性。接下来,我们在调研城市中以P1为基准,对消费者评价数据进行了差分处理。相应地,专家的评价数据也依据消费者调研城市的卷烟品类做类似处理。然后,运用MFA进行消费者与专家抽吸感知强度及适宜度的一致性分析,结果发现,剔除不同消费者对评价标准把控不一致的影响后,虽然消费者与专家的抽吸感知强度及适宜度评价之间的相关性有了一定的提升,但仍然不存在显著的线性相关关系。

2.2 消费者与专家在风味感知强度及适宜度方面的 MFA 分析和原因探析

2.2.1 消费者与专家风味感知强度及适宜度的 MFA 分析

在分析消费者与专家的风味感知强度及适宜度评价的对应关系时,与抽吸感知类似,我们依据测试产品对消费者和专家的评价数据分别进行了分类汇总,得出了消费者和专家对每一个测试产品在风味感知强度指标和适宜度指标方面的平均评价(均值),再进行 MFA 分析,得出了消费者与专家风味感知强度及适宜度的分析结果(图 2)。

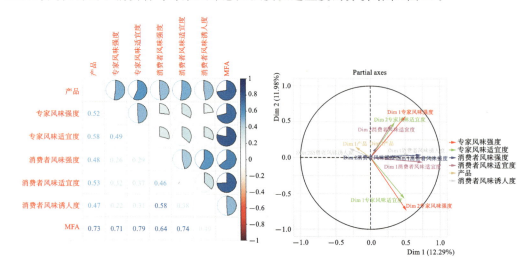

图 2 基于 MFA 的消费者与专家风味感知强度及适宜度的分析结果

由图 2 可以看出,无论是在风味感知强度(适宜度)的指标体系层面,还是在风味感知强度(适宜度)的具体指标层面,消费者与专家的评价均没有表现出显著的线性相关关系,也就是说,消费者与专家在风味感知强度及适宜度方面均不具有一致性。

2.2.2 消费者与专家对风味感知指标评价不一致的原因分析

为了分析造成消费者和专家风味感知强度和适宜度评价不一致的原因,我们针对消费者的风味联想数据进行了文本分析,构建了消费者对卷烟风味 16 种香型理解的知识图谱(图 3)。

从消费者对卷烟风味 16 种香型理解的知识图谱可以看出,木香、豆香和膏香这三种香型自我特征突出,与其他香型有显著差异,消费者对其的认知也形成独立的知识图谱(图 3(a)、(b)、(c));部分消费者对辛香和药草香、烤烟烟香和晾晒烟香的认知有偏差,特别是对烤烟烟香和晾晒烟香在烟草、烟香上的反应和认知偏差较大(图 3(d)、(e));消费者对甜香、烘焙香、奶香、焦香、焦糖香和可可香,以及清香、花香、果香和青滋香的概念理解不清,这些香型相互之间的界限不清晰,造成判断偏差严重(图 3(f)、(g))。

上述结果的产生,是由于消费者不具有相关的专业知识和专业技能,无法像专家一样准确地进行风味感知强度和适宜度的评价。正是消费者与专家在专业知识和专业技能方面的巨大差异,造成了消费者与专家在风味感知强度和适宜度方面的关联性下降。这种差

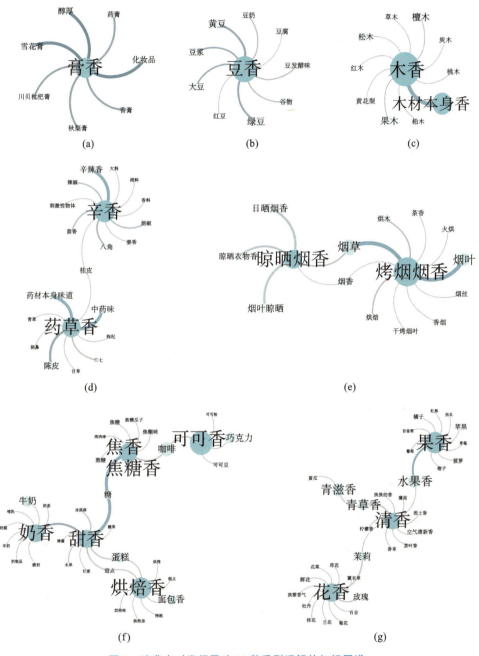

图 3 消费者对卷烟风味 16 种香型理解的知识图谱

距是业余和专业之间的差距,是短时间内无法弥补的。产品的研发必须符合消费者的风味偏好,只有迎合消费者喜好的产品才能更好地打开市场和占领市场,因此,准确地调查和确定消费者的风味偏好至关重要。

2.3 消费者对经常抽吸卷烟的抽吸感知和风味喜好度评价

在进一步的调查中,我们针对消费者对经常抽吸卷烟(俗称口粮烟)的抽吸感知和风味喜好度进行分析,得到表2(10分表示非常喜欢)和表3(10分表示非常好)。

表2 消费者对经常抽吸卷烟的抽吸感知评价

评分	1	2	3	4	5	6	7	8	9	10	总计
个案数	0	0	0	1	0	6	24	98	113	58	300
百分比/(%)	0.0	0.0	0.0	0.3	0.0	2.0	8.0	32.7	37.7	19.3	100
累计百分比/(%)	0.0	0.0	0.0	0.3	0.3	2.3	10.3	43.0	80.7	100	

表3 消费者对经常抽吸卷烟的风味喜好度评价

评分	1	2	3	4	5	6	7	8	9	10	总计	缺失值
个案数	0	1	1	2	3	8	32	94	93	64	298	2
百分比/(%)	0.0	0.3	0.3	0.7	1.0	2.7	10.7	31.3	31.0	21.3	99.3	0.7
累计百分比/(%)	0.0	0.3	0.6	1.3	2.3	5.0	15.7	47.0	78.0	99.3		

在消费者对经常抽吸卷烟的抽吸感知评价中,有97.7%在7分以上,有89.7%在8分以上;在消费者对经常抽吸卷烟的风味喜好度评价中,有94.3%在7分以上,有83.6%在8分以上。上述结果表明,消费者对经常抽吸的卷烟(口粮烟)持高度认可的态度。

3 结论与建议

3.1 结论

(1)在抽吸强度和适宜度把控上,消费者与专家评价呈现出不一致的情况。尽管在消除消费者掌握评价标准不规范因素后,消费者与专家评价的相关性有所增强,但评价不一致状态依然存在。

(2)消费者在风味认知专业知识方面的欠缺,造成其风味感知的偏差和混乱,使消费者和专家在风味感知评价方面出现不一致性。

(3)消费者对经常抽吸卷烟的评价,无论是抽吸感知还是风味喜好度,均持高度认可态度。

3.2 建议

在风味偏好的确定上,采用统一消费者和专家认知的媒介——实体物质做参考依据。实体物质作为消费者日常生活中经常接触的物品,有利于消费者准确把控,也有利于专家将实体物质转化为风味偏好。

在强度和适宜度的把控上,建议用消费者日常经常抽吸的卷烟产品做参考依据,并让专家来进行抽吸强度和适宜度的把控,可以更准确地把握消费者对抽吸感知强度和适宜度的需求。

参考文献

[1] 中华人民共和国国家质量监督检验检疫总局,中国国家标准化管理委员会.卷烟 第4部分:感官技术要求:GB 5606.4—2005[S].北京:中国标准出版社,2005.

[2] 红云红河烟草(集团)有限责任公司等.卷烟 中式卷烟风格感官评价方法:YC/T 497—2014[S].北京:中国标准出版社,2014.

[3] 徐轲.卷烟感官指标消费者评价方法[J].中国烟草科学,2010,31(1):53-55.

[4] 李思源,刘继辉,刘应波,等.消费者卷烟抽吸感知综合评价分析[J].中国市场,2022(26),127-133.

[5] 刘熙.消费者吸烟行为的卷烟感官质量评价研究[J].安徽农业科学,2011,39(18):10995-10997.

[6] 王德平,张胜华,沈军.基于消费者感知的卷烟产品质量影响因素的研究[J].技术经济与管理研究,2008(6),49-51.

[7] 杨剑锋.卷烟新产品开发中消费者需求转化路径研究[J].工业技术经济,2010(9),94-99.

[8] 孙东亮,赵华民.基于消费者感知的细支卷烟轻松感、满足感设计思路[J].中国烟草学报,2017,23(02),42-49.

[9] 金吉琼,居雷,张易,等.基于用户画像的卷烟消费者特征识别和价值评估[J].烟草科技,2023,56(1),105-112.

[10] WORCH T. PrefMFA, a Solution Taking the Best of Both Internal and External Preference Mapping Techniques[J]. Food Quality and Preference,2013,30(2):180-191.

[11] PARTIDASEDAS J G, FERREIRO M N M, VAZQUEZODERIZ M L, et al. Influence of the Postharvest Processing of the "Garnica" Coffee Variety on the Sensory Characteristics and Overall Acceptance of the Beverage[J]. Journal of Sensory Studies,2019.

[12] 陆龙建,陈磊,余苓,等.多元因子分析在卷烟风格特征剖析中的应用[J].烟草科技,2012(10):36-40.

[13] 田欣,张会宁,祁新春,等.快速感官分析技术在葡萄酒香气感官分析中的应用[J].食品与发酵工业,2019,45(21):215-220.

[14] 许晓青,苏庆宇,王冬,等.多重因子分析技术在食品饮料行业感官分析中的应用[J].食品工业科技,2021,42(13):427-434.

Analysis of Consumer and Expert Cigarette Smoking Perception and Flavor Perception Based on MFA

Abstract: Multiple Factor Analysis (MFA) is a statistical method that describes and summarizes complex structured and multi-sourced multivariate data. It proves to be highly effective in sensory analysis of food and cosmetics and in consumer preference research. In this study, MFA is employed to investigate consumer and expert perceptions of cigarette smoking and flavor, analyzing consistency and reasons from intensity and suitability. The results reveal: ① Lack of consistency between consumers and experts in cigarette smoking and flavor perceptions. ② Inadequate consumer expertise is the primary cause of inconsistency. ③ Consumers highly recognize habitual smoking in evaluating smoking and flavor perceptions. Given the above conclusions, it is recommended in flavor preference research to utilize tangible substances to assist consumers in accurately assessing cigarette flavor preferences and to analyze perception intensity concerning habitual smoking.

Keywords: Cigarette smoking perception; Flavor perception; Multiple factor analysis; Knowledge map

Consumer flavor preference has always been a challenging issue for the tobacco industry. In addition, it emphasizes sensory perceptions such as "aroma, taste, irritation, aftertaste, comfort, sweetness, moisten, coolness" that consumers are interested in, or industry-level sensory evaluation requirements such as "luster, aroma, harmony, offensive odor, irritation, aftertaste"[1,2], it is also necessary to collect consumer preferences from the aspect of cigarette flavors, such as cigarette aroma type, personalized olfactory, addictive aroma, and surface aroma characteristics[3-11]. Furthermore, it is crucial to determine whether there is consistency between consumers and experts in cigarette smoking and flavor perceptions and how to translate consumer perceptions into expert perceptions and apply them to product-targeted research and development to improve market success rates. This study is based on research data to analyze the consistency between consumers and experts in smoking and flavor perceptions of cigarettes, dissecting influencing factors and exploring solutions.

1 Data Collection and Analysis Methods

1.1 Data Collection

The initial cigarette smoking and flavor perception investigation was conducted separately through focus group discussions with consumers and industry experts. The aim was to understand the data on the intensity and suitability of cigarette smoking and flavor perception from consumers and experts, analyze the correlation between consumer and expert evaluations of cigarette smoking and flavor perception, and find a bridge between experts and consumers in cigarette smoking and flavor perception to lay a foundation for subsequent product development based on consumer flavor preferences.

1.1.1 Preparation and Requirements for the Preliminary Research

The selection principle for test samples was based on different price categories of cigarette products, covering Class high Ⅲ, Class Ⅱ, Class ordinary Ⅰ, Class junior Ⅰ, Class senior Ⅰ, and Class superior Ⅰ categories, with 5 brands selected for each category, totaling 30 cigarette products. The selected products were required to cover different brands, have differences in aroma types, ensure a certain level of domestic market penetration, and the brand's regional distribution should not be concentrated in a few provinces. Firstly, 30 expert smokers were organized to conduct 5 Sensory evaluation sessions, referring to the industry standard YC/T 497—2014 method[2], to evaluate the 30 product specifications. Then research was conducted in ten large and medium-sized cities in seven regions across China, including East China, South China, Central China, Northwest China, North China, Northeast China, and Southwest China, with 10 focus group discussions organized. Each focus group discussion selected 6 consumers to evaluate 6 products, covering 30 specifications.

In order to avoid the influence of familiarity on the test results, the six products tested in each city will exclude the local top-selling product specifications. In order to reduce the influence of the order of tested products, the test order of each product in different groups is different, specifically using the experimental design of "balancing the presentation order and first-order lag effect in the venue test"[12]. In order to reduce the influence of factors such as brand and packaging on consumers' smoking and flavor perception evaluation, the logo of the tested products is blocked before the test.

1.1.2 Research Content

In the investigation of cigarette smoking perception, evaluations of smoking perception intensity and suitability were conducted in three stages: pre-smoking, during smoking, and post-smoking, focusing on visual perception, olfactory perception, smoking sensation, and post-smoking sensation. In investigating cigarette flavor perception, 14 types of aroma styles were targeted for aroma perception experience through olfaction, and aroma perception intensity, suitability, and attractiveness were evaluated through smoking perception. The specific indicators are shown in Table 1.

Table 1 Consumer and Expert Indicators for Cigarette Smoking and Flavor Perception

Smoking perception indicators			Flavor perception indicators		
Oiliness	Oral irritation	Strength	Flue-cured tobacco aroma	Woody aroma	Cocoa aroma
Aroma quality	Throat irritation	Transparency	Air-dried tobacco	Green aroma	Milk aroma
Aroma quantity	Nasal irritation	Delicate and mellow	Faint aroma	Flower aroma	Cream aroma
Richness	Offensive odor	Smoothness and moisten	Fruit aroma	Herb aroma	Baking aroma
Elegance	Sweetness	Cohesive and mild	Spicy aroma	Bean aroma	
Cleanliness	Concentration				

Note: The indicators of smoking perception are evaluated from two aspects—intensity and suitability. The flavor perception indicators are evaluated from intensity, suitability, and attractiveness.

1.2 Analytical Method

Multiple factor analysis (MFA) is a principal component analysis that can be applied to multiple sets of multidimensional data to explore consistency issues between multiple sets of multidimensional variables. It is helpful in sensory analysis and consumer preference research in food and cosmetics[13-18]. In analyzing consumer and expert cigarette smoking and flavor perception, we use cigarette categories as samples, the smoking perception intensity and suitability of consumers and experts, and the flavor perception intensity and suitability of consumers and experts as variables. We apply the multiple factor analysis (MFA) method to analyze whether consumers and experts have consistency issues in evaluating the intensity and suitability of cigarette smoking and flavor perception.

2　MFA Analysis and Cause Analysis of Consumer and Expert Perception Intensity and Suitability of Smoking and Flavor

2.1　Consumers and Experts' Consistency Analysis Based on MFA in Smoking Perception Intensity and Suitability

In order to analyze the correspondence between consumers and experts in terms of the intensity and suitability of smoking perception, we classified and summarized the evaluation data of consumers and experts based on the test products, obtained the average evaluation (mean) of consumers and experts for each test product in terms of smoking perception intensity and suitability, and then conducted a consistency analysis of smoking perception intensity and suitability between consumers and experts using MFA analysis technology, obtaining the MFA analysis results of consumers and experts in terms of smoking perception intensity and suitability (Figure 1).

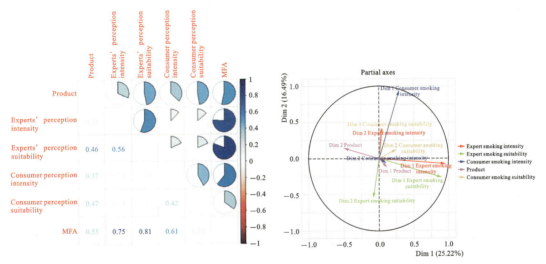

Figure 1　The Analysis Results of Consumers' and Experts' Smoking Perception and Suitability Based on MFA

As can be seen from Figure 1, there is no significant linear correlation between the evaluations of consumers and experts, both at the level of the indicator system for smoking perception intensity (suitability) and at the level of the specific indicators for smoking perception intensity (suitability). That is to say, consumers and experts do not have consistency in terms of smoking perception intensity and suitability. Further, we conducted a differential treatment on the consumer evaluation data in the survey cities based on Figure 1. Correspondingly, the evaluation data of experts were also similarly processed based on the cigarette categories in each survey city of consumers. Then, we used MFA to analyze the consistency between consumers and experts in smoking perception intensity and suitability. After removing the influence of different consumers' inconsistent control over evaluation standards, the results showed that there was a certain improvement in the correlation between consumers and experts in smoking perception intensity and suitability evaluation, and there was still no significant linear correlation.

2.2 MFA Analysis and Cause Analysis of Consumer and Expert Flavor Perception Intensity and Suitability

2.2.1 MFA Analysis of Consumer and Expert Flavor Perception Intensity and Suitability

In analyzing the correspondence between consumers and experts in the evaluation of flavor perception intensity and suitability, similar to the analysis of smoking perception, we classified and summarized the evaluation data of consumers and experts based on the test products, obtained the average evaluation (mean) of consumers and experts for each test product in the flavor perception intensity and suitability indicators, and conducted MFA analysis to obtain the analysis results of flavor perception intensity and suitability between consumers and experts (Figure 2).

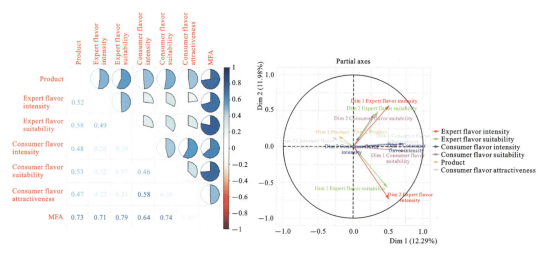

Figure 2 The Analysis Results of Consumers' and Experts' Flavor Perception and Suitability Based on MFA

As can be seen from Figure 2, both from the perspective of the indicator system of flavor perception intensity (suitability) and from the perspective of the specific indicators of flavor perception intensity (suitability), there is no significant linear correlation between consumer and expert evaluations, which means that consumers and experts do not have consistency in flavor perception intensity and suitability.

2.2.2 Analysis of the Reasons for the Inconsistent between Consumers and Experts in Evaluating Flavor Perception Indicators

To analyze the reasons for the inconsistency between consumers and experts in evaluating flavor perception intensity and suitability, we conducted text analysis on consumers' flavor association data. We constructed a knowledge graph of consumers' understanding of 16 cigarette aroma types (Figure 3 for details).

Based on the knowledge graph of consumers' understanding of 16 cigarette flavor profiles, it can be observed that the characteristics of woody, bean, and cream aromas are prominent, showing significant differences from other flavor profiles. Consumers' perceptions also form independent knowledge graphs (Figures 3 (a)、(b)、(c)). Some consumers have misconceptions about spicy aroma and herbal aroma, flue-cured tobacco and air-dried tobacco aromas, particularly significant deviations in their reactions and perceptions regarding tobacco and smoke (Figure 3 (d), (e)). Consumers have an unclear understanding of concepts such as sweet aroma, baking aroma, milky aroma, toasty aroma, caramel aroma, cocoa aromas, faint aroma, floral aroma, fruity aroma, and fresh green aromas. Their unclear boundaries lead to significant judgment biases (Figure 3 (f), (g)).

The above results stem from consumers lacking relevant professional knowledge and skills, making it difficult for them, unlike experts, to accurately evaluate the intensity and suitability of flavor perception. The significant difference between consumers and experts regarding professional knowledge and skills leads to a decreased correlation between consumers and experts in the intensity and suitability of flavor perception. This gap represents the disparity between amateur and professional, which cannot be bridged in the short term. However, product development must align with consumer flavor preferences, and only products that cater to consumer flavor preferences can better penetrate and dominate the market. Therefore, accurately investigating and determining consumer flavor preferences is crucial.

2.3 Consumers' Perception of Smoking Sensation and Flavor Preference for Regularly Smoked Cigarettes

In further investigation, we analyzed consumers' perception of smoking sensation and flavor preference for regularly smoked cigarettes (commonly known as daily cigarettes), as shown in Table 2 (rated on a scale of 1 to 10, with 10 being "very like") and Table 3

卷烟消费市场研究初探

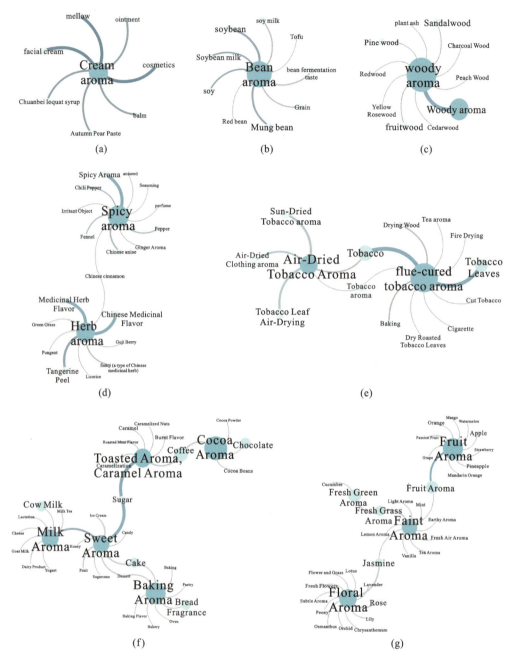

Figure 3　Knowledge map of consumer understanding of 16 cigarette aroma types

(rated on a scale of 1 to 10，with 10 being "very like").

Table 2　Consumers' Evaluation of Smoking Sensation for Regularly Smoked Cigarettes

Score	1	2	3	4	5	6	7	8	9	10	Total
Case No.	0	0	0	1	0	6	24	98	113	58	300
Percentage/(%)	0.0	0.0	0.0	0.3	0.0	2.0	8.0	32.7	37.7	19.3	100

continue

Score	1	2	3	4	5	6	7	8	9	10	Total
Accumulated percentage/(%)	0.0	0.0	0.0	0.3	0.3	2.3	10.3	43.0	80.7	100	

Table 3 Consumers' Evaluation of Flavor Preference for Regularly Smoked Cigarettes

Score	1	2	3	4	5	6	7	8	9	10	Total	Missing
Case No.	0	1	1	2	3	8	32	94	93	64	298	2
Percentage/(%)	0.0	0.3	0.3	0.7	1.0	2.7	10.7	31.3	31.0	21.3	99.3	0.7
Accumulated percentage/(%)	0.0	0.3	0.6	1.3	2.3	5.0	15.7	47.0	78.0	99.3		

In Table 2, consumers' evaluations of the smoking sensation of regularly smoked cigarettes reveal that 97.7% rate it at 7 or above, with 89.7% rating it at 8 or above. In Table 3, consumers' flavor preference evaluations for regularly smoked cigarettes show that 94.3% rate it at 7 or above, with 83.6% rating it at 8 or above. These results indicate a high level of consumer approval for regularly smoked cigarettes.

3. Conclusion and Recommendations

3.1 Conclusion

(1) Consumers and experts show inconsistent smoking strength and suitability evaluations. Although the correlation between consumer and expert evaluations has strengthened after eliminating factors such as irregular evaluation standards, inconsistent evaluation persists.

(2) Due to consumers' lack of professional knowledge in flavor perception, their biases and confusion in flavor perception lead to inconsistencies with expert evaluations.

(3) Consumers' evaluations of regularly smoked cigarettes, whether in terms of smoking sensation or flavor preference, are within a highly approved range.

3.2 Recommendations

In selecting flavor preferences, utilize a medium that aligns consumer and expert perceptions — tangible objects as reference points. Tangible objects, being items consumers frequently encounter in daily life, facilitating consumers' accurate understanding and experts' conversion of tangible objects into flavor preferences.

In controlling smoking strength and suitability, it is advisable to use regularly smoked cigarette products that consumers frequently encounter as reference points. Additionally, allowing experts to control smoking strength and suitability for regularly smoked cigarette products can more accurately meet consumers' needs for smoking sensation intensity and suitability.

References

［1］ General Administration of Quality Supervision, Inspection and Quarantine of the People's Republic of China, Standardization Administration of China. Cigarettes Part 4: Sensory Technical Requirements: GB 5606. 4—2005［S］. Beijing: Standards Press of China, 2005.

［2］ Hongyun Red River Tobacco (Group) Co., Ltd., et al. Sensory Evaluation Method of Chinese-style Cigarette Style: YC/T 497—2014［S］. Beijing: Standards Press of China, 2014.

［3］ XU K. Consumer Evaluation Method of Cigarette Sensory Indicators［J］. Chinese Tobacco Science, 2010, 31 (1): 53-55.

［4］ LI S Y, LIU J H, LIU Y B, et al. Comprehensive Evaluation and Analysis of Consumer Cigarette Smoking Sensation［J］. China Market, 2022 (26): 127-133.

［5］ LIU X. Research on Sensory Quality Evaluation of Consumer Smoking Behavior ［J］. Anhui Agricultural Science, 2011, 39 (18): 10995-10997.

［6］ WANG D P, ZHANG S H, SHEN J. Research on Factors Affecting the Quality of Cigarette Products based on Consumer Perception［J］. Technoeconomics and Management Research, 2008 (6): 49-51.

［7］ YANG J F. Study on the Path of Consumer Demand Transformation in New Cigarette Product Development［J］. Industrial Technology and Economy, 2010 (9): 94-99.

［8］ SUN D L, ZHAO H M. Design Ideas of Relaxation and Satisfaction of Fine Cut Cigarette based on Consumer Perception［J］. Acta Tabacaria Sinica, 2017, 23 (02): 42-49.

［9］ JIN J Q, JU L, ZHANG Y, et al. Identification and Value Evaluation of Consumer Characteristics of Cigarette based on User Profile［J］. Tobacco Science and Technology, 2023, 56 (1): 105-112.

［10］ WORCH T. PrefMFA, a Solution Taking the Best of Both Internal and External Preference Mapping Techniques［J］. Food Quality and Preference, 2013, 30 (2): 180-191.

［11］ PARTIDASEDAS J G, FERREIRO M N M, VAZQUEZODERIZ M L, et al. Influence of the Postharvest Processing of the "Garnica" Coffee Variety on the

Sensory Characteristics and Overall Acceptance of the Beverage[J]. Journal of Sensory Studies, 2019.

[12] LU L J, CHEN L, YU L, et al. Application of Multivariate Factor Analysis in Analysis of Cigarette Style Characteristics[J]. Tobacco Science and Technology, 2012 (10): 36-40.

[13] TIAN X, ZHANG H N, QI X C, et al. Application of Rapid Sensory Analysis Technology in Sensory Analysis of Wine Aroma[J]. Food and Fermentation Industry, 2019, 45 (21): 215-220.

[14] XU X Q, SU Q Y, WANG D, et al. Application of Multivariate Factor Analysis Technology in Sensory Analysis of Food and Beverage Industry[J]. Food Industry Science and Technology, 2021, 42 (13): 427-434.

第 4 章
卷烟消费需求转化机制

卷烟消费者评价与专家技术指标关联性研究

摘要：针对消费者的需求，对卷烟进行设计与改良是卷烟市场化经营的重要基础。为找出消费者评价与专家技术指标的关联性，形成由消费需求指导卷烟设计的转化模型，在对消费者和专家调研的基础上，采用 AHP 层次分析法建立专家技术指标设计层—专家技术指标结果层—消费者指标初步关联模型，然后通过相关分析和基于回归方程的 Shapley 值法对关联模型进行验证与权重分析，最终建立卷烟产品特征属性与消费需求的对接转化模型。该模型的建立实现了卷烟消费者评价、专家评价技术指标、卷烟设计技术指标的对接，有助于把握消费者的需求，增强生产与消费的链接。

关键词：消费需求；产品属性；卷烟指标评价；关联性

烟草行业作为国民经济的重要组成部分，由于其产品的特殊性，过去一直实行"统一领导、垂直管理、专卖专营"的管理体制。然而，随着市场经济的发展，以消费者需求为导向的市场化经营理念逐渐形成。在该经营理念下，了解消费者的需求，并进行针对性的卷烟设计与改良是市场化经营的重要基础。近年来，已有一些烟草企业逐步尝试运用市场经营理念指导卷烟的设计与改良以及生产和营销，并取得了一定成效。但是，烟草行业的发展仍然面临市场化手段不足等问题[1,2]。按照当前市场化经营理念，卷烟产品的设计、生产与营销应该以消费者的需求为导向，根据消费者的消费行为与特征以及评价情况和满意度来制定策略[3,4]。然而,由于烟草行业长期采取专卖经营模式,生产企业对消费需求认识不足。长期以来,消费者群体形成了一套自己的评价卷烟优劣的言辞标准,这套言辞评价标准体现了消费者对卷烟品质的朴素需求,可是截至目前该标准尚未被充分探索并理解。深入分析消费者的言辞评价标准,了解消费者的需求与消费特点,可为卷烟经营者的决策提供重要依据[5,6]。卷烟的消费情况常常因消费者的年龄、职业、收入、地域、卷烟偏好、品牌忠诚度、政策作用而变化,只有把握消费者的消费特点,准确分析其言辞评价标准,才能更好地实现生产与消费的衔接。专业评价一般由从事多年卷烟配方工作且取得烟草及烟草制品感官评价资质的专业人士进行。消费者言辞评价标准与卷烟制造的技术指标不同,与专业品吸评价方式也有所差异。然而,目前尚缺乏一套由消费需求指导卷烟设计的转化模型来实现"消费者评价—专家评价技术指标—卷烟设计技术指标"的对接。因此,市场导向下的卷烟行业亟待开展精准营销和以需求为导向的研发及营销活动,把消费者的需求转化为对产品品质,以及产品设计、包装设计、生产工艺的要求。本研究以市场为导向,拟建立一套行之有效的卷烟技术指标测评体系,使消费者需求与卷烟技术指标之间形成有效联系,探索构建产品测试中反映消费者评价的模型,以指导生产实践,实现研销结合。

1 研究方法

1.1 数据来源

1.1.1 专家评价

本研究邀请9名具有多年卷烟产品配方工作经验,且取得烟草及烟草制品感官评价资质的专业人士组成专家组,采用面对面座谈的形式进行调研。由于本研究旨在构建卷烟产品属性要求与消费需求的对接转化模型,因此必须从专业的角度归纳总结出与消费者评价指标存在关联性的专家技术指标,并在专业意见下初步探索消费者评价指标与专家技术指标的关联性,为后续开展消费者调研提供验证依据。

1.1.2 产品留置测试

(1)消费者调研。本次消费者调研以全国销量排名前40的卷烟产品为测试样品(表1),通过问卷方式对年龄为18~50岁的重度卷烟消费群体(日均吸烟量在10支以上)进行调研,调查范围覆盖全国七大区域,每个区域含两个城市,共计14个城市。每个城市发放10份调研问卷,共计140份,实际收回有效问卷135份,问卷回收率为96.43%。问卷发放地域分布及数量见表2。

(2)专家调研。邀请云南中烟工业有限责任公司技术中心的9位专家,采用专业的设计技术参数,在14 d内完成与消费者调研同一批的卷烟产品品吸与评价打分。

表 1　40 款测试卷烟产品及相关指标

序号	销量前 40 的产品	价格/(元/条)	焦油量/mg	价类	序号	销量前 40 的产品	价格/(元/条)	焦油量/mg	价类
1	白沙(精品)	85	8	三类	21	黄山(硬一品)	55	10	四类
2	白沙(精品二代)	110	10	三类	22	兰州(硬珍品)	180	8	二类
3	白沙(软)	45	10	四类	23	利群(软红长嘴)	220	11	一类
4	白沙(硬)	55	10	四类	24	利群(软蓝)	180	11	二类
5	芙蓉王(硬)	250	11	一类	25	利群(西子阳光)	310	5	一类
6	贵烟(硬黄精品)	130	11	二类	26	利群(新版)	140	11	二类
7	哈德门(精品)	45	11	四类	27	南京(红)	120	11	三类
8	红梅(软黄)	45	10	四类	28	南京(炫赫门)	160	8	二类
9	红双喜(硬)	80	11	三类	29	南京(雨花石)	530	5	一类
10	红塔山(软经典)	75	10	三类	30	七匹狼(红)	150	11	二类
11	红塔山(硬经典)	75	10	三类	31	双喜(软经典)	100	11	三类
12	红塔山(硬经典100)	100	10	三类	32	双喜(硬经典1906)	170	10	二类
13	猴王(金)	55	10	四类	33	苏烟(五星红杉树)	220	11	一类
14	黄果树(长征)	55	11	四类	34	泰山(红将军)	70	11	三类
15	黄鹤楼(软蓝)	190	11	一类	35	玉溪(软)	230	11	一类
16	黄鹤楼(天下名楼)	160	8	二类	36	云烟(软珍品)	230	11	一类
17	黄鹤楼(雅香金)	160	8	二类	37	云烟(紫)	100	10	三类
18	黄金叶(硬帝豪)	105	11	三类	38	中华(软)	700	11	一类
19	黄金叶(硬红旗渠)	105	10	三类	39	中华(硬)	450	11	一类
20	黄山(新制皖烟)	140	11	二类	40	中南海(5 mg)	100	5	三类

表 2　问卷发放地域分布及数量

区域	华东	华北	华南	西南	西北	东北	华中
城市	上海	北京	广州	成都	西安	沈阳	郑州
样本量	11	10	9	11	8	10	9
城市	宁波	保定	深圳	昆明	兰州	哈尔滨	武汉
样本量	10	11	8	10	9	11	8

1.2 分析方法

1.2.1 确定并划分专家技术指标

召开专家工作座谈会,组织专家进行集体讨论,确定并划分了专家技术指标,并进一步探索专家技术指标间的内在联系。为了提高该划分结果的准确度,确保决策依据的可靠性,所选专家均为烟草行业配方专家。经会议讨论,在云南中烟工业有限责任公司技术中心原有专家技术指标的基础上,对产品属性要素的含义进一步明确,将技术指标划分为设计层和结果层两个层次。设计层共9个卷烟设计技术指标,包括烟丝组分、烟叶配方、加料香精配方、加香香精配方、叶处理工艺模式及强度、丝处理工艺模式及强度、烟支物理指标、卷烟材料配方、包装材料配方,用于技术中心产品改进。结果层共21个专家评价技术指标,包括烟气浓度、香气质、喉部刺激、劲头、香气量、干净度、柔细程度、醇和度、生津感、烟气集中性、谐调性、口腔舒适度、烟气圆润性、杂气、回味、透发性、鼻腔刺激、嗅香、丰富性、口腔刺激、开包香,通过专家打分法进行定量调研。

1.2.2 专家技术指标权重分析

针对专家得出的结果,通过AHP层次分析法[7-9]依次确定与特定结果层指标相关的设计层指标的权重。对每一层次结构,设第k个专家认为第i个专家评价技术指标(结果层)对于第j个卷烟设计技术指标(设计层)的相对重要度为$a_{ij}k(i,j=1,2,\cdots,9)$,则共给出9个判断矩阵。用如下公式进行一致性计算:

$$CR = |\lambda_{max} - m|/(m-1) \times RI$$

CR(consistency ratio)为一致性比率,CR值小于0.1则通过一致性判断。上式中,CR=CI/RI,CI(consistency index)为一致性指标;RI(random consistency index)为随机一致性指标;λ_{max}表示判断矩阵的最大正特征值;m表示判断矩阵的个数。

$$CI = (\lambda_{max} - n)/(n-1)$$

在上式中,当CI=0时,判断矩阵具有完全一致性;CI越大,则表示判断矩阵的一致性越差。随机一致性指标RI见表3。

表3 随机一致性指标

n	1	2	3	4	5	6	7	8	9	10	11
RI	0.00	0.00	0.58	0.90	1.12	1.24	1.32	1.41	1.45	1.49	1.51

一致性比率通常用于确定判断矩阵的不一致性的容许范围。一致性比率CR的计算公式如下所示。

$$CR = \frac{CI}{RI}$$

将CI与RI进行比较,可以检验判断矩阵是否具有令人满意的一致性。若CR<0.1,说明判断矩阵的一致性是令人满意的;若CR≥0.1,说明还需要调整判断矩阵,直到令人满意为止。

根据一致性判断的结果,使用如下公式进行权重计算,求出所有专家技术指标权重的平均值。

$$a_{ij} = \sqrt[K]{\prod_{k=1}^{K} a_{ij}^{k}}$$

1.2.3 消费者指标与专家技术指标关联性分析

汇总专家意见,然后形成消费者指标与专家技术指标结果层初步关联模型,通过相关分析和基于回归方程的 Shapley 值法[10,11]进行相关性验证和权重分析。

取消费者和专家对产品综合评分的平均值作为相关分析的原数据,通过 SPSS 软件进行分析。取消费者和专家对产品综合评分的平均值作为基于回归方程的 Shapley 值法分析的原数据,通过计算每个专家指标被纳入模型和未被纳入模型时 R^2 的变化,来确定该指标的贡献度。每个变量的 Shapley 值的计算公式如下:

$$SV_j = \sum_k \sum_i \frac{k!(n-k-1)!}{n!}[v(M_{i|j}) - v(M_{i|j(-j)})]$$

式中,$v(M_{i|j})$ 为模型 i 包含变量 j 时的 R^2;$v(M_{i|j(-j)})$ 为模型 i 不包含变量 j 时的 R^2;$v(M_{i|j}) - v(M_{i|j(-j)})$ 即为 j 变量被纳入模型和 j 变量未被纳入模型时 R^2 的变化;n 为变量总数;k 为不含 j 变量时模型中的变量总数;$\frac{k!(n-k-1)!}{n!}$ 为权重。

2 结果与分析

2.1 专家技术指标关联性分析

汇总专家意见后,形成专家技术指标设计层与结果层初步关联模型(图1)。

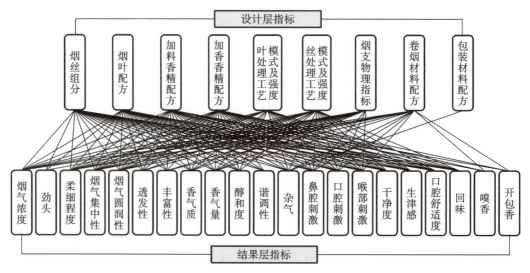

图1 专家技术指标设计层与结果层初步关联模型

同时邀请9位专家,对设计层与结果层各指标进行科学、合理的比较,再通过AHP层次分析法依次确定与特定结果层指标相关的设计层指标的权重,求出所有专家技术指标权重的平均值,获得各结果层相关的设计层指标权重(表4)。

表4 卷烟产品属性设计要素中与结果层关联的各设计层指标权重

序号	结果层指标	设计层指标	权重
1	烟气浓度	烟丝组分	0.27
		烟叶配方	0.23
		卷烟材料配方	0.17
		加料香精配方	0.10
		丝处理工艺模式及强度	0.06
		叶处理工艺模式及强度	0.06
		加香香精配方	0.06
		烟支物理指标	0.04
2	劲头	烟丝组分	0.42
		烟叶配方	0.41
		卷烟材料配方	0.19
		烟支物理指标	0.09
3	柔细程度	烟丝组分	0.19
		加香香精配方	0.15
		卷烟材料配方	0.15
		加料香精配方	0.15
		烟叶配方	0.14
		丝处理工艺模式及强度	0.10
		叶处理工艺模式及强度	0.08
		烟支物理指标	0.04
4	烟气集中性	烟叶配方	0.21
		烟丝组分	0.17
		加料香精配方	0.15
		加香香精配方	0.15
		卷烟材料配方	0.13
		丝处理工艺模式及强度	0.07
		叶处理工艺模式及强度	0.07
		烟支物理指标	0.04
5	烟气圆润性	加料香精配方	0.19
		烟叶配方	0.16

续表

序号	结果层指标	设计层指标	权重
5	烟气圆润性	烟丝组分	0.15
		加香香精配方	0.14
		卷烟材料配方	0.11
		丝处理工艺模式及强度	0.11
		叶处理工艺模式及强度	0.09
		烟支物理指标	0.05
6	透发性	烟叶配方	0.25
		烟丝组分	0.20
		加料香精配方	0.15
		卷烟材料配方	0.14
		加香香精配方	0.13
		丝处理工艺模式及强度	0.12
7	丰富性	烟叶配方	0.24
		烟丝组分	0.21
		加料香精配方	0.20
		加香香精配方	0.18
		卷烟材料配方	0.09
		丝处理工艺模式及强度	0.08
8	香气质	加香香精配方	0.19
		加料香精配方	0.19
		烟叶配方	0.18
		烟丝组分	0.16
		丝处理工艺模式及强度	0.09
		叶处理工艺模式及强度	0.08
		卷烟材料配方	0.07
		烟支物理指标	0.03
9	香气量	烟叶配方	0.19
		烟丝组分	0.19
		卷烟材料配方	0.15
		加料香精配方	0.15
		加香香精配方	0.12
		丝处理工艺模式及强度	0.09
		叶处理工艺模式及强度	0.06
		烟支物理指标	0.04

续表

序号	结果层指标	设计层指标	权重
10	醇和度	烟叶配方	0.25
		加料香精配方	0.21
		烟丝组分	0.20
		加香香精配方	0.16
		丝处理工艺模式及强度	0.09
		叶处理工艺模式及强度	0.09
11	谐调性	加香香精配方	0.35
		加料香精配方	0.32
		烟丝组分	0.17
		烟叶配方	0.16
12	杂气	烟叶配方	0.21
		烟丝组分	0.20
		加料香精配方	0.18
		加香香精配方	0.14
		叶处理工艺模式及强度	0.10
		丝处理工艺模式及强度	0.09
		卷烟材料配方	0.05
		包装材料配方	0.03
13	鼻腔刺激	烟丝组分	0.22
		烟叶配方	0.21
		加料香精配方	0.15
		加香香精配方	0.14
		丝处理工艺模式及强度	0.09
		卷烟材料配方	0.08
		叶处理工艺模式及强度	0.07
		烟支物理指标	0.05
14	口腔刺激	烟丝组分	0.20
		烟叶配方	0.18
		加料香精配方	0.17
		加香香精配方	0.15
		叶处理工艺模式及强度	0.09
		丝处理工艺模式及强度	0.08
		卷烟材料配方	0.07
		烟支物理指标	0.04

续表

序号	结果层指标	设计层指标	权重
15	喉部刺激	烟丝组分	0.20
		烟叶配方	0.19
		加料香精配方	0.17
		加香香精配方	0.15
		丝处理工艺模式及强度	0.09
		叶处理工艺模式及强度	0.09
		卷烟材料配方	0.07
		烟支物理指标	0.04
16	干净度	烟叶配方	0.25
		加料香精配方	0.21
		烟丝组分	0.21
		加香香精配方	0.16
		叶处理工艺模式及强度	0.09
		丝处理工艺模式及强度	0.08
17	生津感	烟叶配方	0.23
		烟丝组分	0.22
		加料香精配方	0.21
		加香香精配方	0.17
		叶处理工艺模式及强度	0.09
		丝处理工艺模式及强度	0.08
18	口腔舒适度	烟叶配方	0.22
		加香香精配方	0.21
		加料香精配方	0.18
		烟丝组分	0.18
		丝处理工艺模式及强度	0.10
		叶处理工艺模式及强度	0.10
19	回味	加料香精配方	0.24
		烟叶配方	0.21
		加香香精配方	0.18
		烟丝组分	0.18
		丝处理工艺模式及强度	0.10
		叶处理工艺模式及强度	0.09

续表

序号	结果层指标	设计层指标	权重
20	嗅香	加香香精配方	0.57
		加料香精配方	0.22
		卷烟材料配方	0.19
21	开包香	加香香精配方	0.57
		加料香精配方	0.22
		卷烟材料配方	0.19

选取平均相关性最高的指标进行连接(平均相关性相同时随机选择一项指标),得到简化后的关联模型作为结果层到设计层转化路径(图2)。

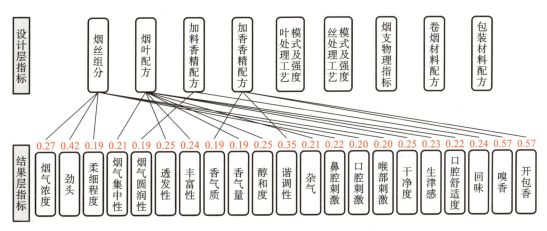

图2　专家技术指标结果层到设计层转化路径

2.2　消费者指标与专家技术指标关联性分析

前期研究[3]得出了一套可用于研究的消费者卷烟评价指标体系,其包括16个消费者指标:烟草纯正程度、嗅香新颖独特程度、嗅香浓淡程度、口腔舒适度、口腔干燥程度、口腔饱满程度、烟气平稳程度、喉咙舒适度、烟气细腻柔和度、烟气顺滑度、劲头、鼻腔舒适度、烟气丰富程度、余味舒适程度、余味干净程度、抽后口腔干燥程度。

2.2.1　消费者指标与专家技术指标结果层初步关联模型构建

将专家意见进行汇总,形成消费者指标与专家技术指标结果层初步关联模型(图3)。

2.2.2　消费者和专家技术指标间的关联性验证

在全国七大区域招募了135位卷烟重度消费者(日均吸烟量在10支以上),同时邀请了9名云南中烟工业有限责任公司技术中心的专家,参与了40款卷烟产品内在属性消费者指标和专家技术指标的满意度调查。分别使用消费者和专家对产品综合评分(打分指标)的平均值来作为相关分析的原数据,通过SPSS软件得出相关分析结果,并采用基于回

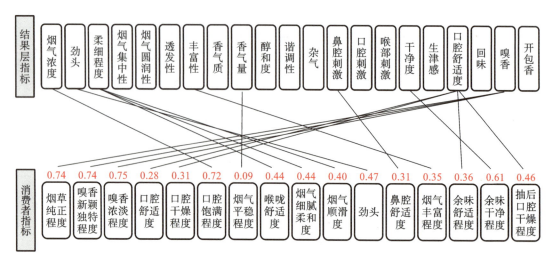

图 3　消费者指标与专家技术指标结果层初步关联模型

归方程的 Shapley 值法计算出与消费者指标相关的专家技术指标权重(表 5)。从表 5 可以看出,专家讨论得出的关联因素(结果层指标)确实与消费者指标间存在较高的关联程度,与各项消费者指标相关的专家技术指标权重如下:"烟草纯正程度"中开包香为重要指标,权重为 0.569;"嗅香新颖独特程度"中开包香为重要指标,权重为 0.549;"嗅香浓淡程度"中开包香为重要指标,权重为 0.545;"口腔舒适度"中干净度为重要指标,权重为 0.139;"口腔干燥程度"中干净度为重要指标,权重为 0.222;"口腔饱满程度"中烟气集中性为重要指标,权重为 0.662;"烟气平稳程度"中香气质为重要指标,权重为 0.084;"喉咙舒适度"中柔细程度为重要指标,权重为 0.373;"烟气细腻柔和度"中柔细程度为重要指标,权重为 0.271;"烟气顺滑度"中劲头为重要指标,权重为 0.345;"劲头"中柔细程度为重要指标,权重为 0.317;"鼻腔舒适度"中柔细程度为重要指标,权重为 0.267;"烟气丰富程度"中香气质为重要指标,权重为 0.268;"余味舒适程度"中干净度为重要指标,权重为 0.273;"余味干净程度"中干净度为重要指标,权重为 0.517;"抽后口腔干燥程度"中口腔舒适度为重要指标,权重为 0.339。

表 5　消费者指标和结果层指标关联性分析结果

序号	目标层(消费者指标)	指标层(结果层指标)	相关性结果	权重
1	烟草纯正程度	开包香	0.793	0.569
		嗅香	0.736	0.431
2	嗅香新颖独特程度	开包香	0.812	0.549
		嗅香	0.771	0.451
3	嗅香浓淡程度	开包香	0.775	0.545
		嗅香	0.739	0.455

续表

序号	目标层（消费者指标）	指标层（结果层指标）	相关性结果	权重
4	口腔舒适度	干净度	0.921	0.139
		口腔舒适度	0.912	0.129
		柔细程度	0.910	0.134
		回味	0.908	0.126
		醇和度	0.897	0.118
		生津感	0.894	0.120
		口腔刺激	0.890	0.115
		烟气圆润性	0.875	0.120
5	口腔干燥程度	干净度	0.906	0.222
		口腔舒适度	0.898	0.202
		口腔刺激	0.885	0.195
		生津感	0.884	0.194
		烟气圆润性	0.865	0.187
6	口腔饱满程度	烟气集中性	0.904	0.662
		烟气浓度	0.741	0.338
7	烟气平稳程度	香气质	0.920	0.084
		干净度	0.898	0.055
		柔细程度	0.897	0.060
		醇和度	0.895	0.056
		回味	0.893	0.055
		杂气	0.891	0.054
		口腔舒适度	0.887	0.052
		生津感	0.884	0.054
		鼻腔刺激	0.883	0.054
		劲头	0.871	0.056
		喉部刺激	0.870	0.051
		口腔刺激	0.869	0.050
		烟气集中性	0.866	0.055
		烟气圆润性	0.861	0.055
		谐调性	0.855	0.051
		丰富性	0.848	0.045

续表

序号	目标层(消费者指标)	指标层(结果层指标)	相关性结果	权重
7	烟气平稳程度	透发性	0.833	0.044
		香气量	0.781	0.039
		烟气浓度	0.628	0.031
8	喉咙舒适度	柔细程度	0.909	0.373
		喉部刺激	0.889	0.336
		劲头	0.846	0.292
9	烟气顺滑度	柔细程度	0.878	0.345
		劲头	0.871	0.341
		喉部刺激	0.861	0.314
10	烟气细腻柔和度	柔细程度	0.893	0.271
		喉部刺激	0.876	0.248
		劲头	0.870	0.257
		烟气圆润性	0.860	0.229
11	劲头	柔细程度	0.910	0.317
		喉部刺激	0.895	0.291
		劲头	0.874	0.277
		烟气浓度	0.614	0.242
12	鼻腔舒适度	柔细程度	0.897	0.267
		醇和度	0.891	0.258
		鼻腔刺激	0.878	0.242
		烟气圆润性	0.869	0.233
13	烟气丰富程度	香气质	0.908	0.268
		醇和度	0.878	0.206
		谐调性	0.861	0.189
		丰富性	0.834	0.174
		香气量	0.809	0.164
14	余味舒适程度	干净度	0.918	0.273
		回味	0.903	0.248
		口腔舒适度	0.902	0.245
		生津感	0.889	0.235

续表

序号	目标层(消费者指标)	指标层(结果层指标)	相关性结果	权重
15	余味干净程度	干净度	0.910	0.517
		口腔舒适度	0.895	0.483
16	抽后口腔干燥程度	口腔舒适度	0.876	0.339
		生津感	0.876	0.323
		回味	0.867	0.338

从相关分析可以看出，一个消费者指标可能与多个专家技术指标相关，且不同参数与指标间存在相关性差异。优先选取关联度较高的专家技术指标来进行改进，可以更科学、高效地实现产品改良。本研究在消费者指标与专家技术指标(结果层)初步关联模型的基础上，依据基于回归方程的 Shapley 值法获得了相关性分析结果，并最终获得消费者评价指标(消费层)—专家评价技术指标(结果层)—卷烟设计技术指标(设计层)的关联模型(图4)。卷烟生产企业可在与各个消费者指标相关联的专家技术指标中，选取相关性最高的指标构建转化路径，用于指导卷烟产品的改良。例如，在进行云烟(软大重九)顾客满意度调查时发现，消费者对于喉咙舒适度这一指标的打分情况较均值偏低，因此在进行产品改良时，需要优先改进这一指标。而根据设计层—结果层—消费层的关联模型，可以得出消费者指标喉咙舒适度与专家技术指标结果层的柔细程度相关性最高，而柔细程度又与专家技术指标设计层的烟丝组分相关，因此在改进喉咙舒适度这一指标时，可以优先改进烟丝组分来提升消费者对这一指标的满意度。

3 小结

本研究通过分析卷烟消费者产品需求的重要性，将卷烟技术指标与消费者产品需求进行关联，建立了卷烟产品特征属性与消费需求的对接转化模型：烟草纯正程度—开包香—加香香精配方；嗅香新颖独特程度—开包香—加香香精配方；嗅香浓淡程度—开包香—加香香精配方；口腔舒适度—干净度—烟叶配方；口腔干燥程度—干净度—烟叶配方；口腔饱满程度—烟气集中性—烟叶配方；烟气平稳程度—香气质—加香香精配方；喉咙舒适度—柔细程度—烟丝组分；烟气细腻柔和度—柔细程度—烟丝组分；烟气顺滑度—劲头—烟丝组分；劲头—柔细程度—烟丝组分；鼻腔舒适度—柔细程度—烟丝组分；烟气丰富程度—香气质—加香香精配方；余味舒适程度—干净度—烟叶配方；余味干净程度—干净度—烟叶配方；抽后口腔干燥程度—口腔舒适度—烟叶配方。该对接转化模型可为今后产品开发提供市场认可的指标转化路径。

此外，为了从消费者角度更加有针对性地对卷烟产品进行改进，卷烟生产企业应对消费者指标评价体系不断进行完善，通过指标评价体系的应用，全面了解产品的优势与劣势所在，并找到其改进路径，从而实现基于消费者体验的卷烟产品设计。

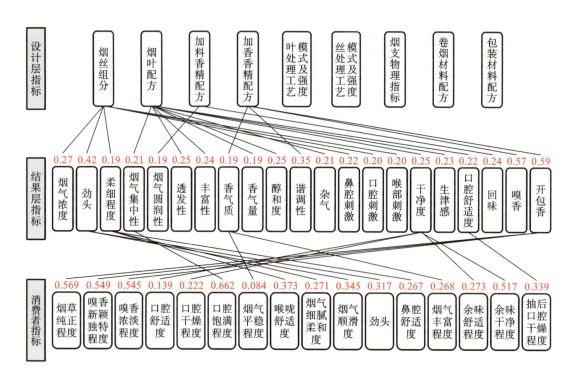

图 4 设计层—结果层—消费层的关联模型

参考文献

[1] 叶奕.面向零售商的烟草货源投放模式研究[D].杭州:浙江工业大学,2012.

[2] 段文婷.经济社会发展对卷烟消费需求的影响[C]//中国烟草学会2016年度优秀论文汇编.北京:中国烟草学会,2016.

[3] 杨蕾,杨乾栩,冯洪涛,等.卷烟产品消费者满意度影响因素实证研究[J].云南农业大学学报(社会科学),2019,13(5):93-101.

[4] 李豪.浅谈区域市场的卷烟消费者研究工作[C]//中国烟草学会2014年度优秀论文汇编.北京:中国烟草学会,2014.

[5] 王昊.卷烟企业顾客满意度指数模型设计及应用[C]//中国烟草学会2014年度优秀论文汇编.北京:中国烟草学会,2014.

[6] 白远良,吴应禄,程晓苏.我国卷烟需求分析:卷烟需求模型实证分析与结论[J].中国烟草学报,2007(4):55-59.

[7] 宇文立平,钱敏,张金锁.AHP法在顾客满意度指标评价中的应用[J].西安科技学院学报,2001,21(2):175-177.

[8] 张瑾,李秉诚.现代营销体系下需求预测的方法探究[C]//上海市烟草学会2020年度优秀论文集.上海:上海市烟草学会,2020.

[9] SAATYT L. Axiomatic Foundation of the Analytic Hierarchy Process[J].

Management Science,1986,32(7):841-855.

[10] 李叔清,周业付.基于 Shapley 模型的农产品供应链利益分配[J].现代营销,2020(4):144-145.

[11] CHAUHAN S,PROTH J M. Analysis of a Supply Chain Partnership with Revenue Sharing[J]. International Journal of Production Economics,2005,97(1):44-51.

Research on the Correlation between Cigarette Consumer Evaluation and Expert Technical Indicators

Abstract: The design and improvement of cigarettes play a crucial role in managing the cigarette market, as they need to meet the demands of consumers. This study transforms consumer demand models to explore the correlation between consumer evaluations and expert technical indicators in cigarette design. Through surveys with consumers and experts, the Analytic Hierarchy Process (AHP) is utilized to establish a preliminary correlation model between expert technical indicators at the design layer, expert technical indicators at the result layer, and consumer indicators. Subsequently, this association model is verified along with weight analysis using correlation analysis and regression equations based on the Shapley value method. A transformation model for aligning cigarette product attributes with consumer demand is established. This model links consumer evaluation and expert evaluation technology indicators with cigarette design technical indicators to better understand consumer demand and enhance production-consumption connections.

Keywords: Consumer demand; Product attributes; Cigarette indicator evaluation; Correlation

The tobacco industry is an integral part of the national economy, and due to the unique nature of its products, it has historically been subject to "unified leadership, vertical management, monopoly franchise" management system. However, with the development of a market economy, there has been a gradual shift towards a market-oriented management approach driven by consumer demand. Under this business philosophy, understanding consumer demand and implementing targeted cigarette design and improvement are crucial foundations for successful market operation. In recent years, some tobacco enterprises have begun to embrace the market management concept in guiding the design and improvement of cigarettes, as well as in production and marketing, resulting in significant achievements. Nevertheless, the tobacco industry still faces challenges, such as a lack of market-oriented strategies[1,2]. According to current market management principles, cigarette product design, production, and marketing should be aligned with consumer demand. Strategies should be developed based on consumers' consumption behaviors, characteristics evaluation, and satisfaction[3, 4]. However, due to the long-standing monopoly management mode adopted by the tobacco industry, production enterprises have insufficient understanding of consumer demand. Over time, consumer groups have established their own set of criteria for evaluating cigarettes that primarily reflect their simple demand for cigarette quality but may not fully capture or understand their preferences. In-depth analysis of consumers' verbal evaluation criteria and understanding of consumers' demands and consumption characteristics can provide essential insights for decision-making among cigarette operators[5, 6].

Cigarette consumption is often influenced by various factors such as consumers' age, occupation, income, region, cigarette preference, brand loyalty, and policy effects. Understanding the consumption characteristics of consumers and accurately analyzing their rhetoric evaluation marks are essential in achieving better convergence of production and consumption. Experts with extensive experience in cigarette formulation and qualification for sensory evaluation of tobacco and products typically conduct professional evaluations. The evaluation criteria used by consumers differ from the technical standards employed in cigarette manufacturing, and the assessment methods for professional products also vary. However, there remains a lack of a transformation model guided by consumer demand to facilitate the alignment of consumer evaluation, expert evaluation technology indicators, and cigarette design technical standards. As such, the market-oriented cigarette industry urgently needs to engage in precision marketing activities and demand-oriented research and development efforts. This will enable the translation of consumer demand into product quality requirements, product design specifications, packaging designs, and production process demands. Guided by market trends, this study aims to establish an effective system for evaluating cigarette technical standards that can effectively link consumer demand with these standards. Additionally it seeks to explore the construction of a model that reflects consumer evaluations in product testing to guide production practices while integrating research with marketing.

1 Research Methods

1.1 The Data Source

1.1.1 Expert Evaluation

The study invited a group of nine qualified professionals with extensive experience in cigarette product formula and tobacco sensory evaluation to participate in face-to-face forums. The study aims to establish the attributes of cigarette products and the model of transfer based on consumer demand. Therefore, it is necessary to generalize professionally to construct relevant technical indicators for experts' and consumers' evaluation indicators. Additionally, preliminary exploration was conducted to examine the correlation between professional opinions of expert technical indicators and the consumer evaluation indicators, providing a basis for validation in subsequent consumer research.

1.1.2 Product Test

(1) Consumer Survey. A survey was conducted using test samples from the top 40 national sales cigarette products (Table 1). The survey targeted heavy smokers aged 18-50 (with an average daily consumption of more than 10 cigarettes) across seven regions, each containing two cities for a total of 14 cities. A total of 140 questionnaires were distributed, with each city receiving 10 questionnaires, resulting in an effective questionnaire recovery rate of 96.43%, as evidenced by the return of 135 completed surveys (see Table 2 for geographic distribution and quantity).

Table 1 Evaluation of 40 Cigarette Products and Associated Indicators

Serial No.	Sales of the initial 40 products	Price/(yuan/piece)	Tar/mg	Price class	Serial No.	Sales of the initial 40 products	Price/(yuan/piece)	Tar/mg	Price class
1	Baisha (premium)	85	8	III	11	Hongtashan (hard classic)	75	10	III
2	Baisha (second generation premium)	110	10	III	12	Hongtashan (hard classic 100)	100	10	III
3	Baisha (soft)	45	10	IV	13	Monkey King (gold)	55	10	IV
4	Baisha (hard)	55	10	IV	14	Huangguoshu (long march)	55	11	IV
5	Furongwang (hard)	250	11	I	15	Huanghelou (soft blue)	190	11	I
6	Guiyan (hard yellow premium)	130	11	II	16	Huanghelou (the towers in the world)	160	8	II
7	Hademen (premium)	45	10	IV	17	Huanghelou (elegant fragrant gold)	160	8	II
8	Hongmei (soft-yellow)	45	10	IV	18	Gold Leaf (hard emgrand)	105	11	III
9	Double Happiness (hard)	80	11	III	19	Gold Leaf (hard red flag canal)	105	10	III
10	Hongtashan (soft classic)	75	10	III	20	Huangshan (newly made Anhui tobacco)	140	11	II

continue

Serial No.	Sales of the initial 40 products	Price/ (yuan/ piece)	Tar/ mg	Price class	Serial No.	Sales of the initial 40 products	Price/ (yuan/ piece)	Tar/ mg	Price class
21	Huangshan (hard first rank)	55	10	IV	31	Double Happiness (soft classic)	100	11	III
22	Lanzhou (hard treasure)	180	8	II	32	Double Happiness (hard classic 1906)	170	10	II
23	Liqun (soft red long mouth)	220	11	I	33	Suyan (five star redwood)	220	11	I
24	Liqun (soft blue)	180	11	II	34	Mount Tai (red general)	70	11	III
25	Liqun (west sunshine)	310	5	I	35	Yuxi (soft)	230	11	I
26	Liqun (new version)	140	11	II	36	Yunyan (soft-treasure)	230	11	I
27	Nanjing (red)	120	11	III	37	Yunyan (purple)	100	10	III
28	Nanjing (xuanhemen)	160	8	II	38	Zhonghua (soft)	700	11	I
29	Nanjing (riverstones)	530	5	I	39	Zhonghua (hard)	450	11	I
30	Seven Wolves (red)	150	11	II	40	Zhongnanhai (5 mg)	100	5	III

Table 2 Distribution and Quantity of Questionnaires Distributed by Geographic Location

Area	East China	North China	South China	Southwest	Northwest	Northeast	Central China
City	Shanghai	Beijing	Guangzhou	Chengdu	Xi'an	Shenyang	Zhengzhou
Sample size	11	10	9	11	8	10	9
City	Ningbo	Baoding	Shenzhen	Kunming	Lanzhou	Harbin	Wuhan
Sample size	10	11	8	10	9	11	8

(2) Expert Investigation. Nine experts from the R&D Center of Yunnan Tobacco Industry Co., Ltd. have been invited to conduct smoking and evaluation of the same batch of cigarette products in conjunction with consumer research within a 14-day period.

This will be achieved through the use of professional design and technical parameters.

1.2 Analysis Method

1.2.1 Identification and Differentiation of Expert Technical Indicators

A forum was convened with expert technical indicators to facilitate discussions among the organization's expert group to identify and differentiate the various indicators. The goal was to explore the intrinsic relationship between these indicators further. Experts specializing in tobacco industry formulas were selected to ensure the accuracy of classification results and the reliability of decision-making. Following extensive discussions during the meeting at the R&D Center of Yunnan Tobacco Industry Co., Ltd., the original expert technical indicators were further clarified based on product attributes. The technical indicators were divided into two layers: design layer and result layer. At the design layer, a total of nine cigarette design specifications were identified, including cut tobacco formula, tobacco leaf formula, adding formulations, favoring formulations, mode and intensity of tobacco leaf treatment process, mode and intensity of cut tobacco treatment process, physical indicators of cigarette, formula for cigarette materials, as well as formula for packaging materials used for improvement by the R&D Center products. At the result layer, 21 expert evaluations of technical indicators were established. These included parameters such as concentration of smoke, aroma quality, throat irritation, strength, aroma quantity, cleanness, softness, mellowness, moisturizing sensation, smoke centrality, harmony, oral comfort, smoothness, offensive odor, aftertaste, permeability, nasal irritation, sniffing, richness, oral irritation, opening aroma. These indicators are utilized in quantitative research through expert scoring methods.

1.2.2 Weight Analysis of Technical Indicators by Experts

The results obtained by experts are determined through the Analytic Hierarchy Process (AHP) to establish the weights of the design layer indicators related to specific result layer indicators. For each level of the hierarchy, if the k-th expert considers the relative importance of the i-th result layer technical indicator to the j-th cigarette design technical indicator (design layer) as $a_{ij}k\ (i,j=1,2,\cdots,9)$, then a total of 9 judgment matrices are provided. The consistency is calculated using the formula:

$$CR = |\lambda_{\max} - m| / (m-1) \times RI$$

Here, CR refers to consistency ratio, if its value is less than 0.1, it passes consistency judgment. Where $CR=CI/RI$; CI represents consistency index and RI stands for random consistency index; $\lambda_{\max}$ denotes maximum positive eigenvalue of judgment matrix; m indicates number of judgment matrices. CI can be calculated as:

$$CI = (\lambda_{max} - n)/(n - 1)$$

In this equation, when CI=0, it indicates complete consistency in judgment matrix; conversely, larger values of CI indicate poorer consistency in judgment matrix. Here λ_{max} represents maximum eigenvalue of judgement matrix and random consistency index RI can be referred from Table 3.

Table 3 Random Consistency Index

n	1	2	3	4	5	6	7	8	9	10	11
RI	0.00	0.00	0.58	0.90	1.12	1.24	1.32	1.41	1.45	1.49	1.51

The consistency ratio (CR) is typically used to determine a judgment matrix's acceptable range of inconsistency. The calculation formula for CR is as follows:

$$CR = \frac{CI}{RI}$$

By comparing CI with RI, we can test whether the judgment matrix has satisfactory consistency. If CR<0.1, it indicates that the consistency of the judgment matrix is satisfactory; if CR≥0.1, further adjustments to the judgment matrix are needed until satisfaction is achieved.

After assessing consistency, using the formula:

$$a_{ij} = \sqrt[K]{\prod_{k=1}^{K} a_{ij}^k}$$

It is used to calculate weights and obtain the average results of all expert technical indicators weights.

1.2.3 Analysis of the Correlation between Consumer Indicators and Expert Technical Indicators

By summarizing expert opinions and forming a preliminary correlation model between consumer and expert technical indicators, the correlation and weight analysis are verified through correlation analysis and the Shapley value method based on regression equation[10, 11]. The average scores of product evaluations by consumers and experts are used as the original data for correlation analysis, which is analyzed using SPSS software. The average scores of product evaluations by consumers and experts are used as the original data for the Shapley value method analysis based on the regression equation. The contribution of each indicator is determined by calculating the change in R^2 when each expert indicator is included or not included in the model. The calculation formula for the Shapley value of each variable is as follows:

$$SV_j = \sum_k \sum_i \frac{k!(n-k-1)!}{n!}[v(M_{i|j}) - v(M_{i|j(-j)})]$$

Where $v(M_{i|j})$ represents the R^2 when variable j is included in model i, $v(M_{i|j(-j)})$

represents the R-squared when variable j is not included in model i, $v(M_{i|j}) - v(M_{i|j(-j)})$ represents the change in R-squared when variable j is included or not included in the model; n represents a total number of variables; k represents a total number of variables in model without variable j; $k!(n-k-1)!/n!$ represents weight.

2 Results and Analysis

2.1 Correlation Analysis of Expert Technical Indicators

After summarizing experts' opinions, a preliminary correlation model was formed between the expert technical indicators at the design and results layers (see Figure 1). At the same time, 9 experts were invited to scientifically and reasonably compare each indicator at the design layer with those at the results layer. Then, the AHP hierarchical analysis method determined weights for specific design-layer indicators related to result-layer indicators sequentially. The average of all expert weight results was calculated to obtain the weights of design-layer indicators for each result layer (see Table 4).

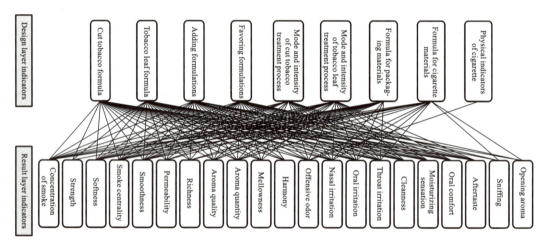

Figure 1 The Preliminary Model of the Initial Association between Design Layer and Result Layer on Expert Technical Indicator

Table 4 The Weights of Each Design Layer Indicator Associated with the Cigarette Product Attribute Design Elements on the Result Layer

No.	Result layer indicators	Design layer indicators	Weights
1	Concentration of smoke	Cut tobacco formula	0.27
		Tobacco leaf formula	0.23
		Formula for cigarette materials	0.17

continue

No.	Result layer indicators	Design layer indicators	Weights
1	Concentration of smoke	Adding formulations	0.10
		Mode and intensity of tobacco leaf treatment process	0.06
		Mode and intensity of tobacco leaf treatment process	0.06
		Favoring formulations	0.06
		Physical indicators of cigarette	0.04
2	Strength	Cut tobacco formula	0.42
		Tobacco leaf formula	0.41
		Formula for cigarette materials	0.19
		Physical indicators of cigarette	0.09
3	Softness	Cut tobacco formula	0.19
		Favoring formulations	0.15
		Formula for cigarette materials	0.15
		Adding formulations	0.15
		Tobacco leaf formula	0.14
		Mode and intensity of cut tobacco treatment process	0.10
		Mode and intensity of tobacco leaf treatment process	0.08
		Physical indicators of cigarette	0.04
4	Smoke centrality	Tobacco leaf formula	0.21
		Cut tobacco formula	0.17
		Adding formulations	0.15
		Favoring formulations	0.15
		Formula for cigarette materials	0.13
		Mode and intensity of cut tobacco treatment process	0.07
		Mode and intensity of tobacco leaf treatment process	0.07
		Physical indicators of cigarette	0.04
5	Smoothness	Adding formulations	0.19
		Tobacco leaf formula	0.16
		Cut tobacco formula	0.15
		Favoring formulations	0.14
		Formula for cigarette materials	0.11
		Mode and intensity of cut tobacco treatment process	0.11
		Mode and intensity of tobacco leaf treatment process	0.09
		Physical indicators of cigarette	0.05

continue

No.	Result layer indicators	Design layer indicators	Weights
6	Permeability	Tobacco leaf formula	0.25
		Cut tobacco formula	0.20
		Adding formulations	0.15
		Formula for cigarette materials	0.14
		Favoring formulations	0.13
		Mode and intensity of cut tobacco treatment process	0.12
7	Richness	Tobacco leaf formula	0.24
		Cut tobacco formula	0.21
		Adding formulations	0.20
		Favoring formulations	0.18
		Formula for cigarette materials	0.09
		Mode and intensity of cut tobacco treatment process	0.08
8	Aroma quality	Favoring formulations	0.19
		Adding formulations	0.19
		Tobacco leaf formula	0.18
		Cut tobacco formula	0.16
		Mode and intensity of cut tobacco treatment process	0.09
		Mode and intensity of tobacco leaf treatment process	0.08
		Formula for cigarette materials	0.07
		Physical indicators of cigarette	0.03
9	Aroma quantity	Tobacco leaf formula	0.19
		Cut tobacco formula	0.19
		Formula for cigarette materials	0.15
		Adding formulations	0.15
		Favoring formulations	0.12
		Mode and intensity of cut tobacco treatment process	0.09
		Mode and intensity of tobacco leaf treatment process	0.06
		Physical indicators of cigarette	0.04
10	Mellowness	Tobacco leaf formula	0.25
		Adding formulations	0.21
		Cut tobacco formula	0.20
		Favoring formulations	0.16

continue

No.	Result layer indicators	Design layer indicators	Weights
10	Mellowness	Mode and intensity of cut tobacco treatment process	0.09
		Mode and intensity of tobacco leaf treatment process	0.09
11	Harmony	Favoring formulations	0.35
		Adding formulations	0.32
		Cut tobacco formula	0.17
		Tobacco leaf formula	0.16
12	Offensive odor	Tobacco leaf formula	0.21
		Cut tobacco formula	0.20
		Adding formulations	0.18
		Favoring formulations	0.14
		Mode and intensity of tobacco leaf treatment process	0.10
		Mode and intensity of cut tobacco treatment process	0.09
		Formula for cigarette materials	0.05
		Formula for packaging materia	0.03
13	Nasal irritation	Cut tobacco formula	0.22
		Tobacco leaf formula	0.21
		Adding formulations	0.15
		Favoring formulations	0.14
		Mode and intensity of cut tobacco treatment process	0.09
		Formula for cigarette materials	0.08
		Mode and intensity of tobacco leaf treatment process	0.07
		Physical indicators of cigarette	0.05
14	Oral irritation	Cut tobacco formula	0.20
		Tobacco leaf formula	0.18
		Adding formulations	0.17
		Favoring formulations	0.15
		Mode and intensity of cut tobacco treatment process	0.09
		Mode and intensity of tobacco leaf treatment process	0.08
		Formula for cigarette materials	0.07
		Physical indicators of cigarette	0.04
15	Throat irritation	Cut tobacco formula	0.20
		Tobacco leaf formula	0.19

continue

No.	Result layer indicators	Design layer indicators	Weights
15	Throat irritation	Adding formulations	0.17
		Favoring formulations	0.15
		Mode and intensity of cut tobacco treatment process	0.09
		Mode and intensity of tobacco leaf treatment process	0.09
		Formula for cigarette materials	0.07
		Physical indicators of cigarette	0.04
16	Cleanness	Tobacco leaf formula	0.25
		Adding formulations	0.21
		Cut tobacco formula	0.21
		Favoring formulations	0.16
		Mode and intensity of tobacco leaf treatment process	0.09
		Mode and intensity of cut tobacco treatment process	0.08
17	Moisturizing sensation	Tobacco leaf formula	0.23
		Cut tobacco formula	0.22
		Adding formulations	0.21
		Favoring formulations	0.17
		Mode and intensity of tobacco leaf treatment process	0.09
		Mode and intensity of cut tobacco treatment process	0.08
18	Oral comfort	Tobacco leaf formula	0.22
		Adding formulations	0.21
		Favoring formulations	0.18
		Cut tobacco formula	0.18
		Mode and intensity of cut tobacco treatment process	0.10
		Mode and intensity of tobacco leaf treatment process	0.10
19	Aftertaste	Adding formulations	0.24
		Tobacco leaf formula	0.21
		Favoring formulations	0.18
		Cut tobacco formula	0.18
		Mode and intensity of cut tobacco treatment process	0.10
		Mode and intensity of tobacco leaf treatment process	0.09
20	Sniffing	Favoring formulations	0.57
		Adding formulations	0.22
		Formula for cigarette materials	0.19

No.	Result layer indicators	Design layer indicators	Weights
21	Opening aroma	Favoring formulations	0.57
		Formula for cigarette materials	0.22
		Adding formulations	0.19

In addition, by selecting the indicators with the highest average corrlation for connection(pick one item at random when average corrlation is the same), a simplified correlation model was obtained as a transformation path from the result layer to the design layer (see Figure 2).

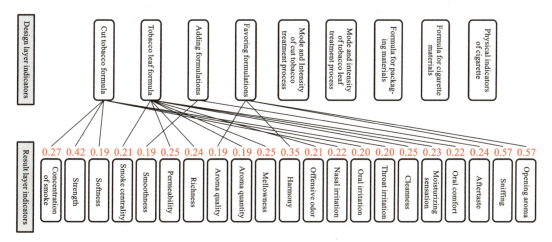

Figure 2   Transformation Path from Results Layer to Design Layer on Expert Technical Indicator

2.2   Consumer Indicator and Expert Technical Indicator Correlation Analysis

Previous research[3] has developed a set of consumer cigarette evaluation indicators that can be used for research, including 16 consumer indicators: purity of tobacco, novelty and uniqueness of sniffing, sniffing intensity, oral comfort, oral dryness, oral fullness, smoke stability, throat comfort, delicacy and softness of smoke, smoke smoothness, strength, nasal comfort, smoke richness, aftertaste comfort, aftertaste cleanliness, and oral dryness after smoking.

2.2.1   Preliminary Construction of the Model for the Initial Association between Consumer Indicators and Expert Technical Indicators

The expert opinions were summarized to form a preliminary model for the association between consumer and expert technical indicators (Figure 3).

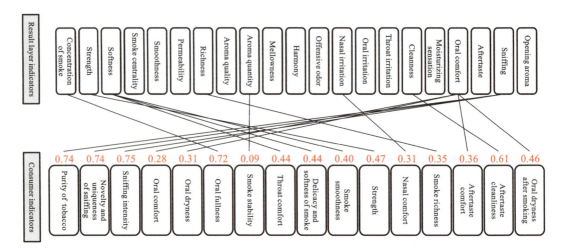

Figure 3　Preliminary Model for the Initial Association between Consumer Indicators and Expert Technical Indicators

2.2.2　Validation of the Association between Consumer and Expert Technical Indicators

A total of 135 heavy cigarette consumers (smoking more than 10 cigarettes per day) were recruited from seven major regions nationwide. At the same time, 9 experts from China Tobacco Yunnan Industrial Co., Ltd. participated in a satisfaction survey on 40 cigarette products' intrinsic attributes based on consumer and expert technical indicators. The average scores given by consumers and experts for product evaluation (scoring indicator) were used as raw data for correlation analysis. SPSS software was used to obtain the correlation analysis results. The Shapley value method based on regression equations was then employed to calculate the weights of expert technical indicators related to consumer indicators (Table 5). From Table 5, there is indeed a high degree of association between the factors discussed by experts (result layer indicators) and consumer indicators. The weights of expert indicators related to various consumer indicators are as follows:

-Regarding the purity of tobacco, opening aroma contributes most significantly with a weight of 0.569.

-For novelty and uniqueness of sniffing, opening aroma holds greater importance with a weight of 0.549.

-Regarding sniffing intensity, opening aroma has the highest contribution with a weight of 0.545.

-Cleanliness contributes most significantly to oral comfort with a weight of 0.139.

-Regarding oral dryness, cleanliness holds the most significant importance, with a weight of 0.222.

—Smoke centrality describes oral fullness best, contributing at an extent level with a weight of 0.662.

—Aroma quality is most important in smoke stability, holding an importance level at an extent level, with weight 0.084.

—Throat comfort relies mostly on softness levels, which hold the greatest importance at an extent level, with a weight of 0.373.

—Softness contributes greatly to the delicacy and softness of smoke, having a high weight of 0.271.

—Strength plays the strongest role in smoothness, having a high weight of 0.345.

—In strength perception, softness holds the highest contribution level, having a high weight of 0.317.

—Nasal comfort relies mostly on softness levels, having the greatest importance level, with a weight of 0.267.

—Aroma quality is most important in smoke richness perception, with a weight of 0.268.

—Cleanliness holds the greatest importance in aftertaste comfort, with a weight of 0.273.

—In aftertaste cleanliness sensation, cleanliness has the highest contribution level with a weight of 0.517.

—Oral dryness after smoking relies mostly on oral comfort, with the greatest importance level with a weight of 0.339.

Table 5　Analysis of the Correlation between Consumer Indicators and Result Layer Indicators

No.	Target Level (consumer indicators)	Indicator Level (result layer indicators)	Correlation	Weights
1	Purity of tobacco	Opening aroma	0.793	0.569
		Sniffing	0.736	0.431
2	Novelty and uniqueness of sniffing	Opening aroma	0.812	0.549
		Sniffing	0.771	0.451
3	Sniffing intensity	Opening aroma	0.775	0.545
		Sniffing	0.739	0.455
4	Oral comfort	Cleanness	0.921	0.139
		Oral comfort	0.912	0.129
		Softness	0.910	0.134

continue

No.	Target Level (consumer indicators)	Indicator Level (result layer indicators)	Correlation	Weights
4	Oral comfort	Aftertaste	0.908	0.126
		Mellowness	0.897	0.118
		Moisturizing sensation	0.894	0.120
		Oral irritation	0.890	0.115
		Smoothness	0.875	0.120
5	Oral dryness	Cleanness	0.906	0.222
		Oral comfort	0.898	0.202
		Oral irritation	0.885	0.195
		Moisturizing	0.884	0.194
		Smoothness	0.865	0.187
6	Oral fullness	Smoke centrality	0.904	0.662
		Concentration of smoke	0.741	0.338
7	Smoke stability	Aroma quality	0.920	0.084
		Cleanness	0.898	0.055
		Softness	0.897	0.060
		Mellowness	0.895	0.056
		Aftertaste	0.893	0.055
		Offensive odor	0.891	0.054
		Oral comfort	0.887	0.052
		Moisturizing sensation	0.884	0.054
		Nasal irritation	0.883	0.054
		Strength	0.871	0.056
		Throat irritation	0.870	0.051
		Oral irritation	0.869	0.050
		Smoke centrality	0.866	0.055
		Smoothness	0.861	0.055
		Harmony	0.855	0.051
		Richness	0.848	0.045
		Permeability	0.833	0.044
		Aroma quantity	0.781	0.039
		Concentration of smoke	0.628	0.031

continue

No.	Target Level (consumer indicators)	Indicator Level (result layer indicators)	Correlation	Weights
8	Throat comfort	Softness	0.909	0.373
		Throat irritation	0.889	0.336
		Strength	0.846	0.292
9	Smoke smoothness	Softness	0.878	0.345
		Strength	0.871	0.341
		Throat irritation	0.861	0.314
10	Delicacy and softness of smoke	Softness	0.893	0.271
		Throat irritation	0.876	0.248
		Strength	0.870	0.257
		Smoothness	0.860	0.229
11	Strength	Softness	0.910	0.317
		Throat irritation	0.895	0.291
		Strength	0.874	0.277
		Concentration of smoke	0.614	0.242
12	Nasal comfort	Softness	0.897	0.267
		Mellowness	0.891	0.258
		Nasal irritation	0.878	0.242
		Smoothness	0.869	0.233
13	Smoke richness	Aroma quality	0.908	0.268
		Mellowness	0.878	0.206
		Harmony	0.861	0.189
		Richness	0.834	0.174
		Aroma quantity	0.809	0.164
14	Aftertaste comfort	Cleanness	0.918	0.273
		Aftertaste	0.903	0.248
		Oral comfort	0.902	0.245
		Moisturizing sensation	0.889	0.235
15	Aftertaste cleanliness	Cleanness	0.910	0.517
		Oral comfort	0.895	0.483

continue

No.	Target Level (consumer indicators)	Indicator Level (result layer indicators)	Correlation	Weights
16	Oral dryness after smoking	Oral comfort	0.876	0.339
		Moisturizing sensation	0.876	0.323
		Aftertaste	0.867	0.338

From the correlation analysis, a consumer indicator may be related to multiple expert technical indicators, and there are differences in correlation between each parameter and indicator. Priority selecting expert technical indicators with higher relevance for improvement can more scientifically and efficiently achieve product improvement. Based on the preliminary correlation model of consumer indicators and expert technical indicators (result layer), this study obtained the correlation analysis results based on the Shapley value method using regression equations and ultimately obtained the association model of consumer evaluation indicators (consumption layer) - expert evaluation technical indicators (result layer) - cigarette design technical indicators (design layer) (Figure 4). Cigarette production enterprises can select the most relevant indicators from the expert technical indicators associated with each consumer indicator to construct a transformation path for guiding cigarette product improvement. For example, during a customer satisfaction survey for Yunyan (soft 99), it was found that consumers rated throat comfort relatively low compared to the average score. Therefore, when making product improvements, it is necessary to prioritize improving this indicator. According to the association model of the design layer - result layer- consumption layer, it can be concluded that throat comfort as a consumer indicator has the highest correlation with the expert technical indicator result layer softness level, which in turn is correlated with the expert technical indicator design layer cut tobacco formula. Therefore, when improving throat comfort as an indicator, priority should be given to improving cut tobacco formula in order to enhance consumer satisfaction with this particular aspect.

3 Conclusion

This study establishes a model for the exchange and transformation of cigarette product characteristics and consumer demands by analyzing the importance of product requirements for cigarette consumers and correlating cigarette technical indicators with consumer product demands. The model includes attributes such as purity of tobacco - opening aroma - favoring formulations; novelty and uniqueness of sniffing - opening aroma - favoring formulations; sniffing intensity - opening aroma - favoring formulations;

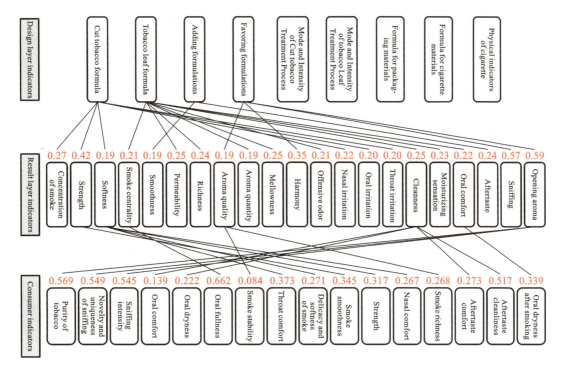

Figure 4　The Associated Model of the Design Layer, Result Layer, and Consumption Layer

oral comfort - cleanness - tobacco leaf formula; oral dryness - cleanness - tobacco leaf formula; oral fullness - smoke centrality - tobacco leaf formula; smoke stability - aroma quality - favoring formulations; throat comfort - softness - cut tobacco formula; delicacy and softness of smoke - softness - cut tobacco formula; smoke smoothness - strength - cut tobacco formula; strength - softness - cut tobacco formula; nasal comfort - softness - cut tobacco formula; smoke richness - aroma quality - favoring formulations; aftertaste comfort - cleanness - tobacco leaf formula; aftertaste cleanliness - cleanness - tobacco leaf formula; oral dryness after smoking - oral comfort - tobacco leaf formula. This exchange transfer model can provide a recognized market indicator exchange path.

Furthermore, to improve cigarette products more targeted from the perspective of consumers' side, the evaluation system should be continuously improved by cigarette production enterprises. Applying this evaluation system makes it possible to fully understand both strengths and weaknesses within products while finding ways to improve them based on consumer experience, thus achieving a more consumer-oriented design for cigarette products.

References

[1]　YE Y. Research on the Supply Mode of Tobacco for Retailers[D]. Hangzhou:

Zhejiang University of Technology, 2012.

[2] DUAN W T. The Impact of Economic and Social Development on Cigarette consumption demand[C]//2016 Annual Excellent Papers Compilation of China Tobacco Society. Beijing: China Tobacco Society, 2016.

[3] YANG L, YANG Q X, FENG H T, et al. An Empirical Study on Influencing Factors of Consumer Satisfaction of Cigarette Products[J]. Journal of Yunnan Agricultural University (Social Sciences), 2019, 13 (5): 93-101.

[4] LI H. Discussion on the Research Work of Cigarette Consumers in Regional Market [C]//2014 Excellent Papers Compilation of China Tobacco Society. Beijing: Chinese Tobacco Society, 2014.

[5] WANG H. Design and Application of Customer Satisfaction Index Model in Cigarette Enterprises[C]//2014 Excellent Papers Compilation of China Tobacco Society. Beijing: China Tobacco Society, 2014.

[6] BAI Y L, WU Y L, Cheng X S. Analysis of Cigarette Demand in China: Empirical Analysis and Conclusion of Cigarette Demand Model[J]. Chinese Journal of Tobacco, 2007 (4): 55-59.

[7] YUWEN L P, QIAN M, ZHANG J S. Application of AHP Method in Evaluation of Customer Satisfaction Index[J]. Journal of Xi'an Institute of Science and Technology, 2001, 21 (2): 175-177.

[8] ZHANG J, LI B C. Research on the method of demand forecasting under modern marketing system[C]//Excellent Papers of Shanghai Tobacco Society in 2020. Shanghai: Shanghai Tobacco Society, 2020.

[9] SAATYT L. Axiomatic Foundation of the analytic hierarchy process. Management Science, 1986, 32 (7): 841-855.

[10] Li S Q, ZHOU Y F. Profit Distribution of Agricultural Product Supply Chain based on Shapley Model[J]. Modern Marketing, 2020 (4): 144-145.

[11] CHAUHAN S, PROTH J M. Analysis of a Supply Chain Partnership with Revenue Sharing[J]. International Journal of Production Economics, 2005, 97 (1): 44-51.

基于层次分析法和 Shapley 值分解方法的卷烟消费者内在质量需求转化路径构建研究

摘要:消费者对卷烟质量优劣的评价直接影响其重复购买意愿。找出消费者评价指标与卷烟产品质量的关系,可有效指导卷烟制造技术的改进。本文结合卷烟生产实际,以行业感官质量评价标准为基础,应用层次分析法建立了卷烟产品属性要素层次结构指标,通过消费者定量调研和专家调研,结合相关性分析,验证消费者评价指标和产品属性设计要素的关联度,并应用 Shapley 值分解方法对路径进行修正及优化,最终完成卷烟消费者内在质量需求转化路径的构建。该路径的建立,可以有效解决卷烟感官质量与卷烟制造技术相关性以及卷烟感官质量与卷烟质量消费者评价指标对应关系的问题,对于通过消费者评价有效指导卷烟产品配方改进,提高消费满意度具有重要意义。

关键词:属性要素;层次分析法;需求转换;路径

长期以来,消费者都有一套评价卷烟优劣与否的语言体系,该语言体系与卷烟制造的技术指标不同,与专业卷烟配方师的评价方式也有所差异。卷烟感官质量好坏依托于卷烟制造技术水平的高低,消费者对卷烟质量的评价往往又与卷烟感官质量有紧密联系。与卷烟制造技术有关的因素众多且复杂,虽然烟草行业建立了相关卷烟感官质量评价标准[1],但有关卷烟感官质量与卷烟制造技术相关性的研究却鲜见报道,同时,有关卷烟感官质量与消费者评价卷烟优劣指标对应关系的研究也鲜见报道。

层次分析法(analytical hierarchy process,AHP)是目前比较成熟的决策分析方法,它引入了分层的概念把复杂问题结构化,是一种将决策者的定性判断和定量计算有效结合起来的实用的决策分析方法[2-4]。经文献查询,层次分析法目前在烟草行业信用体系建立方面有相关应用,譬如,朱军[5]应用层次分析法提出了烟草行业建立信用体系的一些设想和建议,并结合天津烟草进行实证分析;郑晓平等[6]运用层次分析法提出了一个包含 3 个一级指标、10 个二级指标的经营者信用评价指标体系和相应的经营者动态信用评价模型。何儒汉[7]等通过分析烟草专卖零售经营者特征,及其诚信内涵与范畴,应用群组决策和层次分析法构建卷烟零售户诚信评价指标体系。

本文旨在通过层次分析法结合回归 Shapley 值分解方法分析卷烟感官质量指标与消费者评价指标及卷烟制造技术指标间的联系,最终完成卷烟消费者内在质量需求转化路径的构建,从应用层面来看,可以有效解决卷烟感官质量与卷烟制造技术相关性以及卷烟感官质量与卷烟质量消费者评价指标对应关系的问题,从而达到通过消费者评价有效指导卷烟产品配方改进,提高消费满意度的目的。

1 材料与方法

1.1 数据来源

本次调研采取消费者调研和专家调研结合的方式,分别使用消费者指标和产品属性设计要素(专家技术指标)进行抽吸测评。其中,专家调研邀请了云南中烟技术中心产品评吸专家 10 人,消费者调研从全国七大区域招募了 133 位卷烟重度消费者(烟龄在 2 年及以上,日均吸烟量在 10 支以上)。调研覆盖全国七大区域,每个区域两个城市,共计 14 个城市;每个城市问卷 10 份,共计 140 份,每个城市备份问卷 1 份。最终问卷数量 154 份,实际有效问卷 133 份,合格率为 86.3%;问卷答案置信度核查问卷 144 份,合格问卷 133 份,合格比例 92.4%。测试产品选择上,以 2017 年全国卷烟销量排名前 40 的卷烟产品为研究对象,覆盖了一类、二类、三类、四类不同价类,不同价位的卷烟产品。样本分布具体情况见表 1 和表 2。

表 1 定量样本分布情况

区域	华东	华北	华南	西南	西北	东北	华中
城市	上海	北京	广州	成都	西安	沈阳	武汉
样本量	11	10	9	11	8	10	8
城市	宁波	保定	深圳	昆明	兰州	哈尔滨	郑州
样本量	8	11	8	10	9	11	9
合计	19	21	17	21	17	21	17

表 2 40 款测试产品价类及焦油含量分布情况

卷烟价类	产品个数	价类定义	焦油量	产品个数
一类烟	10	零售价为 180 元/条以上	≤8 mg	8
二类烟	10	零售价为 130~180 元/条	9~10 mg	13
三类烟	13	零售价为 60~129 元/条	11~12 mg	9
四类烟	7	零售价为 30~59 元/条		
五类烟	0	零售价为 30 元/条以下		

1.2 指标收集

依据云南中烟卷烟产品企业技术标准,参考工艺专家建议,结合烟草行业建立的卷烟感官质量评价标准[1],初步得出云南中烟产品属性要素。经过专家工作坊讨论,最终将产品属性要素划分为两个层次:设计层(9 个指标,用于产品配方及工艺改进)和结果层(21 个指标,用于感官质量评价)。产品属性要素表如表 3 所示。烟丝组分包括梗丝、膨胀丝添加比例,上、中、下部烟配方比例,薄片添加比例。烟叶配方包括烟叶品种等级。烟支物理指标包括烟支长度、圆周、质量、吸阻、硬度、含末率、含水率、总通风率。卷烟材料配方包括滤棒、油墨、卷烟纸、接装纸、成型纸。包装材料配方包括内衬纸、框架纸、商标、条盒、油墨。

表 3 产品属性要素表

设计层（9个）	烟丝组分、烟叶配方、加料香精配方、加香香精配方、叶处理工艺模式及强度、丝处理工艺模式及强度、烟支物理指标、卷烟材料配方、包装材料配方
结果层（21个）	嗅香、开包香、烟气浓度、劲头、柔细程度、烟气集中性、烟气圆润性、透发性、丰富性、香气质、香气量、醇和度、谐调性、杂气、鼻腔刺激、口腔刺激、喉部刺激、干净度、生津感、口腔舒适度、回味

本研究借鉴前期研究结果,采用一套优化后可用于研究的消费者卷烟内在属性评价指标体系[8],将其中的 16 个消费者指标作为本次消费者内在质量需求转化路径探索研究中的消费者评价指标(见表 4)。

表 4 消费者评价指标

序号	指标名称	指标描述
1	烟草纯正程度	闻起来有烟草的本香,没有香精或添加剂
2	嗅香新颖独特程度	嗅香具有独特的香气,与众不同,有辨识度
3	嗅香浓淡程度	在闻香过程中,香气浓郁或清淡
4	口腔舒适度	卷烟入口柔和,不苦不辣,舌头没有刺激感
5	口腔干燥程度	整个抽吸过程中口腔中没有干燥、燥热和灼烧的感觉
6	口腔饱满程度	抽吸时,烟气在口中饱满、充足的感觉
7	烟气平稳程度	抽吸时,抽第一口到最后一口给人的感觉一致
8	喉咙舒适度	烟气入喉时,喉咙部位没有灼烧、热辣的感觉
9	烟气细腻柔和度	烟气吸入时,喉咙感觉柔和细腻,没有颗粒感
10	烟气顺滑度	烟气能顺利进入喉咙,抽吸不费劲
11	劲头	烟气浓度适中,可以轻松下咽,不顶喉
12	鼻腔舒适度	烟气进入鼻腔时,卷烟对鼻腔产生的灼烧感的强烈程度
13	烟气丰富程度	烟气进入鼻腔时,感受到的烟气丰富、融洽、有层次的感觉
14	余味舒适程度	抽完烟嘴里不发苦、不辣,有回甜
15	余味干净程度	抽完烟嘴里不发涩,没有涂层感
16	抽后口腔干燥程度	抽后感觉不口干,嘴里湿润不起痰

1.3 分析方法

本次卷烟消费者内在质量需求转化路径的构建研究通过两个阶段完成。首先使用

AHP法[3,4],让专家对不同层次指标之间的相对重要程度进行评价,在产品属性指标中的设计层指标、结果层指标以及消费者评价指标之间建立初步联系,并确立各指标的权重。然后通过消费者定量调研和专家调研数据结果,结合相关性分析以及基于回归方程的Shapley值分解方法,验证消费者评价指标与设计层指标、结果层指标的具体关联度,完成卷烟消费者内在质量需求转化路径的修正及优化。

1.3.1 卷烟消费者内在质量需求转化路径的初步构建

(1)构造判断矩阵。

将同一层次的指标分别列入判断矩阵的i行和j列,组织9名云南中烟配方及评吸专家利用轮换打分的方式进行两两对比打分,见表5。

表5 判断矩阵打分示例

项目i行和j列	烟丝组分	烟叶配方	加料香精配方	加香香精配方
烟丝组分	1			
烟叶组分		1		
加料香精配方			1	
加香香精配方				1

为使矩阵中各元素的重要性能够得到定量显示,引入矩阵判断标度(1~9标度法)[9]作为评分体系,各标度含义见表6。

表6 判断矩阵评分体系

标度	含义
1	表示两个元素相比,具有同样的重要性
3	表示两个元素相比,前者比后者稍重要
5	表示两个元素相比,前者比后者明显重要
7	表示两个元素相比,前者比后者极其重要
9	表示两个元素相比,前者比后者强烈重要
2、4、6、8	表示上述相邻判断的中间值

注:若元素i和元素j的重要性之比为a_{ij},那么元素j与元素i的重要性之比为$a_{ji}=1/a_{ij}$。

针对需要比较的元素,如果认为两个元素一样重要,则重要性之比为1∶1,如果认为前者比后者强烈重要,则比值为9∶1,也可以取中间数值6∶1等。通过两两比较,把数值排列成判断矩阵(判断矩阵是对角线积为1的正反矩阵即可)。

(2) 进行一致性检验。

在构建判断矩阵后,项目组对每个成对比较矩阵计算最大特征值及其对应的特征向量,利用一致性指标、随机一致性指标和一致性比率做一致性检验。若检验通过,特征向量(归一化后)即为权向量;若不通过,需要重新构造成对比较矩阵。

判断矩阵通常是不一致的,但是为了能用它的特征根对应的特征向量作为被比较因素的权重向量,其不一致程度应在容许的范围内。如何确定这个范围? 通常会使用以下三个指标来确定这个范围:一致性指标 CI、随机一致性指标 RI、和一致性比率 CR。

① 确定一致性指标 CI。

$$CI = \frac{\lambda - n}{n - 1}$$

当 CI＝0 时,判断矩阵(A)具有完全一致性;CI 越大,判断矩阵(A)的一致性越差(λ 为 A 的最大正特征值)。

② 确定随机一致性指标 RI。

③ 确定一致性比率 CR。

- 一致性比率通常用于确定 A 的不一致性的容许范围。

$$CR = \frac{CI}{RI}$$

当 CR＜0.1 时,A 的不一致性程度在容许范围内,此时可用 A 的特征向量作为权向量。

- 将 CI 与 RI 进行比较,可以检验判断矩阵是否具有令人满意的一致性。
- 若 CR＜0.1,说明判断矩阵的一致性是令人满意的。
- 若 CR≥0.1,说明还应调整判断矩阵,直到令人满意为止。

(3) 计算权重向量。

通过一致性检验后,应利用判断矩阵计算各因素对目标层的权重(权系数),计算过程如下。相关示例如图 1 所示。

① 将 A 的每一列向量归一化。

② 对归一化向量按行求和。

③ 将求和后向量归一化,即近似特征根(权重向量)。

④ 计算最大特征根的近似值 λ。

1.3.2 卷烟消费者内在质量需求转化路径的关联性验证

首先,以消费者和专家定量调研结果为基础,采用消费者和专家对产品综合评分(打分指标)的平均值作为相关分析的原数据,探究卷烟指标与消费者满意度的关联度,并通过 SPSS 软件得出相关性结果。其次,为进一步验证专家指标(产品属性要素中的结果层指标)与消费者评价指标体系间的联系,采用基于回归方程的 Shapley 值分解方法来确定专家指标对消费者评价指标的重要性。通过计算每个专家指标被纳入模型和未被纳入模型时 R^2 的变化,来确定该指标的贡献度。

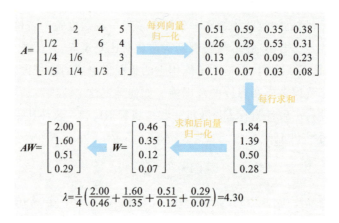

图 1　计算单排序权重向量示例

Pearson 相关系数作为简单相关系数,是用来度量两个变量间的线性关系的,相关系数越大,说明变量间的线性关系越强,其计算公式为:

$$r(X,Y) = \frac{\mathrm{cov}(X,Y)}{\sqrt{\mathrm{var}(X)\mathrm{var}(Y)}} ;$$

$$r = \frac{\sum_1^n (X_i - \overline{X})(Y_i - \overline{Y})}{\sqrt{\sum_1^n (X_i - \overline{X})^2 \sum_1^n (Y_i - \overline{Y})^2}}$$

基于回归方程的 Shapley 值分解方法是在对所有可能的变量组合进行运算后,计算出每个自变量的贡献度,因此相对于普通线性回归而言,Shapley 值分解方法可以化解自变量间的共线性,能够更准确地解释本次研究中专家指标对于消费者评价指标的重要性。其中,每个变量的 Shapley 值的计算公式如下:

$$\mathrm{SV}_j = \sum_k \sum_i \frac{k!(n-k-1)!}{n!} [v(M_{i|j}) - v(M_{i|(-j)})]$$

式中,$v(M_{i|j})$ 为模型 i 包含变量 j 时的 R^2;$v(M_{i|(-j)})$ 为模型 i 不包含变量 j 时的 R^2;$v(M_{i|j}) - v(M_{i|(-j)})$ 即为 j 变量被纳入模型和 j 变量未被纳入模型时 R^2 的变化;n 为变量总数;k 为不含 j 变量时模型中的变量总数;$\frac{k!(n-k-1)!}{n!}$ 为权重。

2　结果与分析

2.1　卷烟消费者内在质量需求转化路径的初步构建

2.1.1　结果层与设计层关联性结果

结果层与设计层关联性探讨结果如表 7 所示。

表7 结果层与设计层关联性探讨结果

序号	结果层	设计层（影响因素）									相关因素个数
		烟丝组分	烟叶配方	加料香精配方	加香香精配方	叶处理工艺模式及强度	丝处理工艺模式及强度	烟支物理指标	卷烟材料配方	包装材料配方	
1	嗅香			●	●				●		3
2	开包香			●	●				●		3
3	烟气浓度	●	●	●	●	●	●	●	●		8
4	劲头	●	●			●	●				4
5	柔细程度	●	●	●	●	●	●	●	●		8
6	烟气集中性	●	●	●	●	●	●	●	●		8
7	烟气圆润性	●	●	●	●	●	●	●	●		8
8	透发性	●	●	●	●	●	●				6
9	丰富性	●	●	●	●	●	●				6
10	香气质	●	●	●	●	●	●	●	●		8
11	香气量	●	●	●	●	●	●	●	●		8
12	醇和度	●	●	●	●	●	●				6
13	谐调性			●	●	●	●				4
14	杂气	●	●	●	●	●	●		●	●	8
15	鼻腔刺激	●	●	●	●	●	●	●	●		8
16	口腔刺激	●	●	●	●	●	●	●	●		8
17	喉部刺激	●	●	●	●	●	●	●	●		8
18	干净度	●	●	●	●	●	●				6
19	生津感	●	●	●	●	●	●				6
20	口腔舒适度	●	●	●	●	●	●				6
21	回味	●	●	●	●	●	●				6

消费者评价指标与结果层关联性探讨结果如表8所示。

表8 消费者评价指标与结果层关联性探讨结果

序号	消费者评价指标	结果层（专家指标共21个）	相关因素个数
1	烟草纯正程度	嗅香、开包香	2
2	嗅香新颖独特程度	嗅香、开包香	2

续表

序号	消费者评价指标	结果层(专家指标共21个)	相关因素个数
3	嗅香浓淡程度	嗅香、开包香	2
4	口腔舒适度	柔细程度、烟气圆润性、醇和度、口腔刺激、干净度、生津感、口腔舒适度、回味	8
5	口腔干燥程度	烟气圆润性、口腔刺激、干净度、生津感、口腔舒适度	5
6	口腔饱满程度	烟气浓度、烟气集中性	2
7	烟气平稳程度	烟气浓度、劲头、柔细程度、烟气集中性、烟气圆润性、透发性、丰富性、香气质、香气量、醇和度、谐调性、杂气、鼻腔刺激、口腔刺激、喉部刺激、干净度、生津感、口腔舒适度、回味	19
8	喉咙舒适度	劲头、柔细程度、喉部刺激	3
9	烟气细腻柔和度	劲头、柔细程度、烟气圆润性、喉部刺激	4
10	烟气顺滑度	劲头、柔细程度、喉部刺激	3
11	劲头	烟气浓度、劲头、柔细程度、喉部刺激	4
12	鼻腔舒适度	柔细程度、烟气圆润性、醇和度、鼻腔刺激	4
13	烟气丰富程度	丰富性、香气质、香气量、醇和度、谐调性	5
14	余味舒适程度	干净度、生津感、口腔舒适度、回味	4
15	余味干净程度	干净度、口腔舒适度	2
16	抽后口腔干燥程度	生津感、口腔舒适度、回味	3

2.1.2 基于AHP层次分析法的权重计算

组织专家集体讨论,收集专家打分及意见。因参与工作坊的每个专家的重要性相等,无须再对专家的重要性进行赋值,最终权重见表9和表10。

从表9可以得出,不同设计层指标,与其相关的结果层指标有所差异,具体表现为:

(1)烟叶配方与劲头烟气集中性、透发性、丰富性、香气量、醇和度、杂气、干净度、生津感、口腔舒适度指标关联度较高;

(2)烟丝组分与烟气浓度、劲头、柔细程度、鼻腔刺激、口腔刺激、喉部刺激关联度较高;

(3)加料香精配方对谐调性、回味的贡献度最大;

(4)加香香精配方对谐调性、嗅香、开包香最为重要。

从表10可以得出,不同消费者评价指标,与其相关的结果层指标有所差异,具体表现为:

(1)对烟草纯正程度、嗅香新颖独特程度、嗅香浓淡程度而言,嗅香和开包香是相关因素,其中嗅香重要性水平更高;

(2)与口腔舒适度相关的结果层指标有口腔舒适度、干净度、回味、生津感、口腔刺激、柔细程度、烟气圆润性和醇和度,其中口腔舒适度重要性水平最高;

表 9 设计层指标到结果层层指标转化路径构建结果

设计层指标	嗅香	开包香	烟气浓度	劲头	柔细程度	烟气集中性	烟气圆润性	透发性	丰富性	香气质	香气量	醇合度	谐调性	杂气	鼻腔刺激	口腔刺激	喉部刺激	干净度	生津感	口腔舒适度	回味
烟丝组分	—	—	0.27	0.42	0.19	0.17	0.15	0.20	0.21	0.16	0.19	0.2	0.17	0.20	0.22	0.20	0.20	0.21	0.22	0.18	0.18
烟叶配方	—	—	0.23	0.41	0.14	0.21	0.16	0.25	0.24	0.18	0.19	0.25	0.16	0.21	0.21	0.18	0.19	0.25	0.23	0.22	0.21
加料香精配方	0.22	0.19	0.10	—	0.15	0.15	0.19	0.15	0.2	0.19	0.15	0.21	0.32	0.18	0.15	0.17	0.17	0.21	0.21	0.21	0.24
加香香精配方	0.57	0.59	0.06	—	0.15	0.15	0.14	0.13	0.18	0.19	—	0.16	0.35	0.14	0.14	0.15	0.15	0.16	0.17	0.18	0.18
叶处理工艺模式及强度	—	—	0.06	—	0.08	0.07	0.09	0.12	0.08	0.08	0.06	0.09	—	0.10	0.08	0.08	0.09	0.09	0.09	0.10	0.09
丝处理工艺模式及强度	—	—	0.06	—	0.10	0.07	0.11	—	—	0.09	0.09	0.09	—	0.09	0.09	0.09	0.09	0.08	0.08	0.10	0.10
烟支物理指标	—	—	0.04	0.09	0.04	0.04	0.05	—	—	0.03	0.04	—	—	—	0.05	0.04	0.04	—	—	—	—
卷烟材料配方	0.20	0.22	0.17	0.19	0.15	0.13	0.11	0.14	0.09	0.07	0.15	—	—	0.05	—	0.07	0.07	—	—	—	—
包装材料配方	—	—	—	—	—	—	—	—	—	—	—	—	—	0.03	—	—	—	—	—	—	—

表 10 消费者评价指标到结果层指标转换路径构建结果

消费者评价指标	嗅香	开包香	烟气浓度	劲头	柔细程度	烟气集中性	烟气圆润性	透发性	丰富性	香气质	香气量	醇合度	谐调性	杂气	鼻腔刺激	口腔刺激	喉部刺激	干净度	生津感	口腔舒适度	回味
烟草纯正程度	0.74	0.26	—	—	—	—	—	—	—	—	—	—	—	—	—	—	—	—	—	—	—
嗅香新颖独特程度	0.74	0.26	—	—	—	—	—	—	—	—	—	—	—	—	—	—	—	—	—	—	—
嗅香浓淡程度	0.75	0.25	—	—	—	—	—	—	—	—	—	—	—	—	—	—	—	—	—	—	—
口腔舒适度	—	—	—	—	0.08	—	0.08	—	—	—	—	0.07	—	—	—	0.09	—	—	0.12	0.28	0.14
口腔干燥程度	—	—	—	—	—	—	0.24	—	—	—	—	—	—	—	—	0.12	—	0.15	0.18	0.31	—
口腔饱满程度	—	—	0.72	—	—	0.28	—	—	—	—	—	—	—	—	—	—	—	—	—	—	—
烟气平稳程度	—	—	0.07	0.06	0.06	0.06	0.06	0.06	0.06	0.08	0.09	0.06	0.06	0.03	0.03	0.03	0.03	0.04	0.04	0.04	0.04
喉咙舒适程度	—	—	—	0.22	0.44	—	—	—	—	—	—	—	—	—	—	—	0.34	—	—	—	—
烟气细腻柔和度	—	—	—	0.11	0.44	—	0.29	—	—	—	—	—	—	—	—	—	0.15	—	—	—	—
烟气顺滑度	—	—	0.14	0.32	0.40	—	—	—	—	—	—	—	—	—	—	—	0.28	—	—	—	—
劲头	—	—	—	0.47	0.18	—	—	—	—	—	—	—	—	—	—	—	—	—	—	—	—
鼻腔舒适度	—	—	—	—	0.28	—	0.20	—	—	—	—	0.21	—	—	0.31	—	0.22	—	—	—	—
烟气丰富程度	—	—	—	—	—	—	—	—	0.35	0.25	0.14	0.11	0.15	—	—	—	—	—	—	—	—
余味舒适程度	—	—	—	—	—	—	—	—	—	—	—	—	—	—	—	—	—	0.24	0.16	0.36	0.24
余味干净程度	—	—	—	—	—	—	—	—	—	—	—	—	—	—	—	—	—	0.61	0.39	—	—
抽后口腔干燥程度	—	—	—	—	—	—	—	—	—	—	—	—	—	—	—	—	—	—	0.34	0.46	0.20

(3) 对口腔干燥程度来说,口腔舒适度、烟气圆润性、生津感、干净度和口腔刺激是相关指标,其中口腔舒适度是最重要的因素;

(4) 口腔饱满程度与烟气浓度和烟气集中性相关,其中烟气浓度较重要;

(5) 烟气平稳程度受各因素影响分布较均匀,相关指标包括烟气浓度、香气质、干净度、柔细程度、醇和度、回味、杂气、口腔舒适度、生津感、鼻腔刺激、劲头、喉部刺激、口腔刺激、烟气集中性、烟气圆润性、谐调性、丰富性、透发性和香气量,其中香气量是最重要的因素;

(6) 与喉咙舒适度和烟气顺滑度相关的指标为柔细程度、喉部刺激和劲头,其中柔细程度最重要;

(7) 对烟气细腻柔和度而言,柔细程度、烟气圆润性、喉部刺激和劲头是相关因素,其中柔细程度是最重要的因素;

(8) 与劲头有关联性的指标包括劲头、喉部刺激、柔细程度和烟气浓度,其中劲头最为重要;

(9) 鼻腔刺激、柔细程度、醇和度和烟气圆润性是与鼻腔舒适度相关的因素,其中鼻腔刺激重要水平最高;

(10) 对烟气丰富程度来说,重要的因素有丰富性、香气质、谐调性、香气量和醇和度,其中丰富性对烟气丰富程度的贡献度最大;

(11) 余味舒适程度的相关因素包括口腔舒适度、干净度、回味和生津感,其中口腔舒适度是最重要的因素;

(12) 与余味干净程度相关的因素有干净度和口腔舒适度,其中干净度较重要;

(13) 对抽后口腔干燥程度而言,口腔舒适度、生津感和回味是相关因素,其中口腔舒适度的重要水平最高。

2.1.3 消费者评价指标到产品属性要素转换路径初步构建结果

综合以上结果,我们将消费者评价指标、结果层指标、设计层指标之间具有关联性的指标进行相连,可以初步构建消费者评价指标到产品属性要素的转化路径,见图2、图3。

由于单个指标可能对应多个指标,从而产生多条转化路径,本文分别从设计层指标到结果层指标的转化路径,消费者评价指标到结果层指标的转化路径中,选取了平均相关性最高的指标进行连接,最终构建出较为精简的初步路径模型图,见图4。

根据路径图结果,可以得出以下结论。

(1) 设计层指标里的"烟叶配方"与结果层指标的联系最多,尤其与"干净度""醇和度""透发性"的关联性较高;"烟丝组分"也与结果层的多个指标相关联,其中与"劲头"的关联性较高。

(2) 结果层指标里的"柔细程度"与消费者评价指标的联系最多,尤其与"喉咙舒适度""烟气细腻柔和度"的关联性较高。

2.2 卷烟消费者内在质量需求转化路径的关联性验证结果

从表11可以看出,各结果层指标与消费者评价指标的相关性普遍较高,大多在0.7以

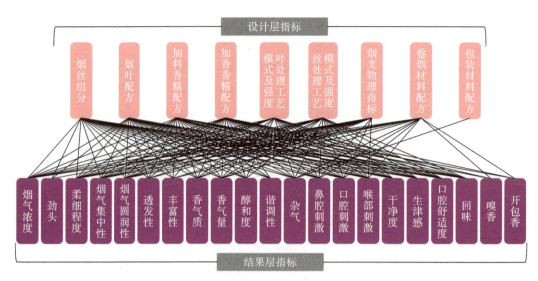

图 2　设计层指标到结果层指标转化路径图

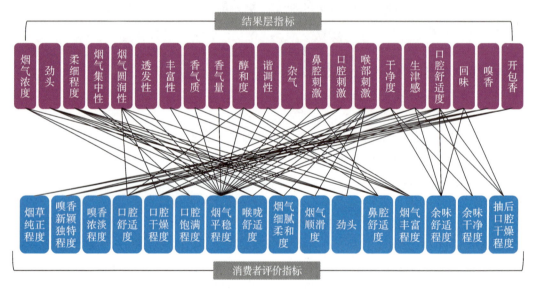

图 3　消费者评价指标到结果层指标转化路径图

上,且结果具有显著性,说明结果层指标与消费者评价指标均高度相关。

从表 12 可以得出,化解自变量间的共线性,能够更准确地解释本次研究中结果层指标对于消费者评价指标的重要性,从而确定该指标的贡献度。

通过上述相关分析和基于回归方程的 Shapley 值分解方法的应用,最终构建出了卷烟消费者内在质量需求转化全路径图(见图 5)。

为简化全路径图,本文选取了平均相关性最高的指标构建出了如图 6 所示的最终全路径图,即单个消费者评价指标到结果层指标再到设计层指标的转化仅保留一条最相关的路径。其中消费者评价指标到结果层指标系数为定量研究得出的权重系数,结果层指标到设计层指标系数为专家工作坊得出的权重系数。

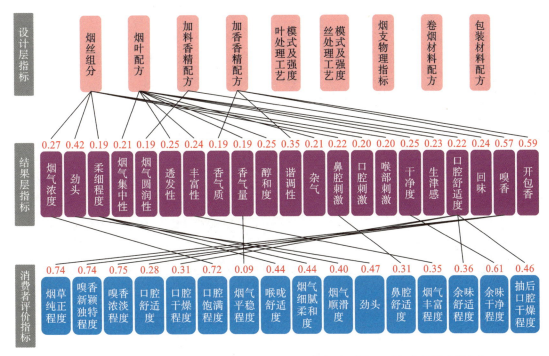

图 4　初步转化全路径图：设计层—结果层—消费者（仅选取平均相关性最高指标）

3　结论

（1）根据最终构建的转化路径，可以得出与消费者对卷烟内在品质评价直接相关的结果层指标，以及与这些结果层指标有关的设计层指标；同时，通过关联系数的值，可以准确得到这些产品属性要素对消费者感官质量评价结果的影响程度。

（2）仅选取权重最高的路径，可以得出 16 个消费者评价指标到结果层指标再到设计层指标的关联性最高的转换路径：烟草纯正程度—开包香—加香香精配方；嗅香新颖独特程度—开包香—加香香精配方；嗅香浓淡程度—开包香—加香香精配方；口腔舒适度—干净度—烟叶配方；口腔干燥程度—干净度—烟叶配方；口腔饱满程度—烟气集中性—烟叶配方；烟气平稳程度—香气质—加香香精配方；喉咙舒适度—柔细程度—烟丝组分；烟气细腻柔和度—柔细程度—烟丝组分；烟气顺滑度—劲头—烟丝组分；劲头—柔细程度—烟丝组分；鼻腔舒适度—柔细程度—烟丝组分；烟气丰富程度—香气质—加香香精配方；余味舒适程度—干净度—烟叶配方；余味干净程度—干净度—烟叶配方；抽后口腔干燥程度—口腔舒适度—烟叶配方。

（3）本文通过工作坊的形式，将卷烟产品属性要素层次结构指标与消费者评价指标进行关联，建立了卷烟产品特征属性与消费需求的对接转化模式。通过将消费者评价指标体系与专家指标相结合，建立起真正的"消费者反馈—消费者需求转化—专家评吸指标对应—产品技术改进"的完整路径，对于产品研发人员了解消费者需求，将其转换成产品研发

表 11 Pearson 相关性分析结果

Pearson相关性	嗅香	开包香	烟气浓度	劲头	柔细程度	烟气集中性	烟气圆润性	透发性	丰富性	香气质	香气量	醇和度	谐调性	杂气	鼻腔刺激	口腔刺激	喉部刺激	干净度	生津感	口腔舒适度	回味
烟草纯正程度	0.736**	0.793**	0.648**	0.870**	0.872**	0.870**	0.860**	0.809**	0.830**	0.892**	0.759**	0.871**	0.833**	0.873**	0.868**	0.852**	0.854**	0.884**	0.873**	0.882**	0.876**
嗅香新颖独特程度	0.771**	0.812**	0.643**	0.872**	0.897**	0.876**	0.880**	0.835**	0.846**	0.922**	0.771**	0.895**	0.865**	0.910**	0.885**	0.887**	0.891**	0.916**	0.897**	0.911**	0.902**
嗅香浓淡程度	0.739**	0.775**	0.637**	0.859**	0.874**	0.878**	0.867**	0.827**	0.822**	0.894**	0.775**	0.874**	0.843**	0.886**	0.866**	0.862**	0.864**	0.895**	0.880**	0.886**	0.882**
口腔舒适度	0.760**	0.804**	0.634**	0.863**	0.910**	0.883**	0.875**	0.830**	0.846**	0.932**	0.771**	0.897**	0.860**	0.918**	0.901**	0.890**	0.893**	0.921**	0.894**	0.912**	0.908**
口腔干燥程度	0.742**	0.796**	0.586**	0.847**	0.909**	0.861**	0.865**	0.811**	0.831**	0.919**	0.745**	0.900**	0.837**	0.903**	0.895**	0.885**	0.886**	0.906**	0.884**	0.898**	0.899**
口腔饱满程度	0.730**	0.762**	0.741**	0.876**	0.823**	0.904**	0.844**	0.869**	0.836**	0.887**	0.854**	0.859**	0.856**	0.872**	0.820**	0.823**	0.819**	0.876**	0.873**	0.861**	0.884**
烟气平稳程度	0.743**	0.790**	0.628**	0.871**	0.897**	0.866**	0.861**	0.833**	0.848**	0.920**	0.781**	0.895**	0.855**	0.891**	0.883**	0.869**	0.870**	0.898**	0.884**	0.887**	0.893**
喉咙舒适度	0.725**	0.795**	0.583**	0.846**	0.909**	0.860**	0.864**	0.809**	0.824**	0.923**	0.741**	0.893**	0.842**	0.903**	0.898**	0.882**	0.889**	0.913**	0.883**	0.898**	0.892**
烟气细腻	0.726**	0.778**	0.609**	0.870**	0.893**	0.864**	0.860**	0.808**	0.818**	0.906**	0.758**	0.889**	0.839**	0.891**	0.872**	0.866**	0.876**	0.908**	0.883**	0.885**	0.889**
烟气柔和度	0.735**	0.793**	0.681**	0.871**	0.878**	0.888**	0.863**	0.843**	0.842**	0.914**	0.800**	0.890**	0.850**	0.894**	0.876**	0.861**	0.861**	0.900**	0.894**	0.890**	0.897**
烟气顺滑度	0.760**	0.804**	0.614**	0.874**	0.910**	0.872**	0.876**	0.820**	0.833**	0.924**	0.762**	0.899**	0.856**	0.910**	0.898**	0.882**	0.895**	0.918**	0.894**	0.904**	0.897**
劲头	0.742**	0.788**	0.634**	0.874**	0.897**	0.884**	0.869**	0.827**	0.832**	0.912**	0.780**	0.891**	0.853**	0.904**	0.878**	0.864**	0.868**	0.913**	0.892**	0.895**	0.894**
鼻腔舒适度	0.743**	0.797**	0.669**	0.872**	0.875**	0.889**	0.857**	0.851**	0.834**	0.908**	0.809**	0.878**	0.861**	0.900**	0.864**	0.851**	0.856**	0.900**	0.884**	0.885**	0.889**
烟气丰富度	0.757**	0.805**	0.638**	0.871**	0.901**	0.881**	0.871**	0.831**	0.846**	0.920**	0.782**	0.898**	0.860**	0.910**	0.888**	0.874**	0.877**	0.918**	0.889**	0.902**	0.903**
余味舒适程度	0.729**	0.790**	0.642**	0.875**	0.889**	0.887**	0.867**	0.832**	0.843**	0.915**	0.801**	0.890**	0.859**	0.901**	0.875**	0.866**	0.867**	0.910**	0.891**	0.895**	0.897**
余味干净程度	0.711**	0.773**	0.595**	0.854**	0.896**	0.857**	0.853**	0.801**	0.818**	0.906**	0.756**	0.880**	0.836**	0.889**	0.873**	0.860**	0.865**	0.899**	0.867**	0.876**	0.876**

注：** 表示在 0.01 水平（双侧）上显著相关。

表 12 基于回归方程的 Shapley 值分析结果

Shapley值分析结果	开包香	嗅香	烟气浓度	劲头	柔细程度	烟气集中性	烟气圆润性	透发性	丰富性	香气质	香气量	醇和度	谐调性	杂气	鼻腔刺激	口腔刺激	喉部刺激	干净度	生津感	口腔舒适度	回味
烟草纯正程度	0.431**	0.569**																			
嗅香新颖独特程度	0.451**	0.549**																			
嗅香浓淡程度	0.455**	0.545**																			
口腔舒适度					0.134**		0.120**					0.118**				0.115**		0.139**	0.120**	0.129**	0.126**
口腔干燥程度							0.187**									0.195**		0.222**	0.194**	0.202**	
口腔饱满程度			0.338**			0.662**															
烟气平稳程度			0.031**	0.056**	0.060**	0.055**	0.055**	0.044**	0.045**	0.084**	0.039**	0.056**	0.051**	0.054**		0.050**	0.051**	0.055**	0.054**	0.052**	0.055**
喉咙舒适度				0.292**	0.373**												0.336**				
烟气细腻柔和度				0.257**	0.271**		0.229**										0.243**				
烟气顺滑度				0.345**	0.341**												0.314**				
劲头			0.114**	0.277**	0.317**												0.291**				
鼻腔舒适度					0.267**		0.233**					0.258**			0.242**						
烟气丰富程度									0.174**	0.268**	0.164**	0.206**	0.189**								
余味舒适程度																		0.273**	0.235**	0.245**	0.248**
余味干净程度																		0.517**		0.483**	
抽后口腔干燥程度																			0.323**	0.339**	0.338**

注：** 表示在 0.01 水平（双侧）上显著相关。

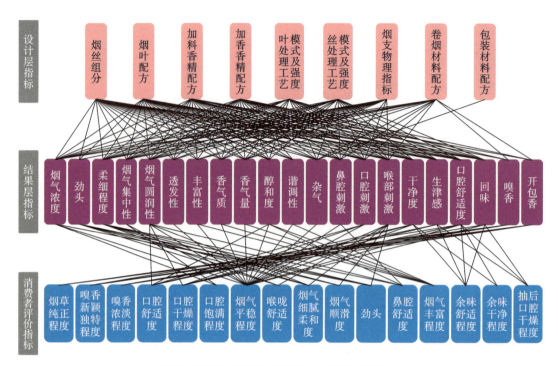

图 5　转化全路径图：设计层—结果层—消费者

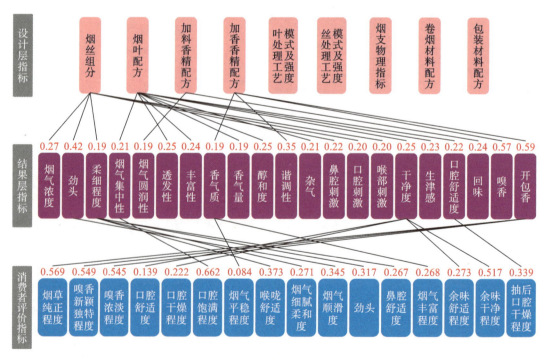

图 6　最终转化全路径图：设计层—结果层—消费者（仅选取平均相关性最高指标）

及维护目标,进一步精确指导配方、进行产品研发及维护具有重要意义。

参考文献

[1] 中华人民共和国国家质量监督检验检疫总局,中国国家标准化管理委员会.卷烟第四部分:卷烟感官技术要求 GB5606.4—2005[S].北京:中国标准出版社,2005.

[2] SAATY T L. Axiomatic Foundation of the Analytic Hierarchyprocess [J]. Management Science,1986,32(7):841-855.

[3] 祁玉龙.基于层次分析法的绩效考核体系研究[J].西安工程大学学报,2008,22(3):125-128.

[4] 谢宣正.层次分析法在绩效管理中的应用[J].中国劳动,2005(11):72-74.

[5] 朱军.烟草行业信用体系构建问题研究[D].天津:天津大学,2006.

[6] 郑晓平,周全,刘易灵.基于层次分析法的烟草专卖零售经营者动态信用评价模型研究[J].重庆与世界(学术版),2016(11):7-11.

[7] 何儒汉,万方名,向俐双等.基于群组决策和层次分析法的卷烟零售户诚信指标体系构建[J].计算机应用与软件,2019,36(12):81-86.

[8] 杨蕾,杨乾栩,冯洪涛等.卷烟产品消费者满意度影响因素实证研究[J].云南农业大学学报,2019,13(5):93-101.

[9] 邱崇宝,徐晓明,郭洪武等.层次分析法在烟草绩效考核指标权重确定中的应用[J].中国新技术新产品,2016(2):156-157.

卷烟消费市场研究初探

Research on the Transformation Path of Cigarette Consumers' Internal Quality Demand Based on AHP and Shapley Value Decomposition

Abstract: Consumers' evaluation of cigarette quality directly affects their willingness to repeat purchase. To find out the relationship between consumer evaluation indicator and cigarette product quality, to effectively guide the improvement of cigarette manufacturing technology. Based on the evaluation standard of the sensory quality of the cigarette industry, this paper establishes the hierarchical structure indicator of attribute elements of cigarette products by AHP. Through the quantitative investigation of consumers and the investigation of experts, combined with the correlation analysis, the correlation degree between the evaluation indicators of consumers and the design elements of product attributes is verified, and the path is modified and optimized by Shapley value decomposition method. Finally, the transformation path of the internal quality demand of cigarette consumers is completed build. The establishment of this path can effectively solve the problems of correlation between cigarette sensory quality and cigarette manufacturing technology, as well as the corresponding relationship between cigarette sensory quality and consumer evaluation of cigarette quality indicators. It is of considerable significance to effectively guide the improvement of cigarette product formula and improve consumer satisfaction through consumer evaluation.

Keywords: Attribute element; AHP; Requirement transformation; Path

For a long time, consumers have a set of their language systam to evaluate the quality of cigarettes, which is different from the technical indicators of cigarette manufacturing and the evaluation methods of professional cigarette formulators. At present, the sensory quality of cigarettes depends on the layer of cigarette manufacturing technology. The evaluation of cigarette quality by consumers is often closely related to the sensory quality of the cigarette. However, there are many complex factors in cigarette manufacturing technology. Although the tobacco industry has established the relevant sensory quality evaluation standard of cigarettes[1], however, there are few reports on the correlation between the sensory quality of cigarette and cigarette manufacturing technology, and the corresponding relationship between sensory quality of cigarette and consumer evaluation indicator of cigarette quality.

The analytic hierarchy process (AHP) is a relatively mature decision analysis method at present. It introduces the concept of layering to structure complex problems. It is a practical decision analysis method that effectively combines the qualitative judgment and quantitative calculation of decision-makers[2-4]. Through a literature search, AHP has been applied in the establishment of a credit indicator system of the tobacco industry. For example, Zhu Jun[5] put forward some ideas and suggestions on the establishment of credit indicator system of the tobacco industry by using AHP, and made a practical analysis combining with Tianjin tobacco; Zheng Xiaoping et al.[6] put forward a credit evaluation indicator system and corresponding dynamic credit evaluation model of operators, which includes three first-layer indicators and 10-second-layer indicators, by using AHP. By analyzing the characteristics of tobacco monopoly retail operators, the connotation and category of credit, He Ruhan et al.[7] applied group decision-making and AHP to construct the credit evaluation indicator system of retail cigarette customers.

Therefore, the purpose of this study is to analyze the relationship between cigarette sensory quality indicator, consumer evaluation indicator and cigarette manufacturing technology indicator by AHP combined with regression Shapley value decomposition method, and finally complete the construction of the transformation path of cigarette consumers' internal quality demand. From the perspective of the application, it can effectively solve the problems of correlation between cigarette sensory quality and cigarette manufacturing technology, as well as the corresponding relationship between cigarette sensory quality and consumer evaluation indicators of cigarette quality, to effectively guide the improvement of cigarette product formula through consumer evaluation and improve consumer satisfaction.

1 Experimental Materials and Methods

1.1 Data Source

This survey adopts the methods of consumer survey and expert survey, using consumer indicators and product attribute design elements (expert technical indicators) for smoking assessment. Among them, the expert survey invited 10 product evaluation experts from Yunnan China Tobacco Technology Center, and the consumer survey recruited 133 heavy cigarette consumers from seven regions of the country (smoking age of 2 years and above, daily average smoking amount of more than ten cigarettes). The survey covers seven regions and two cities in each region, totaling 14 cities; each city has ten questionnaires, totaling 140, and each city has one backup questionnaire. The final number of questionnaires is 154, and the actual valid questionnaire is 133, the qualified rate is 86.3%, 144 verification questionnaires, qualified 133, the qualified rate is 92.4%. In terms of test product selection, the top 40 cigarette products in China in 2017 were selected as the research objects, covering one, two, three, four different price categories, and different price levels of cigarette products. See Table 1 and Table 2 for sample distribution.

Table 1　Distribution of Quantitative Samples

Region	East China	North China	South China	Southwest China	Northwest China	Northeast China	Central China
City	Shanghai	Beijing	Guangzhou	Chengdu	Xi'an	Shenyang	Wuhan
sample size	11	10	9	11	8	10	8
City	Ningbo	Baoding	Shenzhen	Kunming	Lanzhou	Harbin	Zhengzhou
sample size	8	11	8	10	9	11	9
Total	19	21	17	21	17	21	17

Table 2　Price Category and Tar Content Distribution of 40 Test Products

Cigarette price	Number of products	Price class definition	Tar yield	Number of products
Price class Ⅰ cigarette	10	Retail price is more than 180 yuan/piece	≤8 mg	8
Price class Ⅱ cigarette	10	Retail price is 130-180 yuan/piece	9-10 mg	13
Price class Ⅲ cigarettes	13	Retail price is 60-129 yuan/piece	11-12 mg	9
Price class Ⅳ cigarettes	7	Retail price is 30-59 yuan/piece		
Price class Ⅴ cigarettes	0	Retail price is less than 30 yuan/piece		

1.2　Indicator Collection

According to the technical standards of Yunnan China tobacco products enterprises, concerning the suggestions of process experts, and combined with the sensory quality evaluation standards of cigarettes established by the tobacco industry[1], the design elements of the attributes of Yunnan China tobacco products are preliminarily obtained. After expert's discussion, the product attribute design elements are divided into two layers: design layer (9 indicators for product formulation and process improvement) and result layer (21 indicators for sensory quality evaluation), as shown in Table 3. Cut tobacco include adding proportion of expanded tobacco and cut stem, proportion of upper, middle and lower leaf, adding proportion of reconstituted tobacco, Tobacco leaves include leaf grade; Physical indicators of cigarettes include cigarette length, circumference, weight, draw resistance, hardness, dust content, moisture content, total ventilation rate; Cigarette material include filter rod, printing ink, cigarette paper, tipping paper, plug wrap paper; Packaging material include inner-frame paper, outer-frame paper, trademark, carton packing, printing ink.

Table 3 Product Attribute Elements

Design-layer (9 indicators)	X_1: cut tobacco, X_2: tobacco leaves, X_3: spice formula, X_4: flavor formula, X_5: technology of threshing and redrying, X_6: technology of tobacco manufacture process, X_7: physical indicators of cigarettes, X_8: cigarette material, X_9: packaging material
Result-layer (21 indicators)	Y_1: odor, Y_2: packet opening aroma, Y_3: smoke density, Y_4: impact, Y_5: softness, Y_6: cigarette smoke concentration, Y_7: smooth, Y_8: diffusivity, Y_9: abundance, Y_{10}: aroma quality, Y_{11}: aroma volume, Y_{12}: mellowness, Y_{13}: harmony, Y_{14}: offensive taste, Y_{15}: irritancy in nasal, Y_{16}: irritancy in oral, Y_{17}: irritancy in throat, Y_{18}: cleanness, Y_{19}: salivation, Y_{20}: oral comfort, Y_{21}: after taste

This study uses the results of previous studies for reference. It adopts a set of optimized evaluation indicator system of internal attributes of consumer cigarettes that can be used in the study[8], including 16 consumer indicators, as the consumer evaluation indicator in the exploration and research of the transformation path of internal quality demand of consumers (see Table 4).

Table 4 Consumer Evaluation Indicators

Serial number	Indicator title	Indicator description
Z_1	Pure flavor/ aroma of tobacco	It smells of tobacco flavor, no flavors or additives
Z_2	Unique/special odor	The smell has a unique fragrance, which is distinctive and distinguishable
Z_3	Strong & light odor	A firm or light aroma in the process of smelling
Z_4	Oral comfort	The cigarette has a soft entrance, no bitterness, no irritation of the tongue
Z_5	Mouth moist	There is no feeling of dryness and burning in the mouth during the whole suction process
Z_6	Oral richness sensation	When smoking, the smoke in the mouth is full and sufficient
Z_7	Stability	When smoking, the feeling is consistent from the first to the last
Z_8	Throat comfort	When smoke enters the throat, there is no burning or hot feeling in the throat

continue

Serial number	Indicator title	Indicator description
Z_9	Softness, smooth and grainy	When the smoke is inhaled, the throat feels soft and delicate, without the sense of particles
Z_{10}	Smooth	The smoke can enter the throat smoothly, and smoking is not difficult
Z_{11}	Impact	The smoke concentration is moderate, and it can be easily swallowed, not top the throat
Z_{12}	Nasal comfort	The intensity of the burning sensation of cigarettes on the nose when smoke enters the nose
Z_{13}	Abundance	When the smoke enters the nasal cavity, it feels luxurious, harmonious, and layered
Z_{14}	Aftertaste	It is not bitter or spicy after smoking, and it is sweet again
Z_{15}	Aftertaste cleanness	No astringency or coating feeling in the mouth after smoking
Z_{16}	Mouth moist sensation after smoking	The mouth does not feel dry after smoking, and the mouth is moist and cannot produce phlegm

1.3 Analysis Method

The research on the transformation path of internal quality demand of cigarette consumers is completed in two stages, First of all, by using the AHP method[3,4], leting experts evaluate the relative importance of different layers of indicators. Establishing the preliminary relationship between design-layer indicators, result-layer indicators, and consumer evaluation indicators in product attribute indicators, and establishing the weight of each indicator link. Then, through the results of consumer quantitative research and expert research data, combining with correlation analysis and Shapley value decomposition method based on regression equation, verifying the specific relevance of consumer evaluation indicator, design-layer indicator, and result-layer indicator, and completing the modification and optimization of the transformation path of cigarette consumers' internal quality demand.

1.3.1 Preliminary Construction of the Transformation Path of Cigarette Consumers' Internal Quality Demand

(1) Constructing a judgment matrix.

The indicators of the same layer were listed in the row and column of the judgment matrix, and 9 smoking evaluation experts of Yunnan China Tobacco Technology Center and were organized to use the rotation scoring method to compare the two scores. See Table 5.

Table 5　An Example of Judgment Matrix Scoring

i factor	j factor			
	Cut tobacco	Tobacco leaves	Spice formula	Flavor formula
Cut tobacco	1			
Tobacco leaves		1		
Spice formula			1	
Flavor formula				1

In order to show the importance of each element in the matrix quantitatively, the matrix judgment scale (1-9 scale method)[9] is introduced as the scoring system, and the scale meaning is shown in Table 6 below.

Table 6　Judgment Matrix Scoring System

Scale	Meaning
1	Represents the same importance of two elements
3	Indicates that the former is slightly more important than the latter
5	The former is many valuable than the latter
7	The former is more important than the latter
9	The former is most important than the latter
2, 4, 6, 8	Represents the intermediate value of the above adjacent judgments

Reciprocal: if the importance ratio of element i to element j is a_{ij}, then the importance ratio of element j to element i is $a_{ji} = 1/a_{ij}$.

For the factors that need to be compared, if they are considered as equally important, the importance ratio is 1∶1; if they are considered as powerfully necessary, the ratio is 9∶1, and the intermediate value of 6∶1 can also be taken. By comparing the two values, arrange them into a judgment matrix (the judgment matrix is a positive and negative matrix whose diagonal product is 1).

(2) Conduct consistency inspection.

After constructing the judgment matrix, the project team calculates the maximum eigenvalue and its corresponding eigenvector for each pair of comparison matrix and uses the consistency indicator, random consistency indicator, and consistency ratio to test the consistency. If the test is passed, the eigenvector (after normalization) is the weight vector; if not, the pairwise comparison matrix needs to be reconstructed.

The judgment matrix is usually inconsistent, but in order to use its eigenvector corresponding to the characteristic root as the weight vector of the factor to be compared, the degree of inconsistency should be within the allowable range. How to determine the scope? Generally, the following three indicators are used to determine the scope: consistency indicator CI, random consistency indicator RI, and consistency ratio CR.

①Consistency indicator CI.

$$CI = \frac{\lambda - n}{n - 1}$$

When CI=0, the judgment matrix (A) is completely consistent; The larger the CI, the less consistent the judgment matrix (A).

λ is the maximum positive eigenvalue of A.

②Random consistency indicator RI.

③Consistency ratio CR.

• The consistency ratio is usually used to determine the allowable range of A's inconsistency.

$$CR = \frac{CI}{RI}$$

When CR<0.1, the degree of inconsistency of a is within the allowable range, then the eigenvector of A can be used as the weight vector.

• Comparing CI with RI can test whether the judgment matrix has satisfactory consistency.

• If CR<0.1, the consistency of judgment matrix is satisfactory.

• If CR≥0.1, the judgment matrix shall be adjusted until it is satisfactory.

(3) Calculate weight vector.

After passing the consistency test, it is necessary to use the judgment matrix to calculate the weight (weight coefficient) of each factor to the target layer. The calculation process is as follows (see Figure 1).

①Normalize each row of vectors of A.

②Sum the normalized vectors by lines.

③Normalize the sum post vector, i.e., approximate characteristic root (weight vector).

④Calculate the approximate value λ of the maximum eigenvalue.

1.3.2 Relevance Verification of Transformation Path of Cigarette Consumers' Internal Quality Demand

First of all, based on the quantitative survey results of consumers and experts, the average value of overall evaluation scores (scoring indicators) of consumers and experts

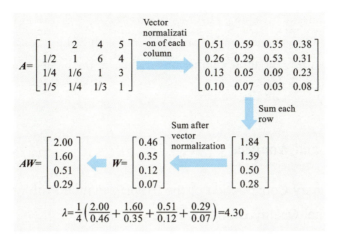

Figure 1　Example of Calculating Single Sort Weight Vector

on products is used as the original data of correlation analysis to explore the correlation between cigarette indicators and consumer satisfaction. The correlation results are obtained by SPSS software. Secondly, in order to further verify the relationship between expert technical indicators (result layer indicators) and consumer indicator system, the Shapley value decomposition method based on the regression equation is used to determine the importance of expert technical indicators to consumer indicators. The contribution degree of each expert indicator is determined by calculating the change of R^2 when it is included in the model and not included in the model. Pearson correlation coefficient, as a simple correlation coefficient, is used to measure the linear relationship between two variables. The larger the correlation coefficient, the stronger the linear relationship between variables. The calculation formula is:

$$r(X,Y) = \frac{\text{cov}(X,Y)}{\sqrt{\text{var}(X)\text{var}(Y)}}$$

$$r = \frac{\sum_1^n (X_i - \overline{X})(Y_i - \overline{Y})}{\sqrt{\sum_1^n (X_i - \overline{X})^2 \sum_1^n (Y_i - \overline{Y})^2}}$$

The Shapley value decomposition method based on the regression equation calculates the contribution degree of each independent variable after calculating all possible variable combinations. Therefore, compared with ordinary linear regression, the Shapley value decomposition method can resolve the collinearity between independent variables, and more accurately explain the importance of expert indicators for consumer indicators in this project. Where the Shapley value of each variable is calculated as follows:

$$\text{SV}_j = \sum_k \sum_i \frac{k!(n-k-1)!}{n!}[v(M_{i|j}) - v(M_{i|j(-j)})]$$

$v(M_{i|j})$ is the R^2 when a model i contains variable j; $v(M_{i|j(-j)})$ is the R^2 when a model i does not contain variable j; $v(M_{i|j}) - v(M_{i|j(-j)})$ is the change of R^2 when j variable is included in the model, and j variable is not included in the model; n is the total number of variables; k is the total number of variables in the model when j variable is not included; $\dfrac{k!\,(n-k-1)!}{n!}$ is the weight.

2 Results and Analysis

2.1 Preliminary Construction of the Transformation Path of Cigarette Consumers' Internal Quality Demand

2.1.1 Correlation Results of Result layer and Design layer.

Discussion results of correlation between result layer and design layer see Table 7.

Table 7 Discussion Results of Correlation between Result Layer and Design Layer

Serial number	Result-layer	Design layer (influence indicators)									Number of relevant indicators
		X_1	X_2	X_3	X_4	X_5	X_6	X_7	X_8	X_9	
1	Y_1			●	●				●		3
2	Y_2			●	●				●		3
3	Y_3	●	●	●	●	●	●	●	●		8
4	Y_4	●	●					●	●		4
5	Y_5	●	●	●	●	●	●	●	●		8
6	Y_6	●	●	●	●	●	●	●	●		8
7	Y_7	●	●	●	●	●	●	●	●		8
8	Y_8	●	●	●	●		●		●		6
9	Y_9	●	●	●	●		●		●		6
10	Y_{10}	●	●	●	●		●	●	●		8
11	Y_{11}	●	●	●	●	●	●	●	●		8
12	Y_{12}	●	●	●	●	●	●				6
13	Y_{13}	●	●	●	●						4
14	Y_{14}	●	●	●	●	●			●	●	8
15	Y_{15}	●	●	●	●	●	●	●	●		8
16	Y_{16}	●	●	●	●	●	●	●	●		8
17	Y_{17}	●	●	●	●	●	●	●	●		8
18	Y_{18}	●	●	●	●	●	●				6
19	Y_{19}	●	●	●	●	●	●				6

continue

Serial number	Result-layer	Design layer (influence indicators)									Number of relevant indicators
		X_1	X_2	X_3	X_4	X_5	X_6	X_7	X_8	X_9	
20	Y_{20}	●	●	●	●	●	●				6
21	Y_{21}	●	●	●	●	●	●				6

Discussion results of correlation between consumer evaluation indicators and result layer see Table 8.

Table 8 Discussion Results of Correlation between Consumer Evaluation Indicators and Result Layer

Serial number	Consumer indicators	Result layer (21 expert indicators in total)	Number of relevant indicators
Z_1	Pure flavor/ aroma of tobacco	Odor, packet opening aroma	2
Z_2	Unique/special odor	Odor, packet opening aroma	2
Z_3	Strong & light odor	Odor, packet opening aroma	2
Z_4	Oral comfort	Softness, smooth, mellowness, irritancy in oral, cleanness, salivation, oral comfort, after taste	8
Z_5	Mouth moist	Smooth, irritancy in oral, cleanness, salivation, oral comfort	5
Z_6	Oral richness sensation	Smoke density, cigarette smoke concentration	2
Z_7	Stability	Smoke density, impact, softness, cigarette smoke concentration, smooth, diffusivity, abundance, aroma quality, aroma volume, mellowness, harmony, offensive taste, irritancy in nasal, irritancy in oral, irritancy in throat, cleanness, salivation, oral comfort, after taste	19
Z_8	Throat comfort	Impact, softness, irritancy in the throat	3
Z_9	Softness, smooth and grainy	Impact, softness, smooth, irritancy in the throat	4
Z_{10}	Smooth	Impact, softness, irritancy in the throat	3
Z_{11}	Impact	Smoke density, impact, softness, irritancy in throat	4
Z_{12}	Nasal comfort	Softness, smooth, mellowness, irritancy in nasal	4
Z_{13}	Abundance	Abundance, aroma quality, aroma volume, mellowness, harmony	5

continue

Serial number	Consumer indicators	Result layer (21 expert indicators in total)	Number of relevant indicators
Z_{14}	Aftertaste	Cleanness, salivation, oral comfort, after taste	4
Z_{15}	Aftertaste cleanness	Cleanness, oral comfort	2
Z_{16}	Mouth moist sensation after smoking	Salivation, oral comfort, after taste	3

2.1.2 Weight Calculation Based on AHP

Through the collective discussion of the experts, collect their scores and opinions. Because the importance of each expert participating in the workshop is equal, there is no need to assign the importance of the expert. The final weight of the transformation path is shown in the following table.

From table 9, it can be concluded that the indicators of different design layers are different from those of their related result layers, accurately as follows:

(1) The tobacco leaves have a high correlation with the indicators of impact, smoke density, diffusivity, abundance, aroma volume, mellowness, offensive taste, cleanness, salivation, and oral comfort;

(2) The cut tobacco was highly correlated with smoke density, impact, softness, irritancy in nasal, irritancy in oral, and irritancy in throat;

(3) The Spice formula has the most significant contribution to the harmony and after taste;

(4) The flavor formula is most famous for harmony, odor, and packet opening aroma.

From table 10, it can be concluded that different consumer indicators and their related result-layer indicators are different, accurately as follows:

(1) In terms of pure flavor/aroma of tobacco, unique/special odor, and strong & light odor, odor and packet opening aroma are related factors, odor is more important than others;

(2) The result layer indicators related to oral comfort include oral comfort, cleanliness, after taste, salivation, irritancy in oral, softness, smooth, and mellowness, among which oral comfort is the most important;

(3) For the degree of mouth moist, oral comfort, smooth, salivation, cleanliness, and irritancy in oral are related indicators, among which oral comfort is more important;

(4) The degree of fullness of the mouth is related to smoke density and cigarette

Table 9 Transformation Path Construction Results from the Design Layer Indicators to the Result Layer Indicators

Design layer indicators	Result layer indicators																				
	Y_1	Y_2	Y_3	Y_4	Y_5	Y_6	Y_7	Y_8	Y_9	Y_{10}	Y_{11}	Y_{12}	Y_{13}	Y_{14}	Y_{15}	Y_{16}	Y_{17}	Y_{18}	Y_{19}	Y_{20}	Y_{21}
X_1	—	—	0.27	0.42	0.19	0.17	0.15	0.2	0.21	0.16	0.19	0.2	0.17	0.2	0.22	0.2	0.2	0.21	0.22	0.18	0.18
X_2	—	—	0.23	0.41	0.14	0.21	0.16	0.25	0.24	0.18	0.19	0.25	0.16	0.21	0.21	0.18	0.19	0.25	0.23	0.22	0.21
X_3	0.22	0.19	0.1	—	0.15	0.15	0.19	0.15	0.2	0.19	0.15	0.21	0.32	0.18	0.15	0.17	0.17	0.21	0.21	0.21	0.24
X_4	0.57	0.59	0.06	—	0.15	0.15	0.14	0.13	0.18	0.19	—	0.16	0.35	0.14	0.14	0.15	0.15	0.16	0.17	0.18	0.18
X_5	—	—	0.06	—	0.08	0.07	0.09	—	—	0.08	0.06	0.09	—	0.1	0.08	0.08	0.09	0.09	0.09	0.1	0.09
X_6	—	—	0.06	—	0.1	0.07	0.11	0.12	0.08	0.09	0.09	0.09	—	0.09	0.09	0.09	0.09	0.08	0.08	0.1	0.1
X_7	—	—	0.04	0.09	0.04	0.04	0.05	—	—	0.03	0.04	—	—	—	0.05	0.04	0.04	—	—	—	—
X_8	0.2	0.22	0.17	0.19	0.15	0.13	0.11	0.14	0.09	0.07	0.15	—	—	—	—	0.07	0.07	—	—	—	—
X_9	—	—	—	—	—	—	—	—	—	—	—	—	—	0.03	—	—	—	—	—	—	—

Table 10 Construction Results of Conversion Path from Consumer Evaluation Indicators to the Result Layer Indicatiors

Consumer evaluation indicators	Result layer indicators																				
	Y_1	Y_2	Y_3	Y_4	Y_5	Y_6	Y_7	Y_8	Y_9	Y_{10}	Y_{11}	Y_{12}	Y_{13}	Y_{14}	Y_{15}	Y_{16}	Y_{17}	Y_{18}	Y_{19}	Y_{20}	Y_{21}
Z_1	0.74	0.26	—	—	—	—	—	—	—	—	—	—	—	—	—	—	—	—	—	—	—
Z_2	0.74	0.26	—	—	—	—	—	—	—	—	—	—	—	—	—	—	—	—	—	—	—
Z_3	0.75	0.25	—	—	—	—	—	—	—	—	—	—	—	—	—	—	—	—	—	—	—
Z_4	—	—	—	—	0.08	—	0.08	—	—	—	—	—	—	—	—	0.09	—	0.15	0.12	0.28	0.14
Z_5	—	—	—	—	—	—	0.24	—	—	—	—	—	—	—	—	0.12	—	0.15	0.18	0.31	—
Z_6	—	—	0.72	—	—	0.28	—	—	—	—	—	—	—	—	—	—	—	—	—	—	—
Z_7	—	—	0.07	0.06	0.06	0.06	0.06	0.06	—	0.08	0.09	0.06	0.06	0.03	0.03	0.03	0.03	0.04	0.04	0.04	0.04
Z_8	—	—	—	0.22	0.44	—	—	—	—	—	—	—	—	—	—	—	0.34	—	—	—	—
Z_9	—	—	—	0.11	0.44	—	0.29	—	—	—	—	—	—	—	—	—	0.15	—	—	—	—
Z_{10}	—	—	—	0.32	0.4	—	—	—	—	—	—	—	—	—	—	—	—	—	—	—	—
Z_{11}	—	—	0.14	0.47	0.18	—	—	—	—	—	—	—	—	—	—	—	0.28	—	—	—	—
Z_{12}	—	—	—	—	0.28	—	0.2	—	—	—	—	0.21	—	—	0.31	—	0.22	—	—	—	—
Z_{13}	—	—	—	—	—	—	—	—	0.35	0.25	0.14	0.11	0.15	—	—	—	—	—	—	—	—
Z_{14}	—	—	—	—	—	—	—	—	—	—	0.14	0.11	—	—	—	—	—	0.24	0.16	0.36	0.24
Z_{15}	—	—	—	—	—	—	—	—	—	—	—	—	—	—	—	—	—	0.61	—	0.39	—
Z_{16}	—	—	—	—	—	—	—	—	—	—	—	—	—	—	—	—	—	—	0.34	0.46	0.2

smoke concentration, among which the smoke density is more important;

(5) The stability is affected by various factors and distributed evenly. The relevant indicators include aroma quality, cleanliness, softness, mellowness, aftertaste, offensive taste, oral comfort, salivation, irritancy in nasal, impact, irritancy in throat, irritancy in oral, cigarette smoke concentration, smooth, harmony, abundance, diffusivity, and aroma volume, of which aroma volume is the essential factor;

(6) The indicators related to throat comfort and smooth are softness, irritancy in throat and impact, among which softness is the most important;

(7) For the softness, smooth and grainy, softness, smooth, irritancy in throat and impact are related factors, among which softness is the most important;

(8) The indicators related to impact include impact, irritancy in throat, softness, and smoke density, and impact is the most important;

(9) Irritancy in nasal, softness, mellowness and smooth are the factors related to nasal comfort, among which irritancy in nasal is the most important;

(10) The essential factors for abundance are abundance, aroma quality, harmony, aroma volume, and mellowness, among which abundance significantly contributes the most to the abundance;

(11) The related factors of after taste include oral comfort, cleanliness, after taste, and salivation, and oral comfort is the most important factor;

(12) The factors related to the aftertaste cleanness are cleanliness and oral comfort, among which cleanliness is the most important;

(13) For the degree of mouth moist sensation after smoking, oral comfort, salivation, and after taste are related factors, and the essential level of oral comfort is the highest.

2.1.3 Preliminary Construction Results of Transformation Path from Consumer Evaluation Indicator to Product Attribute Element

Based on the above results, we connect the indicators with relevance in consumer evaluation indicators, result layer indicators, and design layer indicators. We can initially build the transformation path from consumer indicators to product attribute elements, as shown in Figure 2 and Figure 3.

As a single indicator may correspond to multiple expert technical indicators, resulting in multiple transformation paths, this paper selects the indicators with the highest average correlation for connection from the transformation paths from the design layer to the result layer, and from the transformation paths from the consumer indicators to the result layer indicators, and finally constructs a relatively preliminarily simplified path model diagram. See Figure 4 below.

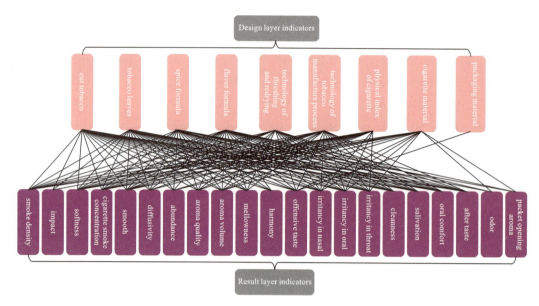

Figure 2　Conversion Path from Design Layer Indicators to Result Layer Indicators

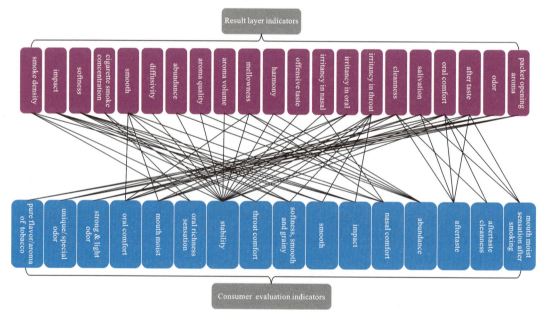

Figure 3　Transformation Path from Consumer Evaluation Indicators to Result Layer Indicators

According to the results of the path map, the following conclusions can be drawn.

(1) In the design layer indicator, the "tobacco formula" is most closely related to the indicators of the result layer, especially with the "cleanliness" "mellowness" and "diffusivity"; the "cut tobacco" is also closely related to multiple indicators of the result-layer, among which the "impact" is strongly related.

(2) The results showed that the "softness" in the result layer was most related to the consumer evaluation indicator, especially the "throat comfort" and "softness, smooth and grainy".

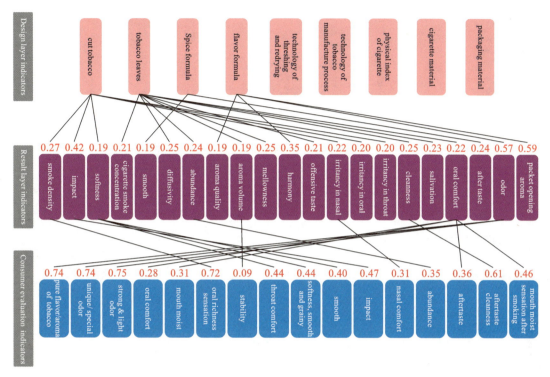

Figure 4　Preliminarily Transformation Path Chart: Design Layer-Result Layer-Consumer

2.2　Correlation Verification Results of the Transformation Path of Cigarette Consumers' Internal Quality Demand

From Table 11, it can be seen that the correlation between each result layer indicator and consumer evaluation indicator is generally high, most of the results are above 0.7, and the results are significant, indicating that the result-layer indicator and consumer indicator are highly correlated.

From Table 12, it can be concluded that resolving the collinearity between independent variables can more accurately explain the importance of result layer indicators for consumer indicators in this project. So as to determine the contribution of the indicator.

Through the above correlation analysis and the application of the Shapley value decomposition method based on the regression equation, a full path map of the transformation path of the internal quality demand of cigarette consumers is finally constructed (see Figure 5 below).

Table 11 Pearson Correlation Analysis Results

Pearson correlation	Y_1	Y_2	Y_3	Y_4	Y_5	Y_6	Y_7	Y_8	Y_9	Y_{10}	Y_{11}	Y_{12}	Y_{13}	Y_{14}	Y_{15}	Y_{16}	Y_{17}	Y_{18}	Y_{19}	Y_{20}	Y_{21}
Z_1	0.736**	0.793**	0.648**	0.870**	0.872**	0.870**	0.860**	0.809**	0.830**	0.892**	0.759**	0.871**	0.833**	0.873**	0.868**	0.852**	0.854**	0.884**	0.873**	0.882**	0.876**
Z_2	0.771**	0.812**	0.643**	0.872**	0.897**	0.876**	0.880**	0.835**	0.846**	0.922**	0.771**	0.895**	0.865**	0.910**	0.885**	0.887**	0.891**	0.916**	0.897**	0.911**	0.902**
Z_3	0.739**	0.775**	0.637**	0.859**	0.874**	0.878**	0.867**	0.827**	0.822**	0.894**	0.775**	0.874**	0.843**	0.886**	0.866**	0.862**	0.864**	0.895**	0.880**	0.886**	0.882**
Z_4	0.760**	0.804**	0.634**	0.863**	0.910**	0.883**	0.875**	0.830**	0.846**	0.932**	0.771**	0.897**	0.860**	0.918**	0.901**	0.890**	0.893**	0.921**	0.894**	0.912**	0.908**
Z_5	0.742**	0.796**	0.586**	0.847**	0.909**	0.861**	0.865**	0.811**	0.831**	0.919**	0.745**	0.900**	0.837**	0.903**	0.895**	0.885**	0.886**	0.906**	0.884**	0.898**	0.899**
Z_6	0.730**	0.762**	0.741**	0.876**	0.823**	0.904**	0.844**	0.869**	0.836**	0.887**	0.854**	0.859**	0.856**	0.872**	0.820**	0.823**	0.819**	0.876**	0.873**	0.861**	0.884**
Z_7	0.743**	0.790**	0.628**	0.871**	0.897**	0.866**	0.861**	0.833**	0.848**	0.920**	0.781**	0.895**	0.855**	0.891**	0.883**	0.869**	0.870**	0.898**	0.884**	0.887**	0.893**
Z_8	0.725**	0.795**	0.583**	0.846**	0.909**	0.860**	0.864**	0.809**	0.824**	0.923**	0.741**	0.893**	0.842**	0.903**	0.898**	0.882**	0.889**	0.913**	0.883**	0.898**	0.892**
Z_9	0.726**	0.778**	0.609**	0.870**	0.893**	0.864**	0.860**	0.808**	0.818**	0.906**	0.758**	0.889**	0.839**	0.891**	0.872**	0.866**	0.876**	0.908**	0.883**	0.885**	0.889**
Z_{10}	0.735**	0.793**	0.681**	0.871**	0.878**	0.888**	0.863**	0.843**	0.842**	0.914**	0.800**	0.890**	0.850**	0.894**	0.876**	0.861**	0.861**	0.900**	0.894**	0.890**	0.897**
Z_{11}	0.760**	0.804**	0.614**	0.874**	0.910**	0.872**	0.876**	0.820**	0.833**	0.924**	0.762**	0.899**	0.856**	0.910**	0.898**	0.882**	0.895**	0.918**	0.894**	0.904**	0.897**
Z_{12}	0.742**	0.788**	0.634**	0.874**	0.897**	0.884**	0.869**	0.827**	0.832**	0.912**	0.780**	0.891**	0.853**	0.904**	0.878**	0.864**	0.868**	0.913**	0.892**	0.895**	0.894**
Z_{13}	0.743**	0.797**	0.669**	0.872**	0.875**	0.889**	0.857**	0.851**	0.834**	0.908**	0.809**	0.878**	0.861**	0.900**	0.864**	0.851**	0.856**	0.900**	0.884**	0.885**	0.889**
Z_{14}	0.757**	0.805**	0.638**	0.871**	0.901**	0.881**	0.871**	0.831**	0.846**	0.920**	0.782**	0.898**	0.860**	0.910**	0.888**	0.874**	0.877**	0.918**	0.889**	0.902**	0.903**
Z_{15}	0.729**	0.790**	0.642**	0.875**	0.889**	0.887**	0.867**	0.832**	0.843**	0.915**	0.801**	0.890**	0.859**	0.901**	0.875**	0.866**	0.867**	0.910**	0.891**	0.895**	0.897**
Z_{16}	0.711**	0.773**	0.595**	0.854**	0.896**	0.857**	0.853**	0.801**	0.818**	0.906**	0.756**	0.880**	0.836**	0.889**	0.873**	0.860**	0.865**	0.899**	0.867**	0.876**	0.876**

**. Significant correlation at 0.01 level (two tails).

Table 12 Results of Shapley Value Analysis based on the Regression Equation

Results of Shapley value analysis	Y_1	Y_2	Y_3	Y_4	Y_5	Y_6	Y_7	Y_8	Y_9	Y_{10}	Y_{11}	Y_{12}	Y_{13}	Y_{14}	Y_{15}	Y_{16}	Y_{17}	Y_{18}	Y_{19}	Y_{20}	Y_{21}
Z_1	0.431**	0.569**																			
Z_2	0.451**	0.549**																			
Z_3	0.455**	0.545**																			
Z_4					0.134**		0.120**					0.118**				0.115**		0.139**	0.120**	0.129**	0.126**
Z_5							0.187**									0.195**		0.222**	0.194**	0.202**	
Z_6			0.338**			0.662**															
Z_7			0.031**	0.056**	0.060**	0.055**	0.055**	0.044**	0.045**	0.084**	0.039**	0.056**	0.051**	0.054**	0.054**	0.050**	0.051**	0.055**	0.054**	0.052**	0.055**
Z_8				0.292**	0.373**												0.336**				
Z_9				0.257**	0.271**		0.229**										0.243**				
Z_{10}				0.345**	0.341**												0.314**				
Z_{11}			0.114**	0.277**	0.317**												0.291**				
Z_{12}					0.267**		0.233**								0.242**						
Z_{13}									0.174**	0.268**	0.164**	0.258**	0.189**								
Z_{14}												0.206**						0.273**	0.235**	0.245**	0.248**
Z_{15}																		0.517**		0.483**	
Z_{16}																			0.323**	0.339**	0.338**

**. Significant correlation at 0.01 level (two tails).

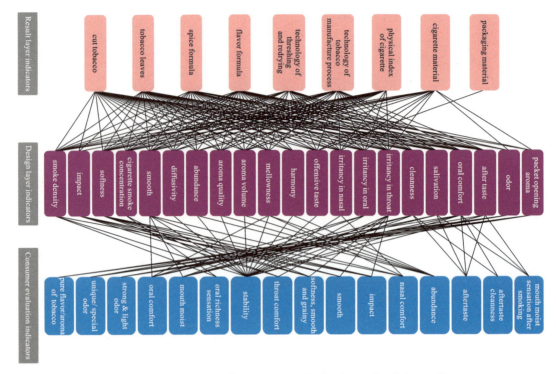

Figure 5 Transformation Full Path Diagram: Design Layer-Result Layer-Consumer

In order to simplify the full path graph, this paper selects the indicator with the highest average correlation to build the final full path graph of Figure 6, there is only one most relevant path for the transformation from a single consumer indicator to the result-layer and then to the design layer.

Among them, the indicator coefficient from consumer indicator to result-layer is the weight coefficient obtained by quantitative research, and the indicator coefficient from the result layer to design layer is the weight coefficient obtained by the expert workshop.

3 Conclusion

(1) According to the final construction of the transformation path, we can get the result layer indicators that directly affect consumers' evaluation of the internal quality of cigarettes and the design layer indicators related to these result layer indicators of cigarette manufacturing. At the same time, we can accurately get the influence degree of these product attribute result layer's factors on the sensory quality evaluation results of consumers through the correlation coefficient value.

(2) Only selecting the highest weight path, we can get the highest conversion path between 16 consumer evaluation indicators to result layer indicators and then to the

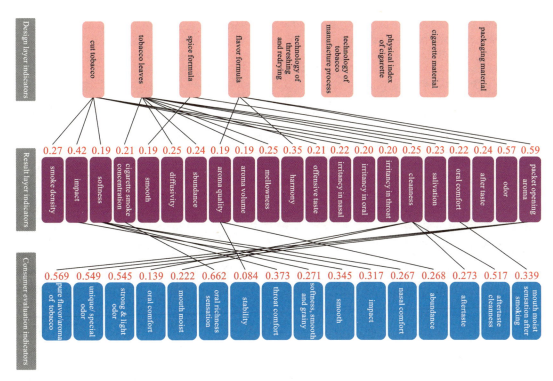

Figure 6　Final Transformation Path Chart：Design Layer-Result Layer-Consumer

relevant indicators of design layer：pure flavor/aroma of tobacco - packet opening aroma - flavor formula；unique/special odor - packet opening aroma - flavor formula；strong & light odor - packet opening aroma - flavor formula；oral comfort - cleanliness - tobacco leaves；mouth moist - cleanliness - tobacco leaves；oral richness sensation - cigarette smoke concentration - tobacco leaves；stability - aroma quality - flavor formula；throat comfort - softness - cut tobacco；softness, smooth and grainy - softness - cut tobacco；smooth - impact - cut tobacco；impact - softness - cut tobacco；nasal comfort - softness - cut tobacco，abundance - aroma quality - flavor formula，after taste - cleanliness - tobacco leaves；aftertaste cleanness - cleanliness - tobacco leaves；mouth moist sensation after smoking - oral comfort - tobacco leaves.

（3）In this paper, through the form of a workshop, the hierarchical structure indicator of attribute elements of cigarette, and the indicators of consumer evaluation are correlated and verified. The docking transformation mode of cigarette product characteristics and consumer demand is established. Through the combination of the consumption evaluation system and expert cigarette evaluation indicator, a real complete path of "consumer feedback consumer demand - transformation expert evaluation indicator - correspondence product technology improvement" is established. For product R&D personnel to understand consumer demand, convert it into product R&D and maintenance objectives, further accurately guide formula, conduct product R&D, and Maintenance is of great significance.

References

[1] General Administration of Quality Supervision, Inspection and Quarantine of the People's Republic of China, Standardization Administration of China. Cigarettes Part 4: Sensory Technical Requirements: GB 5606. 4—2005[S]. Beijing: Standards Press of China, 2005.

[2] SAATY T L. Axiomatic Foundation of the Analytic Hierarchyprocess[J]. Management Science, 1986, 32 (7): 841-855.

[3] QI Y L. Research on Performance Appraisal System based on AHP[J]. Journal of Xi'an University of engineering, 2008, 22 (3): 125-128.

[4] XIE X Z. Application of AHP in Performance Management[J]. China labor, 2005 (11): 72-74.

[5] ZHU J. Research on Credit System Construction of the Tobacco Industry[D]. Tianjin: Tianjin University, 2006.

[6] ZHENG X P, ZHOU Q, LIU Y L. Study on the Dynamic Credit Evaluation Model of Tobacco Monopoly Retail Operators based on AHP[J]. Chongqing and the World (Academic Edition), 2016 (11): 7-11.

[7] HE R H, WAN F M, XIANG L S, et al. Construction of a Credit Index System for Retail Cigarette Customers based on Group Decision and AHP[J]. Computer Application and Software, 2019, 36(12): 81-86.

[8] YANG L, YANG Q X, FENG H T, et al. An Empirical Study on the Influencing Factors of Cigarette Consumer Satisfaction[J]. Journal of Yunnan Agricultural University, 2019, 13 (5): 93-101.

[9] QIU C B, XU X M, GUO H W, et al. The Application of AHP in Determining the Weight of the Tobacco Performance Evaluation Index[J]. China New Technology and New Products, 2016 (2): 156-157.

第 5 章

卷烟市场状态评估与预测

基于 R 语言编程的移动平均方法在卷烟产品销量状态分析中的应用

摘要：产品销量的变化是反映其市场发展状态的重要依据。为了评估上市不满 2 年的新产品的市场状态，指导产品市场策略的制定，本文以 2017—2018 年共 24 个月的卷烟销量数据为基础，采用移动平均方法进行产品销量趋势判断，并利用数据使用表格格式整理结果，在 R 程序平台上自编程构建了产品销量状态分析体系，并以 2017—2018 年全国二类卷烟销量为例进行了运算分析，揭示了常规、细支、中支、短支、爆珠等不同类型卷烟产品市场状态的趋势。运算分析过程表明：该方法体系的运用可以消除传统卷烟新产品销量同比变化判断的不准确性及节假日对销量变化的影响，准确提取产品的正常发展状态；同时，相比传统烦琐的手动分析，运行相关程序进行分析可有效节约时间，提高效率，对于快速掌握市场状态，有效预测产品未来发展趋势，指导产品市场策略的制定具有重要意义。

关键词：产品销量；状态分析；趋势判断；产品策略

产品销量的变化是直接反映产品发展状态的重要指标，销量数据科学分析结果对于指导产品市场策略的制定有重要意义。历史销量数据的研究主要用于未来销量预测，常用的数学分析方法有移动平均方法、指数平滑法、线性回归法等，但在实际应用中，产品的历史销售数据样本量往往有限或不能完全满足线性规律，特别是卷烟产品。不同于一般在售产品,卷烟产品销量受政策、环境、节假日影响较大。基于卷烟产品销量的变化特征,一些数学分析方法(如趋势分析法、时间序列预测方法、ARIMA 模型、BP 神经网络模型等)被大量尝试用于卷烟销量预算的研究分析。

譬如,曹鲁东[1]以国内一类卷烟 2009 年到 2012 年月度销量数据为样本数据,进行季节性时间序列分析,并建立季节性时间序列分析模型,用于预测卷烟未来销量;李嘉霖[2]选取 2004 年至 2016 年全国卷烟销量季度数据,采用时间序列确定性因素分解模型,对其趋势特征和季节波动进行分析,拟合出全国卷烟销量模型;吴明山等[3]以 2006—2017 年全国卷烟销量数据为基础数据,选择 ARIMA 模型、基于梯度下降算法的 BP 神经网络模型、基于 Levenberg-Marquardt 算法改进的 BP 神经网络模型等 3 种模型为单项预测模型,并利用 BP 神经网络对各单项预测模型进行动态加权,构建非线性组合模型对 2018 年 1—4 月全国卷烟销量月度数据进行预测。

然而,目前对于产品的销量状态、销售势能的分析研究较少。过去的研究方法[4-6]在针对具体产品时通常采用年份销量的同比概念来确定产品销量趋势。美国著名市场营销学家菲力普·科特勒提出,产品生命周期包括导入期、成长期、成熟期与衰退期四个阶段[7,8]。对于卷烟产品来说,新品的上市后市场培育阶段,即导入期往往都在 2 年以上或者更长。因此,对于上市后不满 2 年的新品,其销售状态的评价如果仍采用传统同比的方式,很大程度上会导致评价结果的失真,从而不能对卷烟新品销售趋势及未来走势给出相对准确的预判。

为了解决上述问题,提高卷烟产品销量状态、趋势分析的准确性,本文采用移动平均方法进行产品销量趋势判断,并利用数据使用表格格式整理结果,在 R 程序平台上自编程构建了产品销量状态分析体系,以 2017—2018 年共 24 个月的全国不同规格卷烟商业销量数据为基础数据,进行了提取及运算分析,并对云产卷烟四大品牌及其强势竞争对手的具体产品销量数据进行了对比分析,揭示了常规、细支、中支、短支、爆珠等不同类型卷烟产品市场状态的趋势信息,以期为卷烟产品发展变化情况的分析提供更有效和及时的信息反馈,对快速制定产品市场策略具有重要意义。

1 材料与方法

1.1 数据来源

本文以 2017—2018 年全国不同规格卷烟商业销量数据为基础数据,数据格式见表 1~表 3,通过后续的分析体系开发完成卷烟产品销量状态分析展示。

表 1 用于筛选卷烟品类,可作为结果格式输出中分类汇总的前提;另外,它还可以通过对商业销量进行排序,对上四分位数的规格进行筛选,从而确定竞争产品。对云产卷烟的识别主要是针对"云烟""玉溪""红塔山"和"红河"这四大品牌,在卷烟规格指标中对其进行模糊识别。

表1　全国不同卷烟类型数据基础格式样式示例表

卷烟规格	焦油含量	是否细支烟	是否爆珠烟	是否中支烟	是否短支烟	商业销量/(箱/年)
A	10 mg	非细支烟	非爆珠烟	非中支烟	非短支烟	69.25
B	8 mg	细支烟	非爆珠烟	非中支烟	非短支烟	1297.83
C	8 mg	非细支烟	非爆珠烟	非中支烟	非短支烟	0.00
D	11 mg	非细支烟	非爆珠烟	非中支烟	非短支烟	0.00
E	8 mg	细支烟	非爆珠烟	非中支烟	非短支烟	364.18
F	10 mg	非细支烟	非爆珠烟	非中支烟	非短支烟	127.98
G	7 mg	细支烟	非爆珠烟	非中支烟	非短支烟	1270.52
H	6 mg	非细支烟	非爆珠烟	非中支烟	非短支烟	17.64
I	10 mg	非细支烟	非爆珠烟	非中支烟	非短支烟	0.00
J	8 mg	非细支烟	爆珠烟	非中支烟	非短支烟	0.00
K	…	…	…	…	…	…

表2主要用于销量趋势情况的计算分析,以月度数据为基础,通过移动平均方法可以进一步提取产品销量趋势,从而进行判断。

表2　全国月度数据基础格式样式示例表

地区	卷烟规格	年份	月份	商业销量/(箱/月)
北京市	K	2017年	1月	16.57
北京市	K	2017年	2月	7.84
北京市	K	2017年	3月	35.81
北京市	K	2017年	4月	12.98
北京市	K	2017年	5月	10.52
北京市	K	2017年	6月	18.17
北京市	K	2017年	7月	6.81
北京市	K	2017年	8月	6.11
北京市	K	2017年	9月	19.70
北京市	K	2017年	10月	12.80
北京市	K	2017年	…	……

表3用于对特定地区进行筛选,表内的地区内容可以通过对全国趋势的判断进行筛选,也可以根据实际分析需要进行自定义筛选。

表3　特定地区数据基础格式样式示例表

地区
北京市
河北省

续表

地区
山西省
内蒙古自治区
辽宁省
吉林省
黑龙江省
浙江省
安徽省
……

1.2 分析方法

1.2.1 趋势数据提取

本文采用移动平均方法对产品销售趋势进行分析。所谓移动平均,是选择一定的用于平均的时距项数 K,采用对系列逐项递移的方式,对原系列递移的 K 项计算一系列序时平均数,该方法能在一定程度上消除原序列中短期偶然因素引起的不规则变动,从而起到一定的修匀或平滑作用。当序列包含季节变动时,K 应与季节变动长度一致,才能消除其季节变动;当序列包含周期变动时,K 应和周期长度基本一致,才能较好地消除周期波动。

值得注意的是,K 为奇数时,只需要进行一次移动平均,其移动平均值即可作为移动平均项数的中间一期的数值;而当 K 为偶数时,移动平均代表的是偶数项的中间位置的水平,无法对正某一时期,需要再进行一次相邻两平均值的移动平均,才能使平均值对正某一时期,这称为移正平均,也叫中心化的移动平均[9]。

为了消除卷烟销售在春节和中秋等传统节日期间可能出现的销量骤增的趋势影响[10,11],本文利用移动平均方法对表1中具体卷烟产品的月度数据进行趋势提取分析,以两年为一个周期,通过12个月为步长的十二次移动平均及移正平均,最终获得趋势数据。

1.2.2 销量趋势判断

通过上述的十二次移动平均结合移正平均后获得的趋势数据,一般情况下会呈现两种状态:①趋势平顺且明显;②趋势波动,需进行数据截取后判断。具体表现如下。

(1) 趋势平顺且明显,如图1。如果趋势处于上升状态(图1(a)),则利用最高点的销量趋势数据减去最低点的销量趋势数据获得的增量为反映当前卷烟产品的发展状态;如果趋势处于下降状态(图1(b)),则利用最低点的销量趋势数据减去最高点的销量趋势数据获得的减量为反映当前卷烟产品的发展状态。

(2) 趋势波动,需进行数据截取后判断,如图2。如果趋势处于波动状态,则根据趋势出现的拐点数来判断,一般认为具有三个拐点数的趋势波动状态基本能囊括该产品的趋势

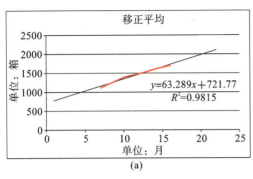
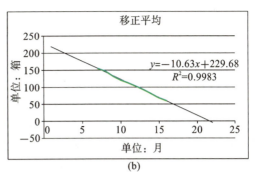

图 1 针对计算后趋势数据平顺且明显的示例图

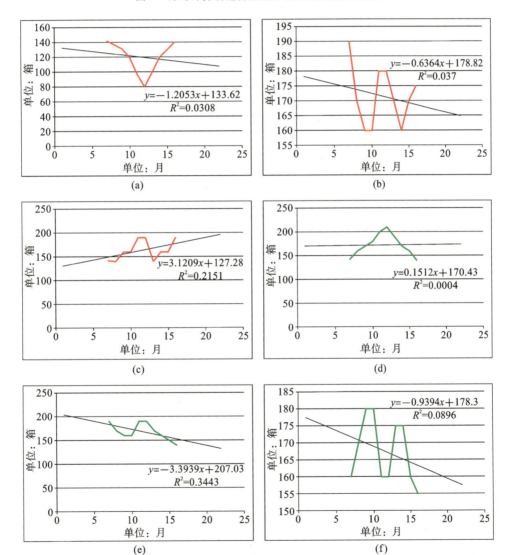

图 2 针对计算后趋势波动,需进行数据截取后判断的示例图

发展状态。判断原则如下:当存在一个拐点时,利用最后趋势点的数据减去拐点所在的数据来表示其趋势发展状态(图 2(a)、(d));当存在两个拐点时,利用最后趋势点的数据减去第二个拐点所在的数据来表示其趋势发展状态(图 2(c)、(e));当存在三个拐点时,利用最后趋势点的数据减去第三个拐点所在的数据来表示其趋势发展状态(图 2(b)、(f))。

1.2.3 基于 R 程序平台的集成实现

将上述的移动平均、产品趋势判断以及相应的结果表格格式整理等,通过 R 平台中自编辑的程序予以实现;并利用 Excel 的 VBA 程序完成重点符号标示的颜色的突出显示(表 4)。具体步骤如图 3 所示。

表 4 销量以及趋势数据可能的趋势表现状态示例表

状态	刚上市	退市	趋势上升	趋势下降	趋势平稳
符号	○	×	↑	↓	—

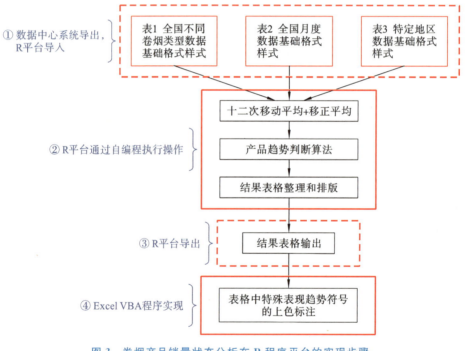

图 3 卷烟产品销量状态分析在 R 程序平台的实现步骤

2 结果与分析

2.1 基于不同价区不同规格产品的结果表格格式

利用表 1 和表 2 中不同价位和规格的卷烟以及卷烟产品销量状态分析集成程序,通过 R 平台运行后可生成表 5。本文以云产二类卷烟为例,进行了相关运算结果的演示。从表 5 中可以得到云产二类卷烟年度商业销量的排序,价位、规格、品类和计算后的趋势量、趋势方向,当前上市的地区数以及上市时间不足两年的新品上市时长等信息。根据这些信息,我们可以快速判断全国范围内云产二类卷烟中销量较高的产品、上市不足两年的新品及特殊品类产品的发展态势、增量快慢、覆盖范围特点等。

表 5　云产二类卷烟销量及时间序列趋势情况

零售价位/(元/条)	卷烟规格	品类	2018年商业销量年累计/箱	两年时间序列趋势及增量	目前上市地区数	上市时间不足两年的新品上市时长/月
130	云烟 A	常规烟	128374.87	46↑	13	—
150	云烟 B	细支烟	101270.43	6218↑	24	15
150	云烟 C	常规烟	34025.57	2085↑	10	15
150	红河 D	常规烟	33588.24	1525↑	18	16
130	红河 E	常规烟	24671.97	−105↓	2	—
150	红塔山 F	细支烟	21090.71	294↑	20	—
140	红河 G	常规烟	17452.82	63↑	1	—
140	红塔山 H	常规烟	8131.87	393↑	7	—
160	云烟 I	常规烟	7956.92	360↑	8	20
180	云烟 J	中支烟	3811.56	208↑	11	10
140	红塔山 K	常规烟	3377.45	−262↓	2	—
150	红塔山 L	常规烟	3052.50	81↑	3	15
150	红塔山 M	常规烟	2309.22	355↑	12	4
140	红塔山 N	常规烟	414.12	−1021↓	2	—
180	云烟 O	常规烟	283.17	−24↓	1	—
160	红塔山 P	常规烟	68.43	−4↓	1	—
140	云烟 Q	常规烟	12.62	退市×	—	21(退市)
160	云烟 R	常规烟	1.7	退市×	—	12(退市)
150	云烟 S	细支烟	0.03	退市×	—	11(退市)
…	…	…	…	…	…	…

2.2　基于特定地区不同价位不同规格产品的结果格式

表 1、表 2 的数据通过 R 平台运行后可生成表 6。本文以零售价位在 150 元/条的二类卷烟为例,在表 5 运算结果的基础上,以北京市及河北省两个特定地区为例,进行了相关运算结果的演示。从表 6 可以看到该价位段云产品牌、竞争品牌以及各个品类卷烟在特定地区的综合趋势说明。我们还可以快速判断零售价位在 150 元/条的云产二类卷烟在这些区域的销售及发展状态,排名在上四分位数的竞争产品规格发展状态以及各品类卷烟的数量及发展趋势。

表6 北京、河北零售价位在150元的二类卷烟销量情况汇总

卷烟销量在过去两年增加700箱以上的省份以及200箱以上的市	云产品牌	竞争品牌	常规烟表述	细支烟表述	短支烟表述	中支烟表述	爆珠烟表述
北京市	1. 云烟B（细支烟）（201.58箱↑）；2. 红塔山F（细支烟）（50.96箱↑）；3. 红河D（常规烟）（−79箱↑）；4. 红塔山M（常规烟）（5.78箱↑）	1. 中南海E（常规烟）（56.34箱↑）2. 长白山F（59.66箱↑）3. 云烟A（201.58箱↑）4. 南京H（9.92箱↑）；5. 红塔山B（细支烟）（50.96箱↑）6. 娇子J（40.87箱↑）	共12个（其中5个趋势增长↑，4个趋势下降↓，1个趋势稳定，2个刚上市，0个云产规格，有2个云产规格（其中1个趋势增长↑，1个趋势下降↓，0个趋势稳定，0个已退市，0个刚上市）	共9个（其中8个趋势增长↑，0个趋势下降↓，1个趋势稳定，0个刚上市，0个云产规格，有2个云产规格（其中2个趋势增长↑，0个趋势下降↓，0个趋势稳定，0个已退市，0个刚上市）	无	共1个（其中0个趋势增长↑，1个趋势下降↓，0个趋势稳定，0个刚上市，0个云产规格，有0个云产规格（其中0个趋势增长↑，0个趋势下降↓，0个趋势稳定，0个已退市，0个刚上市）	共1个（其中0个趋势增长↑，0个趋势下降↓，0个趋势稳定，1个刚上市，0个云产规格，有0个云产规格（其中0个趋势增长↑，0个趋势下降↓，0个趋势稳定，0个已退市，0个刚上市）
河北省	1. 云烟B（细支烟）（301.89箱↑）；2. 红塔山F（细支烟）（32.94箱↑）；3. 红河D（常规烟）（5.73箱↑）；4. 红塔山M（17.54箱↑）；5. 云烟S（细支烟）（已退市×）	1. 长白山F（164.78箱↑）2. 云烟B（301.89箱↑）3. 中南海H（−50.39箱↑）4. 娇子I（81.02箱↑）5. 白沙J（47.71箱↑）6. 黄山K（89.72箱↑）7. 真龙L（细支烟）（73箱↑）8. 红塔山B（细支烟）（32.94箱↑）	共14个（其中3个趋势增长↑，3个趋势下降↓，2个趋势稳定，6个刚上市，0个云产规格，有2个云产规格（其中2个趋势增长↑，0个趋势下降↓，0个趋势稳定，0个已退市，0个刚上市）	共15个（其中13个趋势增长↑，0个趋势下降↓，0个趋势稳定，2个刚上市，0个云产规格，有3个云产规格（其中2个趋势增长↑，0个趋势下降↓，0个趋势稳定，1个已退市，0个刚上市）	无	共1个（其中0个趋势增长↑，1个趋势下降↓，0个趋势稳定，0个刚上市，0个云产规格，有0个云产规格（其中0个趋势增长↑，0个趋势下降↓，0个趋势稳定，0个已退市，0个刚上市）	共1个（其中0个趋势增长↑，0个趋势下降↓，0个趋势稳定，1个刚上市，0个云产规格，有0个云产规格（其中0个趋势增长↑，0个趋势下降↓，0个趋势稳定，0个已退市，0个刚上市）
…	…	…	…	…	…	…	…

3　结论与讨论

产品销量的变化是反映市场发展状态的重要依据。然而,由于卷烟产品的计划性,其销量的变化往往受很多因素的影响,不能完全反映真实的市场状态。本文采用移动平均方法进行产品销量趋势判断,并利用数据使用表格格式整理结果,在 R 程序平台上自编程构建了产品销量状态分析体系,该体系可有效解决上述问题。通过实例验证,该方法体系具有如下优点。

(1) 可以消除传统卷烟新产品销量同比变化判断的不准确性,从而对上市不足两年的新品发展状态及发展趋势给出相对准确的预判。

(2) 使用移动平均方法,有效消除了节假日等因素对卷烟销量变化的影响,提取的产品正常发展水平可信度较高。

(3) 整个产品销量状态分析体系主要通过 R 语言自编程执行实现,相比传统烦琐的手动分析,可有效节约时间,提高效率,对于快速掌握市场状态,有效预测产品未来发展趋势,指导产品市场策略的制定具有重要意义。该分析体系未来可加载到产品销售大数据分析系统中,成为产品市场表现实时监控判断功能的一部分。

但是,该产品销量状态分析体系还存在一定不足,例如,在趋势波动的状态下,目前只针对后部的趋势方向进行了截取,如果和趋势较为明显的产品在同一个层面上比较可能会存在一定偏差。作者将在后续研究中进一步补充,使研究更加完善。

参考文献

[1]　曹鲁东.卷烟销量应用研究——基于时间序列分析[D].昆明:云南财经大学,2012.
[2]　李嘉霖.基于时间序列模型的全国卷烟销量分析[J].社会科学前沿,2018,7(12):1974-1981.
[3]　吴明山,王冰,起亚宁,等.卷烟销量组合预测模型研究[J].中国烟草学报,2019,25(3):84-91.
[4]　杜远宗.烟草一号工程数据采集方案设计与实现[D].北京:北京交通大学,2005.
[5]　刘永久,王志国.哈尔滨市 2004 年卷烟市场动态综合分析[J].新烟草,2005(2):54-55.
[6]　梁彪.关于齐齐哈尔烟草分公司上半年经济运行情况调查报告[J].新烟草,2005(8):28-31.
[7]　王禹,胡伟峰.基于生命周期理论的短视频产品设计规划策略研究[J].大众文艺,2018(12):79-80.
[8]　马颖玥.基于产品生命周期理论的设计要素分析[J].艺术教育,2018(19):192-193.
[9]　袁卫,庞皓,曾五一,等.统计学[M].北京:高等教育出版社,2009:263-266.
[10]　邹亮.怀化市卷烟市场需求时间序列分析[J].中国烟草学报,2007,13(6):51-57.
[11]　白雪梅,赵松山.移动平均法应用之我见[J].统计教育,2001(1):20-22.

Application of Moving Average Method Based on R Programming in the Analysis of Cigarette Product Sales Status

Abstract: Changes in product sales are essential indicators reflecting the market development status. In order to evaluate the market status of new products launched in less than 2 years and guide product market strategies, this paper uses 24 months of cigarette sales data from 2017 to 2018 as the basis. This paper independently constructs a product sales status analysis system on the R programming platform by combining moving average with product sales trend judgment and result data table formatting. Taking the national sales of Class Ⅱ price-category cigarettes in 2017-2018 as an example, computational analysis was conducted to explore the trend information of different types of cigarette product market statuses, including regular, slim, medium, short, and burst bead cigarettes. The computational analysis process shows that the application of this method system can eliminate the inaccuracy of traditional comparative judgments on the sales changes of new cigarette products and the impact of holidays on sales changes, accurately extract the normal development level status of products at the same time, compared with the traditional cumbersome manual analysis, the operation of related programs can effectively save time, improve efficiency, and has significant importance for quickly grasping market status, effectively predicting the future development trends of products, and guiding product market strategies.

Keywords: Product sales; Status analysis; Trend judgment; Product strategy

Changes in product sales serve as crucial indicators directly reflecting the developmental status of products, and scientific analysis of sales data holds significant importance in guiding product market strategies. Research on historical sales data is primarily used for future sales forecasting, with commonly used mathematical analysis methods including moving average, exponential smoothing, linear regression, etc. However, in practical applications, the sample size of historical product sales data is often limited or may not fully conform to linear patterns, especially for cigarette products. Unlike general retail products, cigarette sales are significantly influenced by policies, environmental factors, and holidays. Based on the characteristics of cigarette product sales, in recent years, various mathematical analysis methods such as trend analysis, time series forecasting methods, ARIMA models, BP neural network models, etc., have been extensively attempted in studies analyzing cigarette sales forecasts.

For instance, Cao Ludong[1] utilized monthly data of a specific category of cigarettes sales volume in China from 2009 to 2012 as sample data to conduct seasonal time series analysis and established seasonal time series analysis models for predicting future cigarette sales. Li Jialin[2] selected quarterly sales data of cigarettes nationwide from 2004 to 2016, employing a time series deterministic factor decomposition model to analyze its trend characteristics and seasonal fluctuations, and fitted a national cigarette sales model. Wu Mingshan et al.[3], using national cigarette sales data from 2006 to 2017 as base data, selected three models, including the ARIMA model, the BP neural network model based on the gradient descent algorithm, and the BP neural network model improved based on the Levenberg-Marquardt algorithm as single forecasting models. They utilized the BP neural network to dynamically weight each forecasting model, constructing a nonlinear combination model for predicting monthly data of national cigarette sales from January to April 2018.

However, there needs to be more research on the analysis of product sales status and sales potential. Previous research methods[4-6], when targeting specific products, usually employ the year-on-year concept of sales volume to determine product sales trends. Renowned American marketing expert Philip Kotler proposed that the product lifecycle includes four stages[7,8]: introduction, growth, maturity, and decline. For cigarette products, the market cultivation stage after the launch of new products, i.e., the introduction stage, often lasts over 2 years or longer. Therefore, for new products launched for less than 2 years, if the evaluation of their sales status still adopts the traditional year-on-year method, it will greatly distort the evaluation results, thus being unable to provide relatively accurate predictions for the sales trends and prospects of new cigarette products.

To address the aforementioned issues and improve the accuracy of cigarette product sales status and trend analysis, this study employed the moving average combined with trend judgment of product sales and formatting of result data tables to independently construct a system for analyzing product sales status on the R programming platform. Based on national commercial sales data of different cigarette specifications in 2017-2018 spanning 24 months, the study conducted extraction and computational analysis. It compared and analyzed specific product sales data of the four major brands of Yunnan cigarettes and strong competitors to explore trend information on different cigarette product market statuses. This was done to provide more effective and timely information feedback for analyzing changes in cigarette product development and rapidly formulating product market strategies, thus holding significant value.

1 Materials and Methods

1.1 Data Source

This study utilized commercial sales data of different cigarette specifications nationwide in 2017-2018 as the data basis, with data formats shown in Tables 1-3. Subsequent development of the analysis system was completed to display cigarette product sales status analysis.

Table 1 was used to filter cigarette categories and could be the prerequisite for summarizing classifications in the formatted results output. Additionally, it could be used for commercial sales sorting and filtering of specifications at the upper quartile as competitive products. The identification of Yunnan cigarette products mainly focused on the four major brands "Yunyan" "Yuxi" "Hongtashan" and "Honghe" for fuzzy recognition in cigarette specification indicators.

Table 1 Example of Basic Format Style of Nationwide Different Cigarette Types Data

Cigarette specifications	Tar content	Whether or not slim	Whether or not burst bead	Whether or not medium	Whether or not short	Commercial sales volume/(box/year)
A	10 mg	Non slim cigarette	Non burst bead cigarette	Non medium cigarette	Non short cigarette	69.25
B	8 mg	Slim cigarette	Non burst bead cigarette	Non medium cigarette	Non short cigarette	1297.83
C	8 mg	Non slim cigarette	Non burst bead cigarette	Non medium cigarette	Non short cigarette	0.00
D	11 mg	Non slim cigarette	Non burst bead cigarette	Non medium cigarette	Non short cigarette	0.00
E	8 mg	Slim cigarette	Non burst bead cigarette	Non medium cigarette	Non short cigarette	364.18
F	10 mg	Non slim cigarette	Non burst bead cigarette	Non medium cigarette	Non short cigarette	127.98
G	7 mg	Slim cigarette	Non burst bead cigarette	Non medium cigarette	Non short cigarette	1270.52
H	6 mg	Non slim cigarette	Non burst bead cigarette	Non medium cigarette	Non short cigarette	17.64
I	10 mg	Non slim cigarette	Non burst bead cigarette	Non medium cigarette	Non short cigarette	0.00

continue

Cigarette specifications	Tar content	Whether or not slim	Whether or not burst bead	Whether or not medium	Whether or not short	Commercial sales volume/(box/year)
J	8 mg	Non slim cigarette	Burst bead cigarette	Non medium cigarette	Non short cigarette	0.00
K	...	...	...	...	...	...

Table 2 is primarily used for calculating and analyzing sales trends. The moving average method can further extract product sales trends for assessment by utilizing monthly data as the foundation.

Table 2　Example of Basic Format Style of Nationwide Monthly Data

Regions	Cigarette specifications	Years	Months	Commercial sales volume /(box/year)
Beijing	K	2017	1	16.57
Beijing	K	2017	2	7.84
Beijing	K	2017	3	35.81
Beijing	K	2017	4	12.98
Beijing	K	2017	5	10.52
Beijing	K	2017	6	18.17
Beijing	K	2017	7	6.81
Beijing	K	2017	8	6.11
Beijing	K	2017	9	19.70
Beijing	K	2017	10	12.80
Beijing	K	2017	...	......

Table 3 is utilized for screening specific provincial regions. The provinces listed within can be filtered based on nationwide trends or customized to specific analytical requirements.

Table 3　Example of Basic Format Style of Specific Regions Data

Regions
Beijing
Hebei Province
Shanxi Province
Inner Mongolia Autonomous Region
Liaoning Province
Jilin Province

continue

Regions
Heilongjiang Province
Zhejiang Province
Anhui Province
......

1.2 Analytical Methods

1.2.1 Extraction of Trend Data

In this study, the moving average method is used to analyze the sales trends of products. The moving average refers to selecting a certain number of time intervals K for averaging. By sequentially shifting the series, moving averages are calculated for K consecutive items of the original series. This helps eliminate irregular fluctuations caused by short-term incidental factors to a certain extent, smoothing the series. When the series contains seasonal variations, K should be consistent with the length of the seasonal variation to eliminate its seasonal fluctuations. Similarly, when the series contains cyclical variations, K should match the basic length of the cycle to eliminate cyclical fluctuations effectively.

It is worth noting that when K is an odd number, only one moving average is needed, and its value represents the middle period of the moving average items. However, when K is an even number, the moving average represents the level at the middle position of these even-numbered items. In this case, another moving average of adjacent two values is required to align with a specific period. This is called a centered moving average[9].

To eliminate the trend impact of sudden sales increases during traditional festivals such as the Spring Festival and Mid-Autumn Festival[10-11], this study uses the moving average method to extract trends from the monthly data of specific cigarette product specifications in Table 1. Taking a two-year period as a cycle, trend data is obtained through twelve moving averages with a step size of 12 months and a centered moving average.

1.2.2 Judgment of Sales Trends

Based on the trend data obtained from the twelve moving averages combined with the centered moving average, two general states are observed.

(1) Smooth and clear trend: If the trend is upward (as shown in Figure 1(a)), the difference between the trend sales data at the highest point and the lowest point reflects

the current development status of the cigarette product. If the trend is downward (as shown in Figure 1(b)), the difference between the trend sales data at the lowest point and the highest point reflects the current development status of the cigarette product.

(2) Trend fluctuations requiring data truncation: If the trend shows fluctuations, the number of inflection points is used for judgment. Generally, when there are three inflection points, the trend fluctuation status can be considered to encompass the trend development status of the product. The judgment principle is as follows: when there is one inflection point, the difference between the data at the last trend point and the data at the inflection point represents the trend development status (as shown in Figure 2(a)、(d)); when there are two inflection points, the difference between the data at the last trend point and the data at the second inflection point represents the trend development status (as shown in Figure 2(c)、(e)); when there are three inflection points, the difference between the data at the last trend point and the data at the third inflection point represents the trend development status (as shown in Figure 2(b)、(f)).

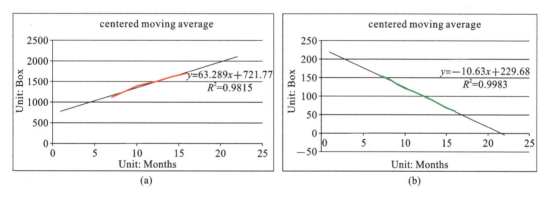

Figure 1　An Example of a Smooth and Clear Trend Data after Calculation

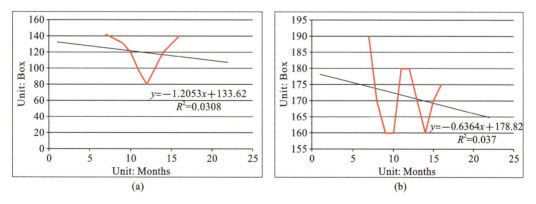

Figure 2　An Example of Data Interception and Judgment for Trend Fluctuations after Calculation

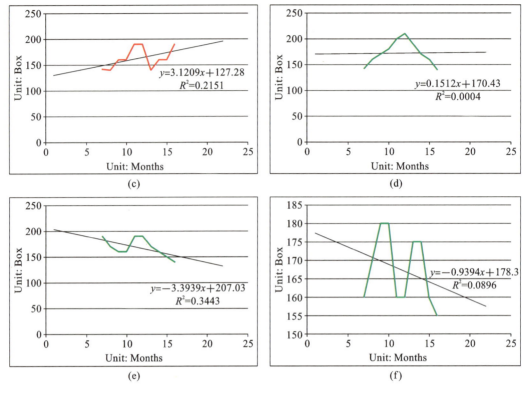

Figure 2

1.2.3 Integrated Implementation Based on the R Programming Platform

The methods of moving average calculation, trend determination of products, and formatting of corresponding results tables are implemented through self-edited programs in the R platform. Additionally, Excel's VBA program is utilized to highlight key symbol indicators with colored emphasis (see Table 4). The specific steps are outlined as follows (see Figure 3):

Table 4 Example Table of Possible Trend Presentations for Sales and Trends Data

Status	Just launched	Delisting	Rising trend	Decline trend	Stable trend
Symbol	○	×	↑	↓	—

2 Results and Analysis

2.1 Results Format Based on Products of Different Price Ranges and Specifications

By utilizing Tables 1 and 2 for different price ranges and specifications, along with the integrated program for analyzing the sales status of cigarette products, Table 5 is

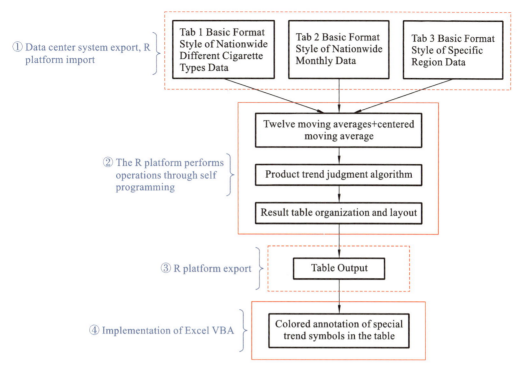

Figure 3　Implementation Steps of Analyzing the Sales Status of Cigarette Products on the R Program Platform

generated as an example through the execution on the R platform. Taking the Class Ⅱ price-category cigarettes produced by Yunnan as an example, the relevant computational results are demonstrated. From the table, the annual commercial sales are sorted by price, specification, category, calculated trend quantity, trend direction, the number of provinces and regions currently listed, and the duration of products on the market for less than two years. Based on this information, we can quickly assess the development trends of products with higher sales volumes, newly launched products less than two years, and special category products within the Class Ⅱ price-category cigarettes produced by Yunnan nationwide, including their growth rates, coverage characteristics, and other attributes.

Table 5　Table of Sales and Time Series Trend of Class Ⅱ Price-Category Cigarettes Produced by Yunnan

Retail price /(yuan /box)	Cigarette specifications	Category	Annual cumulative commercial sales in 2018/box	Trend and increment of two-year time series	Number of regions currently listed	Duration of market presence for products on the market for less than two years/months
130	Yunyan A	Regular cigarette	128374.87	46↑	13	—

continue

Retail price /(yuan /box)	Cigarette specifications	Category	Annual cumulative commercial sales in 2018/box	Trend and increment of two-year time series	Number of regions currently listed	Duration of market presence for products on the market for less than two years/months
150	Yunyan B	Slim cigarette	101270.43	6218↑	24	15
150	Yunyan C	Regular cigarette	34025.57	2085↑	10	15
150	Red river D	Regular cigarette	33588.24	1525↑	18	16
130	Red river E	Regular cigarette	24671.97	−105↓	2	—
150	Hongtashan F	Slim cigarette	21090.71	294↑	20	—
140	Red river G	Regular cigarette	17452.82	63↑	1	—
140	Hongtashan H	Regular cigarette	8131.87	393↑	7	—
160	Yunyan I	Regular cigarette	7956.92	360↑	8	20
180	Yunyan J	Medium cigarette	3811.56	208↑	11	10
140	Hongtashan K	Regular cigarette	3377.45	−262↓	2	—
150	Hongtashan L	Regular cigarette	3052.50	81↑	3	15
150	Hongtashan M	Regular cigarette	2309.22	355↑	12	4
140	Hongtashan N	Regular cigarette	414.12	−1021↓	2	—
180	Yunyan O	Regular cigarette	283.17	−24↓	1	—
160	Hongtashan P	Regular cigarette	68.43	−4↓	1	—
140	Yunyan Q	Regular cigarette	12.62	Delisting×	—	21 (Delisting)
160	Yunyan R	Regular cigarette	1.7	Delisting×	—	12 (Delisting)
150	Yunyan S	Slim cigarette	0.03	Delisting×	—	11 (Delisting)
…	…	…	…	…	…	…

2.2 Results Format Based on Products of Different Price Ranges and Specifications in Specific Provinces

Utilizing data from Table 1 and Table 2, along with the integration program for cigarette sales status analysis in specific provinces, Table 6 is generated after running on the R platform. Taking the example of Class Ⅱ price-category with a retail price of 150 yuan/box, the calculation results are demonstrated based on Beijing and Hebei provinces.

The table shows the comprehensive trend analysis of products produced by Yunnan, competitive brands, and various categories of cigarettes within this price range in specific provinces. This table facilitates a quick assessment of the sales and development status of Class Ⅱ price-category cigarettes priced at 150 yuan/box in these regions, the development status of competitive product specifications ranked in the upper quartile, and the quantity and trend direction of various categories of cigarettes.

3 Conclusion and Discussion

The fluctuation in product sales is a critical indicator reflecting the market's developmental status. However, due to their planned nature for cigarette products, sales fluctuations are often influenced by numerous factors, which may not entirely reflect the true market status. This study addresses these issues by combining moving averages with product sales trend analysis and results in data table formatting, implemented through self-programming on the R platform, to construct a system for analyzing product sales status. Through empirical validation, this methodological system offers the following advantages:

(1) It eliminates the inaccuracy of traditional year-on-year comparisons in assessing new cigarette product sales volume, and provides product sales status, and trends, and relatively accurate predictions for new product launched less than two years.

(2) The use of moving average effectively mitigates the impact of factors such as holidays on cigarette sales fluctuations, enhances the reliability of extracted normal development levels of products.

(3) The entire product sales status analysis system, primarily executed through self-programming in the R language, significantly saves time and improves efficiency compared to traditional manual analysis methods. This system is paramount for swiftly grasping market status, effectively predicts future product development trends, and guiding product market strategies. It is envisioned to be integrated into large-scale product sales data analysis systems, serving as a part of real-time monitoring and judgment functions for product market performance.

However, the product sales status analysis system still has certain limitations. For instance, the current method only truncates the trend direction at the back end in trend fluctuations. This may result in some deviation when comparing products with more apparent trends. In future research, efforts will be made to address these limitations to further enhance the study's comprehensiveness.

Table 6 Summary of Sales Volume of Cigarettes Priced at 150 Yuan/Box in Beijing and Hebei

Provincial regions with a national trend of growth of over 700 boxes and cities with over 200 boxes over the past two years	Products produced by Yunnan	Competitive brands	Regular cigarette expression	Slim cigarette expression	Short cigarette expression	Medium cigarette expression	Burst bead cigarette expression
Beijing	1. Yunyan B (Small cigarettes) (201.58 boxes ↑); 2. Hongtashan F(Small cigarettes) (50.96 boxes ↑); 3. Red River D (conventional tobacco) (−79 boxes ↓); 4. Hongtashan M(regular tobacco) (5.78 boxes ↑)	1. Zhongnanhai E (regular cigarette) (56.34 boxes ↑); 2. Changbaishan F (Slim cigarette) (59.66 boxes ↑); 3. Yunyan A (Slim cigarette) (201.58 boxes ↑); 4. Nanjing H (regular cigarette) (9.92 boxes ↑); 5. Hongtashan B (Slim cigarette) (50.96 boxes ↑); 6. Jiaozi J (Slim cigarettes) (40.87 boxes ↑)	There are a total of 12 product specifications (including 5 trends that increase ↑, 4 trends that decrease ↓, 1 trend that is stable, 2 have been delisted, and 0 have just been listed), with 2 product produced by Yunnan specifications (including 1 trend that increases ↑, 1 trend that decreases ↓, 0 trends that are stable, 0 have been delisted, and 0 have just been listed)	A total of 9 (including 8 trends increasing ↑, 0 trends decreasing ↓, 0 trends stable, 1 has been delisted, and 0 has just been listed), with 2 product produced by Yunnan specifications (including 2 trends increasing ↑, 0 trends decreasing ↓, 0 trends stable, 0 have been delisted, and 0 have just been listed)	None	There is a total of 1 (of which 0 trends are increasing ↑, 1 trend is decreasing ↓, 0 trends are stable, 0 have been delisted, and 0 have just been listed), with 0 product produced by Yunnan specifications (including 2 trends increasing ↑, 0 trends decreasing ↓, 0 trends stable, 0 have been delisted, and 0 have just been listed)	There is a total of 1 (of which 0 trends are increasing ↑, 0 trends decreasing ↓, 0 trends are stable, 1 has been delisted, and 0 have just been listed), with 0 product produced by Yunnan specifications (including 2 trends increasing ↑, 0 trends decreasing ↓, 0 trends stable, 0 have been delisted, and 0 have just been listed)

continue

Provincial regions with a national trend of growth of over 700 boxes and cities with over 200 boxes over the past two years	Products produced by Yunnan	Competitive brands	Regular cigarette expression	Slim cigarette expression	Short cigarette expression	Medium cigarette expression	Burst bead cigarette expression
Hebei province	1. Yunyan B (Small cigarette) (301.89 boxes ↑); 2. Hongtashan F (Small cigarettes) (32.94 boxes ↑); 3. Red River D (conventional tobacco) (5.73 boxes ↑); 4. Hongtashan M (regular tobacco) (17.54 boxes ↑); 5. Yunyan S(Fine Branch Cigarette) (Delisted ×)	1. Changbai shan F (Slim cigarette) (164.78 boxes ↑); 2. Yunyan B (Slim cigarette) (301.89 boxes ↑); 3. Zhongnanhai H (regular cigarette) (−50.39 boxes ↓); 4. Jiaozi I (Slim cigarette) (81.02 boxes ↑); 5. Baisha J (Slim cigarette) (47.71 boxes ↑); 6. Huangshan K (Slim cigarette) (89.72 cases ↑); 7. Zhenlong L (Slim cigarette) (73 boxes ↑); 8. Hongtashan B (Slim cigarette) (32.94 boxes ↑)	There are a total of 14 product specifications (including 3 trends that increase ↑, 3 trends that decrease ↓, 2 trends that are stable, 6 have been delisted, and 0 have just been listed), with 2 product produced by Yunnan specifications (including 2 trends that increase ↑, 0 trends that decrease ↓, 0 trends that are stable, 0 have been delisted, and 0 have just been listed)	There are a total of 15 product specifications (including 13 with an increasing trend ↑, 0 with a decreasing trend ↓, 0 with a stable trend, 2 delisted, and 0 just listed), with 3 product produced by Yunnan specifications (including 2 with an increasing trend ↑, 0 with a decreasing trend ↓, 0 with a stable trend, 1 delisted, and 0 just listed)	None	There is a total of 1 (of which 0 trends are increasing ↑, 0 trends are decreasing ↓, 1 trend is stable, 0 have been delisted, and 0 have just been listed), with 0 product produced by Yunnan specifications (including 2 trends increasing ↑, 0 trends decreasing ↓, 0 trends stable, 0 have been delisted, and 0 have just been listed)	There is a total of 1 (of which 0 trends are increasing ↑, 0 trends are decreasing ↓, 0 trends are stable, 1 has been delisted, and 0 has just been listed), with 0 product produced by Yunnan specifications (including 2 trends increasing ↑, 0 trends decreasing ↓, 0 trends stable, 0 have been delisted, and 0 have just been listed)
⋮	⋮	⋮	⋮	⋮	⋮	⋮	⋮

References

[1] CAO L D. Research on Cigarette Sales Application based on Time Series[D]. Kunming: Yunnan University of Finance and Economics, 2012.

[2] LI J L. Analysis of National Cigarette Sales based on Time Series Models[J]. Social Science Frontiers, 2018, 7 (12): 1974-1981.

[3] WU M S, WANG B, Qi Y N, et al. Study on Combination Forecasting Model of Cigarette Sales[J]. Chinese Tobacco Science, 2019, 25 (3): 84-91.

[4] DU Y Z. Design and Implementation of Data Collection Scheme for Tobacco Project No. 1[D]. Beijing: Beijing Jiaotong University, 2005.

[5] LIU Y J, WANG Z G. Comprehensive Analysis of Harbin's 2004 Cigarette Market Dynamics[J]. New Tobacco, 2005 (2): 54-55.

[6] LIANG B. Investigation Report on Qiqihar Tobacco Company's Economic Operation in the Year's First Half[J]. New Tobacco, 2005 (8): 28-31.

[7] WANG Y, HU W F. Research on Design Planning Strategies of Short Video Products based on Product Life Cycle Theory[J]. Mass Art, 2018 (12): 79-80.

[8] MA Y Y. Analysis of Design Elements based on Product Life Cycle Theory[J]. Art Education, 2018 (19): 192-193.

[9] YUAN W, PANG H, ZENG W Y, et al. Statistics[M]. Beijing: Higher Education Press, 2009: 263-266.

[10] ZOU L. Time Series Analysis of Cigarette Market Demand in Huaihua City[J]. Chinese Tobacco Science Journal, 2007, 13 (6): 51-57.

[11] BAI X M, ZHAO S S. My View on the Application of Moving Average Method[J]. Statistical Education, 2001(1): 20-22.

基于产品生命周期和四象限法的卷烟产品市场状态评价

摘要：为了对卷烟市场状态进行量化评价,使产品的市场状态评估更为合理准确、产品之间的竞争关系更加清晰,本文基于产品生命周期理论,从卷烟销售的市场表现出发,以销量增长优势和销量规模优势指标为坐标,构建了卷烟分类的四象限方法。本文运用该方法对四川省不同规格普一类卷烟(采用"品牌＋字母"表示)的市场状态进行分类,所有在销普一类卷烟的规格被分为进入规格、成长规格、成熟规格和收缩规格四大类,并纵向对比了主要卷烟规格的发展变化,对其在四川省的发展趋势进行了分析。研究结果表明,利群 A、南京 B、天子 C 等 52 个规格为进入规格,包括 29 个新进入规格。天子 A、娇子 A、黄鹤楼 A 等 13 个规格为成长规格。云烟 D、玉溪 H、玉溪 G 等 7 个规格为成熟规格。娇子 C、玉溪 E、苏烟 A 等 49 个规格为收缩规格。同时,2012—2020 年间四川省普一类卷烟 5 个主销规格中,玉溪 G 一直处于成熟期,玉溪 H 和芙蓉王 A 分别在 2015 年和 2017 年进入成熟期,云烟 D 则经历了从成熟到成长再到成熟的状态,天子 A 正处于成长期,对成熟规格构成了强烈的威胁。基于产品生命周期理论的四象限法能够有效反映四川省不同规格普一类卷烟的市场状态与竞争关系,并且连续时间的市场状态指标可以反映卷烟规格的生命周期变化,为市场调控提供量化的数据参考。

关键词：产品生命周期；卷烟；四象限法；市场状态

1 前言

中国的人口总量增长放缓,吸烟率持续下降,控烟环境日益严格,卷烟消费市场逐渐从增量市场的竞争转向日益激烈的存量市场竞争。"把经济平稳运行和保持良好市场状态摆在优先位置"是现阶段卷烟市场调控的要求[1],而对卷烟市场状态进行分析研判是市场调控的前提和基础。

如何准确评估卷烟市场的状态?学者和业界人士已经根据各自的研究和实践经验给出了相关方法。柯先月[2]探索了多指标、多维度地对品牌(规格)进行综合评价,在对品牌(规格)市场表现进行数据量化分析的基础上,构建了品牌市场状态评价指标体系理想模型；李智文和刘立红[3]依托现代化终端信息采集系统,采用灰色层次分析法建立了适合烟草企业的市场状态评估模型,用于评估卷烟零售区域市场状态和品牌市场状态；马骏珍等[4]围绕价格指数、终端存销比、订足率及动销率四项指标,构建了市场、品牌和客户三位一体的市场运行状态评价模型；李子[5]以市场信息采集数据与零售客户订单数据为基础,对北京市的卷烟市场状态进行了评价；李晓梅等[6]基于景气循环理论,建立了包括先行、一致和滞后指数在内的卷烟市场景气指数体系；董晓萍等[7]利用主成分分析方法得出核心指标并建立了卷烟市场运行状态的数学模型；刘颂[8]运用精益管理中的系统图、ECRS 等工具，以及相关性分析、聚类分析、层次分析等数理统计方法，从信息采集、指标选取、模型建立三个方面，系统化研究市场状态精准判断机制；邢阳等[9]利用大数据技术及机器学习算法构建了一种卷烟市场运行状态智能评价模型；刘涛等[10]界定了卷烟品规市场状态评价的核心指标并构造了卷烟品规市场状态综合评价指数与趋势指数；李叶等[11]将层次分析法与灰色评价法相结合，选取销量、市场状态、营销效率、客户满意度等 7 个二级指标，年度卷烟销量、社会存销比、市场净化率、营销服务满意度等 19 个三级指标，构建了一套卷烟市场评价体系；于梦吟等[12]从总量、价位、品规三个维度，给出了以条均行批差、订单需求满足率为核心指标的市场状态评价矩阵，以及品规维度"俏紧平松软"属性评价阈值范围参考；许泓和秦琴[13]使用 Lasso 变量选择方法在国家层指标库中选取市场状态，再分别使用熵值法、变异系数法将指标降维为量、价、存三个类别指标，并使用几何平均原则构建卷烟市场状态综合评价指数。

这些评价方法为我们进行卷烟品牌（规格）的市场状态研判提供了有益的借鉴，但仍然存在着一些不足。①现有评价体系多采用多指标评价，所用指标几乎覆盖了市场监测的所有指标，却忽略了这些指标之间的关联性与主次关系，导致评价结果的差异较小，难以对市场状态形成有效判断；②现有的评价体系以静态评价为主，集中在时点的评价，很少考虑产品本身的生命周期并对其进行动态评价。产品生命周期被广泛运用于成本控制[14]、质量管理[15]等方面，刘小川[16,17]针对卷烟产品，以产品销量、销售额、利润、市场容量等因素确定划分指标，采用经验判断法和聚类分析法等划分产品的生命周期，在利用生命周期理论判断卷烟市场状态方面做出了很好的尝试。但他的方法涉及指标众多，数据收集工作较难，划分缺乏数据标准，不同时期难以对比分析。如何对当前在销的卷烟产品进行生命周期的划分？目前并没有统一的标准方法。本文以生命周期理论[18]为基础，参照赵果庆[19]对产业部门群的研究，以各产品销量的平均占比和产品销量增长率作为参照，使处于不同生命周期的产品呈现出比较优势的周期特征，以坐标系中的每一个象限代表产品比较优势周期的一个阶段，四个象限的产品集合[20]就形成了不同生命周期阶段的产品群，以期对卷烟市场状态做出相对准确的评判，为市场调控提供量化的数据参考。

2 材料与方法

2.1 研究对象

本文使用 2019 年和 2020 年四川省普一类卷烟的销量，对 2020 年的卷烟市场状态进行分类，使用在销的 5 个主要规格近 9 年的销售数据，对其市场状态的变化进行分析。

2.2 研究方法

（1）指标体系构建。

将卷烟产品按价格进行分类，同一价区的卷烟为一个类别。假设某一价类的卷烟共有

n 个规格,第 i 个规格第 t 年的年销售量为 Q_i^t,第 $t-1$ 年的年销售量为 Q_i^{t-1},定义比较增长优势指标 CDA_i^t:

$$CDA_i^t = MQ_i^t - AQ_i^{t-1} = \frac{Q_i^t - Q_i^{t-1}}{Q^t - Q^{t-1}} - \frac{Q_i^{t-1}}{Q^{t-1}}$$

式中,MQ_i^t 为第 i 个规格第 t 年对该价类销量 Q^t(即 $\sum_i Q_i^t$)的边际贡献率,它度量了第 i 个卷烟规格的增量在该价类总增量中所占的份额;AQ_i^{t-1} 为第 i 个规格销量在价类总销量中的份额,它代表第 i 个规格第 $t-1$ 年对价类销量的贡献。

第 i 个规格对价类总销量和价类销量增量的贡献表示了该规格的两种不同优势,这两种优势的组合可确定一个产品(规格)的比较优势生命周期。$CDA_i^t > 0$ 表示第 i 个规格第 t 年的增量贡献率高于第 $t-1$ 年的总量贡献率,即第 i 个规格第 t 年的销量增长率高于价类总销量的增长率,具有比较增长优势。反之,$CDA_i^t < 0$ 表示该规格第 t 年的销量增长率低于价类总销量增长率,处于增长劣势状态。如果 $CDA_i^t = 0$,则意味着该规格既不具有比较增长优势,也不具有比较增长劣势。

定义比较规模优势指标 CSA_i^t:

$$CSA_i^t = AQ_i^t - 100/n$$

式中,AQ_i^t 为第 i 个规格第 t 年在该价类中的市场份额(即销量占比);n 是该价类中的规格数。

如果 $CSA_i^t > 0$,则表示第 i 个规格第 t 年在价类中的份额超过平均水平,该规格具有比较规模优势。反之,则表示第 i 个规格处于比较规模劣势状态。如果 $CSA_i^t = 0$,则该规格既不具备比较规模优势,也不处于比较规模劣势状态。

(2)基于四象限的卷烟产品分类方法。

以产品平均状态为参照系的坐标原点,利用比较增长优势和比较规模优势的组合划分产品的比较优势周期,见表 1。

表 1 卷烟规格的 4 个类型

第 2 象限 ($CDA_i^t > 0, CSA_i^t < 0$) 进入规格	第 1 象限 ($CDA_i^t > 0, CSA_i^t > 0$) 成长规格
第 3 象限 ($CDA_i^t < 0, CSA_i^t < 0$) 收缩规格	第 4 象限 ($CDA_i^t < 0, CSA_i^t > 0$) 成熟规格

进入规格:$CDA_i^t > 0, CSA_i^t < 0$,位于第 2 象限。其规模比较小,尚未达到平均规模,然而,其增长率比较高,呈现出强劲的发展优势。这些规格一般是当年上市的新规格,具有较好的发展潜力。

成长规格:$CDA_i^t > 0, CSA_i^t > 0$,位于第 1 象限。其平均贡献率和边际贡献率都呈递增态势,它既有比较规模优势,又有比较增长优势,因而它对整个价类的卷烟销量增长具有重要作用。这些规格的卷烟正处于扩张期或发展期。

成熟规格:$CDA_i^t<0$,$CSA_i^t>0$,位于第 4 象限。其增长速度已降至价类平均增长速度以下,平均贡献率在下降,但还高于平均水平,销量达到最大值后,会呈现出负增长。这些规格是价类里面的成熟规格,占有较大的份额。

收缩规格:$CDA_i^t<0$,$CSA_i^t<0$,位于第 3 象限。其既无增长优势,又无规模优势。它可能是部分新规格的起点,也可能是某些老规格的终点。

基于四象限的卷烟产品分类方法将产品分为四种类型,进入规格、成长规格、成熟规格和收缩规格大致对应着产品生命周期中的导入期、成长期、成熟期和衰退期,但并非完全对应。产品的生命周期对应着一个产品从诞生到消亡的完整过程,处于导入期的一定是新品(新规格,通常指上市时间不超过一年的产品),处于衰退期的一定是老品(老规格,通常指上市时间超过一年的产品)。四象限法着力于对产品市场状态的判断,产品为进入规格表示产品处于进入市场的状态,可能是新品,也可能是一直发展不顺,进行重塑后的老品,收缩规格不一定全是老品,也有可能是刚刚上市就面临退市的新品。

3 结果与分析

3.1 四川省 2020 年普一类卷烟的分类结果

根据 2019 年和 2020 年四川省普一类卷烟的销量,可以计算出每一个在销规格的比较增长优势 CDA_i^t 和比较规模优势 CSA_i^t,并确定其所在的象限。因本文主要侧重于方法研究,考虑到烟草信息的敏感性,因此产品具体规格采用"品牌+字母"表示,具体的分类结果如表 2 所示。

表 2 四川省 2020 年普一类卷烟市场状态分类

卷烟规格	2020 年销量/箱	2019 年销量/箱	CDA_i^t	CSA_i^t	象限	卷烟规格	2020 年销量/箱	2019 年销量/箱	CDA_i^t	CSA_i^t	象限
天子 A	49864.93	44366.67	11.31	6.63	1	中华 A	0.30	0.00	0.00	−0.83	2
娇子 A	26417.91	15661.27	33.26	3.12	1	云烟 A	0.28	0.00	0.00	−0.83	2
黄鹤楼 A	22236.14	20766.83	1.63	2.50	1	南京 A	0.14	0.00	0.00	−0.83	2
芙蓉王 A	21979.22	20312.42	2.35	2.46	1	云烟 B	0.11	0.00	0.00	−0.83	2
贵烟 A	20986.57	17865.11	7.57	2.31	1	利群 E	5359.58	5331.09	−0.74	−0.03	3
天子 B	20202.50	10473.79	30.66	2.19	1	黄鹤楼 M	4996.95	6162.76	−4.84	−0.08	3
娇子 B	16296.02	10550.40	17.43	1.61	1	娇子 C	4204.08	4388.16	−1.30	−0.20	3
玉溪 A	10995.95	10381.35	0.42	0.82	1	玉溪 C	3691.09	7085.00	−12.38	−0.27	3
黄鹤楼 B	8632.60	7771.98	1.64	0.46	1	玉溪 D	3466.38	6463.96	−10.97	−0.31	3
黄山 A	7997.12	7402.85	0.81	0.37	1	苏烟 A	3417.37	3593.02	−1.15	−0.32	3

续表

卷烟规格	2020年销量/箱	2019年销量/箱	CDA_i^t	CSA_i^t	象限	卷烟规格	2020年销量/箱	2019年销量/箱	CDA_i^t	CSA_i^t	象限
玉溪 B	7418.00	6798.66	0.99	0.28	1	芙蓉王 B	2730.44	2741.66	-0.47	-0.42	3
贵烟 B	6332.11	4318.04	6.01	0.12	1	娇子 H	2687.53	3215.01	-2.25	-0.42	3
大前门 A	6126.71	5558.98	1.01	0.09	1	兰州 B	2664.11	2603.25	-0.21	-0.43	3
利群 A	5122.18	0.00	17.01	-0.06	2	玉溪 E	2637.37	3998.85	-5.15	-0.43	3
利群 B	5112.55	4586.74	1.03	-0.06	2	贵烟 C	2462.01	3501.84	-4.00	-0.46	3
南京 B	4919.88	3569.48	3.93	-0.09	2	娇子 D	2126.90	3492.08	-5.08	-0.51	3
天子 C	4814.09	0.00	15.98	-0.11	2	玉溪 G	1780.80	3047.98	-4.68	-0.56	3
真龙 A	4307.21	1776.22	8.13	-0.18	2	555C	1705.39	1656.40	-0.10	-0.57	3
云烟 C	4236.47	2866.92	4.10	-0.19	2	南京 C	1656.83	1719.62	-0.48	-0.58	3
黄山 B	2868.06	387.88	8.17	-0.40	2	娇子 G	1533.03	2914.81	-5.04	-0.60	3
黄鹤楼 C	2492.50	2275.14	0.37	-0.45	2	娇子 E	1382.17	1833.75	-1.79	-0.62	3
双喜 A	2411.34	1966.63	1.17	-0.47	2	利群 F	957.77	1732.13	-2.84	-0.68	3
七匹狼 A	2050.65	0.00	6.81	-0.52	2	金桥 A	937.70	908.89	-0.05	-0.69	3
利群 C	2006.48	1573.80	1.19	-0.53	2	长城 B	739.00	1614.18	-3.16	-0.72	3
万宝路 A	1916.22	0.00	6.36	-0.54	2	黄鹤楼 G	714.96	1153.38	-1.64	-0.72	3
利群 H	1883.88	0.00	6.26	-0.54	2	长城 C	394.70	1185.56	-2.81	-0.77	3
天子 D	1557.99	0.00	5.17	-0.59	2	利群 G	269.70	860.90	-2.10	-0.79	3
黄金叶 A	1358.60	0.00	4.51	-0.62	2	红双喜 A	216.96	214.02	-0.02	-0.79	3
好猫 A	1197.97	756.26	1.35	-0.65	2	贵烟 D	116.54	596.06	-1.69	-0.81	3
金圣 A	1127.24	0.00	3.74	-0.66	2	红双喜 B	103.60	143.71	-0.16	-0.81	3
长白山 A	1017.30	0.00	3.38	-0.67	2	玉溪 F	101.73	534.96	-1.52	-0.81	3
黄金叶 B	940.00	0.00	3.12	-0.69	2	剑牌 C	86.52	92.42	-0.03	-0.81	3
牡丹 A	882.51	0.00	2.93	-0.69	2	兰州 C	73.98	645.96	-2.00	-0.82	3
555 A	876.04	395.21	1.53	-0.70	2	剑牌 D	66.96	87.34	-0.08	-0.82	3
万宝路 B	793.90	0.00	2.64	-0.71	2	黄鹤楼 H	52.87	86.08	-0.12	-0.82	3
泰山 A	776.04	513.06	0.79	-0.71	2	剑牌 E	24.43	81.39	-0.20	-0.82	3
金圣 A	766.59	482.62	0.87	-0.71	2	七星 A	23.56	76.46	-0.19	-0.82	3
黄鹤楼 D	758.48	0.00	2.52	-0.71	2	骆驼 A	5.20	14.80	-0.03	-0.83	3
真龙 B	702.01	0.00	2.33	-0.72	2	王冠 A	1.80	4.86	-0.01	-0.83	3
黄鹤楼 E	638.32	0.00	2.12	-0.73	2	龙凤呈祥 A	0.30	3350.11	-11.65	-0.83	3
黄鹤楼 F	624.02	0.00	2.07	-0.73	2	万宝路 E	0.18	1375.38	-4.78	-0.83	3

续表

卷烟规格	2020年销量/箱	2019年销量/箱	CDA_i^r	CSA_i^r	象限	卷烟规格	2020年销量/箱	2019年销量/箱	CDA_i^r	CSA_i^r	象限
万宝路C	609.41	454.31	0.44	−0.74	2	黄鹤楼I	0.12	4.02	−0.01	−0.83	3
剑牌A	550.19	375.73	0.52	−0.74	2	黄山B	0.10	387.88	−1.35	−0.83	3
万宝路D	533.77	0.00	1.77	−0.75	2	土楼A	0.08	1277.42	−4.44	−0.83	3
南京D	463.06	0.00	1.54	−0.76	2	天子E	0.04	533.21	−1.85	−0.83	3
剑牌B	336.68	195.10	0.44	−0.78	2	娇子F	0.03	1049.24	−3.65	−0.83	3
爱喜A	284.16	202.80	0.24	−0.78	2	七匹狼C	0.02	198.00	−0.69	−0.83	3
哈尔滨A	261.30	249.02	0.00	−0.79	2	万宝路F	0.02	279.81	−0.97	−0.83	3
哈德门A	258.65	0.00	0.86	−0.79	2	双喜B	0.01	125.66	−0.44	−0.83	3
555B	236.40	0.00	0.78	−0.79	2	万宝路G	0.00	400.50	−1.39	−0.83	3
七星A	81.24	76.46	0.00	−0.81	2	黄山C	0.00	222.80	−0.77	−0.83	3
狮牌A	59.80	4.78	0.18	−0.82	2	芙蓉王C	0.00	193.22	−0.67	−0.83	3
宝亨A	36.19	32.51	0.01	−0.82	2	黄金叶C	0.00	82.62	−0.29	−0.83	3
七星B	25.03	0.00	0.08	−0.82	2	云烟D	133876.78	144349.86	−57.37	19.19	4
御猫A	18.24	17.33	0.00	−0.82	2	玉溪G	80296.08	81654.74	−17.29	11.18	4
长城A	5.00	2.93	0.01	−0.83	2	玉溪H	74054.82	81790.68	−38.49	10.24	4
云烟E	0.71	0.00	0.00	−0.83	2	黄鹤楼J	12580.36	13028.18	−3.53	1.05	4
兰州A	0.10	0.00	0.00	−0.83	2	云烟E	12451.02	12817.17	−3.22	1.04	4
牡丹A	0.05	0.02	0.00	−0.83	2	黄鹤楼K	8937.62	9635.62	−3.83	0.51	4
七匹狼B	0.01	0.00	0.00	−0.83	2	黄鹤楼L	5895.46	7243.19	−5.61	0.05	4
利群D	0.00	0.00	0.00	−0.83	2	合计	668888.16	638770.99			

利用比较增长优势和比较规模优势,可以将普一类卷烟所有的在销规格分为进入规格、成长规格、成熟规格和收缩规格四大类。

进入规格:利群A、南京B、天子C、真龙A、云烟C、黄山B、黄鹤楼C等52个规格为进入规格,包括29个新进入规格。这些规格具有比较增长优势,其中利群A、天子C的比较增长优势最为明显,边际贡献率与总量贡献率的差超过了15%,但规模都比较小,其当年的销量还未达到平均规模。

成长规格:天子A、娇子A、黄鹤楼A、芙蓉王A和贵烟A等13个规格为成长规格。其中,娇子A的比较增长优势最大,其次是天子B,比较增长优势超过了30。此外,娇子B、天子A的比较增长优势比较明显,比较增长优势超过了10。成长规格中,天子A、娇子A、黄鹤楼A的比较规模优势位居前三,比较规模优势均超过了2。综合来看,天子A、娇子A将是四川省内普一类卷烟市场里最具潜力的规格。

成熟规格:云烟D、玉溪H、玉溪G等7个规格为成熟规格,这些规格已经不再具有比较增长优势,但依然具有较大的市场份额。在成熟规格中,云烟 D 和玉溪 H 的危机最大,其比较增长优势最差,分别为 −57.37 和 −38.49,表明边际贡献率远低于总量的贡献率,市场份额出现较大幅度的下降,处于竞争的不利地位。

收缩规格:娇子 C、玉溪 E、苏烟 A、兰州 B、芙蓉王 B 等 49 个规格为收缩规格,不具有比较增长优势,且前一年的销量规模也低于平均规模,面临着退市的可能。

3.2 五种主要规格市场状态的变化分析

本文选取了四川省普一类卷烟中 2020 年在销的 5 个主要规格,其中,云烟 D、玉溪 G、玉溪 H 三个规格为四川省普一类卷烟销量前三的规格;芙蓉王 A 为普一类全国性规格产品,在四川省销售的时间也比较长;天子 A 为四川省 2017 年上市新品。2020 年这五个规格卷烟的销量占到了四川省普一类卷烟销量的 53.83%。依据公式可计算其最近 9 年的市场状态指标,如表 3 所示。

表 3 四川省普一类卷烟主要规格市场状态变化情况

年份	芙蓉王 A		天子 A		玉溪 G		玉溪 H		云烟 D	
	CSA_i^t	CDA_i^t	CSA_i^t	CDA_i^t	CSA_i^t	CDA_i^t	CSA_i^t	CDA_i^t	CSA_i^t	CDA_i^t
2012	0.89	0.35			19.07	3.71	20.65	5.70	29.64	−7.16
2013	1.04	0.79			18.05	−6.65	23.11	15.50	26.94	−17.40
2014	2.03	5.10			18.00	−1.96	24.55	8.17	25.44	−11.82
2015	2.30	1.69			17.98	−2.31	24.51	−2.59	27.73	29.53
2016	2.67	4.69			16.18	−39.46	20.02	−94.09	32.37	91.66
2017	2.68	−2.17	6.17	89.07	13.84	−31.27	15.82	−54.21	29.75	−34.68
2018	2.56	−4.53	5.61	−13.15	12.57	−27.03	13.24	−53.04	25.65	−83.06
2019	2.29	−3.95	6.06	4.98	11.90	−9.08	11.92	−17.16	21.71	−49.88
2020	2.46	2.35	6.63	11.31	11.18	−17.29	10.24	−38.49	19.19	−57.37

从表 3 中比较规模优势和比较增长优势的变化来看,云烟 D、玉溪 H 和玉溪 G 的市场规模优势下降比较快,但依然在四川省普一类卷烟市场中占据重要地位。2012 年,云烟 D 的市场份额接近 30%,但比较增长优势的丧失导致其市场份额下降,至 2014 年下降到了 25.44%。2015 年和 2016 年,由于宏观环境的变化,且本土竞争品牌仅有娇子 H 上市,规格比较单一,还未被消费者熟悉,云烟 D 获得机会,以较大的比较增长优势将市场份额提升到 32.37%,规格从成熟状态回到成长状态。2017 年开始,本土品牌娇子系列、天子系列大量上市,对云烟 D 形成巨大冲击,云烟 D 再次丧失比较优势,步入成熟状态,市场份额继续下降,到 2020 年市场份额已经不足 20%,但仍然是四川省普一类卷烟市场上规模最大的规格。玉溪 H 在 2015 年前处于成长状态,市场份额最高达 24.55%,从 2015 年开始进入成熟状态,比较增长优势下降,市场规模到 2020 年已经降至 10.24%。玉溪 G 2016 年后比较增长优势下降过快,市场规模也随之加速下降。综合来看,2016 年开始,四川省本土品牌

的崛起对云产卷烟造成越来越大的冲击,云产卷烟增长优势不再,市场份额越来越低。目前云产卷烟的三大主销规格虽然还具有一定的规模优势,但恐难以持久。

芙蓉王A也是四川省普一类卷烟市场上在销时间较长的规格,该规格虽然具有较小的规模优势,但总体上看市场份额有所增加,2020年的市场份额为2.46%。从比较增长优势看,芙蓉王A在2017年前一直具有正的增长优势,处于成长状态,但2017年开始,增长优势变为负值,产品步入成熟状态,2020年比较增长优势有所改变,但比较增长优势和比较规模优势的数值变化较小,处于比较稳定的成熟状态。

天子A是四川中烟2017年上市的新品,最近几年在四川省普一类卷烟市场上表现出强劲的增长优势,也具有一定的规模优势,目前处于成长状态。相似的还有2018年上市的娇子A,上市当年的销量达到了9399.67箱,比较增长优势明显(三年的比较增长优势分别为31.52、20.68和33.26),目前的市场份额达到了3.95%,是成熟规格中最强劲的竞争对手。

4　结论与展望

本文在产品生命周期理论的基础上,以卷烟销量为核心指标,构建了以比较增长优势和比较规模优势为基础的卷烟产品四象限分类法,将在销规格分为进入规格、成长规格、成熟规格和收缩规格,使产品的市场状态评估更为合理准确、产品之间的竞争关系更加清晰。对四川省普一类卷烟的分析结果表明,该方法能够有效反映各规格卷烟的市场状态与竞争关系,并且连续时间的市场状态指标可以反映卷烟规格的市场状态变化,并可据此对卷烟规格的发展趋势做出合理判断。

卷烟市场状态的量化评价是货源组织投放、营销策略制定的决策依据,对卷烟市场的调控具有重要的应用价值,也是卷烟市场化取向改革的基础。本文的研究为卷烟市场状态的评价提供了一种简单可行的方法。该方法除了可用于市场状态的评价外,还可用于品牌(规格)的竞争分析。此外,对剔除了周期性和节假日效应的月度销量或周销量数据运用四象限法进行评价,可以大大提高卷烟市场状态评价的时效性,也可为市场监测提供更为及时的信息。

参考文献

[1] 中国卷烟销售公司.搭建综合监测体系精准把脉市场状态[N].东方烟草报,2021-09-27(002).

[2] 柯先月.品牌(规格)市场状态评价指标体系构建及应用探索[C]//中国烟草学会.中国烟草学会2012年学术年会论文集.中国烟草学会,2012:5.

[3] 李智文,刘立红.灰色层次分析法在卷烟市场状态评估中的应用[J].现代商贸工业,2015,36(1):122-123.

[4] 马骏珍,周彩丽,陈耀.基于数据挖掘的市场运行状态评价模型构建及其应用[C]//中

国烟草学会.中国烟草学会 2016 年度优秀论文汇编——卷烟流通主题.中国烟草学会,2016:10.

[5] 李子.北京卷烟市场状态评价方法分析研究[C]//中国烟草学会.中国烟草学会 2016 年度优秀论文汇编——卷烟流通主题.中国烟草学会,2016:11.

[6] 李晓梅,李健,张辉.卷烟市场景气指数编制探索与实践——以广西卷烟市场为例[J].中国烟草学报,2017,23(4):107-113.

[7] 董晓萍,王大刚,邢阳.大数据在卷烟市场状态监测中的应用研究[J].信息技术与标准化,2017(10):65-69.

[8] 刘颂.浅议市场状态精准判断机制构建及应用[J].北方经贸,2017(7):47-49.

[9] 邢阳,黄旭峰,董晓萍,等.卷烟市场运行状态智能评价模型的研究与应用[J].烟草科技,2018,51(7):96-102.

[10] 刘涛,江南,翁春燕,等.卷烟品规市场状态评价指标体系及诊断方案研究——基于重庆实践的视角[J].商场现代化,2020(22):13-17.

[11] 李叶,张晓妮,张云,等.基于多层次灰色评价法的县级卷烟市场评价体系研究——以铜川市卷烟市场为例[J].中国烟草学报,2022,28(3):119-126.

[12] 于梦吟,易瑜,蔡月香.基于系统思维下的消费市场状态评价及调控体系初探——以三维三层卷烟为例[J].商展经济,2021(18):26-29.

[13] 许泓,秦琴.卷烟市场状态综合评价指数构建[J].海峡科学,2021(8):99-105.

[14] 彭昆.浅析产品生命周期下烟草工业企业的精益成本控制[J].财经界,2015(6):47+67.

[15] 潘玉灵,李小兰,陈立新,等.产品生命周期理论在卷烟质量管理中的应用[J].科技创业家,2013(17):201-202.

[16] 刘小川.聚类分析在产品生命周期研究中的应用——以卷烟产品为例[J].江苏商论,2017(8):29-31.

[17] 刘小川.卷烟产品跟踪评估模型研究[J].现代商业,2015(29):121-123.

[18] 吴玉牵.产品生命周期理论指导下的营销渠道管理探析[J].全国流通经济,2017(7):3-4.

[19] 赵果庆.我国产业部门群结构与战略性调整研究[J].财经问题研究,2006(1):19-27.

[20] 陈永国,褚尚军,李宗祥.低碳经济内涵与四象限评价法[J].河北经贸大学学报,2011,32(6):60-63.

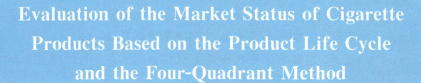

Evaluation of the Market Status of Cigarette Products Based on the Product Life Cycle and the Four-Quadrant Method

Abstract: In order to quantitatively evaluate the state of the cigarette market, make more reasonable and accurate assessments of the market status of products, and clarify the competitive relationship between products, this article is based on the product life cycle theory, starting from the market performance of cigarette sales, constructed a four-quadrant method for classifying cigarette specifications using sales growth advantage and sales scale advantage indicators as coordinates. Using this method, the market status of various cigarette specifications (represented by "brand + letter") in Sichuan Province's ordinary class Ⅰ price-category cigarettes was classified into four categories: entry specifications, growth specifications, mature specifications, and shrinking specifications. The development and changes of the main cigarette specifications were compared longitudinally, and their development trends in Sichuan Province were analyzed. The results showed that 52 specifications, including Liqun A, Nanjing B, Tianzi C, etc., were entry specifications, including 29 new entry specifications. 13 specifications, including Tianzi A, Jiaozi A, and Huanghelou A, were growth specifications. 7 specifications, including Yunyan D, Yuxi H, and Yuxi G, were mature specifications. 49 specifications, including Jiaozi C, Yuxi E, and Suyan A, were shrinking specifications. At the same time, among the five main selling specifications of Sichuan Province's ordinary class Ⅰ price-category cigarettes from 2012 to 2020, Yuxi G has been in a mature stage, Yuxi H and Furongwang A entered the mature stage in 2015 and 2017, respectively, and Yunyan D experienced a state of maturity-growth-maturity. Tianzi A is in the growth stage and poses a strong threat to mature specifications. Based on the product life cycle theory, the four-quadrant method can effectively reflect the market status and competitive relationship of various cigarette specifications in Sichuan Province's Class Ⅰ-ordinary price category cigarettes. Continuous time market status indicators can reflect the life cycle changes of cigarette specifications, providing quantitative data reference for market regulation.

Keywords: Product life cycle; Cigarette; Four-quadrant method; Market status

1 Preface

With the slowdown of China's total population growth, the smoking rate continues to decline, and with the increasingly strict tobacco control environment, the cigarette market is gradually shifting from the competition of the incremental market to the increasingly fierce competition of the stock market. "Putting the stable operation of the economy and maintaining a good market state in the first place" is the requirement of the current stage of cigarette market regulation[1], and the analysis and judgment of the market status of cigarettes is the premise and basis of market regulation.

How to accurately evaluate the market status of cigarettes? Academics and industry professionals have given relevant methods according to their research and practical experience. Ke Xianyue[2] explored the comprehensive evaluation of the brand (specification) from multiple indicators and multiple dimensions based on the quantitative analysis of the market performance of the brand (specification), established an ideal model of the brand market status evaluation index system. Li Zhiwen and Liu Lihong[3] established a market status evaluation model suitable for tobacco enterprises by using the gray analytic hierarchy process, relying on the modern terminal information collection system, for evaluating the market status of cigarette retail areas and brand market state. Ma Junzhen et al.[4] built a market operation status evaluation model of the trinity of market, brand, and customer based on four indicators: price index, terminal stock-to-sales ratio, subscription rate, and sales rate. Li Zi[5] evaluated Beijing's cigarette market based on market information collection data and retail customer order data. Li Xiaomei et al.[6] established a cigarette market cycle index system including leading, consistent, and lagging indexes based on the business cycle theory. Dong Xiaoping et al.[7] used principal component analysis to obtain core indicators and established a mathematical model of the cigarette market operation status. Liu Song[8] systematically studied the accurate judgment mechanism of the market status from three aspects: information collection, index selection, and model establishment, using tools such as system diagrams and ECRS in lean management, as well as mathematical and statistical methods such as correlation analysis, cluster analysis, and hierarchical analysis. Xing Yang et al.[9] built an intelligent evaluation model of the cigarette market operation status using big data technology and machine learning algorithms. Liu Tao et al.[10] defined the core indicators of cigarette product regulation market status evaluation and constructed the comprehensive evaluation index and trend index of cigarette product regulation market status. Li Ye et al.[11] combined analytic hierarchy process with grey evaluation method, selected 7 second-level indicators such as sales volume, market status, marketing efficiency, customer satisfaction, and 19 third-level indicators such as annual cigarette sales volume, social stock-to-sales ratio, market purification rate, and marketing service satisfaction, to construct a set of cigarette market evaluation system. Yu Mengyin et al.[12] presented a market status evaluation matrix with a core indicator of average batch difference and order demand satisfaction rate from three dimensions of total volume, price, and product specification, as well as the reference threshold range of product specification dimension "pretty, tight, flat, and soft". Xu Hong and Qin Qin[13] used Lasso variable selection method to select the market state in country level, and then used entropy method and coefficient of variation method to reduce the index dimension to three categories of quantity, price, and storage, and used geometric average principle to construct a comprehensive evaluation index of cigarette market status.

These evaluation methods provide a useful reference for us to study and judge the market status of cigarette brands (specifications), but there are still some deficiencies. One is that multi-indicator evaluation is often used. The indicators used almost cover all indicators of market monitoring but ignored the correlation and priority between these indicators, resulting in small differences in evaluation results, and it is difficult to form an effective judgment of market status. Second, the existing evaluation system is mainly static evaluation, focusing on the evaluation of time, and seldom considers the product's life cycle and conducts dynamic evaluation. The product life cycle is widely used in cost control[14], quality management[15], and other aspects. For cigarette products, Liu Xiaochuan[16, 17] formulated the division index based on product sales volume, sales revenue, profit, market capacity, and other factors and used the empirical judgment method and cluster analysis method to divide the product life cycle, which made a good attempt to use the life cycle theory to judge the market status of cigarette. However, his method involves many indicators, the data collection is difficult, the division lacks data standards, and it is difficult to compare and analyze in different periods. How to divide the life cycle of the currently sold cigarette products? There is no unified standard method at present. Based on the life cycle theory[18], this paper refers to Zhao Guoqing's study of industrial sector groups[19]. It takes the average proportion of the sales volume of each product and the growth rate of the sales volume of each product as the reference. The products in different life cycles show the periodic characteristics of comparative advantages. Each quadrant in the coordinate system represents a stage of the product comparative advantage cycle, and the product set of four quadrants[20] forms a product group of different life cycle stages. This is expected to make a relatively accurate judgment on the market status of cigarettes and provide quantitative data reference for market regulation and control.

2 Materials and Methods

2.1 Research Object

This paper uses the sales volume of ordinary Class Ⅰ price-category cigarettes in Sichuan Province in 2019 and 2020 to classify the market status 2020. It uses the sales data of the five main specifications in the past nine years to analyze the changes in the market status.

2.2 Research Methodology

(1) Indicator system construction.

Cigarette products are classified by price, and cigarettes in the same price zone are one category. Assuming that there are n specifications of cigarettes in a certain price category, and the annual sales volume of the i-th specification in the t-th year is Q_i^t. The annual sales volume of the t-1st year is Q_i^{t-1}, the comparative growth advantage indicator CDA_i^t is defined as

$$CDA_i^t = MQ_i^t - AQ_i^{t-1} = \frac{Q_i^t - Q_i^{t-1}}{Q^t - Q^{t-1}} - \frac{Q_i^{t-1}}{Q^{t-1}}$$

In the equation, MQ_i^t is the marginal contribution rate of the i-th specification to the sales volume of the price category Q^t in the t-th year (i.e. $\sum_i Q_i^t$), which measures the share of the increment of the i-th cigarette specification in the total increment of the price category; AQ_i^{t-1} is the share of the sales volume of the i-th specification in the total sales volume of the price category, which represents the contribution of the i-th specification to the sales volume of the price category in the t-1st year.

The contribution of the i-th specification to the total sales volume and the increment of the sales volume of the price category represent two different advantages of the specification, and the combination of these two advantages determines the comparative advantage life cycle of a product (specification). When $CDA_i^t > 0$, it means that the incremental contribution rate of the i-th specification in the t-th year is higher than the total contribution rate of the t-1st year, that is, the sales growth rate of the i-th specification in the t-th year is higher than the growth rate of the total sales volume of the price category, which has comparative growth advantage. On the contrary $CDA_i^t < 0$, it means that the sales growth rate of the i-th specification in the t-th year is lower than that of the total sales volume of the price category, which is in a growth disadvantage. If $CDA_i^t = 0$, it means that the specification neither has a comparative growth advantage nor a comparative growth disadvantage.

Defining the comparative scale advantage indicator CSA_i^t:

$$CSA_i^t = AQ_i^t - 100/n$$

Where AQ_i^t is the market share (i. e. sales proportion) of the i-th specification in the price category in the t-th year; n is the number of specifications in the price category.

When $CSA_i^t > 0$, it means that the share of the i-th specification in the price category in the t-th year exceeds the average level. In that case, the specification has a comparative scale advantage. On the contrary $CDA_i^t < 0$, it means that the i-th specification is in a comparative scale disadvantage. If $CDA_i^t = 0$, it means that the specification neither has comparative scale advantage nor is in a status of scale disadvantage.

(2) Classification method of cigarette products based on four quadrants.

With the average state of products as the coordinate origin of the reference system, the combination of comparative growth advantage and comparative scale advantage is used to divide the comparative advantage cycle of products, as shown in Table 1.

Table 1 Four Types of Cigarette Specifications

Second quadrant ($CDA_i^t > 0$, $CSA_i^t < 0$) Entry specifications	First quadrant ($CDA_i^t > 0$, $CSA_i^t > 0$) Growth specifications
Third quadrant ($CDA_i^t < 0$, $CSA_i^t < 0$) Shrinking specifications	Fourth quadrant ($CDA_i^t < 0$, $CSA_i^t > 0$) Mature specifications

Entry specifications: $CDA_i^t > 0$, $CSA_i^t < 0$, located in the second quadrant. Their scale is relatively small and has not yet reached the average scale. However, their growth rate is relatively high, showing strong development advantages. These are generally new specifications launched in the same year with good development potential.

Growth specifications: $CDA_i^t > 0$, $CSA_i^t > 0$, located in the first quadrant. Their average contribution rate and marginal contribution rate are increasing. They have both comparative scale advantages and comparative growth advantages, so they play an important role in the growth of cigarette sales in the whole price category. Cigarettes of these specifications are in the expansion or development period.

Mature specifications: $CDA_i^t < 0$, $CSA_i^t > 0$, located in the fourth quadrant. Their growth rate has dropped below the average growth rate of the price category. Their average contribution rate is declining but still higher than the average level. After-sales reach the maximum, they will show negative growth. These are mature specifications in the price category and occupy a large share.

Shrinking specifications: $CDA_i^t < 0$, $CSA_i^t < 0$, located in the third quadrant. They have neither growth advantages nor scale advantages. They may be the starting point of some new specifications or the end point of some old specifications.

The classification method of cigarette products based on the four quadrants divides products into four types: entry specification, growth specification, mature specification, and shrinking specification. These specifications roughly correspond to the introduction, growth, maturity, and decline periods in the product life cycle but do not completely correspond. The product life cycle corresponds to the complete process of a product from birth to death. The product in the introduction period must be new product (new specification, usually refers to the product with a market time of less than one year), and the product in the decline period must be an old product (old specification, usually refers to the product with a market time of more than one year). The four-quadrant method focuses on the judgment of the market status of products. The product is in the entry specification, which means the product is in the state of entering the market. It may be a new product or an old product after remodeling. The shrinking specification is not necessarily for all old products but may also be for a new product that has just been released.

3　Results and Analysis

3.1　Classification Results of Ordinary Class Ⅰ Price-Category Cigarettes in Sichuan Province in 2020

According to the sales volume of ordinary Class Ⅰ price-category cigarettes in Sichuan Province in 2019 and 2020, the comparative growth advantage CDA_i^t and comparative scale advantage CSA_i^t of each selling specification can be calculated, and the quadrant it is in can be determined. Since this paper mainly focuses on methodology research and considers the sensitivity of tobacco information, the specific product specifications are expressed as "brand + letter," the specific classification results are shown in Table 2.

Table 2　Classification of Ordinary Class Ⅰ Price-Category Cigarette Market Status in Sichuan Province in 2020

Cigarette specifications	Sales volume in 2020/box	Sales volume in 2019/box	CDA_i^t	CSA_i^t	Quadrant	Cigarette specifications	Sales volume in 2020/box	Sales volume in 2019/box	CDA_i^t	CSA_i^t	Quadrant
Tianzi A	49864.93	44366.67	11.31	6.63	1	Zhonghua A	0.30	0.00	0.00	−0.83	2

continue

Cigarette specifications	Sales volume in 2020/box	Sales volume in 2019/box	CDA_i^t	CSA_i^t	Quadrant	Cigarette specifications	Sales volume in 2020/box	Sales volume in 2019/box	CDA_i^t	CSA_i^t	Quadrant
Jiaozi A	26417.91	15661.27	33.26	3.12	1	Yunyan A	0.28	0.00	0.00	−0.83	2
Huanghelou A	22236.14	20766.83	1.63	2.50	1	Nanjing A	0.14	0.00	0.00	−0.83	2
Furongwang A	21979.22	20312.42	2.35	2.46	1	Yunyan B	0.11	0.00	0.00	−0.83	2
Guiyan A	20986.57	17865.11	7.57	2.31	1	Liqun E	5359.58	5331.09	−0.74	−0.03	3
Tianzi B	20202.50	10473.79	30.66	2.19	1	Huanghelou M	4996.95	6162.76	−4.84	−0.08	3
Jiaozi B	16296.02	10550.40	17.43	1.61	1	Jiaozi C	4204.08	4388.16	−1.30	−0.20	3
Yuxi A	10995.95	10381.35	0.42	0.82	1	Yuxi C	3691.09	7085.00	−12.38	−0.27	3
Huanghelou B	8632.60	7771.98	1.64	0.46	1	Yuxi D	3466.38	6463.96	−10.97	−0.31	3
Huangshan A	7997.12	7402.85	0.81	0.37	1	Suyan A	3417.37	3593.02	−1.15	−0.32	3
Yuxi B	7418.00	6798.66	0.99	0.28	1	Furongwang B	2730.44	2741.66	−0.47	−0.42	3
Guiyan B	6332.11	4318.04	6.01	0.12	1	Jiaozi H	2687.53	3215.01	−2.25	−0.42	3
Daqianmen A	6126.71	5558.98	1.01	0.09	1	Lanzhou B	2664.11	2603.25	−0.21	−0.43	3
Liqun A	5122.18	0.00	17.01	−0.06	2	Yuxi E	2637.37	3998.85	−5.15	−0.43	3
Liqun B	5112.55	4586.74	1.03	−0.06	2	Guiyan C	2462.01	3501.84	−4.00	−0.46	3
Nanjing B	4919.88	3569.48	3.93	−0.09	2	Jiaozi D	2126.90	3492.08	−5.08	−0.51	3
Tianzi C	4814.09	0.00	15.98	−0.11	2	Yuxi G	1780.80	3047.98	−4.68	−0.56	3
Zhenlong A	4307.21	1776.22	8.13	−0.18	2	555 C	1705.39	1656.40	−0.10	−0.57	3
Yunyan C	4236.47	2866.92	4.10	−0.19	2	Nanjing C	1656.83	1719.62	−0.48	−0.58	3
Huangshan B	2868.06	387.88	8.17	−0.40	2	Jiaozi G	1533.03	2914.81	−5.04	−0.60	3
Huanghelou C	2492.50	2275.14	0.37	−0.45	2	Jiaozi E	1382.17	1833.75	−1.79	−0.62	3
Double Happiness A	2411.34	1966.63	1.17	−0.47	2	Liqun F	957.77	1732.13	−2.84	−0.68	3
Seven Wolves A	2050.65	0.00	6.81	−0.52	2	Jinqiao A	937.70	908.89	−0.05	−0.69	3
Liqun C	2006.48	1573.80	1.19	−0.53	2	Great Wall B	739.00	1614.18	−3.16	−0.72	3
Marlboro A	1916.22	0.00	6.36	−0.54	2	Huanghelou G	714.96	1153.38	−1.64	−0.72	3
Liqun H	1883.88	0.00	6.26	−0.54	2	Great Wall C	394.70	1185.56	−2.81	−0.77	3
Tianzi D	1557.99	0.00	5.17	−0.59	2	Liqun G	269.70	860.90	−2.10	−0.79	3
Golden Leaf A	1358.60	0.00	4.51	−0.62	2	Red Double Happiness A	216.96	214.02	−0.02	−0.79	3
Good Cat A	1197.97	756.26	1.35	−0.65	2	Guiyan D	116.54	596.06	−1.69	−0.81	3

continue

Cigarette specifications	Sales volume in 2020/box	Sales volume in 2019/box	CDA_i^t	CSA_i^t	Quadrant	Cigarette specifications	Sales volume in 2020/box	Sales volume in 2019/box	CDA_i^t	CSA_i^t	Quadrant
Jin Sheng A	1127.24	0.00	3.74	−0.66	2	Red Double Happiness B	103.60	143.71	−0.16	−0.81	3
Changbaishan A	1017.30	0.00	3.38	−0.67	2	Yuxi F	101.73	534.96	−1.52	−0.81	3
Golden Leaf B	940.00	0.00	3.12	−0.69	2	Kent C	86.52	92.42	−0.03	−0.81	3
Peony A	882.51	0.00	2.93	−0.69	2	Lanzhou C	73.98	645.96	−2.00	−0.82	3
555 A	876.04	395.21	1.53	−0.70	2	Kent D	66.96	87.34	−0.08	−0.82	3
Marlboro B	793.90	0.00	2.64	−0.71	2	Huanghelou H	52.87	86.08	−0.12	−0.82	3
Taishan A	776.04	513.06	0.79	−0.71	2	Kent E	24.43	81.39	−0.20	−0.82	3
Jin Sheng A	766.59	482.62	0.87	−0.71	2	Seven Star A	23.56	76.46	−0.19	−0.82	3
Huanghelou D	758.48	0.00	2.52	−0.71	2	Camel A	5.20	14.80	−0.03	−0.83	3
Zhenlong B	702.01	0.00	2.33	−0.72	2	Crown A	1.80	4.86	−0.01	−0.83	3
Huanghelou E	638.32	0.00	2.12	−0.73	2	Longfeng chengxiang A	0.30	3350.11	−11.65	−0.83	3
Huanghelou F	624.02	0.00	2.07	−0.73	2	Marlboro E	0.18	1375.38	−4.78	−0.83	3
Marlboro C	609.41	454.31	0.44	−0.74	2	Huanghelou I	0.12	4.02	−0.01	−0.83	3
Kent A	550.19	375.73	0.52	−0.74	2	Huangshan B	0.10	387.88	−1.35	−0.83	3
Marlboro D	533.77	0.00	1.77	−0.75	2	Tulou A	0.08	1277.42	−4.44	−0.83	3
Nanjing D	463.06	0.00	1.54	−0.76	2	Tianzi E	0.04	533.21	−1.85	−0.83	3
Kent B	336.68	195.10	0.44	−0.78	2	Jiaozi F	0.03	1049.24	−3.65	−0.83	3
ESSE A	284.16	202.80	0.24	−0.78	2	Seven Wolves C	0.02	198.00	−0.69	−0.83	3
Harbin A	261.30	249.02	0.00	−0.79	2	Marlboro F	0.02	279.81	−0.97	−0.83	3
Hademen A	258.65	0.00	0.86	−0.79	2	Double Happiness B	0.01	125.66	−0.44	−0.83	3
555 B	236.40	0.00	0.78	−0.79	2	Marlboro G	0.00	400.50	−1.39	−0.83	3
Seven Star A	81.24	76.46	0.00	−0.81	2	Huangshan C	0.00	222.80	−0.77	−0.83	3
Lion A	59.80	4.78	0.18	−0.82	2	Furongwang C	0.00	193.22	−0.67	−0.83	3
Baoheng A	36.19	32.51	0.01	−0.82	2	Golden Leaf C	0.00	82.67	−0.29	−0.83	3
Seven Star B	25.03	0.00	0.08	−0.82	2	Yunyan D	133876.78	144349.86	−57.37	19.19	4
Yumao A	18.24	17.33	0.00	−0.82	2	Yuxi G	80296.08	81654.74	−17.29	11.18	4
Great Wall A	5.00	2.93	0.01	−0.83	2	Yuxi H	74054.82	81790.68	−38.49	10.24	4
Yunyan E	0.71	0.00	0.00	−0.83	2	Huanghelou J	12580.36	13028.18	−3.53	1.05	4

continue

Cigarette specifications	Sales volume in 2020/box	Sales volume in 2019/box	CDA_i^t	CSA_i^t	Quadrant	Cigarette specifications	Sales volume in 2020/box	Sales volume in 2019/box	CDA_i^t	CSA_i^t	Quadrant
Lanzhou A	0.10	0.00	0.00	−0.83	2	Yunyan E	12451.02	12817.17	−3.22	1.04	4
Peony A	0.05	0.02	0.00	−0.83	2	Huanghelou K	8937.62	9635.62	−3.83	0.51	4
Seven Wolves B	0.01	0.00	0.00	−0.83	2	Huanghelou L	5895.46	7243.19	−5.61	0.05	4
Liqun D	0.00	0.00	0.00	−0.83	2	Total	668888.16	638770.99			

Using comparative growth advantage and comparative scale advantage, all the sales specifications of the ordinary Class Ⅰ price-category can be divided into four categories: entry specifications, growth specifications, mature specifications and shrinking specifications.

Entry specifications: 52 specifications, including Liqun A, Nanjing B, Tianzi C, Zhenlong A, Yunyan C, Huangshan B, and Huanghelou C, including 29 new entry specifications. These specifications have comparative growth advantages, among which Liqun A and Tianzi C have the most obvious advantages, with the difference between marginal contribution rate and total contribution rate exceeding 15. However, the scale is relatively small, and their sales volume in that year has not reached the average scale.

Growth specifications: 13 specifications, including Tianzi A, Jiaozi A, Huanghelou A, Furongwang A, and Guiyan A, are growth specifications. Among them, Jiaozi A has the largest comparative growth advantage, followed by Tianzi B, with a more than 30 comparative growth advantage. In addition, Jiaozi B and Tianzi A have obvious comparative growth advantages, with a comparative growth advantage of more than 10. Among the growth specifications, Tianzi A, Jiaozi A and Huanghelou A have the top three comparative scale advantages, with a comparative scale advantage of more than 2. Tianzi A and Jiaozi A will be the most promising specifications in the ordinary Class Ⅰ price-category cigarette market in Sichuan Province.

Mature specifications: Yunyan D, Yuxi H, Yuxi G, and the other 7 specifications are mature specifications, which no longer have comparative growth advantages but still have a large market share. Among the mature specifications, Yunyan D and Yuxi H have the biggest crisis, with the worst comparative growth advantages of −57.37 and −38.49, respectively, indicating that the marginal contribution rate is far lower than the total contribution rate, and the market share has declined significantly, putting them at a disadvantageous position in competition.

Shrinking specifications: Jiaozi C, Yuxi E, Suyan A, Lanzhou B, Furongwang B, and other 49 specifications are shrinking specifications, which do not have comparative growth advantages, and the sales scale of the previous year is also lower than the average scale, facing the possibility of delisting.

3.2 Analysis of the Change in the Market Status of Five Major Specifications

This paper selects the five major specifications in the sales of Sichuan Province in 2020, among which Yunyan D, Yuxi G, and Yuxi H are the top three specifications in the sales of Sichuan Province, Furongwang A is a national specification product of the Class Ⅰ ordinary price-category, which has been sold in Sichuan Province for a long time, and Tianzi A is a new product launched in Sichuan in 2017. In 2020, the sales of these five specifications accounted for 53.83% of the ordinary Class Ⅰ price-category cigarettes in Sichuan Province. According to Equations, the market status indicators of the last nine years can be calculated, as shown in Table 3.

Table 3　Market Status Changes of the Main Cigarette Specifications of the ordinary Class Ⅰ Price-Category in Sichuan Province

years	Furongwang A		Tianzi A		Yuxi G		Yuxi H		Yunyan D	
	CSA_i^t	CDA_i^t	CSA_i^t	CDA_i^t	CSA_i^t	CDA_i^t	CSA_i^t	CDA_i^t	CSA_i^t	CDA_i^t
2012	0.89	0.35			19.07	3.71	20.65	5.70	29.64	−7.16
2013	1.04	0.79			18.05	−6.65	23.11	15.50	26.94	−17.40
2014	2.03	5.10			18.00	−1.96	24.55	8.17	25.44	−11.82
2015	2.30	1.69			17.98	−2.31	24.51	−2.59	27.73	29.53
2016	2.67	4.69			16.18	−39.46	20.02	−94.09	32.37	91.66
2017	2.68	−2.17	6.17	89.07	13.84	−31.27	15.82	−54.21	29.75	−34.68
2018	2.56	−4.53	5.61	−13.15	12.57	−27.03	13.24	−53.04	25.65	−83.06
2019	2.29	−3.95	6.06	4.98	11.90	−9.08	11.92	−17.16	21.71	−49.88
2020	2.46	2.35	6.63	11.31	11.18	−17.29	10.24	−38.49	19.19	−57.37

According to the changes in comparative scale advantage and comparative growth advantage in Table 3, the market scale advantage of Yunyan D, Yuxi H, and Yuxi G declined rapidly. Still, it occupied an important position in the ordinary Class Ⅰ price-category of the cigarette market in Sichuan Province. In 2012, the market share of Yunyan D was close to 30%, but the loss of comparative growth advantage led to its market share declining to 25.44% in 2014. In 2015 and 2016, due to the macroeconomic changes, and the only local competitive brand Jiaozi H was listed with a relatively simple specification, and not yet familiar to consumers, Yunyan D gained the opportunity to increase its market share to 32.37% with a large comparative growth advantage, returning the specification from the mature state to the growth status. Since 2017, local brands Jiaozi and Tianzi series have been listed in large quantities, which has greatly impacted Yunyan D. The comparative advantage is lost again, and the market share continues to decline. By 2020, the market share has been less than 20%, but it is still the largest specification in the ordinary Class Ⅰ price-category of the cigarette market in Sichuan Province. Yuxi H grew before 2015, with a maximum market share of 24.55%. In 2015, it entered a mature status, and its comparative growth advantage declined, and the market size fell to 10.24% by 2020. Yuxi G has matured, but the growth advantage has declined too fast since 2016, and the market size has also accelerated. In general, since 2016, with the rise of local brands, Yunnan-made cigarettes have been more and more impacted; the growth advantage is no longer there, and the market share is getting lower and lower. Although Yunnan-made cigarettes' three main sales specifications still have a certain scale advantage, they are feared to last only briefly.

Furongwang A is also a specification that has been sold for a long time in the ordinary Class Ⅰ price-category cigarette market in Sichuan Province. Although this specification has a small-scale advantage, the market share has increased overall, and the market share in 2020 is 2.46%. From the perspective of comparative growth advantage, Furongwang A had a positive growth advantage before 2017 and was in a growth state of products. However, since 2017, the growth advantage has become negative and entered a mature status. In 2020, the comparative growth advantage has changed, but the numerical changes of the comparative growth advantages and comparative scale advantages are small, and they are in a relatively stable, mature status.

Tianzi A is a new product launched by Sichuan Zhongyan in 2017. In recent years, it has shown strong growth advantages in the ordinary Class Ⅰ price-category cigarette market in Sichuan Province and has a certain scale advantage. It is currently in a growth status. Similarly, Jiaozi A, which was listed in 2018, achieved a sales volume of 9,399.67 boxes in the year of listing, with a significant comparative growth advantage (the comparative growth advantages of the three years were 31.52, 20.68, and 33.26, respectively). The market share reached 3.95%, making it the strongest competitor in mature specifications.

4 Conclusion and Prospect

Based on the product life cycle theory, this paper constructs a four-quadrant classification method for cigarette products based on comparative growth advantage and comparative scale advantage, with cigarette sales volume as the core indicator. The cigarette sales specifications are divided into entry, growth, mature, and shrinking specifications, making the market status assessment of products more reasonable and accurate and the competitive relationship between products clearer. The analysis of Sichuan Province's ordinary Class Ⅰ price-category cigarettes shows that this method can effectively reflect the market status and competitive relationship of various cigarette specifications. Moreover, through the market status indicator of continuous time, it can reflect the market status changes of cigarette specifications and make reasonable judgments on the development trend of cigarette specifications.

The quantitative evaluation of cigarette market status is the basis for decision-making for goods organization and marketing strategy formulation, has important application value for regulating and controlling the cigarette market, and is also the basis for reforming the cigarette market. The research in this paper provides a simple and feasible method for evaluating the status of the cigarette market. In addition to evaluating the market status, this method can also be used for brand (specification) competition analysis. In addition, the four-quadrant method is used to evaluate monthly or weekly sales data, excluding the cyclical and holiday effects, which can greatly improve the timeliness of cigarette market status evaluation and provide more timely information for market monitoring.

References

[1] China Cigarette Sales Company. Building a Comprehensive Monitoring System to Accurately Take the Pulse of the Market Status[N]. Oriental Tobacco News, 2021-09-27 (002).

[2] KE X Y. Construction and Application of Brand (Specification) Market Status Evaluation Index System[C]// Chinese Tobacco Society. Proceedings of the 2012 Academic Annual Meeting of Chinese Tobacco Society. Chinese Tobacco Society, 2012: 5.

[3] LI Z W, LIU L H. Application of Grey Analytic Hierarchy Process in Cigarette Market Status Evaluation[J]. Modern Commerce and Trade Industry, 2015, 36 (1): 122-123.

[4] MA J Z, ZHOU C L, CHEN Y. Construction and Application of Market Operation Status Evaluation Model based on Data Mining[C]// Chinese Tobacco Society. 2016 Annual Excellent Papers of Chinese Tobacco Society — Cigarette circulation theme [C]. Chinese Tobacco Society, 2016: 10.

[5] LI Z. Analysis of Evaluation Methods for Beijing Cigarette Market[C]// Chinese Tobacco Society. Chinese Tobacco Society 2016 Outstanding Papers Compilation — Cigarette Circulation Theme. Chinese Tobacco Society, 2016: 11.

[6] LI X M, LI J, ZHANG H. Exploration and Practice of Cigarette Market Prosperity Index Compilation — Taking Guangxi Cigarette Market as an Example[J]. Chinese Journal of Tobacco Science and Technology, 2017, 23 (4): 107-113.

[7] DONG X P, WANG D G, XING Y. Application Research of Big Data in Cigarette Market Monitoring[J]. Information Technology and Standardization, 2017 (10): 65-69.

[8] LIU S. Discuss the Construction and Application of Precise Judgement Mechanisms for Market Status[J]. Northern Economy and Trade, 2017 (7): 47-49.

[9] XING Y, HUANG X F, DONG X P, et al. Research and Application of Intelligent Evaluation Model for Cigarette Market Operation Status[J]. Tobacco Science and Technology, 2018, 51 (7): 96-102.

[10] LIU T, JIANG N, WENG C Y, et al. Research on Cigarette Product Standard Market Status Evaluation Index System and Diagnosis Scheme — Based on the Perspective of Chongqing Practice[J]. Shopping Mall Modernization, 2020 (22): 13-17.

[11] LI Y, ZHANG X N, ZHANG Y, et al. Research on County-Level Cigarette Market Evaluation System based on Multi-Level Grey Evaluation Method—Take the Tongchuan Cigarette Market as an Example[J]. Chinese Journal of Tobacco Science and Technology, 2022, 28(3): 119-126.

[12] YU M Y, YI Y, CAI Y X. Evaluation and Regulation System of Consumer Market based on System Thinking: A Case Study of Cigarettes with Three-Dimensional and Three-Layer Structure[J]. Trade Fair Economy, 2021 (18): 26-29.

[13] XU H, QIN Q. Construction of Comprehensive Evaluation Index of Cigarette Market[J]. Strait Science, 2021 (8): 99-105.

[14] PENG K. Analysis of Lean Cost Control of Tobacco Industry under Product Life Cycle[J]. Finance and Economics, 2015 (6): 47+67.

[15] PAN Y L, LI X L, CHEN L X, et al. Application of Product Life Cycle Theory in Cigarette Quality Management[J]. Science and Technology Entrepreneur, 2013 (17): 201-202.

[16] LIU X C. Application of Cluster Analysis in Product Life Cycle Research: A Case Study of Cigarettes[J]. Jiangsu Business Review, 2017 (8): 29-31.

[17] LIU X C. Research on Cigarette Product Tracking Evaluation Model[J]. Modern Business, 2015 (29): 121-123.

[18] WU Y Q. Analysis of Marketing Channel Management under the Guidance of Product Life Cycle Theory[J]. National Circulation Economy, 2017 (7): 3-4.

[19] ZHAO G Q. Research on the Structure and Strategic Adjustment of China's Industrial Sectors[J]. Research on Financial and Economic Issues,2006(1):19-27.

[20] CHEN Y G,CHU S J,LI Z X. Connotation of Low-Carbon Economy and Four-Quadrant Evaluation Method[J]. Journal of Hebei University of Economics and Business,2011,32(6):60-63.

单规格卷烟月度销量的时间序列预测方法研究

摘要：本文基于回归模型、指数平滑模型、时间序列分解模型、季节 ARIMA 模型和 X13-A-S 方法对某省玉溪（软）卷烟的月度销量进行预测，并对预测结果进行检验。在销量最高的 1 月，预测结果的差异最大，在销量最低的 12 月，预测结果的差异最小。2021 年 1—10 月的实际销量为 49780.79 箱，预测结果最为接近的是季节 ARIMA 模型，其次是 X13-A-S 方法，预测结果差距最大的是时间序列分解模型。在平均相对误差上，X13-A-S 方法的平均相对误差最小，为 8.57%，季节 ARIMA 模型次之，为 10.43%。回归模型的标准误差最小。在销量均值的预测上，季节 ARIMA 模型和 X13-A-S 方法预测的绝对误差和相对误差较低，可以作为卷烟月度销量的通用方法。

关键词：回归预测；指数平滑；时间序列分解；季节 ARIMA；X13-A-S

1 前言

中国的卷烟消费市场已经从高速发展的阶段进入平稳成熟的阶段，新的经济环境也使得单规格卷烟的销量规律弱化。对单规格卷烟销量的精准预测，有助于企业及时把握市场状态，提高企业对市场的响应能力，提升卷烟营销水平。

对于卷烟销量的预测，学者和业界人士已经做过许多研究。在预测的时间类型上，年度数据的预测因周期短，样本少，不用考虑周期、节假日等问题，相关研究最多。季度数据的预测需要解决季节性问题，但是节假日的影响不用单独考虑，因此该类型的研究也较多，如石涛等的研究[1]。月度数据因频率高，波动大，应用需求大，近年来也颇受关注，如罗彪[2]、武牧[3]、吴明山等[4]进行了相关研究。然而，由于周数据获取困难且波动性过大，相关的研究非常少，目前仅见一篇[5]。从预测方法上看，样本量较小的年度预测通常使用灰色模型[6-7]、灰色马尔科夫模型[8-9]、回归模型[10-11]、组合模型[12-13]、系统动力学模型[14]和随机森林算法[15]。在季度预测和月度预测中，数据的周期性必须得到处理，相应的方法有趋势比率模型[16]、季节 ARIMA 模型[17]、时间序列分解模型[18]、组合模型[4,19]和混频模型[1]等。随着大数据技术的兴起，机器学习方法也被运用到卷烟销量预测中，如支持向量机[3]和神经网络[20]等。此外，有学者注意到节假日尤其是农历新年等对卷烟销量的影响，提出了针对性的改进方法[21]。

已有的文献为我们研究卷烟销量的月度预测提供了坚实的基础，但是在以下几个方面仍然存在改进的空间。①现有的月度销量预测集中在一个区域的总销量上，鲜有单规格卷烟的销量预测。②对春节等农历节假日的处理仍不尽人意，春节属于移动假日，其影响的月份不固定，简单地将其设置为虚拟变量难以准确度量春节效应。③在预测方法上，考虑了季节调整、趋势循环、不规则变动和移动节假日的 Census X13-ARIMA-SEATS 方法还未应用到卷烟的月度销量预测中,而该方法是目前最新的季节调整方法[22]。本文拟以某省单一规格玉溪(软)卷烟的月度销量数据为基础,构建和引入 5 种预测方法,对其月度销量进行预测,并选出最优方法。

2 材料与方法

2.1 研究对象

本文使用 2015 年 1 月到 2020 年 12 月共 72 个月的数据进行模型估计及预测,利用 2021 年 1 月到 10 月的实际销量数据进行预测的检验。

2.2 研究方法

2.2.1 回归分析法

回归分析法通过建立变量间的回归方程,根据解释变量的预期值来对被解释变量进行预测[23]。考虑卷烟月度销量的影响因素,假设卷烟销量的长期趋势与周期性之间没有叠加效应,拟建立如下加法回归预测模型:

$$y_t = \alpha_0 + \alpha_1 t + \sum_{i=1}^{11} \alpha_{i+1} S_{it} + \alpha_{13} Z_t + \alpha_{14} D_t + \mu_t$$

式中,y_t 为卷烟月度销量;μ_t 为随机误差项;t 为长期趋势变量,$t=1,2,\cdots,k$;S_{it} 为季节虚拟变量($S_{it}=1$,销量属于第 i 个月;$S_{it}=0$,销量不属于第 i 个月;$i=1,2,\cdots,11$);D_t 为政策变量($D_t=1$,提税顺价(2015 年 6 月)前;$D_t=0$,提税顺价后);参数 α_i 度量了第 i 个变量对月度销量的净影响;Z_t 为春节虚拟变量。

假设春节对销量的影响在春节前是均匀的,计元旦到春节时的天数为 m,则 Z_t 为 $Z_1 \sim Z_{12}$ 的循环取值:

$$Z_1 = \begin{cases} 1, m < 31 \\ 31/m, m \geq 31 \end{cases}, \quad Z_2 = \begin{cases} 0, m < 31 \\ 1-31/m, m \geq 31 \end{cases}, \quad Z_3 = \cdots = Z_{12} = 0$$

若卷烟销量的长期趋势和周期性之间存在叠加效应,还可建立销量预测的乘法回归模型:

$$y_t = \beta_0 + \beta_1 t + \sum_{i=1}^{11} \beta_{i+1} t \cdot S_{it} + \beta_{13} Z_t + \beta_{14} D_t + \mu_t$$

2.2.2 指数平滑法

指数平滑法是一种常用的中短期预测方法,按照平滑的次数,可以进行一次、二次和三次指数平滑。三次指数平滑模型又分为加法和乘法模型。乘法模型主要用于周期性和线性叠加的序列。平滑序列公式为:

$$y_{t+k} = [a(t) + b(t)k]c_{t+k}$$

加法模型主要用于周期变化稳定、线性趋势简单的序列。序列由下列公式给出:

$$y_{t+k} = a(t) + b(t)k + c_{t+k}$$

式中,y_{t+k} 为 $t+k$ 时期的卷烟月度销量;$a(t)$ 为截距;$b(t)$ 为斜率,随时间 t 变化而变化;c_{t+k} 为季节因子。

2.2.3 引入虚拟变量的时间序列分解法

时间序列分解将原始序列拆分为长期趋势变动和循环变动、季节变动和不规则变动[24]。常用的模型有加法、乘法和混合模型。一般卷烟月度销量的趋势和周期性存在叠加效应,多选择乘法或混合模型:

$$y_t = TC_t \cdot S_t \cdot I_t \text{ 或 } y_t = S_t \cdot (TC_t + I_t)$$

式中,y_t 为卷烟月度销量;TC_t、S_t 和 I_t 分别代表长期趋势变动、季节变动和不规则变动。

本文在处理季节因素时,将传统节日设为虚拟变量,构建基于时间序列分解和虚拟回归的改进模型,估测传统节日对序列的影响。用 D_{1t}($D_{1t}=1$,1 月;$D_{1t}=0$,其他月份)和 D_{2t}($D_{2t}=1$,提税顺价前;$D_{2t}=0$,提税顺价后)分别表示春节变量和政策变量,建立卷烟销量长期趋势的回归模型:

$$TC_t = \beta_0 + \beta_1 t + \beta_2 D_{1t} + \beta_3 D_{2t} + \mu_t$$

2.2.4 季节 ARIMA 模型

按照博克斯-詹金斯时域分析方法,建立季节 ARIMA 模型。设季节变化周期为 s,首先用季节差分法消除周期性变化,然后用一阶差分算子去除线性趋势。对于差分后的序列,可能还存在季节效应和随机波动间的交互影响,短期相关性和季节效应之间具有乘积关系,所以季节乘法模型实际上为 ARMA(p,q) 和 ARMA(m_s,n_s) 的乘积[25]。季节乘法模型的形式如下:

$$\Phi_p(L)A_m(L^s)(1-L)(1-L^s)y_t = \Theta_q(L)B_n(L^s)\varepsilon_t$$

式中,L 为滞后算子;$\Phi_p(L)$、$\Theta_q(L)$ 分别是 L 的一元 p 次和 q 次多项式;$A_m(L^s)$、$B_n(L^s)$ 分别是 L^s 的 m 次和 n 次多项式;ε_t 为白噪声。

2.2.5 X-13A-S 方法

X-13A-S 方法是 X-11-ARIMA 与 SEATS 的结合,主要用于经济数据的季节调整。X-13A-S 方法首先建立 RegARIMA 模型,调整原始序列中的极端值和日历效应。RegARIMA 模型是回归模型与 ARIMA 模型的组合,其形式如下:

$$\Phi_p(L)A_m(L^s)(y_t - \sum_i \beta_i x_{it}) = \Theta_q(L)B_n(L^s)\varepsilon_t$$

式中,y_t 为被解释变量;x_{it} 为解释变量;回归残差 $(y_t - \sum_i \beta_i x_{it})$ 为平稳时间序列,满足季节 ARIMA 模型。

X-13A-S 方法运用 RegARIMA 模型对经过预调整后的序列进行向前和向后预测来补充数据,通过移动平均法从原序列中分离出趋势成分、循环成分、季节成分和不规则成分,最后对结果进行诊断。

3 结果与分析

3.1 五种模型的估计和优化选择

如图 1 所示,某省玉溪(软)卷烟从 2015 年 1 月到 2021 年 10 月的月度销量具有明显的周期性,但周期的振幅并没有呈现规律变化,2015 年和 2018 年的峰值明显偏低,趋势变化也不明显,不规则因素的影响较大。

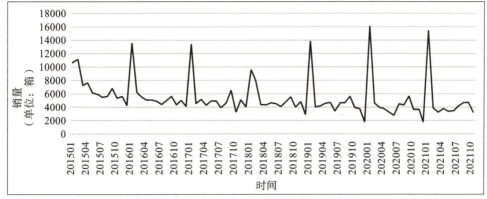

图 1　玉溪(软)月度销量的时序图

3.1.1　回归模型

分别估计加法和乘法回归模型,模型拟合优度分别为 0.9532 和 0.9492,选择拟合优度较高的加法模型作为最终的预测模型,估计结果如表 1 所示。

表 1　回归分析的加法模型估计结果

变量	系数	均方	F	P	变量	系数	均方	F	P
C	4180.3080	312.1649	13.3914	0.0000	S_5	1220.2190	373.3806	3.2680	0.0018
t	−23.9669	4.0627	−5.8993	0.0000	S_6	1073.6920	370.4828	2.8981	0.0053
Z	14809.7500	1326.0610	11.1682	0.0000	S_7	1205.2600	370.2377	3.2554	0.0019
D	1273.9940	346.1046	3.6810	0.0005	S_8	1565.5610	370.0370	4.2308	0.0001
S_1	−3457.0650	1184.2600	−2.9192	0.0050	S_9	2647.5600	369.8809	7.1579	0.0000
S_2	502.0865	424.9917	1.1814	0.2423	S_{10}	870.6722	369.7693	2.3546	0.0220
S_3	1449.7080	373.5574	3.8808	0.0003	S_{11}	1437.7420	369.7024	3.8889	0.0003
S_4	1363.0560	373.4469	3.6499	0.0006					

模型的拟合优度为 0.9532,F 统计量对应的 P 值为 0.000,模型拟合较好,在 1% 的水平下模型显著。解释变量中,除了季节变量 S_2 不显著以外,其余变量均在 5% 的水平下显著,说明虚拟解释变量有较好的解释作用。模型的 DW 值为 2.0577,表明模型不存在随机误差项的序列相关,可用于预测。时间变量 t 的系数为 −23.9669,表明去除周期性和政策影响后,月度销量每月平均下降 23.9669 箱。春节效应变量 Z 和政策效应 D 均显著为正,表明春节所在月份销量确实高于其他月份的销量,提税顺价前的销量也明显高于提税顺价后的销量。

3.1.2　指数平滑模型

分别估计三参数指数平滑加法和乘法模型,结果如下。

加法模型:

$$y_{t+k}=0.05(y_t-c_t(t-s))+0.95(a(t-1)+b(t-1)+b(t-1))k-c_{t+k}(t+k-s)$$

乘法模型：

$$y_{t+k} = \left[(0.06\frac{y_t}{c_t(t-s)} + 0.94(a(t-1)+b(t-1))) + (0.26(a(t)-a(t-1))) + 0.74b(t-1))k\right]c_{t+k}(t+k-s)$$

式中，0.05，0.06 和 0.26 为阻尼因子估计值。

两个模型中的 s 均为"季节性周期"中指定的季节性频率，本文中 s 为 12。加法模型的残差平方和为 83821095，均方误差为 1078.97。乘法模型的残差平方和为 $1.15×10^8$，均方误差为 1261.26。加法季节因子和乘法季节因子见表 2。从均方预测误差来看，加法模型的预测误差更小，选择加法模型作为预测模型。

表 2 指数平滑模型提取的季节因子

月份	1月	2月	3月	4月	5月	6月	7月	8月	9月	10月	11月	12月
加法季节因子	7106.86	786.17	−516.95	−594.13	−727.49	−1076.87	−935.83	−566.05	525.42	−1241.99	−665.44	−2093.71
乘法季节因子	2.3233	1.1220	0.9021	0.8857	0.8692	0.7994	0.8371	0.9048	1.1113	0.7710	0.8784	0.5957

3.1.3 时间序列分解模型的预测结果

考虑到本文中的月度销量趋势和周期性存在叠加效应，因此选择乘法分解模型。首先使用季节指数提取周期性，然后采用线性回归提取趋势，剩余部分归为不规则变动。剔除季节因素后的趋势回归模型为：

$$\hat{TC}_t = 6202.3890 - 30.2538t - 748.4090D_{1t} + 1424.7480D_{2t}$$

式中，D_{1t} 和 D_{2t} 为 1 月和政策的虚拟变量。

经检验，模型整体显著，拟合优度为 0.5251，所有变量均在 5% 的显著性水平下显著。分别对 2021 年 1 月至 10 月的趋势和季节进行预测，然后合并成总的预测，结果如表 3 所示。

表 3 加入虚拟变量的时间序列分解模型预测结果 （单位：箱）

月度	2021M01	2021M02	2021M03	2021M04	2021M05	2021M06	2021M07	2021M08	2021M09	2021M10
趋势预测	3245.45	3963.61	3933.36	3903.1	3872.85	3842.59	3812.34	3782.09	3751.83	3721.6
季节预测	2.6805	1.1024	0.9357	0.8993	0.9241	0.8411	0.8655	0.9531	1.1646	0.8211
合计	8699.57	4369.48	3680.25	3510.11	3578.7	3231.84	3299.69	3604.64	4369.43	3055.62

3.1.4 季节 ARIMA 模型的估计和优化

首先对销量序列进行 1 阶差分去除趋势，然后进行 12 阶差分消除季节性，通过绘制自相关和偏自相关图，确定可以估计 AR(2)、MA(1)、ARMA(1,1)、ARMA(1,12)、SARMA(1,1)×(1,1)$_{12}$ 以及 SARMA(2,1)×(1,1)$_{12}$ 等模型。运用 ML 法估计识别出的所有模型，经模型显著性检验（残差白噪声检验）和参数显著性检验后，SARIMA(1,1,1)×(0,1,

$0)_{12}$,SARIMA$(1,1,1)\times(1,1,0)_{12}$ 和 SARIMA$(1,1,1)\times(0,1,1)_{12}$ 通过检验,可以用来预测。三个模型估计结果的对比见表4。

表 4 SARIMA 模型的优化选择

模型	σ^2	AIC 准则	SC 准则	平稳性	可逆性
SARIMA$(1,1,1)\times(0,1,0)_{12}$	1639119	17.3283	17.4692	平稳	可逆
SARIMA$(1,1,1)\times(1,1,0)_{12}$	1581823	17.3335	17.5095	平稳	可逆
SARIMA$(1,1,1)\times(0,1,1)_{12}$	1484909	17.2971	17.4732	平稳	可逆

模型的选择通常根据信息准则来决定。从表4中可知,SARIMA$(1,1,1)\times(0,1,0)_{12}$ 具有最小的 SC 值,SARIMA$(1,1,1)\times(0,1,1)_{12}$ 具有最小的 AIC 值。因此选择模型通过 LR 检验来进行。以 SARIMA$(1,1,1)\times(0,1,1)_{12}$ 为基础模型,SARIMA$(1,1,1)\times(0,1,0)_{12}$ 为嵌套模型,检验 SMA 项的系数是否为 0 的原假设,其 LR 统计量为 3.84(prob>0.05),因此不拒绝原假设,应该以 SARIMA$(1,1,1)\times(0,1,0)_{12}$ 作为最终的预测模型,其估计结果如下式。

$$(1-L)(1-L^{12})X_t = \frac{1-0.8599L}{1-0.4855L}\varepsilon_t$$

3.1.5 X13-A-S 方法

本文运用 Eviews10 软件中的 Census X-13A-S 程序,对数据不做转换,不考虑交易日影响和移动假日影响(对消费者而言,卷烟销售不存在交易日;前文的研究表明季节效应已经将春节和中秋效应包含在内),由 X-11 Auto 选择 ARIMA 模型,用 X-11 方法进行季节调整,X-13 Auto 进行趋势和季节过滤,可得到一个相对较好的预测结果。

在无季节性影响的假设下,稳定季节性 F 检验的统计量为 18.367,在 1%的显著性水平下存在季节性,稳定季节性非参数检验的 Kruskal-Wallis 统计量为 79.354,在 1%的显著性水平下存在季节性;移动季节性 F 检验(原假设为年变化无影响)的统计量为 1.354,在 5%的显著性水平下没有证据表明存在移动季节性。综合三个检验的结果来看,玉溪(软)卷烟在某省的销量存在稳定的季节性,季节性随月变化,不随年变化。对季节调整后的序列进行季节性检验的结果表明,在 1%的显著性水平下序列中没有剩余的季节性。综上说明,X-13A-S 方法确实能较好地消除卷烟销量中的季节性。

3.2 五种方法的预测结果对比分析

3.2.1 销量的预测结果分析

采用 5 种不同的时间序列预测方法,对某省玉溪(软)2021 年 1 月至 12 月的销量进行预测。结果如表 5 所示。

表 5 5 种方法的销量预测结果   (单位:箱)

月度	实际值	回归分析法	指数平滑法	时间序列分解法	季节ARIMA模型	X13-A-S方法
2021M01	15304.34	10171.31	11458.61	8699.57	15590.15	14313.16

续表

月度	实际值	回归分析法	指数平滑法	时间序列分解法	季节ARIMA模型	X13-A-S方法
2021M02	3830.90	6520.94	5104.47	4369.48	4409.42	4325.49
2021M03	3244.95	3832.50	3767.91	3680.25	3695.09	3663.68
2021M04	3759.82	3721.88	3657.29	3510.11	3498.35	3567.12
2021M05	3370.33	3555.07	3490.48	3578.70	3020.98	3330.31
2021M06	3459.06	3384.58	3107.66	3231.83	2554.30	2725.75
2021M07	4157.25	3492.18	3215.26	3299.69	4228.04	4025.10
2021M08	4644.62	3828.52	3551.59	3604.64	4057.49	4006.14
2021M09	4718.55	4886.55	4609.63	4369.43	5311.88	5135.23
2021M10	3290.97	3085.69	2808.77	3055.61	3391.41	3286.50
2021M11	—	3628.80	3351.87	3545.72	3403.11	3372.81
2021M12	—	2167.09	1890.17	2500.43	1641.04	1602.62
合计	49780.78	46479.22	44771.67	41399.32	49757.11	48378.48

根据表5,各方法的预测基本体现了季节性,符合卷烟销售的周期性特点,1月销量最高,12月销量最低。5种方法在1月的销量预测上差异最大,12月的差异最小。预测差异值和当月的实际销量总体呈正相关。

3.2.2 预测的绝对误差分析

5种方法预测的绝对误差如表6所示。

表6 5种方法预测的绝对误差分析 （单位:箱）

月度	实际值	预测绝对误差				
		回归分析法	指数平滑法	时间序列分解法	季节ARIMA模型	X13-A-S方法
2021M01	15304.34	−5133.03	−3845.73	−6604.77	285.81	−991.18
2021M02	3830.9	2690.04	1273.57	538.58	578.52	494.59
2021M03	3244.95	587.55	522.96	435.3	450.14	418.73
2021M04	3759.82	−37.94	−102.53	−249.71	−261.47	−192.7
2021M05	3370.33	184.74	120.15	208.37	−349.35	−40.02
2021M06	3459.06	−74.48	−351.4	−227.23	−904.76	−733.31
2021M07	4157.25	−665.07	−941.99	−857.56	70.79	−132.15
2021M08	4644.62	−816.1	−1093.03	−1039.98	−587.13	−638.48
2021M09	4718.55	168	−108.92	−349.12	593.33	416.68
2021M10	3290.97	−205.28	−482.2	−235.36	100.44	−4.47
合计	49780.79	−3301.57	−5009.12	−8381.48	−23.68	−1402.31

从表6看,1月预测的绝对误差最大,4月最小。1—10月的实际销量为49780.79箱,

预测最为接近的是季节 ARIMA 模型,相差 23.68 箱,占实际销量的 0.048%,预测差距最大的是时间序列分解法,相差 8381.48 箱,占实际销量的 16.84%。

3.2.3 预测的相对误差分析

相对误差的计算结果如表 7 所示。从结果看,X13-A-S 方法平均相对误差最小,为 8.57%,其中 6 月预测误差最大,10 月最小。时间序列分解法、指数平滑法和回归分析法预测的平均相对误差均较大,主要原因在于 1、2 月份的预测偏差较大。

表 7 5 种方法预测的相对误差 （单位：%）

月度	回归分析法	指数平滑法	时间序列分解法	季节 ARIMA 模型	X13-A-S 方法
2021M01	33.54	25.13	43.16	1.87	6.48
2021M02	70.22	33.24	14.06	15.10	12.91
2021M03	18.11	16.12	13.41	13.87	12.90
2021M04	1.01	2.73	6.64	6.95	5.13
2021M05	5.48	3.57	6.18	10.37	1.19
2021M06	2.15	10.16	6.57	26.16	21.20
2021M07	16.00	22.66	20.63	1.70	3.18
2021M08	17.57	23.53	22.39	12.64	13.75
2021M09	3.56	2.31	7.40	12.57	8.83
2021M10	6.24	14.65	7.15	3.05	0.14
平均值	17.39	15.41	14.76	10.43	8.57

3.2.4 预测的标准误差分析

上述 5 种方法中,指数平滑法和时间序列分解法无法给出预测的标准误差,剩下三种方法预测的标准误差如表 8 所示。

表 8 3 种方法预测的标准误差 （单位：箱）

月度	回归分析法	指数平滑法	时间序列分解法	季节 ARIMA 模型	X13-A-S 方法	月度	回归分析法	指数平滑法	时间序列分解法	季节 ARIMA 模型	X13-A-S 方法
2021M01	719.10	—	—	1338.47	1222.81	2021M07	712.35	—	—	1496.85	1375.76
2021M02	719.10	—	—	1415.96	1319.59	2021M08	712.35	—	—	1501.53	1386.72
2021M03	708.83	—	—	1474.58	1331.02	2021M09	712.35	—	—	1507.14	1397.59
2021M04	708.83	—	—	1474.54	1342.34	2021M10	712.35	—	—	1512.26	1408.38
2021M05	708.83	—	—	1487.17	1353.57	2021M11	712.35	—	—	1517.60	1419.09
2021M06	712.35	—	—	1490.09	1364.71	2021M12	712.35	—	—	1522.80	1429.72

根据表 8,标准误差最小的是回归分析法,在 710 箱左右。季节 ARIMA 模型和 X13-

A-S方法的标准误差相差不大,在1400箱左右。X13-A-S方法的标准误差略低于季节ARIMA模型。

4 结论与建议

本文使用5种时间序列分析预测方法对某省单规格(玉溪(软)卷烟)的月度销量进行了预测,结果显示:回归模型、指数平滑模型、时间序列分解模型、季节ARIMA模型和X13-A-S方法均能有效提取季节因素、趋势和节假日效应,预测结果能较好地反映序列波动性,为未来卷烟的投放提供一定的参考。

卷烟销量主要受长期趋势、周期和节假日因素影响。传统回归模型基于因果关系建立,再通过原因变量的已知或设定值,去估计总体均值[23]。卷烟销售市场监测指标如零售户个数、零售户进货量等和卷烟销量存在高度的同期相关,并不适合做预测,因此本文的回归预测法主要使用可以外推的外生解释变量——时间变量t、月度虚拟变量和政策虚拟变量,避免了预测解释变量带来的误差。但是,回归模型和时间序列分解模型由于不能反映市场结构变化,可能会加大预测偏差。指数平滑法是使用过去若干期销量的加权平均作为下一期的预测,因此其趋势具有滞后性。由于销售策略和春节的影响,单规格卷烟的月度销量在前一年的12月和后一年的1月会出现大幅度的跳跃。而每一年1月的销量预测是上一年最后几个月销量的加权平均,这导致1月的销量预测严重偏低。因此,指数平滑法可能不太适合周期波动比较大的时间序列预测。近年来,受各种因素的影响,单规格卷烟的不规则变动增加,春节效应的规律性减弱,使得单规格卷烟的月度销量预测愈发困难。回归模型、指数平滑模型和时间序列分解模型在可变季节效应和不规则移动节假日效应方面欠缺处理能力,这可能是这三类模型预测误差偏大的原因。

5种预测方法中,季节ARIMA模型和X13-A-S方法在预测均值上拥有相对较小的绝对误差和相对误差。季节ARIMA模型和X13-A-S方法都使用趋势差分和季节差分来提取时间序列中的趋势和周期性,对随机趋势或波动复杂的周期效应更有效。不同之处在于X13-A-S方法增加了预调整、滤波和移动平均等来处理节假日效应、周期效应、趋势以及交易日效应等,从而能对周期性和节假日效应进行更充分的剥离。

在销量均值的预测上,季节ARIMA模型和X13-A-S方法的绝对误差和相对误差在5种预测方法中都相对较低,因此预测效果明显优于其他3种方法,可作为卷烟单规格月度销量均值预测的基本方法和通用方法。

参考文献

[1] 石涛,李根栓,李鹏飞,等.基于混频模型的中部某省卷烟销量趋势预测[J].中国烟草学报,2021,27(4):92-99.

[2] 罗彪,万亮,闫维维.基于PLS及时间序列法的卷烟销量组合预测方法[J].世界科技研究与发展,2012,34(4):699-703.

[3] 武牧,林慧苹,李素科.一种基于支持向量机的卷烟销量预测方法[J].烟草科技,2016,49(2):87-91.

[4] 吴明山,王冰,起亚宁.卷烟销量组合预测模型研究[J].中国烟草学报,2019,25(3):84-91.

[5] 邓超,刘颂,王露笛.基于深度神经网络的卷烟智能投放模型构建方法[J].烟草科技,2021,54(2):78-83.

[6] 岳阳.卷烟销售预测模型初探[J].现代商业,2012(23):22-23.

[7] 陈磊,朱振宏,高逸芸.灰色GM(2,1)模型在卷烟销量预测的应用[J].价值工程,2020,39(6):242-245.

[8] 王伟民,汪沄,张国安.基于灰色马尔科夫模型的全国卷烟需求预测研究[J].中国烟草学报,2009,15(6):66-69.

[9] 杨万,韩亚君,刘辉.基于马尔科夫链模型的湖南省卷烟需求预测[J].现代商业,2018(31):19-22.

[10] 于得水.构建卷烟销售关键指标预测模型——基于Eviews统计预测工具[C]//中国烟草学会2015年度优秀论文汇编.[出版者不详],2015:685-694.

[11] 吴凯.卷烟销售关键指标预测模型(以黄山市公司销售为例)——基于Eviews统计预测工具[C]//中国烟草学会2016年度优秀论文汇编——卷烟流通主题,2016:281-290.

[12] 单宇翔,郁钢,陆海良.基于组合分析模型的市场销量预测——以卷烟厂为例[J].中国商论,2019(2):4-5.

[13] 陈诗.基于组合模型的地市级公司卷烟销量影响因素分析——以湖北省十堰市为例[J].中国产经,2020(15):85-86.

[14] 谭建,陈青梅,林琳.基于系统动力学的卷烟销量预测[J].内蒙古科技与经济,2014(20):42-43.

[15] 高洪利.基于随机森林算法的卷烟销量预测及分析[C]//中国烟草学会学术年会优秀论文集.[出版者不详],2017:1958-1968.

[16] 向美英,何利力.趋势比率模型在卷烟预测中的应用[J].工业控制计算机,2011,24(9):74-75.

[17] 程幸福,陈厚铭,樊红.季节ARIMA模型在企业销售量预测中的应用——以卷烟销售为例[J].中国商论,2016(23):167-168.

[18] 张素平.基于乘法模型的内蒙古乌兰察布市卷烟总销量预测研究[J].内蒙古科技与经济,2012(21):33-34+36.

[19] 赵旻,张丹枫,曾中良.基于组合模型的云南省卷烟需求预测与结果评价研究[J].中国烟草学报,2019,25(1):93-98.

[20] 蒋兴恒,朱素蓉.基于Levenberg-Marquardt算法改进BP神经网络的卷烟销量预测模型研究[J].中国烟草学报,2011,17(5):81-86.

[21] 罗彪,闫维维,万亮.引入虚拟变量的时间序列分解法在卷烟销量预测中的应用[J].计算机系统应用,2012,21(12):215-220+148.

[22] 王书平,朱艳云,吴振信.基于X-13A-S方法的小麦价格季节性波动分析[J].中国管理科学,2014,22(S1):22-26.

[23] 李子奈,潘文卿.计量经济学[M].北京:高等教育出版社,2015.

[24] 王燕.应用时间序列分析[M].北京:中国人民大学出版社,2016.

[25] 杜勇宏,王健.季节时间序列理论与应用[M].天津:南开大学出版社,2008.

A Study on Time Series Forecasting Method for Monthly Sales of Cigarettes with Single Specification

Abstract: Based on the regression model, exponential smoothing model, time series decomposition model, seasonal ARIMA model, and X13-A-S method, the monthly sales of Yuxi (soft) cigarettes in a specific province from were forecasted. The forecast results were then examined. The most significant difference in forecast results was observed in the highest sales month of January, while the slightest difference was seen in the lowest sales month of December. The actual sales from January to October 2021 were 49,780.79 boxes, with the seasonal ARIMA model providing the closest prediction, followed by the X13-A-S method; meanwhile, the time series decomposition method showed the most significant discrepancy. Regarding the average relative error, the X13-A-S method had the slightest average relative error at 8.57%, followed by the seasonal ARIMA model at 10.43%. The regression model had the slightest standard error. For predicting sales mean values, seasonal ARIMA model and X13-A-S methods demonstrated lower absolute and relative errors and can be considered general methods for forecasting monthly cigarette sales.

Keywords: Regression forecasting; Exponential smoothing; Time series decomposition; Seasonal ARIMA; X13-A-S

1 Introduction

The cigarette consumption market in China has transitioned from a stage of rapid development to a stable and mature stage, and the new economic environment has weakened the sales pattern of single-specification cigarettes. Accurate forecasting of the sales volume of single-specification cigarettes is beneficial for enterprises to grasp the market status promptly, improves their response capability to the market, and enhances their cigarette marketing level.

Scholars and industry professionals have conducted numerous studies on cigarette sales forecasting. Regarding time types for forecasting, most researches focus on annual data due to its short period, limited samples, and absence of cyclical or holiday-related issues. There are also considerable studies on quarterly data that need to address seasonal issues but do not require separate consideration for holiday effects[1]. Similarly, there is growing attention towards monthly data due to its high frequency and significant fluctuations[2-4]. However, there is very little research on weekly data due to difficulties obtaining it and its high volatility[5]. In terms of forecasting methods, small sample size annual forecasts typically use grey models[6-7], grey Markov models[8-9], regression models[10-11], combination models[12-13], system dynamics models[14], random forest algorithms[15], etc. Various methods, such as the trend ratio model[16], seasonal ARIMA model[17], time series decomposition model[18], combination model[4, 19], mixed frequency model[1], etc., are used for quarterly and monthly forecasts where periodicity must be addressed. With the rise of big data technology, machine learning methods like support vector machines[3] and neural networks[20] have also been applied in cigarette sales forecasting. Furthermore, some scholars have noticed that holidays, especially the Lunar New Year, can significantly impact cigarette sales, proposing targeted improvement methods[21].

Existing literature provides a solid foundation for our study on monthly forecasted cigarette sales; however, areas still require improvement. Firstly, existing monthly forecasts focus mainly on total regional sales, with few predictions specifically targeting single-specification cigarettes. Secondly, handling lunar holidays such as the Spring Festival remains unsatisfactory since it's a moving holiday whose impact months vary. Setting it simply as a dummy variable makes it difficult to measure the Spring Festival effect accurately. Thirdly, regarding the prediction method, the Census X13-ARIMA-SEATS method, which considers seasonality adjustment trend cycle irregular changes moving holidays, has not yet been applied to monthly cigarette sale prediction despite being the latest seasonally adjusted method[22]. This paper aims to use monthly sales volume data for Yuxi (soft) cigarettes from a specific province as a basis for constructing and introducing five different prediction methods predicting its monthly sales volume and selecting the optimal method.

2 Materials and methods

2.1 Research object

In this paper, 72 months of data from January 2015 to December 2020 are used for model estimation and forecast, and actual sales data from January to October 2021 are used to test the forecast.

2.2 Research Methods

2.2.1 Regression Analysis Prediction Method

Regression analysis predicts the dependent variable based on the expected values of the explanatory variables by establishing a regression equation between variables[23]. Considering the factors affecting monthly cigarette sales, assuming that there is no superimposed effect between the long-term trend and seasonality of cigarette sales, the following additive regression prediction model is proposed:

$$y_t = \alpha_0 + \alpha_1 t + \sum_{i=1}^{11} \alpha_{i+1} S_{it} + \alpha_{13} Z_t + \alpha_{14} D_t + \mu_t$$

Where y_t represents monthly cigarette sales; μ_t represents the random error term; and t represents the long-term trend variable with $t = 1, 2, \cdots, k$; S_{it} represents the seasonal dummy variable ($S_{it} = 1$, if sales belong to month i; $S_{it} = 0$, if not where $i = 1, 2, \cdots, 11$). Z_t represents the Chinese New Year dummy variable D_t represent policy variables ($D_t = 1$, before tax increase (June 2015); $D_t = 0$, after tax increase); The parameter α_i measures the net impact of the i-th variable on monthly sales;.

Assuming uniform impact on sales before Chinese New Year with m representing days from New Year's Day to Chinese New Year. Z_t as Z_1-Z_2 cyclic values:

$$Z_1 = \begin{cases} 1, & m < 31 \\ 31/m, & m \geq 31 \end{cases}, \quad Z_2 = \begin{cases} 0, & m < 31 \\ 1 - 31/m, & m \geq 31 \end{cases}, \quad Z_3 = \cdots = Z_{12} = 0$$

A multiplicative regression model for predicting sales can also be established if there is a superimposed effect between the long-term trend and seasonality of cigarette sales:

$$y_t = \beta_0 + \beta_1 t + \sum_{i=1}^{11} \beta_{i+1} t \cdot S_{it} + \beta_{13} Z_t + \beta_{14} D_t + \mu_t$$

2.2.2 Exponential Smoothing Method

The exponential smoothing method is a commonly used medium-term forecasting method, which can be single exponential smoothing or double exponential smoothing, depending on the number of smoothing applied. The triple exponential smoothing model further divides into additive and multiplicative models. The multiplicative model is mainly used for sequences with cyclical and linear superposition effects with the sequence given by:

$$y_{t+k} = [a(t) + b(t)k] c_{t+k}$$

The additive model is mainly used for sequences with stable cyclical changes and simple linear trends given by:

$$y_{t+k} = a(t) + b(t)k + c_{t+k}$$

Where y_{t+k} represents monthly cigarette sales at period $t+k$; $a(t)$ denotes intercept; b

(t) denotes slope varying over time t; c_{t+k} denotes seasonal factor.

2.2.3 Time Series Decomposition Method with Dummy Variables

Time series decomposition separates the original sequence into long-term trend variation, cyclical variation, seasonal variation, and irregular variation[24]. Commonly used models include additive, multiplicative, and hybrid models. Generally, for monthly cigarette sales where both trend and cycle exist in an overlapping manner, either multiplicative or hybrid models are chosen:

$$y_t = TC_t \cdot S_t \cdot I_t \text{ or } y_t = S_t \cdot (TC_t + I_t)$$

Where y_t stands for monthly cigarette sales; TC_t, S_t, and I_t respectively represent long-term trend change components, seasonal change components, and irregular change components.

In this study, when dealing with seasonal factors, traditional holidays are set as dummy variables to construct improved models based on time series decomposition combined with virtual regression to estimate the influence of traditional holidays on sequences. Using D_{1t} ($D_{1t} = 1$, January; $D_{1t} = 0$, other months) representing Spring Festival variable and D_{2t} ($D_{2t} = 1$, before tax increase; $D_{2t} = 0$, after tax increase) representing policy variables to establish regression model for long-term trends in cigarette sales:

$$TC_t = \beta_0 + \beta_1 t + \beta_2 D_{1t} + \beta_3 D_{2t} + \mu_t$$

2.2.4 Seasonal ARIMA Model

Box-Jenkins' time domain analysis method builds a seasonal ARIMA model where s indicates periodicity, eliminates cyclic variations using seasonal differencing and removes linear trends using the first-order difference operator. Interaction effects between seasonal effects and random fluctuations may still exist for different sequences. Short-term correlation and product relationship exist between them, so the actual form of the seasonal multiplication model becomes ARMA (p, q) multiplied by ARMA (m_s, n_s)[25], whose form looks like this:

$$\Phi_p(L) A_m(L^s)(1-L)(1-L^s) y_t = \Theta_q(L) B_n(L^s) \varepsilon_t$$

Where L stands for lag operator; $\Phi_p(L), \Theta_q(L)$ respectively denote univariate p-th order q-th order polynomial in L; $A_m(L^s), B_n(L^s)$ respectively denote m-th order n-th order polynomial in L^s; ε_t stands for white noise.

2.2.5 X-13A-S Method

X-13A-S method combines X-11-ARIMA and SEATS, primarily used for seasonally adjusting economic data. First, it establishes the RegARIMA model, adjusting extreme values and calendar effects within the original sequence. RegARIMA, being a combination of regression and ARIMA, takes form as follows:

$$\Phi_p(L) A_m(L^s) \left(y_t - \sum_i \beta_i x_{it} \right) = \Theta_q(L) B_n(L^s) \varepsilon_t$$

Where y_t denotes a dependent variable, x_{it} denotes an independent variable, regression residual $(y_t - \sum_i \beta_i x_{it})$ forms stationary time series satisfying seasonal ARIMA model X-13A-S method uses RegARIMA model to forward-backward predict preadjusted sequence supplementing data, separating trending components, cyclical components, seasonal components, and irregular components through moving average, finally diagnosing results.

3. Results and Analysis

3.1 Estimation and Optimization Selection of Five Models

As shown in Figure 1, the monthly sales volume of Yuxi (soft) cigarettes in a specific province from January 2015 to October 2021 exhibits apparent periodicity. However, the amplitude of the period does not show regular changes. The peak values in 2015 and 2018 are significantly lower, and there is no significant trend change, indicating a significant impact from irregular factors.

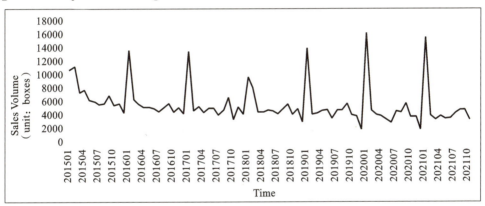

Figure 1 Presents the Time Series Chart of Monthly Sales Volume for Yuxi (Soft)

3.1.1 Regression Models

The additive and multiplicative regression models were estimated separately, with goodness of fit of 0.9532 and 0.9492, respectively. The additive model with a higher goodness of fit was selected as the final predictive model. The estimation results are shown in Table 1.

Table 1 Estimation Results of Additive Regression Analysis Model

Varible	Factor	Mean square	F	P	Varible	Factor	Mean square	F	P
C	4180.3080	312.1649	13.3914	0.0000	S_5	1220.2190	373.3806	3.2680	0.0018
t	−23.9669	4.0627	−5.8993	0.0000	S_6	1073.6920	370.4828	2.8981	0.0053

continue

Variable	Factor	Mean square	F	P	Variable	Factor	Mean square	F	P
Z	14809.7500	1326.0610	11.1682	0.0000	S_7	1205.2600	370.2377	3.2554	0.0019
D	1273.9940	346.1046	3.6810	0.0005	S_8	1565.5610	370.0370	4.2308	0.0001
S_1	−3457.0650	1184.2600	−2.9192	0.0050	S_9	2647.5600	369.8809	7.1579	0.0000
S_2	502.0865	424.9917	1.1814	0.2423	S_{10}	870.6722	369.7693	2.3546	0.0220
S_3	1449.7080	373.5574	3.8808	0.0003	S_{11}	1437.7420	369.7024	3.8889	0.0003
S_4	1363.0560	373.4469	3.6499	0.0006					

The goodness of fit for the model is 0.9532, and the P-value corresponding to the F-statistic is 0.000. The model fits well and is significant at the 1% level. Among the explanatory variables, except for the seasonal variable S_2, all other variables are significant at the 5% level, indicating that the dummy explanatory variables have good explanatory power. The model's Durbin-Watson (DW) value is 2.0577, suggesting that there is no serial correlation in the error terms, and thus, it can be used for prediction. The coefficient for the time variable t is −23.9669, indicating that after removing cyclicality and policy effects, monthly sales volume decreases by an average of 23.9669 boxes per month. Both the Spring Festival effect variable Z and policy effect variable D are significantly positive, indicating that sales in months with Spring Festival are indeed higher than in other months, and pre-tax increase sales volume is also significantly higher than post-tax increase sales volume before tax increase.

3.1.2 Exponential Smoothing Model

The three-parameter exponential smoothing additive and multiplicative models were estimated separately, with the following results.

Additive model:
$$y_{t+k} = 0.05(y_t - c_t(t-s)) + 0.95(a(t-1) + b(t-1) + b(t-1))k - c_{t+k}(t+k-s)$$

Multiplicative model:
$$y_{t+k} = \left[(0.06 \frac{y_t}{c_t(t-s)} + 0.94(a(t-1) + b(t-1)) + (0.26(a(t) - a(t-1))) \right.$$
$$\left. + 0.74b(t-1))k \right] c_{t+k}(t+k-s)$$

Here, 0.05, 0.06, and 0.26 are the estimated values of the damping factor.

The parameter s in both models represents the frequency specified as "seasonal period" in this paper, with s being 12. The sum of squared residuals for the additive model is 83821095, with a mean square error of 1078.97. For the multiplicative model, the sum of squared residuals is 1.15×10^8, and the mean square error is 1261.26. The seasonal factors for both additive and multiplicative models can be found in Table 2. In terms of mean prediction error, it can be observed that the additive model has smaller prediction errors compared to the multiplicative model; therefore, we choose to use the additive model as our forecasting model.

Table 2　Seasonal Factors Extracted by the Exponential Smoothing Model

Month	January	February	March	April	May	June	July	August	September	October	November	December
Additive seasonal factor	7106.86	786.17	−516.95	−594.13	−727.49	−1076.87	−935.83	−566.05	525.42	−1241.99	−665.44	−2093.71
Multiplicative seasonal factor	2.3233	1.1220	0.9021	0.8857	0.8692	0.7994	0.8371	0.9048	1.1113	0.7710	0.8784	0.5957

3.1.3　Prediction Results of Time Series Decomposition Model

Considering the superimposed effect of monthly sales trends and cycles in this paper, a multiplicative decomposition model is chosen. Seasonal indices are first used to extract periodicity, followed by linear regression to extract trends, with the remaining portion attributed to irregular variations. The trend regression model after removing seasonal factors is:

$$\hat{TC}_t = 6202.3890 - 30.2538t - 748.4090D_{1t} + 1424.7480D_{2t}$$

In the equation, D_{1t} and D_{2t} represent dummy variables for January and policy.

After testing, the model is significant, with a goodness of fit of 0.5251, and all variables are significant at the 5% level. Estimates are made for trend and seasonality separately from January 2021 to October 2021, then combined into total estimates, as shown in Table 3.

Table 3　Prediction Results of Time Series Decomposition Model with Dummy Variables　　　　　　　　　　　　　　　　　　　　　　　　　　　　(Unit: box)

Monthly	2021M01	2021M02	2021M03	2021M04	2021M05	2021M06	2021M07	2021M08	2021M09	2021M10
Trend forecasting	3245.45	3963.61	3933.36	3903.1	3872.85	3842.59	3812.34	3782.09	3751.83	3721.6
Seasonal forecasting	2.6805	1.1024	0.9357	0.8993	0.9241	0.8411	0.8655	0.9531	1.1646	0.8211
Total	8699.57	4369.48	3680.25	3510.11	3578.7	3231.84	3299.69	3604.64	4369.43	3055.62

3.1.4　Estimation and Optimization of Seasonal ARIMA Model

Firstly, the sales data series is differenced once to remove the trend, followed by 12-step differencing to eliminate seasonality. By plotting the autocorrelation and partial autocorrelation functions, it is determined that models such as AR (2), MA (1), ARMA (1, 1), ARMA (1, 12), SARMA (1, 1)×(1, 1)$_{12}$ and SARMA (2, 1)×(1, 1)$_{12}$ can be estimated. The ML method is used to estimate all identified models. After conducting model significance tests (residual white noise test) and parameter significance tests, SARIMA (1, 1, 1)×(0, 1, 0)$_{12}$, SARIMA (1, 1, 0)×(1, 1, 0)$_{12}$ and SARIMA (1, 1, 1)×(0, 1, 1)$_{12}$ pass the tests and can be used for prediction. A comparison of the estimation results of these three models is shown in Table 4.

Table 4 Optimization Selection of SARIMA Models

Model	σ^2	AIC criterion	SC criterion	Stationary	Reversibility
SARIMA (1, 1, 1)×(0, 1, 0)$_{12}$	1639119	17.3283	17.4692	Stationary	reversible
SARIMA (1, 1, 1)×(1, 1, 0)$_{12}$	1581823	17.3335	17.5095	Stationary	reversible
SARIMA (1, 1, 1)×(0, 1, 1)$_{12}$	1484909	17.2971	17.4732	Stationary	reversible

The selection of the model is usually determined based on information criteria. From the table, it can be seen that SARIMA (1, 1, 1)×(0, 1, 0)$_{12}$ has the smallest SC value and SARIMA (1, 1, 1)×(0, 1, 1)$_{12}$ has the smallest AIC value. Therefore, the model selection is conducted through LR test. Using SARIMA (1, 1, 1)×(0, 1, 0)$_{12}$ as the base model and SARIMA (1, 1, 1)×(0, 1, 0)$_{12}$ as the nested model to test whether the coefficient of SMA term is zero in its null hypothesis. The LR statistic is 3.84 (prob > 0.05), so we do not reject the null hypothesis and should use SARIMA (1, 1, 1)×(0, 1, 0)$_{12}$ as our final forecasting model. The estimated result is shown in the following equation:

$$(1-L)(1-L^{12})X_t = \frac{1-0.8599L}{1-0.4855L}\varepsilon_t$$

3.1.5 X13-A-S Method

This study utilizes the Census X-13A-S program in Eviews 10 software, without data transformation and without considering the effects of trading days and moving holidays (for consumers, cigarette sales do not involve trading days; previous research has shown that seasonal effects already include the Spring Festival and Mid-Autumn Festival effects). The ARIMA model is selected by X-11 Auto, seasonal adjustment is performed using the X-11 method, and trend and seasonal filtering are conducted using X-13 Auto to obtain a relatively good forecast.

Under the assumption of no seasonal impact, the F-statistic for stable seasonality test is 18.367, indicating significant seasonality at a 1% significance level. The Kruskal-Wallis statistic for the non-parametric test of stable seasonality is 79.354, also showing significant seasonality at a 1% significance level. The F-statistic for the mobile seasonality test (with the null hypothesis of no annual variation) is 1.354, indicating no evidence of mobile seasonality at a 5% significance level. Overall, based on the results of these three tests, it can be concluded that stable monthly seasonality exists in cigarette sales in Yuxi (soft) within a specific province, which does not vary annually. Seasonal testing after adjustment shows no residual seasonality at a 1% significance level. In conclusion, the X-13A-S method effectively eliminates seasonality from cigarette sales.

3.2 Comparison Analysis of Forecasting Results from Five Methods

3.2.1 Analysis of Sales Forecast Results

Five different time series forecasting methods were used to predict Yuxi (soft) sales volume in a specific province from January to December 2021, as shown in Table 5.

Table 5　Sales Volume Forecast Results from Five Methods　　(Unit: box)

Monthly	Actual value	Regression analysis method	Exponential smoothing method	Time series decomposition method	Seasonal ARIMA model	X13-A-S method
2021M01	15304.34	10171.31	11458.61	8699.57	15590.15	14313.16
2021M02	3830.90	6520.94	5104.47	4369.48	4409.42	4325.49
2021M03	3244.95	3832.50	3767.91	3680.25	3695.09	3663.68
2021M04	3759.82	3721.88	3657.29	3510.11	3498.35	3567.12
2021M05	3370.33	3555.07	3490.48	3578.70	3020.98	3330.31
2021M06	3459.06	3384.58	3107.66	3231.83	2554.30	2725.75
2021M07	4157.25	3492.18	3215.26	3299.69	4228.04	4025.10
2021M08	4644.62	3828.52	3551.59	3604.64	4057.49	4006.14
2021M09	4718.55	4886.55	4609.63	4369.43	5311.88	5135.23
2021M10	3290.97	3085.69	2808.77	3055.61	3391.41	3286.50
2021M11	—	3628.80	3351.87	3545.72	3403.11	3372.81
2021M12	—	2167.09	1890.17	2500.43	1641.04	1602.62
Total	49780.78	46479.22	44771.67	41399.32	49757.11	48378.48

Based on Table 5, the predictions of each method generally reflect seasonality, are consistent with the cyclical nature of cigarette sales, with the highest sales in January and the lowest sales in December. The differences in sales forecasts among the five methods are greatest in January and smallest in December. Overall, there is a positive correlation between forecasted differences and actual sales for each month.

3.2.2 Analysis of Absolute Prediction Errors

The absolute prediction errors for the five methods are shown in Table 6.

Table 6 Analysis of Absolute Prediction Errors for Five Methods (Unit: box)

Monthly	Actual value	Absolute Prediction Errors				
		Regression analysis method	Exponential smoothing method	Time series decomposition method	Seasonal ARIMA model	X13-A-S method
2021M01	15304.34	−5133.03	−3845.73	−6604.77	285.81	−991.18
2021M02	3830.9	2690.04	1273.57	538.58	578.52	494.59
2021M03	3244.95	587.55	522.96	435.3	450.14	418.73
2021M04	3759.82	−37.94	−102.53	−249.71	−261.47	−192.7
2021M05	3370.33	184.74	120.15	208.37	−349.35	−40.02
2021M06	3459.06	−74.48	−351.4	−227.23	−904.76	−733.31
2021M07	4157.25	−665.07	−941.99	−857.56	70.79	−132.15
2021M08	4644.62	−816.1	−1093.03	−1039.98	−587.13	−638.48
2021M09	4718.55	168	−108.92	−349.12	593.33	416.68
2021M10	3290.97	−205.28	−482.2	−235.36	100.44	−4.47
Total	49780.79	−3301.57	−5009.12	−8381.48	−23.68	−1402.31

From Table 6, it can be seen that the absolute error is largest in January and smallest in April. The actual sales volume for January to October is calculated to be 49780.79 boxes. The seasonal ARIMA model has the closest prediction with a difference of 23.68 boxes, accounting for 0.048% of the actual sales volume. In comparison, the time series decomposition method has the largest prediction gap with a difference of 8381.48 boxes, accounting for 16.84% of the actual sales volume.

3.2.3 Analysis of Relative Prediction Errors

The results of the relative error calculation are shown in Table 7. It can be observed that the X13-A-S method has the slightest average relative error at 8.57%, with the largest prediction error in June and the smallest in October. The time series decomposition, exponential smoothing, and regression analysis methods all have relatively large average relative errors, mainly due to significant forecast deviations in January and February.

Table 7 Forecast Relative Error Table for Five Methods　　　　　　(Unit: %)

Monthly	Actual value	Regression analysis method	Exponential smoothing method	Time series decomposition method	Seasonal ARIMA model
2021M01	33.54	25.13	43.16	1.87	6.48
2021M02	70.22	33.24	14.06	15.10	12.91
2021M03	18.11	16.12	13.41	13.87	12.90
2021M04	1.01	2.73	6.64	6.95	5.13
2021M05	5.48	3.57	6.18	10.37	1.19
2021M06	2.15	10.16	6.57	26.16	21.20
2021M07	16.00	22.66	20.63	1.70	3.18
2021M08	17.57	23.53	22.39	12.64	13.75
2021M09	3.56	2.31	7.40	12.57	8.83
2021M10	6.24	14.65	7.15	3.05	0.14
Mean	17.39	15.41	14.76	10.43	8.57

3.2.4 Prediction Standard Error Analysis

Among the 5 methods mentioned above, the exponential smoothing and time series decomposition methods cannot provide the standard error of prediction. The standard errors of the remaining three methods are shown in Table 8.

Table 8 Prediction Standard Error Table for 3 Methods　　　　　　(Unit: box)

Monthly	Actual value	Regression analysis method	Exponential smoothing method	Time series decomposition method	Seasonal ARIMA model	Monthly	Actual value	Regression analysis method	Exponential smoothing method	Time series decomposition method	Seasonal ARIMA model
2021M01	719.10	—	—	1338.47	1222.81	2021M07	712.35	—	—	1496.85	1375.76
2021M02	719.10	—	—	1415.96	1319.59	2021M08	712.35	—	—	1501.53	1386.72
2021M03	708.83	—	—	1474.58	1331.02	2021M09	712.35	—	—	1507.14	1397.59
2021M04	708.83	—	—	1474.54	1342.34	2021M10	712.35	—	—	1512.26	1408.38
2021M05	708.83	—	—	1487.17	1353.57	2021M11	712.35	—	—	1517.60	1419.09
2021M06	712.35	—	—	1490.09	1364.71	2021M12	712.35	—	—	1522.80	1429.72

Based on Table 8, the regression analysis method has the slightest standard error at around 710 boxes. The standard errors of the seasonal ARIMA model and X13-A-S method are similar, at around 1400 boxes. The standard error of the X13-A-S method is slightly lower than that of the seasonal ARIMA model.

4 Conclusion and Recommendations

This study used five time series analysis forecasting methods to predict the monthly sales volume of a single specification (Yuxi (soft)) in a specific province. The results show that the regression model, exponential smoothing model, time series decomposition model, seasonal ARIMA model, and X13-A-S method can effectively extract seasonal factors, trends, and holiday effects. The forecasting results can reflect the series' volatility well and provide some reference for future cigarette placement.

The long-term trends and cycles mainly influence the sales volume of cigarettes and holiday factors in economic and social development. Traditional regression models are established based on causal relationships and then estimate the population mean through known or set values of explanatory variables[23]. Monitoring indicators of the cigarette sales market, such as the number of retail outlets and their purchase quantities, are highly correlated with cigarette sales in the same period, making them unsuitable for prediction. Therefore, this paper's regression forecasting method mainly uses extrapolatable exogenous explanatory variables: time variable t, monthly dummy variables, and policy dummy variables to avoid errors caused by predicting explanatory variables. However, regression models and time series analysis methods may increase prediction bias due to their inability to reflect changes in market structure. The exponential smoothing method uses a weighted average of past sales volumes as the forecast for the next period, resulting in a lagging trend. Monthly sales volumes of single-specification cigarettes experience the largest jumps in December of the previous year and January of the following year due to sales strategies and Chinese New Year effects. The forecasted sales volume for January is a weighted average of sales volumes from the last few months of the previous year, leading to a significant underestimation. Therefore, exponential smoothing may not be suitable for forecasting time series with large cyclical fluctuations. In recent years, irregular variations in single-specification cigarettes have increased due to various factors. At the same time, the regularity of Chinese New Year effects has decreased, thus making monthly sales volume forecasts increasingly difficult. Regression model, exponential smoothing model, and time series decomposition model lack handling capabilities for variable seasonal effects and irregular moving holiday effects, which may be why these three models have significant prediction errors.

Among the 5 forecasting methods, the seasonal ARIMA model and X13-A-S method exhibit relatively small absolute and relative errors in predicting the mean. The seasonal ARIMA model and X13-A-S method utilize trend differencing and seasonal differencing to extract trends and periodicity from time series data, making them more effective for complex cyclic effects or fluctuations. The difference is that the X13-A-S method incorporates pre-adjustment, filtering, moving averages, etc., to handle holiday effects, cyclical effects, trends, trading day effects, etc., thus enabling a more thorough extraction of cyclic and holiday effects.

In terms of predicting sales volume means, both the seasonal ARIMA model and X13-A-S method have relatively low absolute errors and relative errors among the 5 forecasting methods. Therefore, their predictive performance is significantly better than the other 3 methods. They can be considered fundamental and general methods for monthly sales volume, which means the prediction of single-specification cigarettes.

References

[1] SHI T, LI G S, LI P F, et al. Based on Mixing Model in the Central Province of Cigarette Sales Trend Prediction[J]. Journal of China Tobacco, 2021, 27 (4): 92-99.

[2] LUO B, WAN L, YAN W W. Cigarette Sales Combination Forecasting Method based on PLS and Time Series Method[J]. World Scientific Research and Development, 2012, 34 (4): 699-703.

[3] WU M, LIN H P, LI S K. A Method of Cigarette Sales Forecasting based on Support Vector Machine[J]. Tobacco Science and Technology, 2016, 49 (2): 87-91.

[4] WU M S, WANG B, QI Y N. Cigarette Sales Combination Forecast Model Research[J]. Journal of China tobacco, 2019, 25 (3): 84-91.

[5] DENG C, LIU S, WANG L D. Construction Method of Cigarette Intelligent Delivery Model based on Deep Neural Network[J]. Tobacco Science and Technology, 2021, 54 (2): 78-83.

[6] YUE Y. Cigarette Sales Forecasting Model[J]. Journal of Modern Business, 2012 (23): 22-23.

[7] CHEN L, ZHU Z H, GAO Y Y. Application of Grey GM (2, 1) Model in Cigarette Sales Forecasting[J]. Value Engineering, 2020, 39 (6): 242-245.

[8] WANG W M, WANG W, ZHANG G A. Prediction of National Cigarette Demand based on Grey Markov Model[J]. Chinese Journal of Tobacco, 2009, 15 (6): 66-69.

[9] YANG W, HAN Y J, LIU H. Based on Markov Chain Model of Cigarette Demand

Forecast in Hunan Province[J]. Journal of Modern Business, 2018 (31): 19-22.

[10] YU D S. Building a Prediction Model for Key Indicators of Cigarette Sales—Based on Eviews Statistical Prediction Tool[C]//2015 Excellent Papers of the Chinese Tobacco Society[Publisher unknown], 2015: 685-694.

[11] WU K. Prediction Model of Key Indicators of Cigarette Sales (Taking Company Sales in Huangshan City as an Example) —Based on Eviews Statistical Forecasting Tool[C]//Compilation of Outstanding Papers of China Tobacco Society 2016—Cigarette Circulation Topics, 2016: 281-290.

[12] SHAN Y X, YU G, LU H L. Market Sales Forecast based on Combinative Analysis Model: A Case Study of Cigarette Factory[J]. China Business Theory, 2019 (2): 4-5.

[13] CHEN S. Analysis of Influencing Factors of Cigarette Sales of Prefecture-Level Companies based on Combination Model: A Case Study of Shiyan City, Hubei Province[J]. China Sankei, 2020 (15): 85-86.

[14] TAN J, CHEN Q M, LIN L. Cigarette Sales Forecasting based on System Dynamics[J]. Inner Mongolia Science and Technology and Economy, 2014 (20): 42-43.

[15] GAO H L. Prediction and Analysis of Cigarette Sales based on Random Forest Algorithm[C]//Excellent Proceedings of the Academic Annual Meeting of the Chinese Tobacco Society. [Publisher unknown], 2017: 1958-1968.

[16] XIANG M Y, HE L L. Application of Trend Ratio Model in Cigarette Prediction [J]. Industrial Control Computer, 2011, 24 (9): 74-75.

[17] CHENG X F, CHEN H M, FAN H. Application of Seasonal ARIMA Model in Enterprise Sales Forecast: A Case Study of Cigarette Sales[J]. Chinese Business Theory, 2016 (23): 167-168.

[18] ZHANG S P. Prediction of Total Cigarette Sales in Ulanqab City, Inner Mongolia based on multiplication model[J]. Inner Mongolia Science and Technology and Economy, 2012 (21): 33-34+36.

[19] ZHAO M, ZHANG D F, ZENG Z L. Model based on Combination of Cigarette Demand Forecast and Evaluation of the Results of Yunnan Province[J]. Journal of China tobacco, 2019, 25 (1): 93-98.

[20] JIANG X H, ZHU S R. Research on Cigarette Sales Forecasting Model based on Improved BP Neural Network based on Levenberg-Marquardt Algorithm[J]. Chinese Journal of Tobacco, 2011, 17 (5): 81-86.

[21] LUO B, YAN W W, WAN L. Application of Time Series Decomposition Method With Dummy Variables in Cigarette Sales Forecasting[J]. Applications of

Computer Systems,2012,21(12):215-220+148.

[22] WANG S P, ZHU Y Y, WU Z X. Analysis of Seasonal Fluctuation of Wheat Price based on X-13A-S Method[J]. China Management Science,2014,22(S1):22-26.

[23] LI Z N, PAN W Q. Econometrics[M]. Beijing:Higher Education Press,2015.

[24] WANG Y. Applied Time Series Analysis[M]. Beijing:China Renmin University Press,2016.

[25] DU Y H, WANG J. Seasonal Time Series Theory and Application[M]. Tianjin:Nankai University Press,2008.